THE COUNTY BOOKS SERIES

A series comprising 58 volumes. It covers every county in England and there will be three books on the mainland of Scotland, two each on the Hebrides, Ireland and Wales, and one each on Orkney, Shetland, the Isle of Man and the Channel Islands

PLEASE WRITE TO THE PUBLISHERS FOR FULL DESCRIPTIVE PROSPECTUS

NOTTINGHAMSHIRE

27161

The County Books Series

GENERAL EDITOR: BRIAN VESEY-FITZGERALD, F.L.S.

NOTTINGHAMSHIRE

by

CHRISTOPHER   MARSDEN

Illustrated and with a Map

Robert Hale Limited
63 Old Brompton Road London S.W.7

First published 1953

PRINTED IN GREAT BRITAIN BY
NORTHUMBERLAND PRESS LIMITED
GATESHEAD ON TYNE

FOREWORD

P L E A S E, a word to clear up any misunderstanding. This, unlike other books in the same series, is not an intimate study, personal and reminiscent, by a native of the place. The county is seen from the outside, by one who came to it as a stranger. It is personal only in so far as the author has arrogantly imposed on his subject his perhaps narrow interests and prejudices—historical, social, literary and architectural. But the fascination of Nottinghamshire's associations, and of its surviving churches and houses, which he feels so strongly and which first drew him there, has been corroborated in his mind by the fact that this was the county chosen as the first to be revealed in Professor Nikolaus Pevsner's incomparable series on *The Buildings of England,* now in process of publication by Penguin Books. The author's debt—as must be that of anyone who visits those parts of the island that have already fallen within the net of this architectural Domesday Book —will be obvious to the reader.

CONTENTS

CONTENTS

ILLUSTRATIONS

Present-day difficulties do not permit of a comprehensive map of the area being included in this book. For more detailed information, readers are referred to the respective Ordnance Survey sheets.

ACKNOWLEDGMENTS

All the above illustrations are reproduced from photographs by J. Allan Cash, F.I.B.P., F.R.P.S., of London, N.W.3.

CHAPTER I

THE COUNTY

WERE one to cast about upon the map of England for some part of it that could be held to contain, within the limits of a single county, the essence of the whole, one would surely direct one's gaze first of all towards the coast. Does not the habitat of an "island-people" necessarily demand a view of the sea? Though this is no place to work out so tedious a sum, it is probable that a glance at the comparative acreages of the seaboard and of the inland counties of England would show a heavy preponderance for those that have a coastline. From this mathematical viewpoint, no doubt, these may be "typical". Yet, thinking deeper of the English and of what they have made of their island, one might after all find oneself wrong in insisting thus hastily on a bit of the sea in a microcosm of England. The presence of the sea affects only the narrowest strip of land. Once out of sight, it is soon out of mind, and cannot, even from only a few miles distance, dictate a special way of life. Islanders, certainly, "we" are: a seafaring race. But, in average experience, it seems always to be some person other than oneself who does the faring. We take the sea more for granted than can, say, the Slovaks or the people of Tibet; but the sea is by no means so essential a part of the everyday lives of all of us as it is, perhaps, among the Melanesians of the Solomon Islands or even the Norwegians. Only to a minority of English people is the sight of the sea not a rather exceptional experience. This is true not merely of the present day. The seaman, even the humble fisherman, has always been a slightly strange person among us, regarded by our ancestors with just the same mild awe as we feel towards him. And the sea has never been a particularly popular calling; it has had its conscripts as well as its volunteers. Again, the mariner's home never was quite like ours. A port, great or little, even a seaside resort, has for most of us a sort of exoticism. No: if one were to be honest—and a little disloyal to accepted tradition—one would not pick upon a maritime county to show the typical life and environment of the mass of English people.

And what, inland? The place we choose must not be exclusively or predominantly farmland, for this is an industrial country. But it must not be all factories, all towns, for we pride ourselves still upon the greenness of our island, our orchards, our deep country lanes, our pleasant pastures. It must be venerable, the county we choose, redolent of the oldness, the continuity of our history; yet not exclusively antique, either, for the last century and a half have heaped a millennium's worth of change upon the face of the island. It may not be mountainous; but must not be too flat. It must have rivers and ponds, but few lakes. Villages and sleeping hamlets must lie embowered in it, with old grey churches, and red manors set in rolling parkland. Yet, surely, coal must be hewn from its bosom, soiling the landscape with its refuse. The poor must still live close-crowded in the streets of its towns, and lordly seats—crumbling, maybe, and empty—must bear witness to the gradualness of our revolution. It must have— God knows!—its share of the ugliness of the present and of the immediate past (the dishonour of ill-conceived construction beside worthy and more recent wounds) as well as of the calm beauty of England's permanent and rustic life and of the accumulated tradition of her vernacular building. Here and there some great medieval shrine must rear itself above the clustering rooftops.

And where shall this epitome be set? Neither north, nor too far south. Is not the south but a vast purlieu of London? And would a Northerner agree to be representative of the whole? Not west: too individual, too personal by far. East Anglia is too Flemish, characteristic of nothing but itself.

Thus tortuously does the writer present his claim for the county to be described. Not that it is the most beautiful of the counties of England—it palpably is not. Not that it is so deeply historic that visitors flood annually into it to see its wonders of architecture and association. On the contrary, Nottinghamshire's figures of external tourists must be among the lowest in the country. The county contains only one object, and that of astonishing dullness, that has as yet fallen under the care of the National Trust. In recent lists of great country houses open to the public Nottinghamshire figured hardly at all in spite of its former wealth in this respect. It contains no remarkable Roman or prehistoric sites. Perhaps evidence of a positively decreasing interest for visitors is provided by the fact that the publishers of a familiar series of red-covered local guide books who used to include a volume devoted to Nottingham and the Dukeries have not thought fit to keep it in print since early in the inter-war period.

On the other hand Nottinghamshire's name is not synonymous with the wealth, the chimneys and drear filth of the black industries: Nottinghamshire is a green and gentle county in spite of the fame of its pits and its miners. It is not the largest county, nor again the smallest. It is not very far north, or south; it is in the middle. It is not mountainous, nor flat. It is precisely because it is nothing special that Nottinghamshire claims special interest. You cannot here by any stretch of the imagination exclaim of its landscape that it is so like Holland, or Norway, or the Riviera (which is done, though with small justification, elsewhere on this island). You would never dream of doing that in Nottinghamshire because Nottinghamshire is like nothing on earth—except England.

Accepting the writer's premiss, then, that this county may be regarded as so English that here one is never tempted to search for exotic overtones as in the south and the east, we may still seek unassimilated reminiscences; let us examine this stretch of English soil, see where it lies and what it bears upon its surface.

Leaf-shaped, it carries its length north- and southwards down the back of England. At the top it is pinched to a point by the converging masses of Yorkshire and Lincoln. Lincolnshire monopolizes its eastern flank and at one point Notts pokes an impertinent finger into that county's soft green side as if it were trying to reach Lincoln itself. On the south it is held scooped in the hand of Leicestershire. Derby runs along most of its straight western length, with Yorkshire taking over the embrace for the last third of the distance. Its neighbours, in thus hemming it in, do not isolate it but rather give it a sense of wider contact. Lincoln gives it awareness of the East Anglian levels and a smell of the sea, and it is through Lincoln that Nottinghamshire's own waterways lead out towards the Wash and towards Hull. Leicester provides immediate links with that very core of England's Midlands from which Nottingham's western neighbour, Derby, snakes up towards those unquestionably northern giants, Lancashire and Yorkshire. The county is thus well situated for an all-round view of the heart of England. And, looking inwards, it finds itself to be the heart.

Nottinghamshire is compounded of the following ingredients. It consists first of a large stretch of the River Trent, which winds its way northwards along the county's eastern edge set in a green vale dotted with villages and hamlets. It consists of Sherwood Forest, within whose limits are both many of the coal-fields and also large areas of woodland, still. It consist of the city of Nottingham, with its proud modern centre, its well-laid array of residential crescents, drives and boulevards, its factories, race-course, cricket-ground, university and castle. It consists of only four other townships that have much name outside the county's limits—Newark, Mansfield, Retford and Worksop. It consists of innumerable villages, none of which can be called among the most dismal in Britain although set among slag heaps, and some that are extraordinary in their remoteness and inaccessibility. It consists of one of the least familiar bishoprics and an important minster, unusual in having no busy cathedral town to go with it. It consists of that series of lordly estates whose collective title is one of the gayest coinages of our language. It consists of an important stretch of the Great North Road. And, among less tangible things, the county offers the scene of the most famous and least substantiated of English folk-tales and legends; a strip of land, between Nottingham and Newark and inclusive of both these places, where the hoof beats and the clash of steel are still faintly audible three hundred years after the clamour of the Civil War has elsewhere faded; a tradition of industrial enterprise and inventiveness and, visibly, an array of great factories that are the lineal descendants of the rows of cottages where all day long the clicking of the early stocking frames used to be heard; a reputation for radicalism, for sturdy non-conformity, and for the brewing of good ale.

This study falls into five distinct parts. First, the city of Nottingham and its immediate environs. Second, there is the valley of the Trent, which embraces the whole of the region south of Nottingham and all of the eastern side of the county. Thirdly, the area of the Nottinghamshire coal-fields and, almost synonymously, the country that is associated with the names of two writers who lived a century apart, Lord Byron and D. H. Lawrence; these are the uplands of the county and take us to the Derbyshire boundaries. Fourth, Newark, with Southwell and its minster. Fifthly, Sherwood Forest and the Dukeries stretching almost the whole width of the county between Mansfield and the Trent. Sixth, and last, the northern tip, from Worksop and Retford to the Yorkshire border.

CHAPTER II

THE COUNTY TOWN AND ITS MAKING

IF a traveller from the south had halted for a while before he crossed the River Trent he would, at almost any period prior to the nineteenth century, have seen in front of him a town dominated by two features. To his left he would have seen the great mass of the castle rock surmounted by its building; on the right, the spire of St. Mary's church. Between, and around, was a town whose pleasantness was a byword among travellers. True, he might have to hold his nose a bit as he passed through the areas near the bridge because of the tanneries which, for a long period were a cause of offence to visitors. But "the famous beautiful town of Nottingham, in the middle of a forest, and sporting country" is how Daniel Defoe described it at the beginning of the eighteenth century, and both earlier and for a long time later, everyone who came to it for the first time praised its cleanliness and pleasant appearance. Also its sense of antiquity. When a certain Herr Memnich, who published an account of his travels in 1799, saw Nottingham he said, "That seems to me the most ancient city that I have yet seen in all England." Nottingham in those days was a clean bright place of red roofs, lofty houses and glittering spires. There seems to have been something almost breath-taking about the view of Nottingham and the Trent valley as it appeared from Ruddington Hill, on the way to Loughborough. The group of windmills that used to stand in a cluster on the plateau atop the Derby road gave their own mark to the skyline but could not detract from the two great sentinels of the landscape, the church and the castle.

I think it is important that anyone who approaches the city for the first time, as perhaps some reader will, should have in his mind a picture of what lies behind the busy centre of industry that now occupies the site on the River Trent. Take, for example, that first and most famous feature. The physical magnificence of the hill on which the castle is built, dominating town, river and surrounding countryside, is in itself enough to give dignity to any city. It is an acropolis; and during the Middle Ages there had arisen there a castle which—though its

5

appearance survives in but few contemporary views—one can presume to have been worthy of the site. A single gateway remains, on the slopes of the hill, to hint at its fabric. One can only guess at the outline it presented against the sky. What is now there suggests how unsuitable to the defensive position on which the medieval castle would have been built is any style other than that commonly associated with a castellated fortress. What has emerged from the accidents of history which we shall touch on in a minute is a pleasantly large country house whose horizontal outline is highly unsuitable to the position. It looks, in fact, little short of ludicrous. The essence of the style of eighteenth-century building which it represents is that the structure should be seen in the distance on the same level as itself. Nottingham Castle occupies the whole of the flat top of the rock. You can't get away from it to look at it: you could only see it properly from a helicopter suspended in mid-air. The whole virtue of its, in itself not inelegant, baroque façade is lost and wasted. There is the additional functional objection that no one in his right mind would build a house or palace of a style whose purpose at least puts comfort above defence, in such an exposed and howlingly draughty position. Aesthetically, the position is too good. English country-house architecture—even Continental palace architecture—is not suitable. The flat top of Nottingham Castle repeats the flat top of the rock. It is remarkable that it has looked faintly silly ever since it was built, as one can tell from the many eighteenth-century engravings of the whole grouping. What is needed are towers, even spires. It was unlucky that its rebuilding, after its destruction by Parliament's orders in 1651, should have had to take place at a time when no other style was capable of being considered than that which held sway throughout Europe—or rather the gentle English version which took the place of the full Continental baroque. In 1674 there could have been no thought of anything but a mansion in the fully contemporary manner. Even a hundred years later there might have been just a chance that the growing antiquarianism might have ventured some castellated towers; or that the Gothic taste might have produced there some sort of a romantic silhouette like the jagged tower of Fonthill. Here on this site is offered the excuse for almost any romantic style however much revived. The happy fate which Windsor Castle suffered at the hands of nineteenth-century improvers gives a hint of what Nottingham Castle might have been made to be. Might have been, but is not.

Now for fact. It was in the year 1068 that William the Conqueror came to Nottingham and ordered the rebuilding

6

Industrial Nottingham from the Castle rock

of the castle which had been a stronghold at least as early as the days in which Danes and Saxons were fighting in England. (According to the *Anglo-Saxon Chronicle*, Alfred the Great and his brother Ethelred went with the West Saxon army into Mercia, as far as Nottingham, there meeting the Danish army "on the works, they beset them within".) It is likely that the works (which were more probably on the site of St. Mary's church than the present castle) used by the Danes in the ninth century, earthworks, had been replaced by nothing more solid than a wooden fort by the time William the Conqueror appeared. The first evidence of a stone building dates from the reign of Henry I, in 1131. The keep of the fortress which then arose certainly stood where now is to be found the castle museum. The Norman fortress received various additions and embellishments during the succeeding reigns. It was for many years a royal station and was visited by almost every English monarch. It was also the place where many parliaments were called together and where privy councils were held, besides being a rendezvous for armies. The castle was at the height of its glory at the beginning of the sixteenth century and had suffered neglect and was already falling into decay at the time that it first enters conspicuously into English history.

Let us try and reconstruct that scene in the late summer of 1643 which is the episode most closely associated with Nottingham's name. Charles I had established his residence at Clare House in the town. The standard which he had had with him was a banner, probably of silk, which had been painted by Robert Large, a local man. Its shape was that of a pennon. One eye-witness of the scene described it as bearing "a red crosse and two lyons passant upon two crowns", though it is elsewhere described as a "bloody flag, the king's arms quartered with a hand pointing to the crown which stands above, with this motto Give to Caesar his Due". The standard was flown from a long staff like a may-pole painted red. It required something like twenty supporters to carry it erect. At first the heralds hung the flag out of the castle turrets, but Charles later had it put in an open space where everyone could come and look at it. It was at about six o'clock in the evening on the 22nd August, 1642, that a solemn procession moved out of the castle—presumably through the still-surviving gateway—out on to what is now known as Standard Hill. The banner itself was borne by the Knights Bannerets and escorted by three troops of horse and several hundred infantry from the county trained bands which had been summoned to the castle by the sheriff, Sir J. Digby. King Charles was accompanied by the

7   B

Judge's lodgings in High Pavement; eighteenth century, refronted about 1830

Prince of Wales, the Duke of York, the Princes Rupert and
Maurice, who had just arrived in England to offer their swords
in their uncle's cause, and a large number of the local Royalist
lords and gentry. The foot of the standard was fixed in a hole
that had been dug with daggers and knives, but it had to be held
firm while the herald read the proclamation aloud. When it was
done Charles suddenly called for pen and ink and made some
last-minute alterations in his own hand to the wording of the
appeal to arms. He laid down his pen; the trumpets sounded;
everyone in the crowd threw their hats into the air, gave a whoop
and cried, "God save King Charles and hang up the Roundheads." Then the standard was taken back in procession to the
castle where it flew from the topmost tower.

One lingers over that scene in order to represent the period
of the Civil War which follows. I don't intend to go over the
story of the activities of the two sides in and around Nottingham, because it would be necessary to say a good deal more about
it when we get to Newark. In fact the war affected only the two
towns of Nottingham and Newark. The rest of the county was, at
times, temporarily affected; but Retford, Worksop and Mansfield
were kept open and discreetly bowed to whatever faction was
locally in power.

The king may have chosen Nottingham in which to raise his
standard at that August 1642; but thenceforward the town's
history belonged to Parliament. Cromwell himself was in Nottingham by May 1643 and in that year John Hutchinson, whose
name will always be associated with the castle, entered the
Parliamentarian army with the rank of Lieutenant-Colonel and
was appointed Governor of Nottingham Castle and town. Hutchinson had been born in Nottingham in 1615 and educated in the
town, at Lincoln Free School, and later at Peterhouse, Cambridge.
Perhaps Nottingham's most remarkable contribution to the
history of the Civil War is of a literary sort, for the county gave to
posterity two extraordinary documents written by women. Not
only did Margaret, Duchess of Newcastle, who will find her place
in these pages a little later, record the life of the county's greatest
royalist commander, her husband the Duke, but Colonel Hutchinson's wife produced the most valuable biographical work to
come out of the whole period. Her memoirs of Colonel Hutchinson's life are conjoined to her own autobiography. This latter
does not take up much room, but its few pages give a strange and
unforgettable picture of an over-trained girl who, when no more
than seven years old, "had at one time eight tutors in several
qualities, languages, music, dancing, writing and needlework,

but her genius was quite averse from all her book". Mrs. Hutchinson wrote her life of her husband for the edification of their children. The picture of the man that she draws is carefully constructed. We meet Colonel Hutchinson first at Peterhouse, where "he was constant at their chapel", and "began to take notice of their stretching superstition to idolatry". We follow him to Lincoln's Inn and to the period of his courtship, in which he gained the hand of a woman considerably above him (she was Lucy, daughter of Sir Alan Apsley, a former Governor of Nottingham), "after about fourteen months' various exercise of his mind, in the pursuit of his love". Mrs. Hutchinson's account of the civil conflict in Nottinghamshire is full of interest. She makes it clear that Hutchinson realized that only the castle and the adjoining town were likely to remain in the hands of Parliament, and that he was long in expectation of a siege, first by Newcastle and then by Prince Rupert. But Hutchinson held his own against these dangers until circumstances changed after the battle of Marston Moor. Yet Hutchinson's worst troubles began after he had come up to London as a Member of Parliament, as part of a definitely republican group, in 1646. His wife's story accompanies through a bewildering period in which, after passing through relations of deep mutual distrust with Cromwell, finally exposed him, as one of the regicides, to the vengeance of the Restoration. She, herself, by her own skilful exertions played a large part in allowing him to escape with his life. But he was falsely accused of treasonable conspiracy in connection with the so-called Yorkshire Plot and in 1622 was confined first to the Tower of London and later in Sandown Castle. He died there in 1664. His wife calls his confinement there the act of "murderers", because, she says, "the place had killed him". If it was the restored Royalists who wreaked their vengeance on Colonel Hutchinson it was Hutchinson himself who dismantled Nottingham Castle, and Cromwell's Council of State which, in 1651, ordered the building to be demolished and the walls blown down with gunpowder. At the Restoration, by a twist of fortune, the Duke of Newcastle bought the site and cleared it of almost every vestige of the old fortress. Then, in 1674, he began to build, on the highest part of the rock, the palatial residence of which one can still get some idea of the outside appearance. It was completed in 1679 by his son, three years after the first duke's death. It consists of a rectangle with projecting wings at the back. The front facing the town is of nine bays, the short sides of three.

The architect of the castle was apparently a Lincolnshire man called March. The cost was computed at fourteen thousand and two pounds, seventeen shillings and eleven pence, which included a hundred and twenty pounds for cedar wood and thirty shillings for a saw to cut it with, likewise fifty-two pounds for marble chimney pieces and three pounds thirteen and fourpence for packing them. Over the north door was carved an equestrian statue—which still exists—of the first Duke of Newcastle. It is said to have been carved out of a single block of stone from Donnington in Leicestershire by a certain Sir William Wilson (Horace Walpole speaks of " Sir William Wilson of Leicester knighted March 8th 1681 was an architect and rebuilt the steeple of Warwick church after it had been burnt "). It is related that Wilson was seduced from art by a rich Leicestershire widow called Lady Putsey, who fell deeply in love with him. However, the lady died before him and since he had lived up to the extent of his apron-stringed state, Sir William was obliged to return to his former occupation of sculptor.

Under the Dukes of Newcastle, Nottingham Castle did no great credit to the town. A visitor towards the end of the eighteenth century describes the inside as being dull, devoid of pictures, and with most of the furniture removed. He writes: " I remember being shown a state bed, thirty or forty years ago said to have been slept on by Queen Anne; but that has journeyed hence, probably to return no more "; and then he adds, mysteriously, " some of the rooms I found occupied by a Miss Kirkby." Apparently a part of the castle at this time was used as a boarding-school. Anyway, until almost the time of its burning, the castle presented a picture of decay, with robins and sparrows as its chief occupants. A little later—somewhere about 1810—the castle was divided into flats and most of the windows were repaired. Apparently until then the townspeople were in the habit of airing themselves in the castle yard, but towards the end of the castle's second period of existence the porters grew surly and, unless bribed, would refuse to let them in.

As I have said, one cannot gain much impression of what the building might look like on a more suitable site because of the difficulty of getting away from it. Anyway, what one now sees is itself only a restoration; if you look carefully at some of the details of the baroque trophies which adorn the parapet you will see that they have been put together like an unsorted jigsaw puzzle. For, in 1831, the mansion was destroyed by fire during riots by the radical townspeople of Nottingham because of the opposition of the House of Lords to the Reform Bill. The Duke of Newcastle at the time was awarded the sum of twenty-one thousand pounds as compensation for the destruction of the building. But he did not use the money to rebuild it. For nearly fifty years the blackened walls alone remained. Then in 1878 the site was let on a five hundred years lease to the corporation of Nottingham. The corporation, with the aid of private subscriptions, thoroughly restored the ruins at a cost of thirty thousand pounds; and when the work was completed the building was opened by the Prince and Princess of Wales—later Edward VII and Queen Alexandra—as a permanent art gallery and a museum of decorative art. It was the first such municipal museum of art in England.

During the late war the castle was requisitioned by the Government and not released until March 1946. A year later the top floor of the castle was reopened to the public. When I was last there the ground floor and what had been the textile gallery were still shut. At the outbreak of war the contents of the museum had been dispersed, but enough is now on show to give an idea of how remarkable a collection it must have been (although from time to time one sees in the local Press complaints about the comprehensiveness of the collection of paintings which it contains. A few years ago at a meeting of the City Council a speaker declared " our municipal gallery is not an art gallery, it is a scrap book and a hotch-potch of little-known works "). It seems to me an unusually enjoyable museum even in its post-war state. It avoids parochialism in that the accent within its walls on purely Nottingham matters is relatively slight. To be sure you would do well to come here if you wanted to see a good example of the Nottinghamshire alabaster work of the Middle Ages. In the fifteenth century there was an immense export trade from Nottingham in alabaster reredoses to France, Spain and Germany. The only complete example of Nottinghamshire alabaster work in London, a reredos now in the Victoria and Albert Museum, came back from Germany, and such scarcity makes it all the more creditable that the Nottingham Castle Museum should have so fine a specimen. Again, there are pictures here by what may be claimed as local artists, Paul Sandby and his brother Thomas, and Richard Parkes Bonington, Henry Dawson and James Orrock (how and to what extent they are local I will discuss later), and there are such things as a painting of Nottingham by Turner. But, on the whole, it is a place of general instruction. Here, in an atmosphere far removed from the deadness and stuffiness of many provincial museums are to be seen sculptures, ceramics (strongly stressed), furniture and byegones as well as paintings and drawings. The museum has moved with the times. The whole collection is pleasingly displayed, making use of well-lighted wall cases, and well signed and lettered in the modern "exhibition" manner.

I don't think you will find Nottingham Castle in any way exhausting; but if you have had your fill of it you can come out and stand on the parapet and look down over the busy roofs of the city and over the Trent, or you can sit among grassy lawns on the seats provided. Or let me lead you by the hand and take you out through the gateway down Castle Road to a place that you must surely have heard of, to the Trip to Jerusalem Inn which, quite apart from its oddness in being built out of, or rather into, the rock on which the castle stands, really is in part medieval, so that its crusading title may indeed date back to the middle ages. It may be doubtful whether the dramatic capture of Edward Mortimer and the guilty queen in 1330 really took place through the underground passage below the castle known as Mortimer's Hole, but certain it is that for centuries good beer has been conveyed into the castle through the hole from what used to be known as Brewhouse Yard. It is not like going into an ordinary pub to disappear, as you do, through a perfectly conventional outside into a hole in the rock. In earlier times, of the two public houses which stood in Brewhouse Yard, one had a parlour cut in the rock with a hole at the top for the admission of light which was hence called Star parlour, while the second had a kitchen and two other large chambers cut in the rock. This an eighteenth-century writer described as "once an asylum for fanatics". There are many other excuses in the city for making your way to a pub. As you go down the hill from the castle towards the centre of the city you shouldn't miss the Salutation Inn, at the corner of St. Nicholas Street and Houndsgate. This ancient inn gives some idea, in its exterior appearance, of what the Nottingham buildings of the sixteenth century must have looked like. Take a glance, likewise, at the Windmill Inn at Weekday Cross; or, with reservations, at the very much restored and dressed-up Flying Horse Hotel in the Poultry, which retains some of its old gables. Though Nottingham is still famous for its pubs, a lot of the inns and taverns which have played their part in the city's history are no longer to be found. There is, indeed, the admirable Black Boy in Long Row, but where is the Black Moor's Head which used to stand at the south-west corner of Pelham Street? It was here that Byron's body rested in state before its final journey to Hucknall Torkard, in a room built in a corner of the courtyard. It seems to have been closed down about 1830. Vanished in the same way is the White Lion at the east end of Long Row, with an opening into what is now Clumber

Street and used to be called Cow Lane. Here in the mid-eighteenth century was to be found a cockpit; here the London coaches drew up and here in 1776 was held a meeting (of which we shall hear later) which resulted in the building of the first grandstand on Nottingham's race-course. Gone, too, the Crown in Long Row beside which, at much the same time, Nottingham's first newspaper began. Gone the Ram, gone the King's Head, gone the Bull's Head, where Bishop Corbett stayed in 1630. What other inns are there to mention? Early in the nineteenth century, it was remarked that the two principal taverns of the town were the Punchbowl and the Peacock, in and near Peck Lane, that many resorted to the old Angel at the end of St. Mary's Gate, facing the County Hall, and that it possibly stood on the site of an ancient dwelling called Bugge Hall, that the Feathers Inn had been the scene of the meeting of the stockingers during the famous strike of June 1779.

But we are down the hill now and in the centre of the city. The centre of an industrial town which, still bright and clean, differs markedly from the darkness of many of its midland neighbours. The central feature has always been the market-place which was one of the largest of its kind in England. Though it has ceased to be a market-place, the great open space, covering nearly six acres and having a circumference of close upon three-quarters of a mile, still provides the city with one of the grandest centres in the country. One of the reasons why the old town had so large a market was that the area comprised the market-places of the two boroughs of which Nottingham once consisted, the survivors of the Saxon and the Norman settlement, one on the castle hill and the other on the opposing eminence on which St. Mary's church stands. Market days in Nottingham are still Wednesdays and Saturdays, but the area between Long Row and South Parade is no longer filled with ranks of canvas-roofed stalls, nor is it here any longer that, on the first Thursday in October and for the next two days, the traditional Goose Fair, a pleasure fair in all but name, is held. Nowadays one must go up to the great green area north of Forest Road, which contains the Forest recreation ground, to that part of it which lies between Gregory Boulevard and Noel Street. The market-place is dominated by the Council House, an imposing public building of a rather conventionally grandiose neo-baroque character, which was opened on the 22nd of May, 1929, by the Prince of Wales, now Duke of Windsor. A lofty dome, bearing on its front a most useful and reliable clock, looks down on the broad pavements and the four enclosed lawns which have taken the place of the picturesque

13

medley of canvas stalls. The architect of the Council House was T. Cecil Howitt and his structure contains an interesting feature in that its centre is a shopping arcade of great height with a glass roof. In addition, shops run all along the ground floor on the north and south sides. The main front of the Council House consists of an arcade and portico on ground level which is surmounted by a porticoed and pedimented frontage to the main storey. The pediment is supported by eight ionic columns. Behind the columns are the seven tall windows of a great banqueting hall which opens on to the terrace overlooking the old market-square. The pediment itself is elaborately ornamented with figures in high-relief representing the activities of the city council, while right across the building under the pediment is a frieze in bas-relief portraying local crafts and industries. The building which this twentieth-century structure replaced was a simpler and duller affair, pedimented but domeless, though again equipped with an outsized clock. It was the site of the eighteenth-century New Change, which was built in 1724 from the designs of Major Marmaduke Pennell. The clock was the work of a well-known local eccentric of the name of Woolley, who came from Codnor in County Derby. The Change was a brick building ornamented with stone, some hundred and twenty feet long, supported by a range of stone columns forming a sort of parade or piazza under the building. On the centre of the top there was a figure of Justice. A number of niches in the front had been intended to hold statues of King George I and the then Prince and Princess of Wales, but the cost of the building, two thousand four hundred pounds, did not permit of the completion of this design. Behind the Change stood the butchers' shambles and if you went through the folding doors and up the stairs into the principal "long room", which contained an opening from which fairs and other events were proclaimed, one was standing over the thirty-four butchers' stalls of which the shambles consisted. In the south-west corner of the old shambles was a square room "wainscotted and seated about" where the mayor and the sheriffs used to meet in order to make their ceremonial perambulation of the Saturday market. In this room, also, there used to sit all day long, whenever there was a market, the steward and his deputy in order to enter auctions and take bail. All through the eighteenth and nineteenth centuries, the Nottingham market was one of the sights of the country. It was formerly divided lengthwise in two by a wall breast high which had openings at intervals for you to pass through. On the north, that is the Long Row side, were sold corn, malt, oatmeal and salt; and here were situated the stalls and booths used by milliners, pedallers, sailshops, hardware men, bakers, turners, brasiers, tinmen, chandlers, collarmakers and gardeners. On the south side between this dividing wall and what is described as "a large hanging bank" was the horse-market. This, unlike the other part of the market, was not paved and went by the name of the Sands. At the east end of the bank, in the eighteenth century, were sold all sorts of sawn timber—boards, planks, quarters, panels and all kinds of material for carpenters, joiners and coopers; in consequence the handsome row of houses built along the bank was known as Timber Hill. On the remaining part of the bank were sheep-folds for the use of country people bringing their flocks into the town to sell.

West of the horse-market, that is alongside Angel Row, was the beast-market whose memory survives to-day in that part of the west side of the market-place between Angel Row and Wheeler Gate. The swine-market lay between the edge of the beasts and sheep-folds. It is interesting to see the gradual changes that took place as the eighteenth century passed into the nineteenth in the arrangement of stalls and commodities. At the time of the battle of Waterloo, for instance, the gardeners more or less monopolized the north side of the market with their fruit and vegetables, while the corn-market was then lower down and near the centre. Here, between noon and two o'clock on Saturdays, were to be found farmers from all over the southern part of the county not with their goods in bulk, but carrying samples in their pockets. The sheep and swine were still to be found between the corn and the beast-market; northwards you could look for butter, between the last row of stalls in Long Row for basket chairs and barrels; if you moved eastwards from the barrels you ran into fish; and close to the baskets was earthenware. The beasts had been moved, after various vicissitudes, to a position in Parliament Street where, from the beginning of the nineteenth century, stallions were also shown, consequent upon a countrywoman's having been killed by one in the market-place. Fowls, obviously, in Poultry. By this time the market was nearly surrounded by arcades and one had a nice sheltered walk going round it.

The old Change has gone, but there still survives from the eighteenth century the Shire Hall on the south side of High Pavement. This was built in 1770 by Gandon, who was the architect of the Dublin Customs House. It is a small but strong, if slightly heavy-looking, stone building in respectable taste with an attached ionic portico and some late nineteenth-century extensions. After it was first built there was much complaint about the bad acoustics, the vibration and echoes in the two courts, each with public galleries, which the hall contained. Let us look around for other reminders of Nottingham's pre-industrial past. First to be mentioned are Collin's almshouses in Friar Lane, a delightful group of two-storeyed houses, which even at the time were considered to "look like a gentleman's house". Abel Collin had died in 1704 and left money to provide, for twenty-four poor men and women, what has survived as one of the best almshouses of its date in England. The Plumtre Hospital in Plumtre Square has not been so fortunate. This was a very old foundation, dating back to about 1415, and the building of 1650, a somewhat irregular brick structure with earlier stone remnants of a chapel, survived until the early nineteenth century. The present building with a central pediment and, in contrast, perpendicular windows, dates from 1823.

In Low Pavement and westward up to the castle there are many great eighteenth-century houses and one of them, Newdigate House, deserves special attention because of an extraordinary and long-remembered episode in Nottingham's history which centred round it. It is No. 7 in Castle Gate—the best street, architecturally, in Nottingham—and dates back to the late seventeenth century with stately alternating window pediments and admirable ironwork railings and gates. I don't know who Mrs. Newdigate was, but she is of little importance compared with a temporary resident who was one of the most fascinating and certainly the most exotic character in the city's history. He was Marshal Tallard—or, to give him his full name and, I fancy his correct spelling—Camille D' Hostun duc de Tallart, Marshal of France. He, born in 1652, had fought under Condé in Holland and under Turenne in Alsace during the years 1674-5. He had become a brigadier in 1677, a Marechal de Camp the following year and Lieutenant-General in 1693; later he was sent as envoy-extraordinary to William III's court in London. In the final struggle against Marlborough and Prince Eugene of Savoy, Marshal Tallard was in command of the French and the Bavarians when they were defeated at the battle which is known on the Continent as Hochstadt and to us as Blenheim. On the 13th of August, the allies, English and Austrian, lost some twelve thousand men, and the French and Bavarians over thirty thousand killed, wounded and prisoners. Among those taken prisoner was the enemy commander-in-chief himself (surely one of the quite rare occasions on which a C-in-C *has* been taken prisoner) and with him the following—a list which has a certain local interest for all these officers were destined to accompany the Marshal to Nottingham: the Marquis de Montperroux, General of Horse;

the Marquis de Hautefeuille, General of Dragoons; Comte de Blanzar, Lieutenant-General; five Major-Generals, the Marquis de Valsème, Marquis de Seppeville, Marquis de Silly (the Nottingham populace must have enjoyed some crude fun at his expense), the Marquis de Vallière and the Chevalier de Crossy; then there was a brigadier, a colonel of dragoons and a certain Comte de Horne.

This party of twelve noblemen with, one supposes, an ample train of batmen, horseholders and other servants—amounting perhaps to fifty Frenchmen in all—provided Nottingham with a pleasantly strange addition to its population during their sojourn of seven or eight years in the first decade of the eighteenth century. They were detained in London for a few months, then, just six months after the battle on the grounds that it was not safe to leave Marshal Tallard in reach of a seaboard, he was moved to a place which was presumably chosen as being absolutely central and as completely inland as could be found. This was on the 22nd of February, 1705. The move alone is said to have cost the country two thousand and fifty pounds. The route was by way of Market Harborough and Leicester. At Market Harborough Tallard's party and escort lodged at the Swan. (Would this be the present Three Swans, in recent times enlivened by the proprietorship of Mr. John Fothergill?) Reports were promptly received in London that Tallard's party had been set upon by a mob, but later dispatches from Market Harborough were reassuring: it was "only occasioned by a few drunken fellows who, when they had seen the Marshal, were satisfied and went away". The reports contained some more general information about the progress of the party: "the French gentlemen have all their victuals dressed by their own cooks, who make in particular excellent soup. They travel but a few miles in a day, having a great equipage with them." Arrived in Nottingham, Marshal Tallard was accommodated, as we have seen, in what was then known as Mrs. Newdigate's house; and the Frenchman, established in Castle Gate, was neither a destructive nor a passive tenant. He improved Newdigate House and laid out the gardens behind it, which became in time one of the sights of Nottingham. Nowadays, our only way of judging its appearance is from the plan printed in Deering's early nineteenth-century *History of Nottingham*. This suggests that Newdigate House must have been a delightful little town estate. The house and garden fill the space between Castle Hill and Houndsgate and ran from Castle Road to Jew Lane. Inside the estate there was a gate on to Castle Gate opposite St. Nicholas church. A contemporary account reads: " When Marshal Tallard was taken prisoner the government gave him this pretty town of Nottingham as his prison; and in the seven years he stayed there he made very fine gardens to the house he lived in, which he gave to his landlord at his departure." It is presumably from this date that there is to be found the origin of a distich from a ballad circulated about the perennial excellence of the Nottingham beer:

> If he'll take t'other boat, we'll let Tallard out;
> And much he's improved, let me tell 'ee;
> With Nottingham ale at every meal,
> And good pudding and beef in his belly.

Marshal Tallard seems to have stuck in the minds of eighteenth-century Nottingham. He was the high-level prisoner par excellence—a sort of Hess: when, as late as 1745, Horace Walpole, speaking of another French Marshal, made prisoner at Hanover, writes, " he has been sent to Nottingham à la Tallarde ", the reference obviously needed no explanation.

Tallard himself settled down at Newdigate House; but it is a strange fact that the whole body of French officers other than Tallard himself seemed promptly to have vanished into thin air. They appear to have left Nottingham soon after the arrival there of the party. There are no records, for instance, of the marriages of any of these Frenchmen in the neighbouring parish registers.

An interesting light on the civilized attitude of the eighteenth century towards prisoners of war (or is it merely a reflection of the international scale of the importance then associated with title and rank?) is given by a letter, addressed to Tallard by a certain Thomas Cooke. Cooke, writing from St. James' Place, London, where he is described as a " vice chamberlain ", on the 17th April, 1705—a month or so after Tallard's arrival in Nottingham—in a strangely apologetic manner: " I have hazarded sending you fifty bottles of champagne and as many of Vosne, by the coaches that have left here for Nottinghamshire this morning, and which will arrive Friday evening." And Cooke goes on in the same apologetic vein: " I should hardly pretend to send you champagne and burgundy, knowing how much they fail to be so good as those which are drunk in France. But having found that which we esteem good in this country passably good . . ." and Cooke proceeds to dispatch some to Nottingham. The official position of this useful communicant of Marshal Tallard's seems to have been " one of the terrors of her Majesty's (that is Queen Anne's) exchequer ", so it is clear that Tallard was being kept in these luxuries at the public expense. However, the wines sent from London by this almost obsequious Whitehall civil servant were not good enough for Tallard. Another Whitehall official called E. Lewis, writes to Tallard at this time: "Monseigneur. I have this morning been to the Commissioners of Customs to acquaint them of the Queen's intentions of allowing your wine to pass through . . . so that M. de Santigni has only to tell them the name of the ship which is entrusted with it, and means will be found to allow it to enter without giving you any difficulty. . . ."

The ensuing correspondence shows that the officer detailed as British liaison officer or A.D.C. to the captive Marshal in Nottingham was a Captain John Wroth. There survives a letter from him, describing himself as "Captain-in-waiting to Marshall Tallard", addressed to the same Thomas Cooke in London, thanking him for the loan of books.

Marshal Tallard and his officers were obviously allowed a fair amount of freedom within a given radius of Nottingham. We hear, for instance, of the Marshal having dined, "together with three French officers and four English gentlemen" at the Earl of Chesterfield's seat near Burton-on-Trent.

But Tallard's legacy to Nottingham was his garden; and since it appears in many eighteenth-century and later references to Nottingham, and in plans of the town, it is worth dwelling on for a moment.

There were, we are told—and it is easy to believe in 1705—few gardeners and no skilled ones, in Nottinghamshire until the arrival of Marshal Tallard. One effect of his imprisonment was that "encouragement was given to men of industry to render themselves useful by raising all kinds of garden stuff".

Tallard has been credited with the discovery of celery. Certainly the introduction of celery into the English menu dates from this time. It has been suggested either that Tallard's men found this crisp and delicious vegetable by accident when they were looking for pot herbs for soup or salads; or, alternatively, that, aware of it from France, they searched for it and found it growing wild. (The village of Lenton is specified in some accounts as the place where the wild celery roots were discovered.) However, it is a much more likely story that these eighteenth-century Frenchmen introduced the cultivated plant into their Nottingham gardens and that the wild specimens that have been found, from time to time, in the neighbourhood of the town were escapes from this imported seed.

Marshal Tallard must have employed a considerable number of workmen on this garden, and had drawn up the plans (they are

19

believed to be of his own inspiration) very quickly, for the garden was ready for inspection by the benighted and gardenless inhabitants of Nottingham by about the month of August 1705, that is only six months after Tallard's arrival in the town. According to some authorities, an admission fee was charged to those citizens who wished to inspect this sample of eighteenth-century civilization that had been so unexpectedly brought to their doorsteps. The plan of the Nottingham garden appears to have been twice engraved: in the second edition of Louis Liger's *Le Jardiner Solitaire*, published in Paris in this same year, 1705, and in the English translation of this work by G. Loudon and H. Wise, under the title of the *Retired Gardener*, which was published in London by Jacob Constant.

Certain indications of what the gardens looked like survive. There was, we are told, a *parterre*, "with angles, squares, semi-circles and branch-work, of *gazon coupé* (or cut-works in grass)" which, incidentally, cannot have been very "mature" as the house agents say, by the end of 1705. The *parterre* was covered, oddly enough, "with red sand or brick dust". As other ingredients of the garden the contemporary account gives: "the slug of pit-coal fine beaten, yellow sand; spar, from the lead-mines, or cockle shell beaten very fine; the walks in fine gravel of different colours." Marshal Tallard's garden must at least have had colour and pattern; in addition, we are told, "there were borders of flowers, slopes, steps, terraces, pyramids and gravel paths". No mention is made of any statuary: perhaps it was too much to ask of these outlandish Midlanders to produce any such ornaments, and even the obsequious Cooke evidently could not insinuate a shipload of them through the customs in time for the first showing of the garden that autumn.

Daniel Defoe saw Tallard's garden (he refers to it in his *A Journey through England in Familiar Letters from a Gentleman here to his Friend Abroad*) and comments, "'Tis said that this gallant gentleman left behind him some *living* memorandums of his great affection and esteem for the English ladies": as to whether this was so or not I can offer no evidence. Just at the time the Tallards' garden was open to the public a certain J. Taylor published a travel book called *A Journey to Eden-borough*. Under the date 11th of August, 1705, we find when Taylor visited Nottingham that he noted "the French prisoners lived very privately, the Marshal paying only fifty shillings per week for his apartments". Of the already famous garden in Castle Gate Taylor observed that "it is but small but it is very neat". Taylor and his friends caught a glimpse of the Marshal and saluted him with a bow which, they reported, " he returned very obligingly ".

There is something pleasantly remote from our abusive and insult-ridden age in this courteous curiosity about a hostile leader. Perhaps the change was to come only a full century later, when the age of dictators began. Neither Tallard nor his master, Louis XIV, could be thought of as " *le monstre* ", which is one of the ways the English described Napoleon. Or was it only the fact that the greater Napoleon was the first Continental captain since William the Conqueror actively to threaten these shores?

To gain some picture of what the town that Marshal Tallard saw around him looked like we might begin with some geographical facts and some statistical matter, taken from a little after Tallard's time, in the 1740's and 50's. In the town as a whole there were " streets, lanes, courts, rows, etc., beside yards, to the number of ninety ". Far the longest street was Back Side, which boasted two hundred and fourteen houses, containing some thirteen hundred-odd souls. Back Side, which formed the extreme northern limit of urbanization, is now made up of Upper and Lower Parliament Street from its present western end, the junction of the Derby Road and Chapel Bar, to where Lower Parliament Street is crossed by Broad Street (which was then known as Broad Lane). The south-north axis through the town led up London Road, round past the east end of St. Mary's, up Stoney Street, up Broad Street, across Back Side which petered out, east of this crossing, into Coal Pitt Lane, leading past orchards and a brick yard to the junction with Goose Gate. The River Leen (now the Notts Canal) formed the southern limit of urbanization. The line of the present Manvers Street and Brook Street provided the eastern limits, beyond which there was nothing but fields. On the west, of course, the castle on its slopes formed the limit of building. The most highly populated area was between Upper Parliament Street and the line of Chapel Bar and Long Row. Here are a few figures. In Castle Gate there were ninety-two houses containing about four hundred and fifty-two people. In Rotten Row and Cuckstool Row (which formed, respectively, the north and south sides of what is now South Parade) there were twenty-three houses containing a hundred and twenty-three people. In High Pavement there were no fewer than forty-eight houses containing two hundred and forty people; while around the castle and Brewhouse Yard (close to the Trip to Jerusalem) there were eighteen houses with sixty-seven people in them.

There were materials ready to hand for the building, decorating and repairing of these increasingly numerous houses. First, it is worth glancing at the price of bricks in the mid-eighteenth century (most of the Nottingham houses of this period are brick). Common bricks cost ten shillings a thousand; dressed brick seventeen shillings a thousand; flat tiles fifteen shillings; pantiles thirty shillings a thousand. This was at a time when prices in the Nottingham market for more familiar commodities may be gathered from the following: meat (of all sorts), averaging 3s. for a fourteen-pound joint; butter, 4d. to 6d. a lb.; eggs, 4d. a dozen; small beer, 1½d. a gallon; salmon, 4d. to 1s. a lb.; Lincolnshire oysters, 4d. to 6d. a score; coal (which cost 23s. a ton in London) brought to your door in Nottingham for 10s. a ton. Consequently it will be seen that bricks, the fundamental building material, were not outrageously expensive. Building in Nottingham had been confined, until the time of Henry VIII, to wood and plaster. It is recorded that the first tiled house in the town was built in 1503: it belonged to a Mr. Stanton and the building was at one time occupied by the Unicorn Inn.

Passing from brick to stone, there was freestone to be had from Mansfield and a stone that was considered not unlike the fashionable Bath stone, which was quarried at Gedling. (A word about this village as it is the best opportunity of noticing its existence. It contains a pleasant church with an unusually fine stone spire and a modern crescent of almshouses designed by T. Cecil Howitt who, you may remember, was the architect of Nottingham's Council House. Gedling is also notable for being the birthplace of two celebrated cricketers—Arthur Shrewsbury, whom W. G. Grace called the greatest batsman of his age, and Alfred Shaw, known as "the Emperor of Bowlers". The two went four times together to play in Australia, and when they retired they together opened an athletic outfitter's shop in Nottingham.)

After stone, lime. Lime was obtained from four places locally. First, from Linby. (Quite a celebrated place, this colliery village— because, at the Castle Mill, a battlemented structure on the edge of the village, whose water-wheel is a hundred feet and more in circumference, the great James Watt set up, in 1785, the first engine to power a cotton mill. This mill is the most interesting feature of Linby, which is anyway a charming village, with its stone cottages, its stream along the high street, two village crosses, and church of St. Michael with some Norman survivals and a fragment of fourteenth-century stained glass. The castellations of the mill, with embattled corner towers, pointed door and quatrefoil openings, is presumed to be part of the improvements in the

Nottingham: the " Trip to Jerusalem" under the Castle rock

YE OLDE TRIP TO
JERUSALEM INN
1189. A.D

THE OLDEST home
brewed
INN IN ENGLAND

district of Papplewick close at hand, of which we shall hear in a moment. The mill is fun to look at; but to work it poor London children were imported wholesale, and the Linby churchyard contains a hundred and sixty-three graves of children killed by forced labour.)

The neighbouring Papplewick is a place worth dwelling on for a moment, not only because of its contribution of lime to Nottingham. Let us go, first, to the church. This, a rarity in these times, was, when I visited it recently, in almost painfully good condition, tremendously clean and redecorated, with new wooden pews in the nave and a new central-heating system. To get to the church you make your way down a long narrow approach from the main road: the church is some distance from the village of Papplewick. From a distance you might take it for the usual medieval Nottinghamshire village church whose western tower has Decorated bell-stage openings. But the curved corners of the battlements of the nave and the sort of central pediment over the south porch give the building away as a piece of late eighteenth-century Gothic. The newness and present good condition of the church is due to the generosity of the Chadburn family, of the Mansfield brewery, who now live at the charming house which lies not far across the fields from the church. This house, like the rebuilding in the Gothic manner, in 1795, of the church of St. James, dates back to the Honourable Frederick Montagu, a Lord of the Treasury, and a friend of the poets Thomas Gray (of the *Elegy*) and William Mason who wrote part of his *The English Garden* here. Though modest in size and discreet in decoration, Papplewick Hall is an admirable building of stone, with a rusticated ground floor and large pilasters above, supporting a pediment. There may well be fact behind its traditional attribution to the brothers Adam. In the grounds are to be seen an urn to the memory of Gray and a little Tuscan temple in memory of Mason. Frederick Montagu's initials are carved over the church porch and, in the churchyard, his curious tomb, like a solid, sensible, outdoor table with six square fluted legs. Montagu, friend of poets, was a versifier himself, and is said to have composed the following lines to go under the bust of the Marquis of Rockingham, which he placed in his library at Papplewick:

> Gentle, intrepid, mild and just,
> These heartfelt titles grace his honoured bust.
> No fields of blood by laurels ill-repaid,
> No plundered provinces disturb his shade.

*Nottingham: the modern Council House overlooking
the site of the ancient market*

But white-robed peace composed his closing eyes,
And joined with soft humanity his sighs.
They mourn their patron gone, their friend no more,
And England's tears his short-lived power deplore.

In addition, Montagu was one of those who helped to prepare the impeachment of Warren Hastings.

Although not far from Nottingham, Papplewick still lies in delicious and nearly unspoilt rolling country. It might be worth quoting a description of the surroundings of the house just after it was built: "The situation of the house is well chosen, from whence there is a most pleasing and extensive view; the ground, formed by nature into swells and declivities which slope smoothly into a plane without any abrupt or broken parts, has been laid out with infinite taste and judgment. Here a variety of beautiful scenes open to the view which, with that necessary appendage, a strong foreground, and the fortunate combination of wood and water, form the most picturesque scenery imaginable. A walk of about two miles surrounds these improvements and a ride of four miles is carried through well-cultivated fields enriched with a variety of spreading trees and takes in the whole of what may truly be called a 'a farm orné'"—— And that indeed may truly be called a perfect contemporary expression of the picturesque attitude towards nature and of those "improvements" carried out in the second half of the eighteenth century which, to so large an extent, created the apparently natural but, in fact, man-made "English landscape" which we have inherited.

We have digressed from the prosaic matter of the sources of lime for the houses of eighteenth-century Nottingham. . . . Next on the list after Linby and Papplewick is Bulwell—a large village that has become a suburb of Nottingham. It contains a church of 1850; a house, Bulwell Hall, now an Approved School, a stuccoed place with a central Venetian window and wings connected with curving colonnades, dating from 1770; and an old school, Strelley House, in Commercial Road, dating from 1667. It has curved and stepped Dutch gables, was a grammar school and has recently been used as a recreation centre by The Association of Unemployed Workers.

Finally, lime came from Nuthall—and here sadness and a little bitterness must creep into our account. For there used to be at Nuthall an object of interest and beauty which brought connoisseurs of architecture into the county from far afield. Nuthall Temple, one of the most delightful, and also one of the smallest, houses in the whole country was demolished in our own lifetime.

The disappearance of the loveliest of the half-dozen or so direct English descendants of the villas of Palladio is indeed "a disgrace", as Professor Pevsner calls it, to the county and to our epoch: the building was destroyed in 1929.

A word about the village first. Nuthall was, at the time of the Norman Conquest, called Nuthole. It contains a church dedicated to Saint Patrick, a thirteenth-century affair with a low tower; it contains some good heraldic glass and one of the Nottinghamshire alabaster monuments, to a certain Sir Robert Cokefield, who died at the end of the fourteenth century. At the end of the eighteenth century, the lordship of Nuthall was owned by the Honourable Henry Sedley and it was his family which built, with the same inspiration as produced Lord Burlington's villa at Chiswick, a domed and porticoed temple in direct imitation of Palladio's Villa Rotunda. Now, alas, no more remains of it than its appearance preserved in many engravings and in the minds of architectural historians, and the memory of superb stucco work inside which included reliefs of pheasants and ducks and swags of fruit. Consequently, to recreate this gay and elegant villa (whose only relic on the site is a small Gothic summer-house) it might be well to turn again to an eighteenth-century view of the setting and the building:

"The seat of the Honourable Henry Sedley stands on a fine plain an easy distance from the village. It is a modern-looking building in a style of singularity, and stands unsheltered from storms and tempests." (The writer, of course, has hit on the two objections to the transplantation to our northern clime of any purely Mediterranean style of habitation—that it *looks* as though it must be cold and draughty, however chic and "modern". The same objection applies equally to an eighteenth-century imitation of Palladio as to a twentieth-century "modern" villa with verandahs and flat roof for sun-bathing.) The eighteenth-century account continues: "if the dwelling were backed by lofty woody screens it might, in some measure, take from its temple semblance and prevent the sight of distant objects, and the surrounding landscape seen from the eminent look-out on the crown of this seat. The woody scenery on the right and left of the temple, although apparently somewhat formal at a distance, possesses a pleasing diversity.

"Its doom within," the eighteenth-century account goes on in an awful way—awful until we realize that "doom" is just dome —"its doom within is a beautiful display of fancy work [these were the reliefs of game and fruit] and deserve the peculiar attention of the stranger. The gallery is supported by handsome pillars.

This part of the interior of the dwelling, taking only a transient view around, has a light, airy and pleasing effect. Bacchus, the God of Wine, welcomes the visitor with a cheerful countenance."

The Sedleys of Nuthall, incidentally, included the famous Sir Charles, the poet of Charles II's reign who was known as Apollo's Viceroy and died in 1701 at the age of ninety.

What led us to Nuthall in the first place was the fact that it was the last of four places which contained limeworks whose products were used in the construction of the houses of Nottingham.

Plaster, too, of course, was much needed—especially for plaster floors, which were used extensively in Nottingham houses before the nineteenth century. The plaster came chiefly from Gotham and from Cropwell.

Cropwell Bishop has an old church with ten carved benches dating from the beginning of the fifteenth century, ornamented with poppy-heads. The plaster, which has brought us here, we find to be made in a mill by the Grantham canal, alongside which is a gypsum well. Close by is the village of Cropwell Butler, whose name is said to be taken from that of an old family, the Botillers. Here are to be found a couple of cottages which are among the few surviving examples in the county of timber-framed construction.

You might perhaps expect the town, and the county, with the oaks of Sherwood at its disposal, to be especially rich in timbered building. It is not so; and a moment's thought suggests why. There were great timbered mansions, rows of oaken houses and shops, churches with wooden steeples, no doubt. But this is a county which has never had a "great past": it has always lived in the present and its prosperity, if changing in basis, has been continuous. Money was constantly available in the locality to take advantage of new fashions and methods of building, and there was no need to hold on to outmoded structures. Timbered survivals are decidedly rare here. There springs to mind, certainly, the carved timber frame of what used to be the White Hart Inn in the market-place at Newark; the wooden turret of the old church at Markham Clinton; not much else. The oak of Sherwood either grows in the ground still or has vanished altogether. In the eighteenth century, timber was obviously not a scarce commodity for Nottingham. Nevertheless, even in the 1750's there were "good old days", pre-war days so to speak, to be looked back on. "Oak timber," wrote a local commentator of that period, "will not allow the people to be so lavish as to waste it as former ages have." But he adds that "according to the present manner of building, we want not a necessary quantity about us, the property of private gentlemen, of whom it may be purchased at reasonable rates." And foreign timber—including, presumably, the mahogany from Jamaica, Cuba and Honduras that had gradually, since George I's reign, ousted the national oak from the fashionable cabinet-maker's shop—" as to what wood is used of foreign product the Trent conveys hither by way of Hull." Regional patriotism was eager to suggest to the great landlords, busy adorning their mansions in the Dukeries and elsewhere, that " those whose affluence of fortune will allow them to decorate their houses with marble, may be supplied with divers sorts of almost all colours, by our neighbour the county of Derby, which in some places falls little short of the foreign ". Paving stone for courtyards and halls, which had formerly been taken out of the bed of the Trent itself, was in the eighteenth century and later brought in ample quantities from Keyworth and near by. But we were discussing the even closer sources of material, " little inferiour to the Plaister of Paris ", for the floors of Nottingham houses, rich or poor.

Next we move to a place whose occupation, besides mining, is still the preparation of plaster—Gotham. It's not a very exciting village to look at but it is famous throughout England because of its so-called Merry Tales, which recount how the Wise Men of Gotham dragged a cart to the top of a barn to shade the roof from the sun, burnt down a forge to get rid of a wasp's nest, tried to drown an eel in a pond and performed other illogical experiments. But it is for building a hedge round a cuckoo to keep it from flying away that the wisdom of Gotham is best known, and you can refresh yourself at the Cuckoo Bush Inn where this exploit is supposed to have taken place. Nobody seems to know exactly how these stories originated, but a tradition claims that the inhabitants of Gotham were anxious that King John should not build there a threatened hunting-lodge, with all its concomitant impositions, or make a public road across their meadows, so they *pretended* to act foolishly in order to encourage the king to go elsewhere. Needless to say this flattering theory is largely a local one. On the derogatory proverb, " As wise as a man of Gotham ", the learned Thomas Fuller wrote in his *Worthies of England* (1662), " it passes publicly for the periphrasis of a Fool, and an hundred fopperies are feigned and fathered on the townfolk of Gotham. Here," says Fuller in his discursive way, " two things may be observed. One. Men in all ages have made themselves merry with singling out some place and fixing the staple of stupidity and stolidity therein. Thus the Phrygians were accounted the fools of all Asia, and the anvils of other men's wits to work upon. In Greece take a single city, and then Abdera in Thracia carried it away for dullheads. But for a whole country commend us the Boetians for blockheads and Boetium ingenium is notoriously known. In Germany auris Batava is taken by the poet for a dull ear which hath no skill in witty conceits. Two. These places thus generally slighted and scoffed at afforded some as witty and wise as the world produced. Thus Plutarch himself (sayeth Erasmus) was a Boetian, and Erasmus a Batavian or Hollander and therefore (his own copyhold being touched in proverb) he expoundeth auris Batava as a grave and severe ear. But," writes Fuller at last, " to return to Gotham it doth breed as wise people as any which carelessly laugh at their simplicity. Sure I am Mr. William de Gotham, fifth Master of Michaelhouse at Cambridge, anno 1336, and twice chancellor of the university was as grave a governor as that age did afford. And Gotham is a goodly large lordship, where the ancient and well-respected family of St. Andrew have flourished some hundreds of years, till of late the name is extinct."

So wrote Fuller in the seventeenth century, and if his justification of Gotham's wisdom is not altogether watertight at least he points the way into the church of St. Lawrence at Gotham whose remarkable thirteenth-century steeple towers over the working-class estates of Nottingham, which are beginning to encroach on Gotham. In the church are some monuments to the St. Andrew family, particularly that of John St. Andrew, who died in 1625. This touching monument has John St. Andrew's children kneeling, a row of diminutive figures, in front of their parents with a baby in its cradle on the extreme left.

A passage might certainly be added about Nottingham and Nottinghamshire sayings, most of which have to do with either places or people. We have been discussing the building and the building materials of the city of Nottingham from the mid-eighteenth century onwards and we ought certainly to add that " Nottingham once stood on Mapperly Hills "—a reference to the fact that most of the bricks of which Nottingham was constructed, anyway after the mid-nineteenth century, were made on these hills. Then there is the curious expression, " The little smith of Nottingham Who does the work which no man can ". This expression was current from about 1620 onwards, and Fuller made a most erudite suggestion as to its origin. He put forward a theory that " Nottingham was merely a corruption of the Greek *nemo autis* " meaning a person who never was. Of the expression, current, we are told, in mid-Victorian times amid the lower classes, " Who shall be Johnny Arnold? ", meaning " Who shall be the stake-holder?", we find that Johnny Arnold was by no means *nemo autis*: he was apparently a well-known local eccentric, who was very partial to making bets of small amounts, but for which he would always hold the stakes himself. Then, of old, one might find someone in these parts saying to you, "Don't be like David Lowe and get into prison for dreaming". This expression appears to have its origin in an historical event. In 1757 a certain Wilson, a hawker, lived in Narrow Marsh, Nottingham (Narrow Marsh is represented to-day by Cliff Road—while Broad Marsh, which was roughly the continuation eastwards of Narrow Marsh, still retains its name). Wilson had his house broken into and, we are told, his silver plate stolen (which seems to suggest that the profession of barrow-boy was as lucrative then as it is now). Wilson had a neighbour, by name David Lowe, who came one morning to Wilson's home shortly after the burglary and declared that he had dreamt that Wilson's plate was in a certain pigsty that he was ready to point out. There, sure enough, the plate was found. It is the consequence of this revelation that gave rise to the saying, "Don't be like David Lowe and get into prison for dreaming", because the unfortunate Lowe was, in fact, jailed for two weeks, and only discharged in the end because of his good character and the fact that, except for his embarrassingly accurate dream, there was no evidence against him whatever.

A personality of a kind familiar in most country towns is recalled in the phrase, "Being shown the High Street by old Rushton". The particular tavern from which one could expect to be bounced by Rushton was the Elephant and Castle.

A local character who must not be confused with David Lowe was David Love, the pedlar-poet or "flying stationer". He was born in Scotland in 1750 and was brought up as a beggar. He turned miner for a while, in the pits at Culross, and then, in 1790, enlisted in the Duke of Buccleugh's South Fencibles, at the beginning of a time of national emergency when the French threat to British security was growing. He assumed the pack and traversed England from end to end with books and stationery. As a sideline he sold rhymed tracts in the streets. He saved £3 and married a woman called Thompson. Almost simultaneously he turned author and published a heartfelt composition called *The Pride and Vanity of Young Women*. Having been discharged from the Fencibles, where discipline was very lax, in about 1793, he continued his tramping and ultimately hawked only his own compositions. In 1796, David Love was abruptly "converted" while at Newbury and his tracts took on a markedly religious tone. He kept a bookseller's shop, sold quack medicines, was jailed for nomadism, and made his living by selling rhymes, acrostics and hymns at a ½d. each. Ultimately he settled in Nottingham, where he had always found the bulk of his patronage and where most of his books were printed. He lived mainly in the neighbourhood of what was then called Leen Side and is now Canal Street. Here is his own description of his coming to Nottingham. "When we arrived here, we took a furnished room in Chandlers Lane and there my wife brought me a second son. A short time before the storm of 1814 we all four went into St. Mary's workhouse, was there above three months, then came out and took an empty house, 66 Plumb Street, Turncalf Alley, where we resided some years." (Turncalf Alley is now Sussex Street.) Love died in 1827, but his third wife, who had married him, she said, "for his scholarship" and whose "silk wheel" in part supported him, was still to be met in the town less than a hundred years ago, for she did not die, at the age of eighty-three, until 1853. Love's own autobiography (with portrait) was one of his most successful, self-travelled, productions. It went through five editions. As a sample of Love's poetic style here are some lines about the city which he made his home and in which he died:

> When first to Nottingham I came
> I found it was a town of fame;
> This place I loved exceeding well,
> As here I many books did sell.

Not so constructive, nor so commercial as David Love, but clearly the possessor of a certain imaginative wit, was a Nottingham character of the next generation—he who was known as "General Monk", but whose name was in fact Benjamin Mayo. Mayo was a round-shouldered idiot about four feet nine inches tall, who had been born in Nottingham about 1779 and suddenly, at the age of sixty, took to wearing a very conspicuous military headdress. He enlarged upon this idiosyncrasy by periodically running through the streets of his native town shouting, "Here's the grand and noble speech as the Duke o' York made yesterday." Upon prevailing on some uninitiated passer-by to enquire further, General Monk would press upon him a blank sheet of paper, adding as explanation, "the Duke said nowt". This inoffensive and witty fellow fell peculiar victim to the rising cost of living in the hungry forties, for he got it into his head that, as the price of everything increased, so he must increase the number of matches he sold for a 1d. It is therefore not surprising that he died, in 1843, in the workhouse. A memorial tablet to him was placed in the general cemetery.

We have time to note in passing James o' Burns or Burnes, otherwise known as Shelford Tommy, from the place where he had settled. He was a ventriloquist and was sent to jail for sending a young girl into a fit from her alarm at the squeals of a baby which he made to come as if from her feet.

We cannot very well leave the matter of eccentricity without recalling an oddity concerning one resident of Nottingham which was none the less remarkable because the fame it brought him was so completely posthumous. All Nottingham at one time had heard of Moore's Concretion, and it seemed to exert a fascination on townspeople of an enquiring and curious mind. What was it? Let me tell you, by means of a contemporary account of its discovery in the year 1792. Let me say that the architectural opening of the story gives no hint of the personal denouement: "An extraordinary occurrence happened this year in St. Mary's churchyard. It was found necessary to improve the passage by the side of the churchyard leading to the County Hall, which could not be erected without taking down some houses on the churchyard wall which stood on the south side of the church; and the better to widen the road it was also necessary to use a part of the churchyard. The ground being much higher here than in the street, when the fence wall was removed, there happened, one night, a heavy shower of rain, which washed away a considerable portion of earth from the churchyard. In consequence several coffins were left bare of covering, and some removed; amongst which was one that contained the remains of Mr. William Moore, who sometime lived at the Sign of the Black Swan near the church, and who had been buried about twelve years. The coffin being broken there was found in his remains a concretion not unlike a pumice stone, but rather whiter, and as large as the liver of a fox, pieces of which are in the possession of several people of Nottingham." (Did they, one wonders in parenthesis, use them as paperweights, or as objects of interest, if hardly of beauty, on their mantelpieces; and must there surely not have been one for proud display in the parlour of the Black Swan?) Mr. Moore, one remembered, after this sensational discovery, had been remarkable for having a large belly which projected more on one side than on the other. He was often heard to observe to his friends that he had been conscious of a hard substance forming inside him since he was about twenty and that the object had grown steadily from then on. He died at about the age of seventy. Mr. Moore was also heard to say that he felt but little pain from this sub-

31

stance but found it troublesome. This is how the contemporary account ends, "it may be worthy remark that the ribs on the side the concretion grew, were much bowed outwards. Three doctors had examined him while living several times; to the survivor of whom he had promised his body to be opened when dead: but he happening to survive these gentlemen, his body was interred without being opened. Nothing—says my informant, Mr. Walker, a respectable builder in Nottingham, under whose immediate inspection the fact happened—nothing would have brought this curious phenomenon to light had it not been for this accidental discovery." The account gives an illustration of a "piece of this substance", supplied by the courtesy of Mr. Walker, the Nottingham builder. This piece is described as being very porous and weighing about two ounces.

While on such mortuary matters, it might be remarked of another Mr. Walker, John Walker, an engineer of Bridgeford on the Hill, that his local fame, such as it is, is also only posthumous. But though his achievements as an engineer are forgotten, his epitaph, carved on his tombstone, in the matter-of-fact modernity of its thought, remains:

> My engine stopped, my valves are bad
> And lie so deep within,
> No engineer could there be found
> To put me new ones in. . . .
> But Jesus Christ converted me
> And took me up above.

This memorial dates from the year 1877.

Chapter III

NOTTINGHAM
AND SOME OF ITS INDUSTRIES

I AM NOT going to detain you long with personalities before resuming a haphazard perambulation of the city. But every county town has, in local memory, a few notable crimes and criminals that local justice has had to deal with. Not to know one or two of them is to be without local background. Listen, then, to the incident of William Andrew Horne, of Butterley Hall, Derbyshire, Esquire. This man was executed in 1759 at Nottingham for a crime he had committed thirty-five years earlier. He had been convicted some time before but his case had dragged on, respited from time to time, because of the extraordinary circumstances. The principal evidence was Mr. Horne's own brother. He had had some share in the crime for which Horne eventually died and had repeatedly blackmailed his brother, threatening to see him hanged if he refused him money whenever he asked for it. However, some years before the murder came to light, Horne's brother had applied to a magistrate and given an account of the whole transaction. This is apparently what had happened. Mr. Horne had taken from its mother an illegitimate child, carried it to a remote farmyard in Nottinghamshire and there smothered it under a haystack. The child's body was discovered next morning by a servant man who stuck the prongs of his fork into it and was too terrified at the discovery to make it public. It was not until thirty-five years later that justice was done.

Another crime used to be recorded locally as an outstanding verification of the early adage of " the biter being bit ". Here it is.

A stocking-maker who lived near Nottingham town bought a piece of veal, some time in May 1762, in Nottingham market, took it home and asked his wife to have it ready for dinner at twelve o'clock. The obedient wife cooked the veal and, as her husband did not come in punctually and she wasn't feeling well, she put it on one side without tasting it. The husband came in at about four and brought with him this time some beefsteaks which he demanded to be cooked for him there and then. His wife fried the steaks in the veal dripping; the man ate his dinner and was almost immediately taken ill. In a state of great alarm he questioned his wife about the cooking of the veal and when he heard that the steaks had been fried with veal dripping, cried, " I am a dead man." Soon he was: but not before confessing that he had rubbed the veal all over with arsenic in order to do away with his wife. The surgeon who examined the veal reported that it contained enough poison to destroy a hundred people.

This criminal, so anxious to become a widower, was a stockinger, and it is necessary thus early that we should become acquainted with the industry which has given Nottingham part of its fame and which in its later development from stockings to lace still survives as an important feature of the city. The story of its origins are familiar and hackneyed but they must be told again. To see the place where it began means going out, north of the city, through Arnold to Calverton. There, among the modern colliery housing of fifteen years ago you will be shown— what you can see in many of the villages round Nottingham—the stocking-knitter's cottages with the typical broad upper window behind which the stocking frames stood. In this village, nearly four hundred years ago, the Reverend William Lee ministered and invented. The legend about him is this: that he was making his addresses to a shrew who was indifferent to his attentions, and who, when he came to call upon her, infuriated him by sitting in front of him engrossed in her knitting, only the click of her needles breaking the silence. In his exasperation Lee is supposed to have given up everything—including, presumably, the care of his flock—in order to invent a device which would make it impossible for ladies of the future to emphasize the coldness of their emotions by this particular means. Anyhow, whether or not there is any truth in that story there is no doubt that the Reverend William Lee, after some seven years work, did produce the first stocking frame, mechanical knitting being entirely an original conception and his machine the first ever devised for manufacturing a looped or knitted fabric. What Lee produced was a piece of machinery of the utmost complexity—by any standard—comprising more than two thousand accurate lead and steel parts. His frame was the forerunner of all the hosiery and lace machines at present in use and has proved so adaptable that its principles are still employed in most of the power frames of the present day. But the curate of Calverton received no encouragement from Queen Elizabeth, though—or possibly because—his machine could produce work as fine in quality as the best hand-knitted products and at ten times the speed. Maximum production by hand is about one hundred loops a minute; with Lee's earliest and least efficient machine one could produce between a thousand and fifteen hundred loops in the same time.

A fact that tallies in some degree with the Lee legend is that this invention does seem to have been—unlike most others—a truly sequestered, isolated and spontaneous domestic affair unrelated to developments elsewhere. Lacking encouragement from his own sovereign, Lee, on the invitation apparently of Henri Quatre himself, left the country and went to France where he died in 1610. His brother James went abroad with him but returned to his native Nottingham after William Lee's death.

Despite his failure to interest the queen, Lee had sown well the seeds of a new industry. Forty years later, at the time of the outbreak of the Civil War, the stocking frame was providing work for a large proportion of the population of Calverton, Woodborough and several neighbouring villages, while hosiery capitalism in the form of two "master hosiers" had already established itself in Nottingham town. Fifty years later, the number of stocking frames in England as a whole is put at about six hundred and fifty, four hundred of them being in London and only a hundred in Nottingham. Some of these hundred were making use of worsted spun locally from wool produced in the neighbourhood of Sherwood Forest. By 1714 there were four hundred frames in Nottinghamshire itself, and later figures of the county's share in the rapidly expanding industry are three thousand in 1739, nine thousand two hundred and eighty-five in 1812, ten thousand five hundred in 1833, and sixteen thousand four hundred and eighty-two in 1844.

Naturally, at the beginning, the invention was much resented by hand-knitters; but its future values soon became evident and attempts by foreigners to take it abroad had to be circumvented. Until the end of the seventeenth century the stocking-frame industry remained an exclusively English craft; while there was, of course, a valuable export trade in finished stockings—to France and Portugal in particular. (We are referring, remember, at this stage, to the *silk* stocking industry.) In 1696 an Act of Parliament was passed imposing a fine of forty pounds—and the forfeit of the machine—on anyone attempting to export a stocking machine or any part of one.

The removal of the industry's centre of gravity from London back again to the scene of its origin dates from the early part of the eighteenth century. Between the years 1732 and 1750 something like eight hundred frames were taken from London to Nottingham. But the year 1730 also introduces, independently, a new phase in the industry's history. It was then that cotton hose became fashionable and the wearing of them more widespread. Unfortunately, the Nottingham frame industry at first showed itself incapable of adaptation to mechanical cotton spinning. At this crucial moment two great names enter the story. Richard Arkwright and James Hargreaves moved in 1768 to Nottingham, Arkwright having produced the spinning frame the previous year, providing the warp for a spinning jenny which Hargreaves had invented a year earlier. Hargreaves built a small factory in Mill Street, but the yarn he produced was at first poor and lumpy. Arkwright obtained financial assistance from a person called Samuel Need, who was a hosier, and from his partner, Jedediah Strutt. The next factory, built with this backing, was at Hockley, where Arkwright carried out his experiments till his triumph in 1775.

Arkwright's backer, Need, you will notice, is described as a hosier. In the eighteenth century a hosier was a capitalist as indeed Need, by being in a position to finance Arkwright, proved himself to be. He would own a number of frames—a hundred or more—some of which would be worked under his immediate supervision in his own workshop, while others, and the majority, were let out on hire to workmen who used them in their own homes. It is because of this latter circumstance that the clicking sound of the stocking machines became so all-pervading and inescapable a characteristic of every little Nottinghamshire alley and of streets and lanes in the outlying villages. In addition to this dual body of workmen employed directly by the hosier, there would also be an unlimited or unspecified number of poor people who were equally his paid workmen in all but name. The hosier would give out the raw materials to men who paid a rent for the use of the frames either in his shop or in their own homes. In addition, he farmed out work to private owners of frames, many of whom were master stockingers, themselves employing a number of journeymen. Finally, the capitalist hosier would sell his finished articles, either in a shop of his own, or to wholesalers.

Such an arrangement is known as the "domestic" system of framework knitting and it obtained in and around Nottingham from the Restoration onwards until nearly the end of the eighteenth century. Earlier in the seventeenth century the trade had been carried on both by hosiers who made their own goods and sold them in retail shops of their own, and by smaller men who made the goods and then sold them either by taking orders from local customers or by passing them to retail hosiers. There is evidence that at the time of the Civil War the Nottingham hosiers held stalls in the market-place where, presumably, they also dealt in hand-knitted goods.

By the eighteenth century it is possible to provide personal examples which indicate the local importance, and pomp, which a successful hosier could achieve. There was, for instance, Samuel Fellowes, who had been robbed of his patrimony by a conspiracy of unscrupulous relatives. Looking around for a means of recoupment—he was quite young—he became apprenticed to a frame-knitter. This was in 1706. Fifty years later he was mayor of Nottingham, having been elected to that office in 1755. He had, when his apprenticeship was over, duly become a hosier and for many years before the mayoralty put the seal on his success he had been living in a substantial house on High Pavement where, as we have already noticed, some of the roomiest as well as the most attractive specimens of Nottingham's post-Restoration and Georgian architecture is to be found. Fellowes accumulated a considerable fortune, and his grandson founded Hart and Fellowes Bank. This was in the early years of the nineteenth century. It is worth remarking while on the subject of houses, that pretty well any issue of the *Nottingham Journal* (of whose origins I shall write in a minute) during this period—1750's and 60's—carry advertisements for the sale of houses in the town which had large rooms suitable for use as a hosier's warehouse.

There is another name, in the generation succeeding that of Mayor Fellowes, which spells success in the hosiery business far more clearly and more lastingly than does his. R. and I. Morley were originally yeoman farmers of Sneinton, now part of the city. They turned to hosiery. In about the year 1790 they set up a London warehouse in Russia Road, Cheapside, and more extensive London establishments followed in the first decade of the nineteenth century. In Nottingham, a warehouse had been set up in Greyhound Yard, where the work of packing and dispatch was carried on. During the period of 1840 and 1860, when many branches of the hosiery business went through a period of depression, Morleys continued to prosper, thanks to the business acumen of the philanthropist, Samuel Morley. The basis of the Morley success was still the cottage system of work and the best-wrought products were still produced on the narrow hand frame. A change, however, came in the middle of this period. Already, by the invention of the Dawson wheel in 1791 which gave to warp knitting the advantage of laying the threads in any direction and thus giving greater scope for variety of design in patterns and colour; by the patenting by Sir Marc Brunel in 1816 of his *tricoteur* which made possible circular knitting; and indeed by Jedediah Strutt's placing a second set of needles at right-angles to the first enabled rib-work to be done: by all these means the Rev. W. Lee's original frame had been much improved on. Then, in 1851, William Cotton of Loughborough patented his straight-bar power knitting machine and perfected it ten years later. Its effect on the industry was immediate and could be seen in the case of the firm of Morley, who built their first Nottingham factory in Manvers Street in 1866. The factory system created a revolution in the industry: not that the actual value of the frames in the possession of a single individual or firm had been negligible before this. In 1812 for instance, Hayne of Nottingham personally owned frames to the value of some twenty-four thousand pounds.

The industry, like so many others, had exposed itself earlier to the dubious activities of a "middleman". The system of "putting out" developed to such an extent that towards the end of the eighteenth century the master stockinger was little more than the agent of the hosier, an intermediary between him and the actual hosiery operative. The master stockinger assumed the duty and remuneration of sub-letting the frames, taking out and bringing in the work, and to some extent making himself responsible for supervising the quality of the products—which included, through the long history of the industry, gloves, pantaloons, drawers, white cotton tops and half hose, besides the long stockings themselves, which had been and remained the basis of the industry from its beginning until the dramatic change-over to lace.

An important turning-point in the history of the industry can be found in the year 1874—only eight years after the first Morley factory had been built—when frame-rents were abolished by law. The domestic industry finally gave way to the factories and the sounds of Nottingham began to change. The old rattle and click gradually died away and were replaced by a louder and more concentrated whirr as the new factories found space within the neighbourhood of the slopes around St. Mary's church.

Nottingham's share in the world's story of lace dates from the latter half of the eighteenth century, when many attempts were made here to manufacture a net on the stocking frame which could be used as a background for what is called pillow-lace. Sufficient modification was made in the stocking frame to produce a lace mesh by mechanical means, but such net was not entirely satisfactory as it unravelled very quickly. In 1808, John Heathcote invented the bobbin net machine. This apparatus was a departure

Race-course, Nottingham

from the principle of the stocking frame and substituted a twisting motion which has remained an essential part of the three main types of modern lace machine. Four years later another type of machine was invented by John Leavers; this used the same twisting principle but did away with the necessity of traversing. Leaver's system was originally intended for the manufacture of plain net, but in 1834, through an adaptation of the jacquard pattern apparatus, it was made applicable to the production of an endless variety of fancy designs and figures. The fancy lace section of the industry is still called the "Leavers section", after the name of the inventor; present-day machines have, of course, greatly increased in size and speed, but their main principles remain unchanged.

These lace machines, invented in Nottingham and first built over a hundred years ago, are now used all over the world. In fact one can say that all the lace machines in the world have been made in Nottingham. All the French plants, for instance, were made here, and at the plant of the largest lacemaking firm in the world, at Philadelphia in the United States, there are as many as three hundred of these Nottingham machines. They are a bit on the dear side; to-day such a machine costs at least six thousand pounds.

The existence of these lace machines is one reason why you sometimes find Nottingham people in unexpected parts of the world. When a machine leaves Nottingham to go to a country abroad as often as not there go with it some skilled people to set it up and give it its initial operation; many of these people have settled down and stayed with the machines.

The lace industry, apart from the manufacture of the machine, is made up of a group of different divisions. I've mentioned the Leavers or fancy lace industry. There are, in addition, the Palin Net or Bobbin Net; the Warp Lace; the Hair Net; and the Lace Furnishing or Curtain industries.

Let's have a closer look at this last one. The furnishings section of the industry is located quite close to the city, with some factories and warehouses within the city itself, in the adjacent areas of Basford, Beeston, Bobbers Mill, Radford, Sandiacre and at Southwell. The machines in Nottinghamshire amount to some three hundred; and in addition there are between sixty and seventy machines owned by two Nottingham companies and situated near Glasgow and in Ayrshire. It was this branch of the industry that was responsible, during the war, for providing the army with its camouflage veiling and enormous quantities of mosquito, sandfly and other netting for tropical and sub-tropical

Nottingham Race-course: Colwick Hall, by Carr of York, 1776

theatres of war. This also remains a big item of export. The netting has to have a fineness and wearing quality of the highest order. The shape of the holes—which are hexagonal—is absolutely uniform so that no insect can penetrate them.

The Lace Furnishing industry is one that feels very intensely the special circumstances of the post-war economy. Since 1948 the industry's selling effort has been concentrated on the overseas markets and the export targets have been substantially exceeded. It is felt, however, that the starving of the British housewife of even the plainest lace furnishings may mean, quite apart from consequent or independent changes of taste, that, in the industry's words, "when lace furnishings are more freely available at home, their outstanding merits will possibly require restatement".

Within the industry a good many changes have been taking place. Let me quote an official statement again. "No attempt can be made to assess the gradual and subtle changes in the outlook of the individual 'Machine-holder' as a result of his perforce intimate wartime association with erstwhile competitors. The pre-war attitude—still largely one of *laissez-faire* and individualism—is now superseded by frank recognition of the need for a judicious leavening of the bread of untrammelled competition." To this end, activities within the industry are now being coordinated on such subjects as the recruitment, training, welfare and labour; scientific research; improvement in production and costing methods and further exploration of overseas markets. Since the war there have been instituted, at the Technical College, classes for young twist hands and other lace-workers. There they have the advantages of fully equipped model machinery, a fulltime instructor and release from their factory duties during two half-days a week. The Manufacturers Association have also promoted a successful course for designers and draughtsmen at the College of Arts and Crafts. The industry showed considerable enterprise during the war years when the production of lace was, naturally, substantially curtailed, in reviewing its circumstances and by such measures as the inauguration of scholarship schemes to bring new blood into the trade. These operate through the Nottingham College of Arts and Crafts and the city's education authorities. There is also a recently established Research Council which has the approval and support of the Department of Scientific and Industrial Research. This body is converted into an Incorporated body under the style of the Lace Research Association, and a statuary levy has been introduced at the request and with the approval of the industry to provide the necessary funds and maintain the body at a high level of efficiency.

The Nottingham lace factories are built of brick, most of them a single storey high with a high roof built in slanting bays, each bay having glass on one side and slate on the other. Inside the sheds the lace machines stand in rows—tall iron frames of massive weight. Machines weighing upwards of fifteen tons are used to manufacture this most delicate of materials. The web of lace is woven upright. One man looks after each frame. The pattern of lace is formed at about the height of the man's eye. He stands on a wooden step or platform that runs the whole length of the machine. In all the lace factories the floors of the shed are of wood, shiny and black as a rule, and apt to be covered with the "trodden graphite" which is used for lubricating the machine, and also with the wooden cases and baskets—or skips as they are called in the textile industry—full of cotton yarn, spun in Lancashire and wound into tight cheese-shaped bundles. The sheds have to be kept warm, because the lace has to be made in the constant temperature of about sixty-five degrees. This temperature must not be allowed to vary, as the long strings that control the threads and which are operated by the jacquard system are very subject to the atmosphere and might expand or contract—"run-up" or "run-down" as they say here—and this would interfere with the perfect control of the pattern. The men who operate the machines in Nottingham call themselves twist-hands and, indeed, the lace machine twists the threads rather than weaves them. There is no shuttle. There are hundreds of disc-shaped brass bobbins. The yarn is wound into them as the ribbon of a typewriter is wound into its spool, but these discs are only about as thick as a large coin. These disc-like brass bobbins move pendulum-wise between the upright pillar of threads of the warp, and the upright threads as they are drawn sideways, to and fro, to form a pattern.

Nottingham, as a lace manufacturing city, owes a lot to its fortunate water supply. Owing to the large deposits of Bunter sandstone in the locality an abundant supply of pure bright water is available from artesian borings. It is only necessary to sink wells to a moderate depth to get water that is free from all organic matter and the impurities that are always found in water from surface sources. This local water contains small quantities of chlorine and free ammonia which particularly help in the bleaching processes of the industry. This water produces the fine "clear" white that is not liable to subsequent discoloration.

In the narrow street called Stoney Street there is to be found the Nottingham lace market, and the offices and warehouses of the lace firms have been built on each side of it. The office and counting-house belonging to the oldest lace firm of all has its own chapel, its own parson and its own choir.

This discreet and paternal Victorian organization was rather different from the circumstances of the predecessors of the lace-makers, the hosiery operatives of the previous century. During the eighteenth century the wages they earned had been less relatively than in the seventeenth. In 1686, when the framework knitters (then of silk stockings exclusively) had been comparatively affluent, it was recorded that " they had been observed seldom to work on Mondays or Tuesdays, but to spend their time at the ale-house . . . among the weavers, tis common in them to be drunk on Monday, have their headache on Tuesday and their tools out of order on Wednesday ". During the first thirty or so years of the eighteenth century the most skilled (that is, the fine silk) workers in the Nottingham area got between half a crown and three and sixpence a day, while the embroiderers might earn up to five shillings. The cost of living was low: board and lodging for a single man was something like sixpence or eightpence a day, no more. Thus the complaint that among these silk workers it was possible to earn enough in two or three days to keep themselves, and to keep themselves in the alehouses for the rest of the week, seems to some extent justified.

On the other hand, among the workers in cotton and worsted dire penury prevailed, and by 1750 the phrase " poor as a stock-inger " was common currency well beyond the immediate area of this county. A typical budget of the period must have been such as that of William Hallam of Nottingham. In about 1778 Hallam produced a dozen pairs of worsted hose every week. For these he was paid sevenpence a pair, so that his weekly earnings were seven shillings. His expenses, however, were considerable. For the rent of his frame he had to pay ninepence a week; he had to pay threepence for "standing room"; needles, each week, came to fourpence; he had a weekly charge of twopence to pay—presumably to someone at an even lower level of subsistence than himself—for " pulling worsted out of slips "; fire and candles—he had to work far into the night to produce his dozen pairs of stockings a week—cost him fivepence; and the stockings he made had to be put out for seaming, the cost of which, a further sevenpence, he had to stand. Thus from his seven shillings earnings a full half-crown a week had to be subtracted, leaving only four and sixpence to provide for the week's food and rent and for clothes and other necessaries. There would not be many visits to the alehouse for him.

The wages that could be earned by the various categories of machine workers varied considerably. Take first him—and at this period it would almost certainly be him and not her—who produced stockings of fine worsted. Compared with Hallam's dozen pairs of coarse ones, the fine worsted worker could only produce eight, or at the most nine pairs a week. But instead of Hallam's sevenpence or eightpence, the fine worsted stockings would bring in one and fourpence or one and fivepence a pair. So this man's gross earnings would range between ten and eightpence and twelve and ninepence according to his productivity and the price he got for his wares. This would probably leave him between eight and twelve shillings a week nett. A further case to be considered is that of a worker in silk hose. He got, on an average, half a crown a pair for his stockings; but he could only produce four, or at the most five, pairs a week. This would give him a gross weekly wage of between ten and fifteen shillings, which represented something between seven and ten shillings a week to spend. Such are the figures that have been estimated from what is known of the actual productive capacity of these three categories of hosiery workers. There was, however, a different contemporary opinion about their theoretical capacity which, as might be expected, came from the employers. The person called Need, who has already entered into this account as having provided financial backing for Arkwright—he was the proprietor of a factory in Nottingham and owned a large number of frames in the hosiery village of Arnold—made himself exceedingly unpopular by offering a gratuitous estimate of what could be done by an ideally industrious hosiery worker. He took the lowest-paid category, that of the coarse cotton worker. Need said that a man, if he worked twelve hours a day, could earn as much as two shillings in the day—fourteen shillings in a seven-day week; that his wife could make four shillings a week by seaming stockings; that a child of eight ought to be able to earn one and sixpence a week; and that constantly a family of husband, wife and two or three children should be enjoying more than one pound a week gross. It is easy to understand that this exaggerated estimate brought great odium upon its originator.

In the mid-eighteenth century there was a short-lived innovation in the industry. The craft of making gloves on the stocking frame was introduced into this country, from Cordova in Spain. It became for a while a very lucrative Nottinghamshire side-line, particularly at Mansfield, where a speciality was made of silk mittens. However, a sudden change in London fashion virtually put an end to the industry: when the vogue of black kid gloves seized the captial the knitted Nottinghamshire gloves were put completely out of countenance.

Clearly the industry as a whole was always at the mercy of changes of fashion. However, it was not only fashion but "man's inhumanity to man" which accounted for the appalling conditions among the hosiery—and later the lace—workers in the nineteenth century. At the time of the Chartist movement, Nottinghamshire stockingers, living in overcrowded slums, insanitary and disease-ridden, endured, literally from the cradle to the grave, lives of unrelieved privation. The men who made the stockings were too poor to afford any kind of leg covering for themselves. Almost all stockingers' children went about without shoes, stockings and caps. We read that the people of Sutton-in-Ashfield (this was in the early '40s) "had not so much as one acre of common ground for the use or amusement of the poor, not a bathing place to which the people had access without trespassing; and of the five thousand people, three thousand, owing to the want of trade, had not had sufficient food for several years past". The state of affairs was the same when, at the time of the Luddite Riots, to which we shall inevitably come in a moment, Lord Byron described the stockingers as "meagre with famine, and sullen with despair".

By the middle of the nineteenth century conditions were even worse, particularly among the children in what had then become largely a lace industry. A country magistrate is reported to have said at Nottingham that children of nine and ten years old were dragged from "their squalid beds at two or three or four o'clock in the morning and compelled to work for a bare subsistence until ten, eleven, or twelve at night. 'What,' this magistrate added, 'can we think of a town which holds a public meeting to partition that the period of labour for men shall be diminished to eighteen hours a day?'" This observation, taken from the *Daily Telegraph*, January 18th, 1860, was quoted by Karl Marx in his "Capital".

Such circumstances, existing at a time when the nineteenth century had passed its centre point, should not be taken as indicating that the stockingers, at any time during the previous hundred years, had accepted their misfortunes with complete passivity. If we look back over their history we find our attention arrested by the events of a single year—1779. The period just preceding this moment had been one of great inventive activity in the stocking industry, and one of considerable technical advance. For one thing, Hargreaves and Arkwright had recently migrated to Nottingham. The eyelet hole machine had come into being, a device on which elaborately fashioned gloves and waistcoat pieces could be made; as had also the Derby Rib machine. Between about 1776 and 1777 "point net lace"—a web of hexagonal mesh —was first made on the stocking machine.

But such new technical enterprise brought little material advantage to the stockingers themselves. There was among them a growing determination to draw attention to their plight, and at this time the stockingers of the Midlands combined with their fellows among the Londoners and together partitioned Parliament to regulate their wages on an agreed basis. This was in 1778. The hosiers, the owners, promptly formed a counter association under a Nottingham lawyer named Samuel Turner. They opposed the Bill in Parliament and it was rejected. The stockingers could hardly have expected any other outcome and did not despair. The men held a meeting on the 4th of August, 1778, and it was decided to partition Parliament again. The meeting took place on the race-course.

The Nottingham race-course. Let us not confuse the issue by imagining this gathering as taking place in surroundings identical with those which, to-day, made so pleasant a sporting centre of Nottingham in the flat racing season. Colwick Hall, whose handsome presence, its river side adorned with a portico of four attached ionic columns and a graceful central cupola, lends dignity to the present scene, had just been completed for its Musters owner by a local builder, Samuel Stretham, of Nottingham, working to the designs of John Carr, the great "Carr of York". He built, conspicuously, Harewood House in Yorkshire, and his surviving contributions to the elegance of eighteenth-century Nottinghamshire are Clifton Hall, remodelled in 1779; Grove Hall; and the Palladian Town Hall with its Tuscan columns and pediment, in the market-place at Newark, dating from 1773. It was not until the present century that Colwick Hall left the possession of the Chaworth Musters family and became the catering centre for the present race-course. But it seems to have been these same two men, Carr and Stretham, who collaborated in 1777, in the construction of the grandstand for the Nottingham race-course, which was one of the finest buildings of its sort in the country at the time. It was where the Forest Recreation Ground now is and does not survive. The patron of the scheme which brought it into being was a certain Sir Charles Sedley. It must have been, to judge by the engravings of it, an admirable building. It was based upon a nine-arched colonnade with round-headed windows behind, surmounted by a handsome upper structure with seven arched windows; and on top of all was a neat balustrade. The grandstand's front and ends were supported by pillars which formed what the eighteenth century called a piazza, under which, we are told, "many a dashing female screens her dress from the disordering effects of a shower". (Presumably the word "dashing" is to be understood here in its literal, mobile sense.) A meeting had been held at the White Lion Inn and a subscription was entered among the local gentry for the building of a grandstand. No one was permitted to put up less than twenty guineas, which minimum sum entitled the subscriber on the completion of the building to two silver entrance tickets, transferable and available for use by both ladies and gentlemen. In the list of subscriptions we find many names still of local interest and which will recur in the course of this account. The Duke of Newcastle, the Lord Lieutenant of the county, put up £200; so did Lord Portland and Lord Edward Bentinck; in the £100 list were John Musters of Colwick, Lord Middleton and Lord George Savile; Sir Gervase Clifton of Clifton disgorged £60, Lord George Cavendish £30, and Sir Thomas Parkyns, Bart., of Bunny, the minimum of £20.

Thus it was beneath the shadow of a handsome, aristocratic and well-endowed grandstand that the Nottingham stockingers assembled on the 4th of August, 1778, a grandstand which by that time should already have enjoyed its first summer meeting. The stockingers, as we have seen, decided to send a further partition to Parliament. Abel Smith, the son of a banker and described as "a brother frame-work knitter", represented them. He was Member of Parliament for the borough of Nottingham. His election was the occasion for an impressive demonstration and, of course, a procession. The flag of the Association was carried alongside the Union Jack, followed by the officials of the Framework Knitters Company, the Committee of the Association, the main body of the framework knitters marching two abreast, with a band of clarinets and French horns to provide—it would be interesting to know what—musical support. The procession, we are told, moved in perfect order and there were no irregularities.

Shortly afterwards, however, Abel Smith died, and his brother, Robert Smith, stood for election in his place as the representative of the stockingers. A new petition was submitted, giving evidence of appalling sweating and asking for a modest increase of wages. The bill this time passed its first reading with only one dissentient vote. There were great rejoicings in Nottingham, where the tradespeople of the town showed their full support of the stockingers.

When the time for the bill's second reading came round, Robert

Smith spoke on its behalf, moderately and persuasively. The measure, he said, was intended to do no more than prevent unfair competition between the opulent masters and the poor journeymen. This time it received a majority of only one vote. Then Need—that same Need, the powerful hosier and joint owner of Arkwright's cotton mill, whose Bedaux-like insistence on a fantastic productive capacity among the stockingers had brought him such notoriety—sought, and obtained, the support of certain venal Cornish Members of Parliament, and the bill was lost.

The bad news reached Nottingham on 10 July, 1779. The news of the bill's rejection spread rapidly through the slums and poorer quarters of the town, and within a very short time the market-place was filled with people. The first hint of what was to follow was the sound of breaking glass: the windows of a house in Parliament Street, belonging to another obnoxious hosier of the Need category, were being systematically smashed. Then, every window, shutter and tile on the house and mill belonging to Need and Arkwright went the same way. The disturbances continued all through the next day, and the Riot Act was read. Soldiers stationed in the castle were called out to quell the mobs. From the neighbouring villages and from the countryside round Nottingham stockingers poured into the town. Two prisoners were taken but were subsequently released.

On 17th July a formal meeting between the two elements took place, this time at the Feathers Inn. It lasted for five hours, but the deadlock between the men's representatives and the hosiers got no further towards being broken. No sooner was the meeting over, and its negative result known, than further outbreaks of rioting took place in the town. Bands of stockingers patrolled the streets, entered houses indiscriminately and declared their intention of breaking every stocking frame they found working that day. Events then followed according to a carefully prepared plan. At six o'clock in the evening a sham attack—in order to distract the attention of the soldiery—was staged against the town factory of " the villain Need "; and when the feint was in progress a large body of stockingers set out for the village of Arnold. . . .

To-day, although Nottingham has encroached almost to the point of swallowing Arnold as a separate entity, the modern development has taken place away from the old, so that the village centre is pretty well preserved. You ought to have a look at the church. It contains one of the Easter sepulchres characteristic of the county and its neighbours. Unfortunately it is in a very bad state and no longer has the sculpture which formerly adorned it. Originally, says Professor Pevsner, it must have been similar to the Easter sepulchre at Horton, of upright shape, tripartite, with crocketed ogee gables and tall pinnacles. But the plain surfaces are still partly adorned by diaper work, patterns of square flowers as will be seen again at Southwell, on the stone rood-screen. What else at Arnold and close by? There's Manor Farm, with a mid-eighteenth century front; Gadsby's Farm, a three-storey building dating from about 1700, two miles north of the village; at Hollinwood Hall, there's a rectangular hill fortress originally with a double fosse and with two entrances on each of the long sides, which may date from the iron age or may be Roman; at Redhill an old brick farmhouse stands by the side of the old North Road and was where the coaches stopped to change horses. The old stable was still there, and the clock and the look-out balcony. Then, in Arnold itself, you will find that local pride will direct you to No. 79 the High Street. In this mid-eighteenth century house, which contains its contemporary staircase, the painter Bonington was born, who is claimed by many Nottingham people as the county's most distinguished painter. Indeed, he would on any count be an admirable artist to have to one's credit. The county can certainly claim, without any likelihood of dispute, Bonington *père*, of Arnold, who was, variously and at different times, the notably unsuccessful governor of a jail, a painter—he actually exhibited at the Royal Academy—and a lace-maker. It was apparently something to do with this last, and quite temporary profession which took him to Calais and to Paris in about the year 1817. With him went his son, then a boy of about fifteen, who never, before his death in 1828, at the age of only twenty-six, returned to Nottingham, and whose claim to be a Nottinghamshire painter, as distinct from a native of the county, is consequently not very great. But he was, to be sure, an infant prodigy and had certainly begun to sketch before he left for France. He had been born in 1802 in this quiet Arnold High Street, in the big three-storeyed house that still rises above its neighbours and is distinguished by a bronze plaque let into the wall. Arrived with his father in France, young Bonington set to work making copies of paintings in the Louvre and entered the École des Beaux Arts. Later, studying under Louis Francia and the Baron Gros, he attracted the notice of the great Delacroix by the brilliance of his sketches. In 1822 he began to exhibit at the Salon and in 1824 was awarded a medal there. The bulk of Bonington's paintings, as is well known, are the result of his French study and those that are not "historical" are of French and Continental scenes. He is, perhaps rightly, regarded by the French as rather more than half their property. But in the realm of landscape painting at this time the two countries were closely inter-connected. It is reasonable to say that much of the best in contemporary French landscape painting dates from Constable's copies of Claude; but a great deal has to be allowed to the great influence of Bonington. Although his fame has continued to grow with time, he enjoyed great esteem during his short life. His "Henry the IV receiving the Spanish Ambassador" was bought by Lord Hertford for over eighty thousand francs, and his "Grand Canal, Venice" and his "Fish-market, Boulogne" also realized high prices. He exhibited several pictures at the Royal Academy. In London, you can see a good selection of his water colours in the Wallace collection and, at the National Gallery, two canvases, "Piazzetta, St. Mark's, Venice" and "Sunset". At the Tate Gallery there are two Boningtons—a water colour of a London subject, "Cheney Walk", and a mountain landscape in oil. Bonington's early death was the result of "brain fever", caused by exposure to the sun while sketching. As is only suitable, the Nottingham Castle museum has made a special effort to provide itself with some worthy record of this local son. It possesses a Bonington self-portrait as well as a portrait of Bonington by Thomas Phillips (1770-1845). The museum has also three characteristic Bonington landscapes—they are "Fisher folk on the coast of Normandy", "Coast Scene" and "Undercliffe"—this last claiming to be Bonington's final drawing before he died. Bonington of Arnold, yes; but in local memory, the name of Arnold is still largely associated with the frame-breakers and with the disturbances which began with the events we were describing.

The reason for the journey of the special contingent of frame-breakers from Nottingham on the evening of July 17, 1779, was that the "villain" Need had a house and several frames there. When the rioters arrived these latter were systematically defenestrated. A band of cavalry was dispatched from Nottingham but by the time it arrived the frame-breakers had dispersed. The next move on the side of authority was the swearing-in of three hundred special constables who were publicly instructed in their duties through the columns of the *Nottingham Journal*. Then sixty-five of the principal hosiers of the town issued a manifesto denouncing the rioters.

Meanwhile the stockingers had burnt and completely destroyed the house of a certain Wilkinson, particularly unpopular master stockinger. He was the proud possessor of a "marvellous apprentice", a sort of early Stakhanovite, who declared that he could make eighteen pairs of hose a week—whereas, as we have seen, nine was considered good going among the best of the fine-worsted workers, and four or five the maximum possible among those who worked in silk. This model youth must indeed have been irksome to the rioters, and it is remarkable that the "marvellous apprentice" got away with his life when his master's house was burnt.

But there the story virtually ends; for its climax, considering the times in which it took place, was, surprisingly, almost a happy one. For, though the Mayor of Nottingham, William Huthwaite, proclaimed a regime of severity against all offenders, and the rioting immediately ceased, the magistrates, when the time came to dispense punishment, were unexpectedly mild. Even a man called Mephringham, who was charged with the then capital offence of arson—of burning Wilkinson's house—received no more than a fine of six shillings and eightpence, together with three weeks' imprisonment for frame-breaking; while a man who had wounded a Justice of the Peace with a stone was, on begging the J.P.'s pardon, set free.

But however sympathetically and leniently the magistrates may have behaved, the "owners", the hosiers themselves, were unquestionably left masters of the situation. They did their best to wreak vengeance on the officers of the men's committee, whose names—Pilkington, Wright, Herring—are preserved as those of the heroes of an unsuccessful incident. For when, in 1787, a new wages agreement was made—an agreement which gave the stockingers little or no improvement in their lot—it stood for more than twenty years, some distance into the nineteenth century—without change.

A hint of the state of feeling in Nottingham during the final years of the eighteenth century may be gathered from a contemporary account of the incidents—they were no more than that—which took place during 1792 and 1794. The first episode, that of 1792, was very brief and was confined to the airing of a particular grievance. In May of that year there was a riot on account of the high price of butcher's meat. A crowd converged on the Shambles, breaking doors and shutters, and moved on to burn books and other goods found on the stalls of the market-place. The second rising, two years later, was a little more serious. It took place on July 2nd, 1794.

Would you object for a line or two of historical background? During the previous month, while in Paris the terror was sharpened, under Robespierre, and in seven weeks getting on for fifteen hundred people were put to death in the capital, the French revolutionary armies were achieving some of their most startling successes against the allied coalition. The Austrian armies were retreating rapidly eastwards towards the Rhine, and the British were withdrawing equally rapidly northwards. The Austrians had lost the decisive battle of Fleurus; the consequent fall of Charleroi opened the way for the French to Brussels; and soon they were to gain Antwerp as well. Pressing on further, the French were soon to be acclaimed by the republicans of Holland, cross the ice and seize the Dutch fleet, and then the whole of Holland, and William of Orange was to flee to England.

It was at the beginning of such a stirring period that what our recorder calls "this disagreeable news from the Continent" arrived at Nottingham. An account of these military events reached the market-place, he says, towards the evening of the 2nd of July, 1794. A serious disturbance took place. Certain people of the town, "evil affected showed signs of pleasure at the news, wearing on their hats emblems of the meanings of their hearts". These emblems were presumably tricolours. The loyal riposte was prompt, but smacked somewhat of undergraduate behaviour. A party, composed of Royalists, ducked "several supposed disaffected people" in the River Leen: there seems an element of doubt even in the official account as to whether they got the right victims. But not stopping there, a mob at night set fire to some outhouses in a cotton mill where a party of "Jacobins", as, of course, they were called, had taken shelter and whence some shots were said to be coming. But the vigilance of the magistrates and their friends—and of the Light Horse from Nottingham barracks—prevented anything worse happening than the burning of a few more premises. We are told that the next day too was "a day of ducking and disorder".

Early the following year the Nottingham mob rose again, in consequence of the high price of provisions. The outcome of the rising was according to pattern: the troops of Nottinghamshire gentlemen yeomen assembled in full accoutrement and were joined by a troop of heavy dragoons from the barracks, which combination secured about thirteen of the ringleaders and restored peace.

Before continuing with this sketch of the Nottinghamshire labour troubles, before entering the century which saw in our county an uprising of sufficient moment to bring Nottingham, its frames and its frame-breakers into the general history books, it might be worth retracing our steps for a moment, back to 1779 and to the first of these movements to be noted here. It may be remembered that the special constables who were enrolled to deal with the frame-breakers at Arnold and in the city that year were "instructed in their duties through the columns of the *Nottingham Journal*". Since that was the first appearance in these pages of any mention of the journalism of the county, it is perhaps worth examining the circumstances of this particular periodical at the time of which we are writing. For Nottingham is by no means least among the provincial centres of early journalism; and with J. M. Barrie and Mr. Graham Greene among those who have in recent times practised the craft there, a certain literary eminence seems well maintained.

It was in about the year 1710, nearly sixty years before the first of the events we have been describing, that a Mr. William Ayscough began business as a printer in a house in the west side of Bridlesmith Gate, between Pepper Street and St. Peter's Gate. That was one event. Towards the end of the next year, 1711, one John Collyer began printing a newspaper in a house on what was then called Timber Hill and is now South Parade. The paper that Collyer started was called the *Nottingham Post,* and it was in existence from the month of December 1711. (One might remark that the *Worcester Postman* had been among the first in the field of provincial journals, being issued in 1690; while the *Lincoln, Rutland and Stamford Mercury* followed close behind it in 1695.) Collyer's *Nottingham Post* continued until 1732, when George Ayscough, the son of William Ayscough, began the *Nottingham Courant,* which he issued from his father's house in Bridlesmith Gate. The next development was in 1757, when a certain Samuel Creswell of Nottingham, with a John Gregory of nearby Leicester, combined to produce a *Leicester and Nottingham Journal,* which was printed at Leicester and published at Nottingham at a stated hour on the day of its arrival there. The *Leicester and Nottingham Journal* lasted until 1769, when Creswell bought out Ayscough's *Nottingham Courant* and converted it into the *Nottingham Journal,* which he published from a house situated at the south end of the Exchange. As we approach the date of the early disturbances among the stockingers when, as we have seen, the *Nottingham Journal* played a part on the side of repression, we find, in 1772, the first appearance of a *Nottingham Chronicle.* This was the creation of one of the town's earliest book publishers, a George Burbage, who had his establishment in Long Row, two doors west of the Crown Inn. The two newspapers, the *Chronicle* and the *Journal,* ran concurrently until 1775, when Creswell and Burbage combined, killed the *Chronicle* and ran the *Journal* jointly. This, then, was the paper that was instructing the constables against the frame-breakers. The two men who ran it were people of strongly marked character—

Samuel Creswell, as befitted the grandson of Thomas Hawksley, a well-known Jacobite, had the reputation of being a determined Tory. Burbage—for thirty years the *Journal's* printer and publisher—is represented by tradition as being very close in money matters. His dress, apparently, was "after the old fashion and very imposing", his manners very polite; and the story goes that success once attended the originator of a bet that Burbage would pompously and with effusive phrases *thank* a little girl sent to get from him two half-pennies in exchange for a penny. Similarly, it was said that if one were to rouse him at his shop over which he lived, at dead of night, and ask him for a $\frac{1}{2}$d. sheet of paper one would still get profuse thanks for the purchase. Burbage was also reputed to have killed, in the columns of his *Journal*, more French soldiers than the whole French army mustered. When, in August 1786, his partner Creswell died, Burbage did his best to deprive Creswell's widow of her interest in the *Journal*. Burbage was certainly, for a long period, its sole proprietor. When Burbage himself eventually died the paper passed into the possession of his son-in-law, George Stretham.

One further paper appeared in this period. This was the *Nottingham Gazette*. Its publisher was a writing master called Henry Cox whose premises were at the Weekday Cross end of Low Pavement. But the career of the *Nottingham Gazette* was short. It was given up within the first year, and the *Journal* once again held the field alone. To-day the *Nottingham Journal* and the *Nottingham Guardian* are the two morning papers, with the *Evening News* and the *Nottingham Evening Post* for the later part of the day.

The first decade of the nineteenth century was passed before the next and most famous outbreak of industrial disturbance shook the county. The Luddite Riots of 1811 have been described as a reply to oppression by men who had been deprived of all other means of resistance. The industrial historians Cole and Postgate insist that the riots were not in the proper sense a "mass movement", that it was not an uprising of the bulk of the population in the area in which the rioters operated—a large area which included portions of Lancashire, Yorkshire and Cheshire as well as Nottinghamshire itself which was, however, the centre of the movement. For it was somewhere in Sherwood Forest that there was supposed to lie the office of the person alleged to be called Ned Ludd by whom the rioters claimed to be directed—you will observe how the alleged facts are here hedged about with qualifications, for it is not known whether, in fact, anyone called Ned Ludd ever existed, and if he did it is not known who or what he was. The historians suggest that the movement undoubtedly had some capable organizing brain behind it, which is hardly consistent with the traditional association of the name of Ned Ludd with an idiot boy of Leicestershire, who, unable to catch someone who had been tormenting him, destroyed some stocking frames in a fit of temper.

The Luddite campaign in Nottinghamshire itself began in the spring of 1811, was in full swing by November and lasted until February 1812. It was asserted by the House of Lords' Committee on the Riots that the movement was directed against the introduction and use of new machinery in the stocking trade. But modern historians declare that this was not so, that the rioters' purpose was to draw attention, rather, to the abuse of old machinery. The French Revolution and the Napoleonic Wars had practically brought ruin to the frame knitters and conditions were worsened by the fact that the owners were trying to keep up their dwindling profits by selling on a large scale "cut-outs" made on "wide frames".

These expressions may need a bit of explanation. While the ordinary stockingers' frame was narrow, of sufficient width only for the making of hose, there was in existence a large number of much wider frames, which had been used for knitting pantaloons or fancy stockings called "twills". Now at this period twills had gone out of fashion and pantaloons, whose chief market was the Continent, could not be sold because of the war. What was happening in Nottingham was that unscrupulous owners were making their weavers produce large pieces of materials on the now idle wide frames and then cut the stuff up with scissors into the shape of stockings and gloves and so on. These stitched-up products, cut-ups, as they were called, had no selvedges like true stockings, and so rapidly fell to pieces. But this shoddy, sold at low prices, was ruining the market, and hundreds of the true stocking frames were rendered idle.

That autumn and winter of 1811 the Luddites appeared in village after village, smashing the wide frames and any other frames worked by unapprenticed labour. A fair number of the masters, it is said, if they could not approve the methods at least regarded the Luddite cause as reasonable and to some degree accepted the results. Troops sent into the affected areas are described as running up and down helpless, baffled by the silence, connivance and solidarity of the workers. In the town of Nottingham itself as many as a thousand "illegal" frames were destroyed and a large amount of the cut-out material destroyed. The first results were positive and satisfactory. The cut-up trade

The new Arts Centre in Nottingham
Wollaton Hall, 1580-88

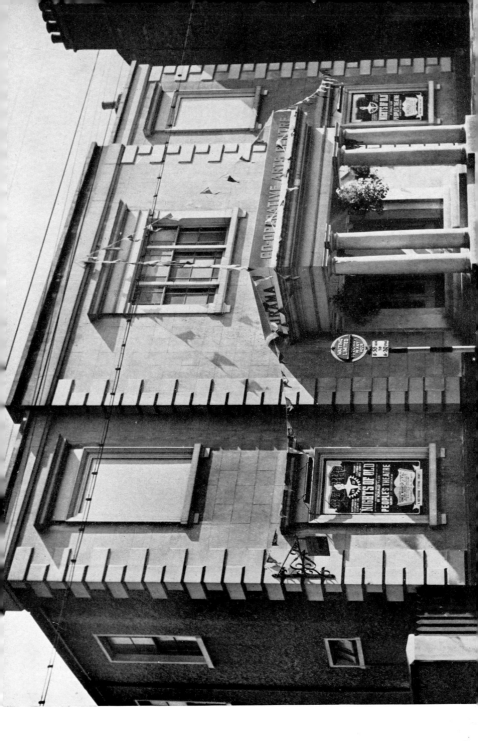

was checked, and the frame knitters' wages temporarily rose by as much as two shillings per dozen pairs of stockings.

On the other side of the picture was the Act passed by Parliament as a result of the rising. Frame-breaking, up to this point, was punishable by a term of fourteen years transportation to " one of his Majesty's plantations ". The new law made frame-breaking a capital offence. Fortunately most of the Luddites had been captured and tried before the new law had actually come into effect. Seven men were found guilty but they came before an upright judge—Mr. Justice Bailey—who sentenced them to between seven and fourteen years transportation. Mr. Justice Bailey even took it to higher authority with the request for leniency— this, however, was refused.

It is in such circumstances, as a creditable, if ineffective character in this drama, and not merely playing the fool in the Monk's Parlour, that I would prefer to introduce the most striking character we shall meet in this account. In the House of Lords on the 27th February, 1812, he rose to make his maiden speech. Referring to the Bill we have just heard of, authorizing the death penalty for frame-breaking, he spoke as follows :

" Suppose it is passed," he said. " Suppose one of these men, as I have seen them—meagre with famine, sullen with despair, careless of a life which your Lordships are perhaps about to value at something less than a stocking frame—suppose this man (and there are a thousand such from whom you may select your victims) be dragged into court to be tried for this new offence by this new law, still there are two things wanting to convict and condemn him—twelve butchers for a jury and a Jeffreys for a judge." Then he turned to the efforts of the military to suppress the Nottingham riots, and poured on them this ridicule :

" Such marchings and counter-marchings!—from Nottingham to Bulwell, from Bulwell to Bamford, from Bamford to Mansfield! And when at length the detachments arrive at their destination in all ' the pride, pomp, circumstance of glorious war ', they came just in time to witness the mischief which had been done, and ascertain the escape of the perpetrators, to collect the *spolia optima* in the fragments of broken frames, and return to their quarters amid the derision of old women and the hooting of children."

Lord Byron was in his twenty-fifth year when he made what appears to have been an intrinsically moving speech—though not one that had any effect on the voting of their Lordships. Byron reports that Lord Holland and Lord Grenville, particularly the

The main buildings of Nottingham University
Boots' factory at Beeston, from Clifton Grove

latter, paid him some high compliments in their speeches, and that he had had many marvellous eulogies repeated to him since, in person and by proxy, "from diverse persons *ministerial*, yes, *ministerial*, as well as oppositionists". Lord Holland, the nephew of Charles James Fox, was at that time Recorder of Nottingham, and he said to Byron that he (Byron) would beat them all if he persevered; Lord Grenville remarked that the construction of some of Byron's periods was very like Burke's; and Sir Francis Burdett said it was the best speech by a *Lord* since *Lord* knows when!

What, besides making this speech and enjoying this flattery, was Byron doing in this year 1817? The previous year—in July—he had returned from Athens. His mother, that dreadful woman, had died. Byron had expressed to his friend Francis Hodgson his fear of insanity, and in the early months of the following year he suffered from considerable depression. But life at Newstead Abbey was resumed. It was not quite so carefree as when he had first been able to invite his friends to this ancestral house between the ruined church and the lake. But perhaps there was a sense of responsibility that was not there before, which can be set beside that Luddite speech as a less obvious, but more than usually worthy aspect of the Byronic character. Take this as evidence: he is writing to John Cam Hobhouse, the friend of Cambridge days, and companion in the Mediterranean, writing from Newstead on the 14th October, 1811. He was twenty thousand pounds in debt and says: "I must mortgage for that and other expenses, so that altogether my situation is perplexing." Then he adds: "If I chose to turn out my old bad tenants, and take monied men, they say Newstead would bear a few hundreds more from its great extent; but this I shall hardly do. . . . It contains three thousand eight hundred acres, including the Forest Land, the Rochdale Manor, eight thousand two hundred and fifty-six acres of Lancashire which are larger than ours. So there you have my territories on the earth, and 'in the waters under the earth'; but I must marry some heiress, or I shall always be involved." But in spite of the temporary blight which "poverty" and the death of his mother cast upon life at Newstead (for though he never loved her he was shocked by her sudden death) he had, by the autumn of 1811, begun to organize his life at Newstead once again more or less for pleasure. Here he is writing again on the 25th September of that year:

"I am plucking up my spirits and have begun to gather my little sensual comforts together. Lucy is extracted from Warwickshire; some very bad faces have been warned off the premises, and more promising substituted in their stead; the partridges are plentiful, hares fairish, pheasants not quite so good and the girls on the manor . . . (this part of the letter was denied posterity by Byron's first editor) . . . just as I had formed a tolerable establishment my travels commenced, and on my return I find all to do over again; my former flock were all scattered; some married, not before it was needful. As I am a great disciplinarian, I have just issued an edict for the abolition of caps; no hair to be cut on any pretext; stays permitted but not too low before; full uniform always in the evenings; Lucinda to be commander—*vice* the present, about to be married (*mem.,* she is thirty-five with a flat face and a squeaking voice) of all the makers and un-makers of beds in the household)."

Thus it was in the later months of the year 1811. The depression of the first months was to be succeeded by the onset of those astonishing " Years of Fame " which are without equal in literary history. The vigorous maiden speech on the Luddites, and its agreeable reception, preceded by only two or three days that morning at the beginning of March 1812, when, upon the publication of the first and second cantos of *Childe Harold's Pilgrimage,* Byron " awoke to find himself famous ".

The form of celebrity he enjoyed was at first mainly social, and confined to London. The time when he was to be a European figure enjoying the shocked admiration of every capital from Paris to St. Petersburg, the object of all shades of honour, from the respect of a Goethe in Weimar to the dark and flashing glances of every Venetian courtesan, was still in the future. But for the time being, in London, as Byron's most recent editor says: " He became the lion of the season, the hero of every drawing-room and the talk of every dinner-table." From loneliness, poverty and obscurity he was raised overnight to the height of fame and fashion.

To what extent, though—and it is really the most important question here—can Lord Byron's connection with Nottingham be sustained? He is accepted as unquestionably its greatest national, indeed international, figure. Newstead was quite rightly accepted, and is administered by, the Corporation of the City of Nottingham, and has been made, as we shall see, into a worthy place of pilgrimage. But the question must remain in the sceptical mind approaching Byron for the first time, whether he is in fact any more the Nottinghamshire poet-in-chief than Bonington is its chief painter. The " Song for the Luddites ", which is his immediate poetical connection with the revolutionary movement we have been looking at, is contained, characteristically, in one of his first letters from Venice. It was written immediately on his arrival there for the long sojourn that was to last until his departure for Ravenna in 1819 with Teresa Guiccioli, which was itself the "prelude to the beginning" of the final wanderings that were to end with Greece and death. The "Song" is contained in that best, almost, of the letters to Tom Moore in those early Venetian days. It is that one dated December 24th, 1816, in which, after a couple of delightful amorous anecdotes—readers of Byron will remember them as the one about the Irish Colonel and his return after a quarter of a century to his Italian inamorata; and the one about Count Fersen and the travelling orchestra—Byron goes on to make one of his—one must admit—rather often repeated descriptions of his first important Venetian acquisition, Mariana Segati, "two and twenty, married to a merchant well to do in the world, and has great black oriental eyes and all the qualities which her eyes promise. . . ." Then Byron breaks out, you may recall, into impromptu verse. First, with the lines:

> What are you doing now,
> What are you doing now,
>   Oh Thomas Moore?
> Sighing or suing now,
> Rhyming or wooing now,
> Billing or cooing now,
>   Which, Thomas Moore?

After which there comes the remark, suddenly, to Moore, "are you not near the Luddites? By the Lord, if there's a row, but I'll be among ye! How go on the weavers—the breakers of frames —the Lutherans of politics—the reformers?" he asks; and then come the verses:

> As the Liberty lads o'er the sea
> Bought their freedom, and cheaply, with blood,
> So we, boys, we,
> Will *die* fighting, or *live* free,
> And down with all kings but King Ludd.

> When the web that we weave is complete,
> And the shuttle exchanged for the sword,
> We will fling the winding sheet
> O'er the despot at our feet,
> And dye it deep in the gore he has poured.

> Though black as his heart its hue,
> Since his veins are corrupted to mud,
> Yet this is the dew
> Which the tree shall renew
> Of liberty planted by Ludd!

"There," declares Byron to Moore of this rather dreadful (and, I dare say, to many susceptibilities, tastelessly facetious) effort, "there's an amiable chanson for you—all impromptu. I have written it," he goes on, "principally to shock your neighbour who is all clergy and loyalty—mirth and innocence—milk and water. . . ." Then, of course, he is off again, in his airy way:

> But the carnival's coming,
> Oh Thomas Moore,
> Masking and mumming,
> Fifing and drumming,
> Guitaring and strumming,
> Oh Thomas Moore.

Luddite emotions, even in this unkindly dispassionate sense, extolling action which the hereditary nobleman in Byron would really have been the first to abhor, don't last long. Yet there are other, quite emphatic statements of Byron's sense of belonging to the county and to the movement whose genuine spokesman he had been, which are not open, as the "Song for the Luddites", to the charge of facetiousness and levity. A month after the letter just quoted he is writing to Thomas Moore again. It is January; and the carnival he had heralded is now on. "Venice," he says, "is in the estro of her carnival"; and he proceeds to record the famous incident of the appearance in his apartment of the sister-in-law of Marianna Segati ("a well-looking, and for an Italian, *bionda* girl of about nineteen"), followed by a high-class row. You may remember it: first, Marianna, having seized her sister-in-law by the hair and given her about sixteen slaps, "which would have made your ears ache only to hear their echo", went into fits in Byron's arms and "in spite of reasoning, eau-de-cologne, vinegar, half a pint of water and God knows what other waters beside, continued so till past midnight", after which her husband appeared. Well, it is in that letter that Byron makes the remark to Moore, apropos of nothing: "I think of being in England in the spring (in fact, of course, he never returned) and if there is a row, by the sceptre of King Ludd I'll be there; and if there is none, and only a continuance of this 'meek, piping time

59

of peace ', I will take a cottage a hundred yards to the south of your abode, and become your neighbour; and we shall compass such canticles, and hold such dialogues, as shall be the terror of the Times (including the newspaper of that name), and the wonder, and honour, and praise, of the *Morning Post* and posterity."

The only other quotation from Lord Byron I should like to make at this stage is considerably later in date. It comes from the time when he had moved from Venice to Ravenna in the company of Teresa Guiccioli. He is writing about the political situation in Italy, and says of the Liberals—with whom Left-Wing admirers of Byron like to remember he sided and associated to such an extent that he was under Austrian surveillance by means of spies and agents throughout his period of residence in Italy— " the Liberals have delayed till it is too late for them to do anything to the purpose ". Then he goes on: " The worst of all is that this devoted country will become, for the six thousandth time, since God made man in His own image, the seat of war. I recollect Spain in 1809, and the Morea and part of Greece in 1810 to 1811, and a small stretch also of *my own county of Nottingham* under the Luddites, when *we* were burning the frames, so that I have a tolerable idea of what may ensue." A bit fanciful, perhaps, but the comparison may help to give posterity an idea of the warlike atmosphere of Nottingham in those years. We shall leave them, now, and Lord Byron, until we meet him again in his ancestral habitat a little later.

To the Radical tendency that Nottingham has displayed since it first became so early a nursery of advanced industry, must be added the liking for varied and dissenting religions. Before we pay our necessary respects to the churches of Nottingham (which are not, in all honesty, one of the most exciting features of the city) it seems right that we should note the places of worship other than those of the Church of England. The surviving building, or site, rather, with the longest history of dissent is the chapel of the Socinians or Unitarians in High Pavement. It was originally a Presbyterian meeting-place to which a free school had been attached at the time of the Declaration of Indulgence in 1672. (This was Charles II's gesture, suspending penalties against Protestant dissenters and also allowing Catholics to worship in their houses, which licensed, within the first year of its existence, some fifteen hundred dissenting preachers and released many Quakers.) You can get some idea of the importance of the High Pavement chapel from the fact that in 1717 its regular congregation was 1,400, approximately one-sixth of the total population of the town at the time. The moving spirit in the erection of what was originally an unexciting square brick building had been John Whitlock (whose memorial floorstone you can see in St. Mary's church). He had had as his associates William Reynolds and John Barnett, who were joint ministers of St. Mary's during the Commonwealth. The High Pavement meeting was built in 1662. A little more than a hundred years later there came to it an important Nottingham figure, the Reverend George Walker, an eminent mathematician, a fellow of the Royal Society, and friend of the chemist and divine Joseph Priestley. Walker stayed for twenty-five years, during which time he was the acknowledged leader of Nottingham's religious and intellectual life. With Gilbert Wakefield, in the late 1780's, Walker formed a literary club among the dissenters. The High Pavement Meeting, as it was called, underwent considerable repairs in 1805. Then, in 1876, the Gothic building with its prominent spire, which stands now on the site, was erected to the design of the Bristol architect, named Stuart Colman. If, architecturally, the building leaves us rather cold, at least its east window deserves a careful look because this was designed by Edward Burne-Jones and the work of the stained glass carried out by the firm of William Morris and Company, whose place in the history of English taste is secure and important. This work, consisting of twenty-three figures in three tiers, dates from 1890. Of the two other windows in the High Pavement chapel that in the north transept dates again from 1890 and was made at Düsseldorf, and that in the north aisle, work of 1925, by Towers.

The Castle Gate church is a building which was built originally in 1688, on a site which had been a Calvinist or Congregational chapel thirty years earlier than that. Now it is the radiating centre of congregational activities in the city and has, I believe, the distinction of being the first church to have been wired for broadcasting. On the south side of Park Street was built a spacious and well-lighted meeting-house for the baptizing Calvinists. This should not be confused with the mother church in Nottingham of the General or Armenian Baptists, in George Street, which was open in 1740 and recently closed, being replaced by the tabernacle in Mansfield Road, better known as Regent Hall. The Hockley Street Methodist chapel still exists. It has had, however, a period of existence as a warehouse. It was, in the early nineteenth century, the largest of the dissenting places in Nottingham. In this lofty, but usually crowded building, austerely plain, dating from 1872, John Wesley preached his last sermons before his death in 1791. The Wesleyan Methodists were the centre of several religious disruptions in Nottingham during the late eighteenth and early nineteenth centuries and there was a considerable changing of hands among their various centres of worship, and the history of the individual buildings is confusing to follow. The octagonal brick building originally erected in 1760 for the Wesleyans became a chapel for the Baptists who, by 1799, had already moved to a new chapel at the lower end of Plumtre Street. The Wesleyans had moved from Hockley Street, in 1814, to the George Street chapel. A schism among the sect had taken place in 1805, when a small party retired from Hockley Street to a schoolroom in Malt Mill Lane. They afterwards joined some Scottish Baptists and together bought the Broad Street chapel. Again, the followers of Wesley had, in 1762, built a tabernacle in Milton Street. Twenty years later they sold it to the general Baptists who, in turn, sold it to a cowkeeper. Shortly afterwards it was pulled down. Nottingham had also a Sion chapel, built in 1761 by a group that had split off from the Unitarians, and a place of meeting, in Houndsgate, for the Sandemanians, from 1778. The Quakers had built, in 1737, at the cost of £337 1s. 7d., a meeting-house facing the north-east end of Collin's almshouses, in Friar Lane, which was described as "like the people who attended, neat within and without". One ought not, of course, to omit due mention of the fact that the founder of the Salvation Army, William Booth, was born in 1829, at Notintone Place, Sneinton, and the Booth Memorial Halls in Edward Street are a tribute to his memory. The headquarters of the Nottinghamshire and Derbyshire section of the Salvation Army are situated at Low Pavement, and there are nine other Salvation Army quarters in the city and its immediate environs, including halls at New Basford, Bulwell, Arnold and Astbury, a goodwill centre in Sneinton, and a men's industrial home at Aberdeen Street in the city. William Booth himself was converted at the Wesley chapel in Broad Street, where a memorial tablet which marks the spot where he knelt is visited annually by large numbers of people.

For the Roman Catholic community Nottingham is the centre of a diocese which comprises the counties of Nottingham, Derby, Leicester, Lincoln and Rutland. Thus the Catholics have within the city a cathedral, which the Church of England has not. Their cathedral cannot, I feel, be described either as a beautiful or as an impressive building, though I am prejudiced in its favour by the interesting character of its architect, Augustus Welby Pugin, who is one of the most striking spokesmen, theorists and executants of the early Victorian episode of the Gothic revival. Prior to the existence of the building which is Pugin's memorial in Nottingham, the Catholics had had a small place of worship in Stoney Street. St. Barnabas' cathedral in the Derby Road was consecrated on August 27th, 1844, having been begun two years earlier. It is a hundred and ninety feet long, cruciform in shape, and designed in a severe and, to my eye, rather forbidding version of the Early English, that is to say thirteenth-century, Gothic. But it is made of good and solid material, the masonry is admirable, and there is something noble about the hundred-and-fifty-foot steeple above the central crossing. Unfortunately, its position on the traffic-laden slope of the Derby road—which gives always the impression of bearing people in transit and having no time for that actual part of the city—is not worthy of a cathedral. Nor have I, in spite, I repeat, of an affection for Pugin, been able to find genuine pleasure in its interior. Its pattern is modelled on local architectural habit, with octagonal piers and twice as many windows in the clerestory as there are arcade openings. I think one can see that there is something impressive about the lancet windows of the transept. The east end is square with an ambulatory and chapel. What is worth careful attention by all students of Puginesque Gothic are the altars and furnishings of these eastern chapels and of the chapel of the Holy Sacrament which are typical of the conscientious, elaborate and yet somehow sensible work of Pugin. The cathedral is rendered brilliant by seventy-six windows of stained glass, all designed by Pugin, including a rose window over the sanctuary. The cathedral very largely owes its existence to the piety and financial benefactions of the then Earl of Shrewsbury who contributed handsomely to the fifteen thousand pounds needed for its erection. I have omitted to add that a previous Roman Catholic church, dating from 1828, can be seen in Broad Street, where it is now the premises of Messrs. Halstead. Before we reach the three Nottingham churches which deserve individual attention, let me list some of those in the city and close around, mainly Victorian, but by some of the leading church architects of the period which the specialist might visit. I have arranged them roughly in chronological order. From 1812 dates St. Peter's in Old Radford. Here is a church of the eighteenth century surviving into a later date, square, and characteristically Georgian in appearance but with windows of a mild and unemphatic Gothic. It has no gallery. The chancel dates from 1871. A local architect with the appropriate name of Surplice, built the stone church, with lancet windows, of St. John the Evangelist in Mansfield Road, Carrington, in 1843. At about the same time a church of St. John the Baptist in Canal Street was built in an uninteresting Early English style. It was badly damaged during the war. Another St. John the Baptist, in Chilwell Road, Beeston, was rebuilt in 1844 and, like the last, is the work of the great—or if you prefer it, infamous—Sir Gilbert Scott, working with his partner Moffatt (this collaboration, at the outset of Scott's career, lasted only for ten years, and Scott's first church, at Lincoln, was built in 1838, so that these two Nottingham examples have a certain documentary interest). The Beeston church has a large south-west tower and a dull Perpendicular interior. The chancel of the earlier church was left standing, much lower than Scott's new building. Quite different is the 1844 St. Paul's in Hyson Green. This is an aisleless, undecorated church with single lancet windows. Others from succeeding years are Holy Trinity, Trinity Square by Stevens, a large rectangular church with galleries on three sides narrowing to the chancel; this dates from 1841. St. Stephen's, Sneinton, though mostly built by Hare in 1912, retains its large Early English style tower of 1837-39. St. Matthew's, Talbot Street, 1853, has a tall octagonal spire and two very low turrets on the west front. St. Mark, Huntingdon Street, is perpendicular in manner with turrets at the four corners after the fashion of King's College, Cambridge. Stevens of Derby, who built St. Paul's in Hyson Green, was also responsible for Christ church in New Radford, built in 1847. Professor Pevsner says of Stevens that he "built many sound churches in and around Nottingham, all characterized by great restraint in the use of decoration". Christ church, New Radford, has one single, wide, low-pitched roof covering both nave and aisles; the aisled east end is lower than the rest of the church and ends in a polygonal apse.

There are a few later Victorian churches to mention. First, St. Paul's, Daybrook, dating from 1896 and built by Pearson who designed the dark grey and heavy-looking cathedral at Truro in Cornwall. This Daybrook church has an almost identical tall spire on the pattern of that of the cathedral at Coutances in the department of La Manche in France, which is one of the finest examples in Normandy of the early Pointed style of Gothic architecture. . . . Then there is the church of St. George in Kirk White Street West. This is 1897 again but this time by G. F. Bodley, one of the major figures of church architecture at the end of Queen Victoria's reign, who had begun as a pupil in the office of G. G. Scott but later broke away from his teachings. He was the architect of Washington cathedral. His St. George's in Nottingham is quite an impressive affair, tall and plain with a very tall separate altar niche possessing only one window high up on the wall.

So we turn, having reversed the usual order and taken the later —if not necessarily minor—churches first, to the three tolerably well-known ecclesiastical buildings in the city itself.

St. Mary's church, the mother church of Nottingham, is almost cathedral-like in size and majesty. It stands on a prominent eminence—against a background, now of the towering brick blocks of the early and mid-Victorian warehouses and hosiery factories which climb up the hills around it—some ninety feet above the Nottingham Meadows, which seems to have been utilized for religious purposes since the very earliest times. Norman relics have been found under St. Mary's during repairs and alterations and though it is not known how many churches succeeded each other before the present structure was erected in the fifteenth century, there is evidence that two, or possibly three, churches have preceded the present building since the Conquest. There are existing records, for instance, of an earlier church, which, with its lands, tithes and appurtenances, was granted to the Abbey of Lenton in about 1100. You can find what is probably a fragment of the twelfth-century church in two arches built into a plain mid-Victorian wall in Broadway at Jacoby's warehouse; these arches—a matter of technical interest—have no capitals between jambs and voussoirs.

With the exception of the west front and the tracery on the clerestory level, which are both by Sir Gilbert Scott, dating from 1843, and are in imitation of what had been there originally, the church is almost entirely of fifteenth-century construction and belongs to the period of greatest prosperity for the English spinning and weaving towns. The church consists of a nave of six bays and aisles, an originally aisleless chancel (the south chancel chapel is by Temple Moore of 1912-15) and transepts. The badly weathered south porch is one of the oldest portions of the building and dates from the last quarter of the fourteenth century. The stone roof, with four rolls as transverse arches, is interesting and the lion's head above the doorway seems to be there out of compliment to Richard II, who bore a lion's head on his arms. The inner doorway of the porch is enriched by niches placed diagonally in a way that is typical of fourteenth-century work. The voussoirs of the arches are decorated with large square fleurons. The bronze doors, illustrating the life of Christ in relation to the Virgin, were erected in 1905 in memory of a late-Victorian vicar of the church, the Rev. Francis Morse. Inside the church, on the third pier from the west on the south side of the nave, will be seen faint traces of an eighteenth-century inscription, "Pray remember the poor". And on the fifth pier from the west on the same side are certain curious little crosses, which, if they are not masons' marks, are votive crosses celebrating some vow or pilgrimage.

In plan the church is cruciform, and both inside and out now probably looks much as it did prior to 1726 when a rebuilding of the west end took place and a classical piece was stuck on to the Perpendicular. Sir Gilbert Scott reversed the process. The broad and lofty embattled tower is the most striking feature of the exterior, and there is a magnificent view to be got from the summit. The tower contains a peal of ten bells, some of which are nearly three hundred years old. The church is remarkable both for the number and for the size of its windows, and especially for the magnificence of those of the transepts and west end. There are fragments of fifteenth-century glass in several windows of the south chancel aisle, while the nineteenth-century windows in the bulk of the church are unusual in their extent and completeness.

The towers rest on broad composite piers—which were rebuilt in the nineteenth century—and has a fan vault inside. Outside it is of three stages, the first with a blank arcade, the second with one large window on each side, the third with four arcades, of which the two middle ones are pierced and the others blank. The tower is crowned by battlements and eight pinnacles. The body of the church is also castellated, the chancel plainly, the nave and aisles with panelled battlements. The panelling extends to the buttresses too. The rectangular panelling of the walls is what gives the church its special character. The panels are framed by plain rolls. This gives the effect of the windows of the aisles, for example, being set into this framework.

One usually gives some—to my mind often meaningless—figures in connection with a building of this magnitude; so, for what it is worth, the length of the church is two hundred and ten feet, its breadth at the transepts ninety-five by thirty feet, the roof is pitched at an altitude of fifty feet and the tower is more than twice that height.

The church is not very rich in monuments. Those that it undoubtedly contained in earlier times have been either removed or mutilated. You will find, in the north aisle, a battered alabaster figure, and in the transepts the tomb of John Samon, who died in 1416 having been three times Mayor of Nottingham. This, again, is of the local alabaster. Opposite, in the north transept, is a recess with niches and mutilated angel figures in the gable, which was perhaps erected for the tomb of Thomas Thurland who died in 1474. In it there now rests an alabaster tomb chest made probably for John de Tannesley (died 1414) and his wife. It is

decorated with quatrefoil panels with shields and small figures of
the Annunciation. Who were these people? Thomas Thurland
was a Nottingham magnate of the time of the Wars of the Roses.
His name is preserved in Thurland Street, in the centre of the
city, which runs down parallel to Clumber Street into Pelham
Street. It was in this position, covering pretty well all of what
is now Thurland Street, that there stood Thurland Hall, which
Thomas Thurland, who was several times Mayor and was a
merchant of Staple, had built for himself about the year 1458.
Opposite it, in succeeding centuries, stood the Blackamoor's Head
stables. This ancient stone building passed by purchase to Sir
John Horace, who was created the first Earl of Clare when James I
paid his last visit to Nottingham. It was called Clare Hall for
some time. Charles I stayed here when he came to Nottingham
to raise his standard at the outset of the Civil War. Among the
upper servants in the house, ten years later, was an ardent Royalist and one of Nottingham's literary notabilities, Robert Loveday,
the translator of Calprenède and author of an interesting series
of *Loveday's Letters Domestick and Foreign*. In a letter to his
brother, Loveday wrote of his service here with Lord Clare:
"My employment is something too great for an unseasoned
servant. . . . I attend him in his chamber, and usher his lady,
write his letters, and whatever else that unbeseems not his command or my obedience." Clare was then Recorder of Nottingham and Loveday presumably his private secretary. Neither the
medieval building of Thurland himself nor the seventeenth-
century frontage which was put on by Francis Pierrepont, third son
of Robert Earl of Kingston, in the late 1650's survives; but Thurland Hall was long pointed out as one of the oldest domestic
buildings in the town. Only two-thirds—the centre and one
wing—of the original plan was left. The street front was decorated with a double row of ornamental pilasters and a flight of
steps led up to the entrance door eight feet above street level.
The windows were framed in heavy stonework and the four
storeys were crowned with curved and pointed Jacobean gables.
In the eighteenth century Thurland Hall seems to have served
a number of public purposes. "The rooms are spacious but
gloomy," we learn, "the walls are castle-like thick; here, on
particular public occasions, the noble and gentlemen of the
county dine in the great room." Eventually Thurland Hall became the property of the Duke of Newcastle, and some time
before 1830 it was demolished. Thomas Thurland was a former
Mayor, so was John de Tannesly whose tomb now usurps Thurland's recess in St. Mary's. But the Purbeck marble mensa or

slab which lies on Tannesley's tomb probably commemorates yet another wealthy Nottingham merchant, one William d'Amyas, a wool merchant of the fourteenth century, who may have been the builder of Gedling church.

St. Mary's, of course, contains its usual quota of unimportant eighteenth and nineteenth-century memorials and tablets. Worth noting for a local name, is the monument to Thomas Smith, a member of the great banking family, who died in 1727. His memorial blocks the entrance to a stairway which, in pre-Reformation days, led to the Rood loft, the Singing Gallery on top of the screen which used to stretch across the church. In the north transept, under a window which retains a few fragments of sixteenth-century glass displaying the Tudor rose, will be found monuments to the great family of Plumtre to whom Nottingham owes so much. We have already met the name of this family in Plumtre Hospital, the almshouses originally founded in 1415 which survive in the early nineteenth-century building in Plumtre Square.

Nothing whatever to do with the history of Nottingham or with the church itself but worth mentioning for its presence here is a painting of a madonna and child, at full-length, which is to be seen here, having been given to the church in 1839. It is the work of Fra Bartolommeo (1475-1517).

St. Peter's church down to the south, down Wheelergate, is one of the oldest in the city though it has been many times restored. It is of a typical Nottinghamshire appearance of a kind you will see duplicated in the larger villages all over the county. It probably dates from the first quarter of the fifteenth century and is known to have replaced an earlier church. It has a western steeple with pairs of angle buttresses and a tall thin spire (which shows the marks of repeated repairs) rising above the battlements. The west door is very elaborate, decorated with pinnacles and niches. The tracery of the windows is mainly Perpendicular. In the south arcade are thirteenth-century columns with grotesque capitals. The capitals of the columns in the north arcade are worth looking at for their curious mouldings cut in the form of a battlement. During the Civil War, St. Peter's church received considerable damage as it was bombarded by the Parliamentarians based on the castle, in order to dislodge a party of Royalists who took refuge in it.

A much more drastic fate overtook the church of St. Nicholas, in Castle Gate, which we approach a few yards south of St. Peter's. This church was razed to the ground by the Parliamentarian commander in the castle, Colonel Hutchinson, because, from its spire, the Royalists were able to annoy the defenders of the castle. The materials of the old church, which was considerably larger than the new one which eventually took its place, were converted to private uses: the boxes in the kitchen of a certain inn in the town (that means the high-backed seating partitions of the bar, the descendant of the true "kitchen") were made out of some of the pews, and the bells were, by Colonel Hutchinson's orders, removed to his own village of Owthorpe where his house, Owthorpe Hall, was destroyed during the Civil War but rebuilt immediately after-wards, and where, in the church, he was buried in 1662, after his death at Sandown Castle. (Colonel Hutchinson's house has gone now, but from the church of St. Margaret, which was largely re-built about 1705—incorporating some of the materials of the older church, for instance the charming bracket above the west entrance with two angels holding a shield—the early eighteenth-century clock still strikes the hours for the benefit of the men working in the fields all around; for Owthorpe church is now isolated from its village and stands, rather overgrown and tumbledown on the outside, but neat and tidy with a strip of carpet on the floor within, by itself in the meadows behind a farm; and the clock's chimes mingle with the drone and clatter of modern agricultural implements.) Well, Colonel Hutchinson destroyed St. Nicholas', but soon after the Restoration, in 1671, a new church was begun and finished in 1678. It was built of brick with stone facings and in spite of the period of its building—a moment as unfriendly to the Gothic as any, with the tradition lost and the revival not yet beginning, the west tower was given crocketed pinnacles (which were blown down in 1714-15 and though apparently replaced are not there now) and decidedly Perpendicular bell-openings, which are still there. The church was considerably enlarged during the eighteenth century and it gets its present agreeable Georgian appearance from the addition first of a south aisle in 1756 and then, by a subscription raised in 1783 amounting to nearly five hundred pounds, a north aisle was added with a new gallery, the church was to a large measure re-pewed and a pleasant pulpit—which survives—added. These aisles have large round-headed windows and battlements and are separated from the nave by Tuscan columns. It has a great deal of character this brick church of St. Nicholas, more, in spite of its comparative modernity, than has either St. Mary's or St. Peter's, and it has the luck to have fared better in its position than have either of the others. For, while St. Mary's great eminence has been built up to by the push-ful undeserving and St. Peter's is almost swamped, St. Nicholas', on the ascent to the hill where the castle stands, still has wide views out over the Trent to the south (even an eighteenth-century lover of the picturesque could write: " From St. Nicholas church-yard there is a fine prospect of the distant and adjacent country. Belvoir Castle, which must be at the distance of twenty miles, is an object of beauty, on the left and near objects such as one sees from the castle are delightful distractions. I have, on my visits to Nottingham, frequently, on a summer's day, walked to this churchyard for the benefit of its refreshing and salutary air, as well as for its extensive prospect.") To-day, though the views are more limited than that, the quarter is still peaceful, the air no doubt quite salutary, and the church screened from the busy street by the trees which grow in its churchyard.

Quiet, that churchyard; but Nottingham is, in spite of its stir and its movement and its industrial activity, by no means a place that one cannot get, if one wants it, a quiet sit down and a rest within a moment or two's walk of the city centre. It is, while retaining to far greater degree than most midland or northern centres the agreeable characteristics and grace of its pre-industrial past, a notably well-planned city and, as we shall see in a moment, contains some large and remarkable examples of organized urban design. It has therefore got the best of both worlds, the old and the new, for look at this complaint of a visitor to Nottingham in the seventeen-eighties:

" When it is said," he complains, " that Nottingham is delight-ful, the air salubrious and the town one of the pleasantest in the Kingdom it must be lamented that the new buildings are erected many of them without any design of forming regular streets. Well contrived streets and passages are highly conducive to health and cleanliness; but here, if one may be allowed the expression, is a resurrection of buildings, generally without order, seated like clusters of mushrooms in a field, cast up by chance. Here the gathered filth within doors is scattered, daily, in the dirty passages without, in front of the dwellings, *delightful* to the sight and odorous to a sensitive nose. Yards, in which such good things should be treasured for agriculture, are not, it may be supposed, always thought of when buildings are erected here. What may be denominated streets or lanes before some of these new erections, are, many of them, without any sort of pavement, consequently without regulated water courses, and consequently pregnant with mischievous effect."

That complaint was made in the last decade of the eighteenth century. It was only about thirty years later that there began to be laid out, on ground immediately west of the Castle Rock, the Park Estate, a piece of planning which, for its early date and its

A Victorian Gothic country house by Gilbert Scott: Kelham Hall, about 1860
Bunny: the strange tower of Bunny Hall designed by its owner, Sir Thomas Parkyns

MONSTE AUDET

Quem modo trivisti longo in Certamine Tempus
Hic Recubat Britonum Clvis in Orbe Pugil;
Iam primum stratus, procfor Te Vicerit omne
De Te etiam Uictor quando Resurgit erit

Tempus edax rerum

That Time at LENGTH did throw him it is plai
WHO lies in hopes that he Should RISE again

ΚΑΙΡΟΣ Ο ΠΑΝΔΑΜΑΤΩΡ

Here lieth Sr Thomas Parkyns Barronet one of His Maties Justices of ye Peace & one of the Deputy Lieutenants both for ye Count
of Nottingham & Leicester Second Son of Sr Tho: Parkyns Barronet & Anne ye Sole Daughter & Heiress of Thos Creswell
in ye County of York Esqr whose Ancestors came in with William ye Norman ye said Sr Tho Parkyns Married
Elizabeth ye Grand Daughter & Heiress of John Sampson Esqr Alderman & Citizan of London, with whom he had
fee-farm Rent of 130l 16s 8d per Annu paid out of ye Mannor Borough & Park of Beverley & ye Waterton
& superiorities in that County also ye fee-farm Rent of 130l 16s 8d issuing out of ye Mannor & Castle of Bolsover, in ye Count
of Derby ye Copies of ye Deeds of Purchase are Enrolld in Chancery & in Money about 3000l was Educated at West-min
Sr brook & Trinity Colledge Cambridge An Greys Inn of Court 7 years who purchased ye whole Tythe of Bradmore & part of Keyworth
formerly ye Duke of Rutlands Also A Rent of 60 Marks per Annu payable out of ye Tythe of Bunney, Also ye Mannor & Estate in Ruddington
& Sr Thos Widford Barr Also ye Mannor & Estate in Est-Leake with ye Mannors & Copt-Lands of Cortlingstock Wysall, Thorpe & Willoughby
by Armstrongs with other Estates in Barron Sub Soar, Gotham & ye forsaid before mentioned. He Next Roofed this Chancel, built
which & erected this Monument, gave 4 Tuneable Bells to ye Church, Built ye School House & Hospital, which ye Lady Anne Endowed with
her Anni he Gave to ye Poor 100l of ye Followers of Bunney & Bradmore 12s yearly in Bread to be Distributed every Sunday in Bunney
Church, He Builtt ye Mannor Houses in Bunney & East-Leake, ye Daity of Uberidge House & most of ye Farm Houses in Bunney & Bradmore
He Studied Physick both Gallenick & Parracelsick for ye benifit of his Neighbours, had a Competent Knowledge of most part of the
Mathematicks, especially Architecture & Hydrostaticks, & Contriving & Drawing all his Plains without an Architect, He wrote the
ΠΡΟΓΥΜΝΑΣΜΑΤΑ or Cornish Hugg Wrestle, & was buried March ye 22 Anno 1741 aged 78 years, He had two Sons by
Said Elizabeth his Wife (viz.) Thos who was buried September ye 14 Anno 1706 aged 19 years, & Sampson
who was buried April ye 17 Anno 1713 and 22 ys also who had two Sons & two Daughters by Alice his wife (viz.)
Tho who Died an Inft. The Inst. & Hanna, His Sister Anne Parkyns Spinster gave 200l for ye putting
forth poor boys Apprentices in ye Towns of Bunney, Bradmore, & Cortlingstock, was buried
August the 31 Anno 1743 aged 79 yeares

The abovesaid Sr THOMAS PARKYNS in 1727 married a second Wife JANE, Eldest Daughter of
Mr GEORGE BARNARD one of the Aldermen of the City of York by whom he had Issue
two Sons and one Daughter THOMAS the present Baronet, and GEORGE and ANN now living
She departed this Life August the 4th In the Year of our Lord 1740 and the 33d Year of her Age

success in imposing on the city a pattern and quality of layout which was duly followed later, is an important feature of the place.

The Park Estate had been forest land until the beginning of the nineteenth century. The first house was built in 1827 and activity followed along the north-east fringe of the area. In Park Terrace and Rope Walk you can see stuccoed villas of late Regency or very early Victorian date, while some of the buildings now forming part of the General Hospital, built originally as wealthy villas, date from the same time or even perhaps from 1815 to 1820. Slightly further north, by Canning Terrace (which, with its Italianate classical features forms the entrance feature to the neo-Greek general cemetery in Alfreton Road, begun in 1837) and along Derby Road and Ilkeston Road, houses were obviously going up in the 1830's. Let us hear Professor Pevsner on the Park Estate. "The Park itself was only laid out after 1850, presumably under some influence of Nash and his original dream of scattering villas at generous distances all over Regents Park. The Nottingham Park did not keep to the generous distances, and moreover did not reach actual building, until the whiteness and the pilasters and the columns of Nash's 'compo' fronts had given way to brick or Gothic or Tudor detail. 1854 is the date at which building began properly, an unfortunate date for packing houses into a landscape. Even so, as a piece of planned villa siting so close to the city centre the Nottingham Park is something that historians of 'urbanism' should take more notice of. It has its Victorian picturesque aspects too. About 1850 a tunnel entrance down from the Derby Road was made but later discarded. On the other hand an alderman with a house in Rope Walk made his own tunnel in his garden about 1856 and embellished it by having roaring lions carved out of the cave-like walls."

At a house called The Elms in the Rope Walk there died one of the two Nottingham poets that one cannot very well leave out of this account. Neither of them, at the moment, draw a great deal of response, I fancy, even from residents of their native town; and I doubt whether in Nottingham from year to year a very large number of copies are sold either of the works of Henry Kirk White (with whom we shall deal in a moment), or of Philip James Bailey, who died at The Elms in the Rope Walk in 1902. Bailey, "Festus Bailey", was born at a house near the church at Weekday Cross—the building, a warehouse, was, after Bailey's death, honoured with a plaque commemorating this event of 1816—the son of Thomas Bailey, himself a man of letters in a mild way. Mild is

Sir Thomas Parkyns on the tomb he designed for himself in Bunny Church
Kingston-on-Soar: the Babington Chantry, about 1550

the last word you would apply to Festus Bailey, for his single work, the enormous poem *Festus,* written mostly at Basford, was conceived and executed on an heroic scale, achieved tremendous popularity and has now suffered total oblivion. I have a feeling that, however much the critical barometer may change, *Festus* will never completely "come back" because its lofty moral tone is something that is not likely to be swallowable in any epoch except the Victorian; yet, in spite of its crashing faults, the blank verse of which most of its exhausting length is composed has occasional passages of striking brilliance of diction and versification. Since, except in a book about Nottingham, no one in the mid-twentieth century is likely to think about P. J. Bailey at all, we'd better at least recall what the poem was about. First, Bailey's life can be dismissed in a sentence. From Nottingham, at the age of nineteen, he went to London and entered Lincoln's Inn, but did not take up the law seriously; in 1839, when he was twenty-three, he published *Festus*; the rest of his life was spent in watching the development and decline of the popularity of that work, which went through dozens of editions both here and in the United States.

The late George Saintsbury who wrote quite sympathetically, though far from reverently, about Bailey draws attention to the fact that many of Bailey's contemporaries of undoubted poetical competence—for instance Tennyson—accepted, indeed welcomed Bailey and his *Festus* as they never accepted Martin Tupper and his *Proverbial Philosophy,* which has become almost synonymous both with commonplaceness and bathos, and with *Festus.*

Festus? A version of *Faust,* as the poem is a version of the Faust story. Bailey's hero has as his accompanying tempter Lucifer, he has a number of Gretchens, but, being a Victorian, Faust does not precisely seduce any of them but does eventually marry one of them, Clara. I cannot resist quoting Saintsbury's comments on the episode of Clara. "A sort of battle of Armageddon, followed by the consummation of all things, interrupts their honeymoon. In the enormous interim, Lucifer, for purposes not always obvious, personally conducts Festus about the universe—and all the universes; and once creates a really poetical situation by himself falling in love with a girl whom he has thought to use for ensnaring Festus. Usually the Tempter indulges in speeches of great length, replied to with tenfold volubility by Festus, who might have claimed to have 'talked the devil dead' inasmuch as Lucifer himself at least once cries for mercy. . . . Between 1839 and 1850 *Festus* had a comparatively fair field open to it; *The Angel World,* a sort of satellite of *Festus,* was not received cordially; *The Mystic* and *The Spiritual Legend* (1855) still less so; and when an entirely new poetical period had thoroughly set in, the *Universal Hymn* in 1868 least of all. No one but a very curmudgeonly person quarrels with a parent, poetical or other, for standing by his unpopular children. But the way in which Bailey acted towards his was without precedent, and, one may hope, will never be imitated. He stuffed large portions of the unsuccessful books into what was becoming the not very popular body of *Festus* itself, which, thereby, from a tolerably exacting individuality of twenty thousand lines or thereabouts, became an impossible sausage of double the number."

Saintsbury, you see, doesn't like *Festus,* and I think you would find it, even in the original version, and less still in the later composite "sausage", almost impossible to get through; certainly to enjoy. I think we must accept Saintsbury's judgment, delivered nearly forty years ago, as still holding good for our generation and perhaps for ever. He admits that the blank verse has—either in mere single lines or short fragments, but occasionally in more sustained pieces—unashamed purple passages of undoubted brilliance. But he writes of the form of the poem in general: "The greater part of it is couched in a curiously loose blank verse, neither definitely originally nor clearly imitated from anybody else. It drops occasionally into couplet or into semi-doggerel anapaestics—generally bad—while it is, in one part frequently, in others sometimes, interspersed with lyrics of extraordinary weakness. . . ." But enough of poor Bailey. Let us leave him living at The Elms in the Rope Walk and dying there, it is to be feared, quite a long time after he had seen the death and critical interment of his precious *Festus.* Let us leave him in due kindliness with the remark of Alfred Tennyson's to Edward Fitzgerald in 1846: "Order it and read: you will most likely find it a great bore, but there are really very grand things in *Festus.*"

There are really not, I am afraid, any grand things at all in the works of either of our other two Nottingham poets, Henry Kirk White and Robert Millhouse. Festus Bailey's reputation was not only national, it was world-wide. Neither Kirk White nor Millhouse really belong now, much outside their own county. Let us have a look first at the life and career of that "Burns of Sherwood Forest", Robert Millhouse. He was born in the parish of St. Mary, Nottingham, on the 14th of October, 1788, the second child of a John Millhouse who had married, in 1785, Ann Burbage. The place of Millhouse's birth appears to have been what was then called Mole Court off Milton Street, a part of the city

which is now absorbed in the site of the Victoria Hotel and railway station. Robert Millhouse—it was nothing unusual—was
put to work at the age of six. When he was ten he had started
work on a stocking loom. But he was also being educated. He
went to a Sunday school and at the age of ten was a singer in
St. Paul's church. His acquaintance with poetry began this way.
When he was in his teens he saw at a friend's house two small
statues. They were of Shakespeare and of Milton, and under one
he read the lines from *The Tempest*: " The cloud-capped towers,
the gorgeous palaces . . . leave not a wrack behind." Millhouse
turned to his elder brother and said, " Is it not scripture? " He
received an informative answer as to the origin of the lines and,
according to tradition, immediately sat down and began to read
verse. In 1810, Millhouse joined the Nottinghamshire militia
and it was when billeted at Plymouth as a soldier that he wrote
his " Stanza Addressed to a Swallow " and " On Finding a Nest
of Swallows ", which were published in the *Nottingham Review*.
This was followed, in 1812, by a " Poem of Nottingham Park ".
In 1814 his regiment was disembodied and Millhouse returned to
the stocking loom. But three years later he was back with his old
unit, now rechristened the Royal Sherwood Foresters. In 1818 he
married for the first time, at St. Mary's, a girl called Eliza Saxby
whom he described, somewhat tritely, as " the pride of Sherwood's
maids ". His married life was necessarily interrupted by the calls
of military duty (a time, this, of almost universal peace) which
called for poetic comfort:

> Hark, my love, the trumpets call:
> Wipe those foolish drops away;
> Safe, perhaps, from sword and ball,
> We shall meet another day.

Millhouse's poem *Vicissitude* came in 1821, and *Blossoms* in 1823.
That year an appeal on behalf of the then Corporal Millhouse
was made to the committee of the Royal Literary Fund and in the
columns of the *Gentleman's Magazine*. As a result Millhouse did
receive some charitable assistance which bouts of ill-health made
all the more necessary. In 1827 there appeared his *Sherwood
Forest and Other Poems*, the title work, in three cantos, consisting of nearly a hundred verses. Millhouse, now out of the army,
had returned once more to the stocking frame; but in 1832,
through the kindness of friends, he was found a post in a savings
bank. That year he published his *Destinies of Man*. At this time,
too, his wife, who was always ailing, died, leaving him with the

five survivors of the eight children that had been born to them. In 1836—Millhouse was now forty-eight—he married again, a Marion Mure, a girl of twenty-five who was described as " a blooming young woman ". But by now, there was added to Millhouse's chronic penury the misery of a fatal intestinal disease. His friends rallied round and the savings bank paid him a pension of four shillings a week, but on April 13th, 1839, Robert Millhouse died and was buried on the east side of the Nottingham General Cemetery nearly opposite the chapel.

Because, one presumes, of his alternations between the hosiery and the military life, Millhouse and his wives seem to have undergone an unusually large number of changes of address. Millhouse is recorded as having lived at different periods in Charles Street (off Colwick Street), in Mole Court (where he had been born), in Mount East Street, in St. Anne's Street, Nile Street, Nile Row, Gedling Street, and in Walker Street, Sneinton. Not, I fancy, that anyone is now going to try and decide the exact chronology of these migrations.

As he was dying, Millhouse said to his friend and benefactor, that notable Nottingham writer and character Spencer T. Hall, " Spencer," he said, " my family belonged to my country; my fame I leave." If that ambiguous phrase has any meaning it seems to suggest that Millhouse was sure of some sort of standing in posterity. A few hours before he died he said, " My name, Spencer, is linked with Sherwood Forest."

It is. But the Burns of Sherwood Forest has not survived far beyond its limits. Although the author of *The Song of the Patriot* has some claim to be described as " the artisan poet of Notts" and to be discussed in the same breath with Bloomfield and Clare, it is, surely, only because of the lowliness of his origins. His verses have not sufficient universality in them to carry them beyond his native haunts. But if you are looking for a local poet you will find one in Millhouse; celebrating in his rather stiff sonnets and lyrics what are still " the sights " of the neighbourhood. The titles of his verses give you a clue to what you will get from them: *Composed in Nottingham Park*; *To Larkdale—a Favourite Scene in Early Life*; *To Sherwood Forest*; *Written in One of the* (supposed) *Druidical Caves in Nottingham Park*; *The Maid of Trent's Shore*. Meet her, as a sample:

> The sun had bid a sweet farewell
> To Clifton's height and topmost tree
> The blackbird ceased its tale to tell
> No more was heard the humming bee;

With hasty step I took my way,
To meet the maid whom I adore,
Nor had I long in doubt to stay
We met on Trent's delightful shore.

Not very good, is it? Perhaps a shade more feeling is to be found in his best-known poem, *The Song of the Patriot,* in which, speaking of the haunts of his infancy, he writes:

For there my sire first told me I was free,
And bade me love my country and my God;
And taught that paths of kind humanity
Should by the mingling sons of men be trod;
And early wished my soul to hate oppression's rod.

It comes as something of a surprise to learn that this suffering, invalid ex-soldier was, almost to the end of his days, a noticeably florid-looking man about five feet nine and a half in height with a ruddy complexion and light brown curly hair. His friend, Dr. Spencer Hall, however, has left a, no doubt, unintentionally forbidding picture of a poet whom one suspects one would have little enjoyed meeting. This is what Hall says: "In person of average height, with somewhat grave and striking but not unpleasant features; an attitude most erect, a deliberate utterance and sonorous voice; the whole presented a remarkable correspondence to his prevailing mental mood, in which a proud dignity had considerable, but playfulness or trifling very little, part. In conversation he was sententious and aphoristic. As a husband and father he strove to do his duty."

After that formidable tribute there seems little to add on the subject of Robert Millhouse. So we will turn now to Henry Kirk White, the youthful poet concerning whose early death Byron wrote:

Unhappy White! While life was in its spring,
And thy young muse just waved her joyous wing,
The spoiler swept that soaring liar away
Which else had sounded an immortal lay.

Henry Kirk White used to be considered worthy of a plaque which was placed on the little house right in the centre of the city, now covered by the great bulk of the Council House, in which he was born in an upper room of what was then, and remained until its demolition, a butcher's shop, on March 21st,

1785, three years before Millhouse. Kirk White was an infant prodigy but his circumstances did not allow his talent to develop. At the age of fourteen he was removed from school and, as he didn't like the idea of going into his father's butcher's shop, he was sent to a stocking frame to learn the business of a hosier. But this was not to his taste either and he was articled to a firm of lawyers, who were the Town Clerks of Nottingham. But in the law he found that not so much disinclination as the deafness from which he suffered was an obstacle to advancement to the Bar, so, through the assistance and encouragement of a curate at St. Mary's church, he went up to Cambridge as a Sizar at St. John's College. At Cambridge he greatly distinguished himself, but it was at the expense of his health and on the 24th October, 1806, at the age of twenty, he died and was buried at All Saints', Cambridge. Robert Southey, soon to be Poet Laureate, whose protégé to some extent Kirk White was, wrote of him, "there never existed a more dutiful son, a more affectionate brother, a warmer friend, nor a more devoted Christian. Of his powers of mind it is superfluous to speak; they were acknowledged wherever they were known. It would be idle to say what hopes were entertained of him, or what he might have accomplished in literature" —which is pretty much what Byron, who had gone up to Cambridge, to Trinity, in 1805, and was writing his first series of poems in the year of Kirk White's death, said in the lines I have quoted.

Kirk White's first volume of poems, entitled *Clifton Grove*— thrashing, you see, the same old beauty spots as Millhouse— appeared in 1803 when he was eighteen years old. It was not at all well received by the critics, but one can see that it had certain qualities which caused Southey and Byron to think so highly of him. To-day, if he is remembered at all outside the county, it is as the author of a couple of hymns—"The Star of Bethlehem" and the (in modern hymnals) much altered "Oft in danger, oft in woe"—and some quite pretty second-rank lyrics on non-sacred subjects. He had, of course, if one can put it callously, the enjoyment of certain enviable characteristics which made for his appearing to his contemporaries a touching and memorable figure in the correct romantic formula of the period. He was a good, a very good young man with decent literary taste, who died young after a life, if not exactly miserable or penurious, at least fraught with the resented menaces of butchery and hosiery. He was a thoroughly poetic figure: he was, in fact, like Keats. And Byron, towards the end of his life, did not hesitate to write of the two poets in the same breath. He did not like Keats or his poetry but, of the *Quarterly* article which Shelley accused of killing

Keats, " I do not envy the man who wrote the article: your *Review* people have no more right to kill than any other footpads. However, he who would die of an article in a review would probably have died of something else equally trivial." The same thing nearly happened to Kirk White, who afterwards died of a consumption.

CHAPTER IV

WOLLATON AND CLIFTON

FROM quite close to the scene of Kirk White's birth in the old Shambles you can get one of those frequent and convenient buses which take you out along the Derby road, past the Roman Catholic cathedral through New Lenton and past the big crossroads where the Derby road is intersected by the Middleton and Clifton boulevards. Middleton and Clifton. Each of these names are full, here, of colour and meaning and history, much more so than are the twin halves of Kirk White Street West and Kirk White Street East, which lie between Nottingham station and the River Trent. Clifton, as we have learnt from information almost too readily offered by our poets, means the Grove and the beauty spot and walks among the trees. In a few moments we must make our enquiries there. And Middleton? Middleton boulevard leads us geographically and historically to Wollaton. Take the bus on past the crossing and get out at the point where the Derby road meets, branching off to the southwest, Beeston Lane. On the north side of the road, before the boulevard crossing, you will have noticed perhaps a large turreted entrance lodge looking somewhat purposeless and out of place in the Derby road leading, as it does, only to tidy streets of houses in a modern residential "estate". Though a far later date, the style of this entrance lodge gives some hint of the architecture of what is certainly the city's as it is the county's most famous, most discussed and most belittled building. The style of Wollaton is overpowering and when, in about 1804, the gatehouse on the Beeston as well as the Lenton edges of the Park came to be built by Jeffry Wyatt (later Wyatville) that architectural romanticizer—to whose very great credit is the splendid silhouette of George IV's Windsor Castle—his own taste could conveniently fall in with the pepper-pot turrets and sculptured gables of Wollaton itself.

The history of Wollaton and its origins is one whose peculiar interest lies in the fact that, although ancient, its beginnings were abrupt, almost upstart, having a flavour of the *nouveau riche* which is reflected, as we shall see, in the architecture of the building. Yet the Willoughby family, whose seat Wollaton Hall was for more than three hundred years, had been prominent in the county for almost as long a period before Wollaton was built. The founder of the family fortunes was a wealthy Nottingham merchant with the solid but perhaps hardly resounding name of Bugge. About 1240 Ralph Bugge purchased an estate at Willoughby-on-the-Wolds, a little village at the extreme southern edge of the county, where part of the old home of the Bugges can be traced in the structure of a farmhouse and cottage near the church and where, in the north transept of the church itself, are some medieval effigies of the highest beauty and importance. Ralph Bugge's grandson was knighted as Sir Richard de Willoughby and the old name was dropped. The tombs in Willoughby church include one, a cross-legged knight, supposed to be Sir Richard himself, who died in 1326. There are other even older tombs which, although exceedingly worn, display the greatest elegance. The oldest portray two ladies wearing wimples—the conventionalized drapery indicates a date in the first half of the fourteenth century—and a couple notable for their slimness, a cross-legged knight and a fashionably dressed lady. These earliest Willoughby effigies are of stone. The later ones are of alabaster, of a Richard Willoughby, a judge, who died in 1362, with a beautifully carved face and exquisite detail of costume, and of a Sir Hugh, who died in 1445, with his wife, lying together on a tomb chest with mitred angels holding rectangular shields. At the west end of this tomb is a Trinity and at the east end a seated figure of the Virgin, both quite admirably carved. There isn't, perhaps, much more to say about Willoughby itself, except to note that it was the scene of the last Civil War battle in Nottinghamshire when, in 1648, the Royalists under Sir P. Monckton defeated the Parliamentarian troops of Colonel Rossiter. Anyway, by this time, Wollaton Hall had been standing, in all its ostentation, for nearly a hundred years, and even when Sir Hugh and his wife were laid to rest at Willoughby church the marriage of the second Sir Richard Willoughby, a grandson of old Ralph Bugge, had married Isabella, heiress of the de Morteins of Wollaton, and thus acquired the Wollaton estates, where the family eventually settled in a manor house near the church. It was not until several generations later, long after Wollaton Hall had been built, that marriage with a Freville heiress, a descendant of Roger Mortimer, brought to the Willoughbys the Middleton estates in Warwickshire, from which the first baron chose to take his title in 1711.

It is generally accepted that Wollaton Hall is one of the most important Elizabethan houses in the whole county. This does not mean (even if one ever uses the word in this connection at all) that it is one of the most beautiful. Wollaton has come in for a great deal of objurgation, not least from present-day architectural critics. I am not for one moment denying that its showiness, its quite blatant vulgarity, prevents it from being breath-taking in anything but a sense of slightly horrified astonishment. This does not mean that grandeur, for the sake of being grand, for the sake of displaying all that was then the latest in the craft of building and external decoration, for displaying all that could be imported from the architectural fashions of Italy, France and the Netherlands, has necessarily to be belittled. Wollaton is distinguished from all other Elizabethan houses in England by its all-round symmetry and by the enormous cost of its building, which is unashamedly displayed in its material, and its ornamentation. The builder of the hall, Sir Francis Willoughby, who was born about 1546 and died in 1596, had none of the, to us, characteristic Elizabethan interest in poetry or learning or science. But—and it brings us close, again, to the course of the county's own development—he was a coal magnate. It was this fact, together with the general growth of the Willoughby family fortunes which made the expensive luxury of the building of Wollaton Hall possible between the years 1580-88, its completion coinciding with the year of the Spanish Armada.

Since it is very characteristic of the county that its greatest Renaissance building should have been built, literally and metaphorically upon coal, and, at the other end of the county's history of building, that the erections and excavations of the fifth Duke of Portland should have been achieved partly through the same useful material, it is necessary at this stage to say something about the early history of the coal industry in this district. For it is a part of England which shows uniquely early and continuing examples of wealth, title and lordly magnificence derived not from land—not, at least, from land in the older, surface, or agricultural sense—but from the greatest of industries.

It is as early as the reign of King Edward I (who ruled from 1292 to 1307) that we first hear of coal being mined in the county. On the extreme west of the area, a narrow strip of magnesium limestone forms a continuation of the Derbyshire hills. This constitutes the only high ground in Nottinghamshire, and it is on this western border, where it touches north-east Derbyshire, that the Nottingham coalfield lies, and, further north, the south Yorkshire coalfield, in the Doncaster area. Nowadays the collieries extend to Harworth on the south Yorkshire border, thus converting a large part of south Yorkshire and north Nottinghamshire which, a few decades ago, was purely an agricultural district, into a continuation of the coal area with its attendant industries; but the original coal edge of the county was at Cossall (a place worth visiting to-day to see the delightful group of Willoughby almshouses, of brick, dating from 1685, with a saddleback roof in the centre and gabled posts on the sides) and at Selston, on the verge of the Annesley upland. (St. Helen's church at Selston is worth remarking, in this connection, for the tomb of a Sir William Willoughby, who died in 1630, and his wife, their two recumbent alabaster effigies on a large plain tomb-chest, the background with black columns. Sir William's helmet is to be seen opposite the tomb against the chancel wall.) At the end of Edward I's reign there was a serious contention in the area about the operations of the coal-mining pioneers. In Queen Elizabeth's reign (by which time coal was fast becoming a mainstay of English export, and a Newcastle fleet of two hundred ships was supplying London, though the Queen herself forbade the fumes near her palace) the Selston mines were the property of Sir Charles Moryson, who, with a neighbour, Sir J. Byron, was also interested in iron mills located in the same area. We won't go much further, at this stage, into the history or location of the colliery works in the county. By the beginning of the seventeenth century mining was still centred round Wollaton Strelley (where, by 1610, four pits were in action and were making the Strelleys of Strelley the main industrial rivals of the Willoughbys of Wollaton), Bramcote, Bilborough and Trowell. The coal was transported on the Trent to Newark and further afield. This last, by the way, was the community chosen as the "Festival Village" in 1951.

Sir Francis Willoughby began the building of the hall, then, in 1580, and a couplet engraved on the south side of the building records the time it took to complete:

En has Francisci Willughbi militis aedes
Rara arte extructas Willughbaeisq(ue) relictas.
Inchoatae 1580 et finite 1588.

that the building that Sir Francis constructed with such rare art, and which he bequeathed to the Willoughbys that came after him, was begun in 1580 and finished in 1588.

This long period (and it is certainly a reasonable one if it is to start from the time the stone was first quarried and to end when the last piece of sculptured and painted decoration was complete) has been transferred by popular tradition to the building of the wall around the Park which was said to have taken seven men, with seven boys serving their apprenticeship on the work, seven years, and to be seven miles in length. The enclosure of this park engulfed, and caused the total disappearance of, the village of Sutton Passeys, which in the Middle Ages existed somewhere between Wollaton and Lenton, and was last mentioned in a subsidy roll of 1558. Already, when the first history and description of the county came to be written, by Thoroton, in the 1670's, no trace even of its site could be found; but the name of this sacrifice to the Elizabethan magnificence of the Willoughbys is now commemorated in Sutton Passeys Crescent on the Wollaton Park estate. (One ludicrous anecdote about Cossal and its Willoughby connections. About the year 1780, when a Miss Willoughby who lived in Nottingham died, an old vault in the chapel was opened to receive her body. "When the workmen entered it"—I am quoting from an account written at the time—"they were surprised at a luminous appearance at the further end of the vault: a candle being brought to examine it the extraordinary light disappeared, which much heightened their astonishment; on the candle being taken away, it appeared as bright as before. It turned out, however, to be nothing but a human skull covered with a greenish light-coloured mauve, of a downy nature, which, where it was fingered, turned black.")

Wollaton Hall was said to have been brought from the Lincolnshire quarries of the Ancaster stone by pack horses which, on the return journey, were laden with coal from the Wollaton pits. Presumably, therefore, the material cost Sir Francis nothing in cash; even so, Cassandra, Duchess of Chandos, who was a daughter of a later Francis Willoughby, 1635-72 (a famous naturalist and friend of John Ray, whose instruments, library, and natural history collections were long preserved at Wollaton Hall), wrote that the total expenditure on the building amounted to eighty thousand pounds in the currency of the time. This was an enormous sum: to get any idea of its modern equivalent you have to multiply it by at least six.

If the stone cost nothing it must have been the architects and craftsmen who were expensive. The responsibility for the design has been the cause of considerable discussion, owing to the existence of two pieces of evidence which have been taken as of equal standing. First, a mural monument in Wollaton church, a severely architectural affair, square and undecorated, records: " Mr. Robert Smythson, gent., Architector and Surveyor unto the most worthy House of Wollaton with diverse others of great account, he lived in the faith of Christ seventy-nine years and then departed this life the fifteenth October, 1614." Secondly, there exists, in the Soane Museum in London, a collection of drawings by a certain John Thorpe which includes a ground plan of the Hall and half the front elevation. Cassandra Willoughby, Duchess of Chandos, in her account of the house, written in 1702, stated that Sir Francis sent to Italy for the master workmen who built the house and also for most of the stone figures that adorn it. On the strength of this Soane Museum drawing, J. A. Gotch, in his notable and influential books about English Renaissance architecture, attributed the design of the house to Thorpe, who was regarded as one of the first and greatest of Elizabethan architects and to whom had been attributed the design of such buildings as Kirby Hall and Rushden in Northamptonshire, Buckhurst House in Sussex, Longford Castle in Wiltshire, Holland House in Kensington and Audley End in Essex. This being so, Smythson, in spite of the assertion on his monument in Wollaton church, had to be relegated to the subordinate role of a sort of foreman of the works. But later scholars have considered that Thorpe's fairly accurate plan of the house and his half-elevation, which is very inaccurate, were almost certainly made from memory and perhaps at a distance after the house had been built, and could not possibly have been part of an architect's design of a building yet to be created. There exists, moreover, among the Smythson papers, plans and drawings, now in possession of the Royal Institute of British Architects, a drawing of one of the pavilions at Wollaton that is far more accurate than Thorpe's sketch. The researches of Mr. John Summerson have proved Thorpe—born in 1563 and died in 1655 in London at the great age of ninety-two—to have been merely a painstaking draughtsman and clerk who was sent all over the country as a royal commissioner making surveys for the settlement of boundaries of estates and establishing the legal rights of landlords. His personal interest in buildings and his gift for making delightful drawings was given full scope, so that during his travels he sketched the elevations and drew plans of the great houses which he saw in the course of erection everywhere around him. Many of them, such as survive in his sketchbook, are very rough and, as in the Wollaton case, inaccurate; executed presumably either at a hurried visit on the spot or from memory on his return home to London, where he lived about 1607 onwards. Of his relations with the building of Wollaton, the establishment, for the first time, of the date of his birth, 1563, at the village near Stamford, Northamptonshire, where his father and grandfather had been master masons, is overwhelming evidence: John Thorpe was only seventeen when Wollaton Hall began building.

We have, all the same, to be careful about the exact position of Robert Smythson. On his tablet at Wollaton he is called " architector ", but there is no proof that he ever provided designs for a whole house, and the role of architect in Elizabethan times seems to have been indistinguishable from that of a mason or builder, who would make designs for windows, porches or chimney pieces, perhaps with some latitude in detailed execution of comprehensive designs.

We can, with some safety, dismiss as more or less irrelevant the contribution to the argument of the Duchess of Chandos. The part played in the construction of Wollaton by any Italian workmen must have been a minor and probably sculptural one; tradition at least supports the theory of their existence with a story that one ship laden with statues was wrecked on its way to England.

But if we do not accept the Italians at all, or John Thorpe at all, or Smythson as an " architect " in our full modern sense, then who was the designer of Wollaton Hall? The evidence that has been produced—and it is still remarkably untilled ground—about the building of the great Tudor houses suggests that not enough attention has been paid—except in the most flamboyantly assertive and individualist instances like that of Bess of Hardwick—to the role of the owner himself. It seems now most likely that, in a broad and unprofessional sense, Sir Francis Willoughby was his own designer, an interpretation quite consistent with the phraseology of the Latin inscription carved upon the house: " Has Francisci Willughbi militis aedes rara arte extructas."

The site for the hall was admirably chosen, on gently rising ground which gave a beautiful view of the surrounding country in all directions, and this advantage was fully exploited by the unusual four-square design with generous windows on every front. Tradition asserts that the windows number three hundred and sixty-five and that the hall has fifty-two doors. The square, two-storeyed house with its corner pavilions rising to a third storey, and the great tower of the central hall erected proudly of expensive alabaster stone in the centre, is a striking departure from the usual Elizabethan E or H-shaped plan. Apart from the tower's conspicuous external position it implies a break with the traditional position of the main hall which was still, in Elizabethan times, the most important dwelling and stateroom in the house as it had been virtually the sole chamber of the medieval house, being reached by a centrally placed entrance but extending asymmetrically parallel to the main frontage. An obvious comparison, here, can be made with Hardwick Hall across the Derbyshire border where the hall in this case lies not parallel but at right-angles to the façade and stretches across the building. In style, however, though Robert Smythson is believed to have been concerned with its building also, Bess of Hardwick's grandest house, in spite of the ostentatiously initial cornices, is simplicity itself compared with Wollaton. Wollaton is a mass of ornament: strapwork in the gables, bands round the pilasters on all four sides, busts of Plato, Aristotle, Virgil, Diana, Hercules and many other people in circular niches framed by cartouches. There are said to be nearly two hundred statues and busts and still many of the niches are empty. The corner towers are ornamented with gables, pinnacles and statues, and their chimneys are ingeniously curved to meet in the middle in the form of a crown. The central tower, however, is allowed to make its effect by a force of sheer massiveness. Apart from a balustrade it is plain, adorned only with undecorated cylindrical turrets. A wide flight of steps, with a mounting block at each side, leads up to the great front door on the north side, while from the salon on the south a double flight of steps descends from the terrace. Professor Pevsner, who leaves the question of Robert Smythson's part in the building of the house open, gives a special reason for it being "highly desirable to know the name of the designer (not the builder)". He says that the character of the raised hall, and some of its details, just as those of the "keep" at Bolsover across the county border which was designed by another member of the Smythson family, are clearly evidence of a conscious romantic medieval revival (Pevsner draws attention to the tracery of the windows and the angle tourelles), "a most remarkable thing", he says, "in Elizabethan architecture though perhaps paralleled in Elizabethan court ceremonial and literature".

We have heard already of Italian influences and craftsmanship at Wollaton; and although it may be said that there is a strong kinship between Wollaton and Longleat, the most Italian of all the great English houses of the sixteenth century, there are other Continental precepts and examples at work on it too. The Italian resemblances are largely structural and have to do with the essential framework of the building beneath the superficial imposition of the ornamentation. Italian influence can be seen in the horizontal emphasis of the whole structure, the use of superimposed orders and in the preponderance of window over wall space, as well as minor but quite prominent structural features such as the chimneys in the shape of columns without entablatures

The Nottingham University School of Agriculture at Sutton Bonington

and the circular niches for busts under the windows. But besides these features, which, although they may have come to England via France (as, example, from Blois), must have been derived ultimately from Italy, there are elements at Wollaton which were exclusively French developments of the Renaissance manners, while it is from the Netherlands that the gaudy ornamentation, particularly the gables and their strapwork, derives. It was most probably from the pages of manuals of architectural instruction that the craftsmen employed at Wollaton got many of their Continental ideas. The Flemish element can be traced, in part at least, from the publications of Vredeman de Vries (1527-1608), who was a notable painter of perspective views and helped to decorate the triumphal arches erected for the entry of the Emperor Charles V and his son Philip into Antwerp. His best-known publications were his "Perspective" and "Architecture" published in Antwerp in 1559 and 1563. Both contain, as well as good straightforward architectural drawings, a large number of detailed designs for chimney pieces, gateways, reredoses, and monuments overloaded with grotesque and excessive ornamentation of just such a kind to seem deeply intriguing to the unsophisticated English craftsman. His strapwork interlacements have been described as "nothing short of engineering feats of Heath Robinson ingenuity which cannot be termed art".

A French book which had a far wider and more fundamental influence on English architects and craftsmen was one called *Les Plus Excellents Bastiments,* by du Cerceau, which had been published only four years before the walls of Wollaton Hall began to rise. Let me quote a recent writer, Mr. Lees-Milne, on these triple influences: "The influence of du Cerceau is seen in the square plan with four protruding corner pavilions, obviously copied from those of St. Maur-les-Fossés and Ancy-le-Franc, here used for the first time in England, but to become with the Georgian Palladians a recognized method. In the ornamental detail and above all the plethora of it at Wollaton we at once notice a departure from classical restraint to a crowded and effective expression of ornament, in fact an enrichment of Italian with French and chiefly Flemish forms. In addition to niches in the Roman manner and gondola rings on the dies of the pilasters of the ground floor, to say nothing of the heads of the tower windows, of a Venetian character, we detect the influence of Serlio (Sebastiano Serlio, 1475-1554, author of *Architectura,* 1584, one of the most inspired sources of information of the history of the Italian Renaissance) in the treatment of the pilasters with

87   G

Colston Basset and its "Cross"

wide jewelled bands and a French derivation in the absurd
tourelle with pepper-pot lids like those at Blois at the corners
of the tower. The chief inspiration between the Wollaton ornamentation is, however, clearly de Vries's *Architectura*, of which
some plates are reflected in the flamboyant strapwork cartouche,
particularly in the gables and the aprons below the windows.
How far Smythson personally was given latitude in the application of these details we do not know, but his bias presumably had
veered from Italian classicism to northern mannerism, when
engaged at Wollaton. Wollaton Hall was finished in 1588, by
which time we like to think that Robert Smythson was glad to
regret his capitulation to French and Flemish tastes, which had
possibly been imposed by his fashion-ridden client Sir Francis
Willoughby. He certainly left behind him in Wollaton Hall the
most notable monument to Elizabethan bad taste." That is the
judgment, and it is the usual one, of Mr. Lees-Milne, who is
an authority on the more elegant age of the later eighteenth
century dominated by the brothers Adam. It might not, perhaps, be inappropriate to set beside his learned and extremely
helpful statement an opinion of Wollaton dating from that
very period. "Lovely art thou fair Wollaton; magnificent are
thy features! in years now venerable, thy towered crested presence eminently bold seated, strikes the beholder with respect-
ful awe. Unlike many of the visionary edifices of the present
day, designed with but little variation of style, and uniform
in disordering architectural order, thee we must admire,
chaste in thy component part and presenting an harmonious
whole."

Let us now peer inside. We shall find no difficulty in gaining
access since Wollaton Hall, the park and its mansion now
belong to the Corporation of Nottingham. The woodwork
of the beautiful hammer-beam roof is designed, coloured and
carved to look like stone, and is decorated with numerous
coats of arms. In, or about, 1820, it underwent alteration
at the hands of Jeffry Wyatt(ville) who built the gate houses.
Its towering height is unquestionably impressive, in spite of the
blankness of the walls up to the point where windows become
possible, but the chamber is not really a thing of beauty at all;
proportion, and, one would have thought, comfort and usefulness,
have been entirely sacrificed to ostentation. But at least it has
been spared division into several floors, and remains to give some
sketchy impression of what the interior of the house must have
looked like in earlier times. There is really very little else which
can direct our minds backwards. Where, for instance, is " the

Prynce's chamber " and the " Quines's chamber " which are known once to have existed? On the two large staircases that lead to the upper floor of the body of the house are to be found paintings, in both cases on the ceilings, and in one case on the wall beside the staircase. These decorations have been attributed either to Verrio (1639-1707) or to Laguerre (1663-1721). Verrio was master gardener to King Charles II and painted decorations at Windsor, Hampton Court, Chatsworth and Burghley. Laguerre, working a little later than Verrio, whose chief assistant he was, is generally reckoned the better painter of the pair. Laguerre's masterpiece is probably to be found in the saloon at Blenheim Palace, which has architecturally treated walls and a ceiling emblematically representing John, Duke of Marlborough, in the career of victory arrested by the hand of peace. Laguerre was to have painted the dome of St. Paul's Cathedral, but the commission eventually went to Sir James Thornhill. Verrio has been much objected to for the ebullience and expansiveness of his cloudy and mythological paintings. In Queen Anne's drawing-room at Hampton Court, for instance, not satisfied with filling in the compartments of the ceiling, he omitted the divisions as well as the cornice and often rounded over the angle of the wall and ceiling so that his painting could be spread over the whole surface without apparent break. Laguerre does not create quite such confused Olympian scenes, but the two painters have always been thought of together ever since Alexander Pope coupled them in his famous epistle on the subject of taste to the architect, the Earl of Burlington. These are Pope's lines:

On painted Ceilings you devoutly stare,
Where sprawl the Saints of Verrio or Laguerre,
On gilded clouds in fair expansion lie,
And bring all Paradise before your eye.

The Verrio-Laguerre paintings at Wollaton include a scene on the north staircase which led to the dining-room, which was over the entrance hall and armoury, representing Prometheus stealing fire from heaven and his subsequent punishment.

The most interesting room in the upper part of the house can be reached only by a narrow spiral staircase of sixty-eight steps. This room is directly over the great hall and is now called the prospect room, from the magnificent views commanded from the windows on all sides. At one time it was known as Bedlam, being a dormitory for visitors' servants, and is also said to have been used on occasions as a ballroom. In the later part of Wollaton's period as a private residence it became a kind of museum of rare pieces of furniture.

As so often happens in houses of this date that have been extensively altered, one has to go to the service quarters to find the most comprehensive traces of the old layout of the house. As usual, they were in the basement here; but this was better lighted at Wollaton than was frequently the case, owing to the height of the hall floor above ground level. Down here you can still see the old kitchens and wine cellars, and a bewildering number of other rooms (equipped, most of them, with cupboards built into the walls) leading into each other, or opening off long rambling passages with unexpected little staircases. One room was constructed, and presumably employed, as a prison cell—a convenience which few, even of the largest private houses, are usually supplied. It has a barred window, a very large bolt on the outside of the door, and a little grille for the inspection of the occupant. Down a flight of rough steps from the north-east basement begins a series of subterranean passages, formerly used for the storage of beer, ice and other household commodities, the first part enclosed in brickwork, probably of the Stuart period, and the rest cut out of the living rock. Here also is a well of ice-cold water, so cold as to be completely sterile, in which no form of life can exist, and there is further along the tunnel, and connected with the well by culverts to carry the overflow, a reservoir in which a particularly hardy member of the Willoughby family, an admiral, is said to have taken his daily bath. Let us not forget that the Willoughby family has provided its country with many notable explorers, not least the famous Sir Hugh Willoughby, who perished in the Arctic in 1554 on an expedition to discover a north-east route to Cathay and India.

An eighteenth-century description of the contents of the house, after telling of the grandeur of the hall and the extent of the rooms and corridors, adds that there was to be seen "a family piece by Smith, in which one of the figures represents Sir Hugh Willoughby who was frozen to death in the North Passage"; a moment's thought reassures us that even the remotest corridors of Wollaton Hall cannot have been quite as cold as that. Incidentally, although this painting "by Smith" is no longer there, several portraits of members of the family appear on the Verrio, or more probably Laguerre, paintings on the north staircase. Here, while the ceiling depicting the mythological heavens, teeming with gods, introduces the story of Prometheus, and on the left-hand wall Prometheus is seen animating a female statue, and on the right suffering punishment in the infernal regions, the facing wall depicts a Roman sacrifice to Apollo in which many of the celebrants and bystanders took their features from members of the family.

Some six years ago an important part of Wollaton Hall, which had not been included in the purchase made by Nottingham Corporation in 1925, passed into the keeping of one of the city's greatest institutions. Late in the year 1947, in the hall of what was still then University College, Nottingham, Lord Middleton transferred that part of the Middleton collection of manuscripts still in the hands of the family to the college, not the university, on permanent loan. These documents, which form one of the most exciting and comprehensive collections of material about the details of life in a great English house in various periods, were originally at Wollaton, but were later removed to Birdsall, another of Lord Middleton's properties. It was while they were still at Wollaton, in 1911, that the Royal Commission on Historical Manuscripts issued a celebrated report which drew attention for the first time to the wealth of fascinating material which they contained. One can, for instance, form some idea of life in the hall in the time of Sir Francis Willoughby, its first owner, and, as we have suggested, its designer. Among the documents is a " check-rolle of the number of persones in household the seven of August 1598 ". It was obviously compiled by some official, some form of steward of the household, and begins with " my master and my mistress", continues with six other members of the family, descends then to Mr. Doctar, runs through the names of eight waiters or footmen, passes to Mistress Margery Shelton, who may have been the housekeeper, to Mistress Willoughby's maid, notes one in the buttery, four people in the kitchen (including " Symon Setter, the slaughterman "), two in the brewhouse, two in the stable, three maids in the dairyhouse, various others of unspecified occupations, and ends with " Mr. Doctar his boye", adding "total number is forty-six persons ". Even more revealing in the light it throws on the day-to-day duties and routine of the staff of a big Elizabethan mansion is a copy that Cassandra Willoughby made of some orders to be observed by Sir Francis Willoughby's servants at Wollaton in about the year 1572; that is to say when the family was still living at the old, now long vanished, hall in Wollaton village near the church. According to these rules it was, in the first place, the duty of a person called the usher to see that the hall was kept clean, to notify his master if guests " of the better sort " arrived, " that they may be entertained accordingly. If of the meaner sort, to know the cause of their coming to the end that they may be answered of their business." The usher, again, must see that "no stranger be suffered to pass without offering him to drink, and that no rascal or unseemly person be suffered to tarry there". When food was brought into the hall, when Sir Francis and his family were at table, the usher was to precede the servers, carrying a "little fine rod" as a badge of his office, and to appoint a yeoman in winter to carry the torch before the service. After the private dining-room was served, the usher must arrange the seating in the great hall of all noblemen's men and gentlemen, according to the rank of their masters. If there were no strangers present, the lower servants were to wait upon the upper and to feed upon the remains afterwards. Any food left over must be put on to the alms table, for distribution to the poor later. Drinks of various sorts were all served through the buttery hatch. The usher, moreover, was responsible for order in the hall, and for seeing that no meat was filched. Similar detailed instructions are given to an underling of the ushers, the butler, assisted by the under-butler, for keeping clean the buttery, and providing fire and lights for the great chamber; and the hours at which the buttery door must be opened are set down. From an account book of the same period it can be seen that Sir Francis Willoughby's household expenses for a period of fourteen months amounted to £1,394 18s. 8½d., which, as we have seen, must be multiplied by at least six to give any impression of its present-day value.

There is not a great deal more that need be said about Wollaton. To anybody interested in architecture and, I suggest, in English social history, a visit to Wollaton is an essential part of their education. It need not, as a matter of fact, be an enormously prolonged visit, because unless some different and irrelevant interest draws you to the natural history collections contained within the building it is only the outside, plus a brief glimpse at the great hall and its screen, that need detain you. (I ought to add, in parenthesis, for those who *are* interested, that the natural history collection, which was previously housed for many years at the old University College, is considered one of the best provincial collections of its sort in the country. As at present arranged at Wollaton, the ground floor is devoted to vertebrates, among which is a good series of Nottinghamshire birds, mammals and fishes. The collection of invertebrates is equally large and valuable and includes one of the finest collections of exotic butterflies in the kingdom, as well as large collections of all the other orders of British and foreign insects. Again, the assembling of samples of local insects is a special feature. In addition, the museum includes comprehensive cases of British fossils and of British and foreign mollusca, and there is a good series of minerals and rocks: the museum's range of microscope slides of rock slices ranks as one of the most important in the kingdom. Finally, there is a decent-sized herbarium of British and foreign plants. It has been possible to complain that, in spite of the ample daylight provided by Wollaton's huge windows on all sides, the contents of the museum have been denied the chance of exerting all their intrinsic fascination by the rather dull, unselective, crowded, old-fashioned and somewhat depressing way in which they have been displayed. Recently, however, the committee in charge of the museum has been reorganizing the exhibits with a view to showing fewer specimens but with better descriptions, lighting and appropriate backgrounds. A special collection of mammals—the Cockburn collection—has been arranged in a separate room, another room has been set aside for British birds in specially prepared habitat cases, and the committee is reorganizing the whole collection along these lines.) Unless, as I say, stuffed grouse and bottled newts attract you there is no need to spend long inside the hall. But choose a fine day because you will find that you will want to spend a long time first walking round the outside of this extra-ordinary building and then standing in front of each façade in turn to inspect in detail the incredible, monstrous encrustment of ornament and craftsmanship. I suggest that you walk to it across part of the park. Come in by the Beeston entrance and head north-westwards, taking care to upset neither the herds of gentle deer nor more irritable golfers. The park amounted in all, when the Corporation bought it, to just over eight hundred acres. It had been well laid out, in the best traditions of English land-scaping under the Lords Middleton in the later part of the eighteenth century, and the many fine trees are now in the full glory of their growth. Of this acreage something over five hundred acres were retained by the city as park or for plantations and playgrounds. The remainder, rather over two hundred and fifty acres, was sold for building developments. It is obviously gratifying for the Corporation to be able to report that the sales of land on the estate have fully recovered for the Corporation the price of the purchase of the whole, so that the very substantial estate remaining represents a profit on the original investment of permanent value. It is the eastern, citywards side of the park, incorporating the old main approach through Sir Jeffry Wyat-ville's Lenton lodge, which is now laid out as a residential estate; but just beyond Middleton Boulevard, with its wide dual carriage-way, there remains, intact, the noble avenue of lime trees which leads to the hall, and although the municipal golf course lies on either side of the roadway, the aspect in a westward direction is still that of an unspoilt park. Certainly one sees no longer the very ancient breed of wild cattle which used to graze here, spotted, hornless, and with black on their noses and inside their ears; but there are deer still. The roadway skirts the east side of the hall and its gardens, divided from them by a ha-ha, and curves round to the main north front of the hall, from which a shorter avenue leads northwards to the gate in Wollaton village, the spire of whose church, which we shall visit briefly in a moment, rises above the trees. The south terrace is laid out as a formal garden, with statues and a lily pond inhabited by large and slow-moving goldfish. A flight of steps leads down to a rose garden. On the west side of the hall the ground slopes down to the lake which is bordered by a plantation known as Thompson's Wood. On this side too, just below the house, is an attractive camellia house and a pleasant and rather Continental-looking self-contained stable block, built in the eighteenth century, with a handsome clock and carved coat of arms under the pediment which forms the central feature of its dignified, mildly classical front.

Take now, for a moment, the north-westward avenue to have a look at Wollaton village. Its nucleus consists of early eighteenth-century stone and brick houses, but there is a medieval cottage lying to the west of the church which is perhaps connected with the old manor house of which traces have recently been found underneath the rectory. The church, which is dedicated to St. Leonard, has the steeple usual in this part of the world, with battlements, surmounted by a slim spire. Most of the body of the church dates from the late fourteenth century, although there is earlier masonry in the chancel and a south doorway of as early as 1200. The north aisle was renewed about 1500, and the south aisle nearly four hundred years later, in 1885, by an architect of the name of Hodgson Fowler, who worked intermittently elsewhere in the county between the eighties and the first decade of the following century, and whose handiwork can be seen in the village churches of Averham, Grove and Sturton-le-Steeple. A striking feature of Wollaton church which the visitor should on no account miss is the seventeenth-century reredos, of a sort rare both in the county and in English churches as a whole. It is a classical composition with fluted corinthian columns dividing the side portions from the centre, which is given emphasis by a broken segmental pediment. All three parts of the reredos are filled with large geometrical designs of strapwork in the sixteenth-century manner. In spite of this the reredos can be attributed to the later part of the seventeenth century. The real wealth of Wollaton church, however, lies in its monuments. The series begins with two brasses on a raised stone slab with a rotting corpse shown below it. The tomb is of Richard Willoughby, who died in 1471, and his wife. It has an ornate canopy over it and over the horizontal top of the recess in which the tomb is placed are three demi figures of angels, an elaborate cresting surmounting them, with a panelled canopy containing three niches for statuettes on top of all. Henry Willoughby (died 1528) and his wives are buried beneath a tomb situated between the chancel and the south chancel chapel and visible from both sides. Their tomb-chest has openwork pointed arches, three of them on each side, between four statuettes of mourners of unusually fine quality of carving. If you look through the tracery of the sort of windows between them you will see a skeleton lying inside. The effigy of Henry Willoughby lies on the tomb-chest and those of his four wives in pairs, head to toe, on the left and right of him portrayed at half his size so as to get them in neatly. Above the tomb is a very simple canopy. Two later Willoughby monuments are worth mentioning—that of Henry Lord Middleton who died in 1800 and is commemorated by an urn on a large pedestal with vases on each side of it adorned with attractive floral garlands. This monument without figures is the work of the younger of two sculptors of the name of John Bacon. Then there is a monument to Henry, the sixth Lord Middleton, who died in 1835. This is a design by Westamacott of two genii bending towards each other. A last note about Wollaton church. Since about 1460 the Rectors of Wollaton have had in their keeping a manuscript volume of antiphons, that is, of short pieces of plain song to be sung by the choir, dating from the first half of the fifteenth century, which was originally prepared for a member of the Chaworth family of Wiverton whose church disappeared completely as a result of the enclosures of land in the seventeenth century. This manuscript music book is known to those who care about such things as the Wollaton Antiphonary.

To get to Wollaton church from the hall we went northwards. Let us now reverse our gaze and consider what lies to the southeast of the Derby road which forms the bottom limit of Wollaton Park. A large area of further parkland carries us southward past Lenton House (a pleasant building of about 1800) across Cutthrough Lane to the buildings of the University of Nottingham. The University Park at Highfields is one of the most recent acquisitions of the city and its one hundred and fifty acres make it the third in size of Nottingham's very numerous and varied parks; it includes a boating lake of about fourteen acres in extent, dominated by the buildings of the university. The park is divided by the University Boulevard, and on one side the ground is given over to games such as cricket, hockey, football, rugby and tennis, while on the other side people play bowls and croquet, there is a putting green and there is the boating lake. It was a good idea that the youngest citizens of Nottingham should, by the facilities provided for them, be brought in close and constant contact with the city's most advanced centre of education and learning. For while small children are provided for by a playground and a paddling pool with clean water flowing through it, beside them are the athletic grounds of the students of the university whose buildings, on rising ground facing the University Boulevard, are within sight from all parts of the park. The university buildings were opened in 1928 and were designed by Morley Horder, an architect who is well known for the design of country houses. The university building is of a classical nature and is carried out in a most dignified manner in a pleasant grey stone. There is not much ornament on the long front, which has round-headed windows on the ground level, but the centre is emphasized by a four-columned portico surmounted by a pediment with carvings within it, and above that a tall clock tower looking rather like an Italian campanile, with a weather vane at the top. Close to it is a large modern hostel, a plain and unshowy building with decent Georgian windows, and among the other halls of residence as they are called, close to the main university building, is one which incorporates Lenton Hall, a castellated house with a Gothic porch. It was on 20th August, 1948, by a grant of a charter of incorporation, and new statutes, that Nottingham became a full university. It was a most important post-war development in the history of the British universities, for Nottingham's was the first university college to be so advanced since before the war. It has become, now, the twelfth university in England and the seventeenth in the United Kingdom. Nottingham's successful elevation to this new status is likely to be the first of several changes to take place during the fifties. Among the places suggested as suitable places for new universities are York and Stoke-on-Trent, and there are obviously other university colleges which would like to follow Nottingham's example and be granted charters by the Queen. It seems generally agreed that the problem of Britain's excess undergraduate population can only be solved if there are more universities and, moreover, if these universities are able to become fully residential.

I hear Nottingham has notably fulfilled this important condition, so far as present circumstances make it possible. There are something like 2,500 students at Nottingham, of whom getting on for a third are quartered in residential halls. In addition to the three already mentioned—two for women and one for men—a fourth has been for some years under construction. In addition, of the 220 students at the School of Agriculture—one of the university's more important schools, formerly the Midland Agricultural College, situated at Sutton Bonington, a village we shall hear about shortly—about ninety per cent of the students are in residence. A public appeal has been made for raising about £1,000,000 towards the cost of the university's development and extension during the coming years. The aim is a wholly residential university, with five residential halls for men and four for women. In a speech made at the installation of the university's first Chancellor, the Vice-Chancellor, speaking of the christening of the university, spoke of the University of London as a foster parent, the University Grants Committee as a godparent, and the universities of Oxford, Liverpool, Manchester, Birmingham, Leeds, Sheffield and Reading as uncles. He said that the university's parents were the University of Cambridge and the City of Nottingham.

It was the Corporation of Nottingham which, in 1881, erected the large Gothic building in Shakespeare Street, designed by Lockwood and Mawson, as a university college. Its foundation was the result of a general feeling that so prosperous a city should be able to satisfy the needs of its citizens for higher education. The provision of the building came directly from the request that the Corporation should provide accommodation suitable for University Extension Lectures to be given by the University of Cambridge and for the science classes which had previously been held in the Mechanics Institution which had been established as long ago as 1837. Eight years after University College had been opened (the building includes the central public library), the Government first decided to grant financial assistance to university colleges and Nottingham was one of the thirteen thus recognized, receiving what seems now the ludicrously small sum of £1,400 a year from the Treasury. In 1902 the Treasury Inspectors reported that the college " exhibits the nearest approach of all colleges we have visited to a people's university ". The Charter of Incorporation granted the following year established a Court of Governors consisting of the President and Vice-presidents of the college and the Mayor, Aldermen and Citizens of Nottingham acting by the City Council. Between then and 1928, when King George V formally opened the new buildings of University College in their park at Highfields, the town of Nottingham had continued to develop its industry and its importance and the work of the college in Shakespeare Street and in its technical and other extensions had developed widely; but what most of all made possible the building of so imposing a university had been, of course, the munificence of the first Lord Trent.

A bust of Lord Trent, placed imposingly on a pedestal and surrounded by impressive monumental stonework and statuary, is so sited as to lie between the university buildings and the huge factory half-way between there and the River Trent. "Before him," we read, "a monument to his industry, behind an everlasting monument to his benevolence."

There they are, then, the three great buildings of the west side of Nottingham. They stand almost in a line with each other, in enfilade as it were, each isolated and in its separate way rather splendid among the surrounding green emptiness—Wollaton Hall, the university and the great Beeston factory of Boots. Jesse Boot, the first Lord Trent, the twentieth-century representative of that very element in Nottingham's history which produced Sir Francis Willoughby, caused to arise within a thousand yards of Willoughby's Wollaton a more discreet, less selfish monument to his magnificence, and a thousand yards south of that again the teeming symbol and centre of his own industrial enterprise.

Briefly, very briefly, his career. Jesse Boot was born in Nottingham in the year 1850. As a boy he worked in a herbalist's shop owned by his mother. After about fourteen years he had achieved a chemist's shop of his own in Goose Gate which prospered to the extent that in 1883 he could form the company of J. Boot & Co., which became one of the first "chain stores" in the country. Five years later, in 1888, the firm became Boots Pure Drug Co., and in that year began manufacturing its own drugs on a small scale in Nottingham. The first factory was at Island Street, relatively close to the centre of the city, on the south-eastern edge of the old town between Canal Street and the railway. The Island Street plant has now been very much enlarged and it now specializes in fine chemicals and biological products. By 1896 the firm owned sixty shops in thirty different towns all over England. Boot, who was an active Liberal in politics, was knighted in 1909 and created a peer in 1929. To-day the great Boots factory, or group of factories, at Beeston, covers an area of more than 250 acres. It is one of the largest chemical plants of the kind in Europe and is no negligible piece of architecture either. It was built in two parts, in 1932 and 1938, but the

designer of both was Sir Owen Williams. The earlier part is
considered as a milestone in modern architecture, and especially
in the large-scale external employment of concrete in building
in Britain. It has a south front 550 feet long, all cantilevered out
over the unloading dock. The projection is 30 feet and has
half a dozen or so three-faceted bays above it. Inside is the
packing hall, open all the way up to the top of the building with
galleries built round it, rather like a huge department store. The
1938 part has an even longer frontage of 700 feet, but the design
is considered less bold and perhaps less successful than the earlier.
It consists of a large multi-storey portion and single-storey part,
again with overhangs, this time up to nearly 50 feet. In addition to the huge Beeston factory which is visible from many parts
of the surrounding countryside (not least, now, as the most conspicuous object to be seen from Clifton Grove), a special factory
was built during the last war at Daleside Road, further out in a
south-easterly direction from the Island Street building. The
purpose of this branch was the surface culture production of
penicillin and it operated on behalf of the Government. By June
1944 it was producing one-third of the country's total supply of
this new drug. The Daleside Road factory has now turned
over to the manufacture of penicillin by the deep culture method.
More than 10,000 people are employed in these three factories.
In 1949 a new branch was opened at Airdrie in Scotland, for the
manufacture and packing of pharmaceutical products.

We are, surely, in duty bound to pay our respects to this hugely
important feature of Nottingham enterprise, so we might glance
at a few aspects of the business. While one of the key sections of
the organization is the analytical department which was one of
the first analytical laboratories in the pharmaceutical industry,
and came into existence as early as 1895, the fine chemical department has more direct interest to the lay mind. This came into
being during the 1914-18 war, by the end of which period such
important and now familiar chemicals as aspirin, saccharine,
acriflavine and chloromine T., none of which had previously been
manufactured at all in Great Britain, but which were all vital to
the war effort, were being produced by the company. Since that
time the plant allotted to the manufacture of these products,
particularly saccharine and another essential chemical, potassium
permanganate, had been greatly increased and Boots has now
become one of the major suppliers of these products overseas as
well as at home. To these have now been added such later
developments as the various "sulpha" drugs while Boots were
one of the first British manufacturers of insulin, claiming that

their continuous research and improvement in methods of manufacture have had a marked influence in maintaining the price
of insulin at a reasonably low level. They are particularly proud,
again, of the discovery of Heparin, a non-toxic anticoagulant used
in blood transfusions and thrombosis, and also used in operations
to prevent clotting in the blood vessels.

It was not long before the outbreak of the second world war
that the bulk of the company's manufacturing activities were
transferred to the new works at Beeston. All was ready, as it
happened, for the utilization of a considerable part of this
factory's production by the Ministry of Supply on behalf of the
War Office while the conflict raged. You can get some idea of
the scope of its resources by the figures of production in various
chemical commodities during these war years: more than 5,000
tons of potassium permanganate were produced; over 3,000,000
lbs. of saccharine, which is apparently equivalent in sweetening
properties to more than 73,000 tons of sugar, while, in addition,
more than 14,000,000 saccharine tablets were compressed in Boots'
own works; something like 4,000,000 tablets of the various
"sulpha" drugs were produced, in addition to hundreds of tons
in powder form; sufficient mepacrine hydrochloride—used in the
treatment of malaria—was made to compress over 350,000,000
tablets, in addition to the tableting of another 350,000,000 from
supplies by another manufacturer; millions of water-sterilizing
tablets, millions of tubes and jars of anti-gas ointment . . . you
might think that an enormous amount of such products as the last
go to waste. Perhaps they do. But to some extent, at least, Boots
have been conspicuously successful in adapting the products of
wartime research to peacetime uses. Take, for instance, some
stuff called BAL; this, which stands for British Anti-Lewisite, was
originally prepared as an antidote for Lewisite poisoning but
since the war has been found to be extremely valuable in many
forms of metallic poisoning; and BAL is now the standard treatment for arsenic, gold and mercury poisoning. Again, nitrogen
mustard, a form of mustard gas, which you would not have
thought, if you have encountered it, would make a particularly
welcome addition to a sickroom, has been found to have useful
properties in the palliative treatment of leukaemia and in
Hodgkin's disease, and its developing anaemia. Finally, a
formula bearing the initials DFP, which was being studied
during the war for possible use in gas warfare, has unexpectedly
proved of value in the treatment of certain eye diseases.

We might delay our departure from the subject of Boots just
long enough to take note—purely as a further sample—of one

more department, or indeed sub-department. It goes without saying that in an organization so big as this, and with such responsibilities to the Government and to the public, a research department would be a section to which the firm would pay special attention. Well, in the years following 1945, the research department of Boots has been under the direction of Sir Jack Drummond, F.R.S., who was chief scientific adviser during the war to the Ministry of Food, and under whom work seventy quali-fied scientists and a total staff of more than 300. Out of the various compartments into which Boots' research department is sub-divided—chemistry, bio-chemistry, pharmacology, bacteri-ology, horticulture and agriculture—I am going to pick, for a moment's glance, at the section devoted to veterinary science. My reason is quite capricious and has nothing to do either with Boots or an interest in animals. My reason is that it introduces us, in rather unexpected circumstances, to a place some twelve miles north-east of Nottingham which is interesting for reasons quite other than veterinary or pharmaceutical. In the expansion of Boots' veterinary science division since 1950 it became necessary to find quarters for the enlarged staff and their equipment. Con-sequently an old house called Thurgarton Priory was taken over and now houses the main part of the veterinary research unit. The house, with its 120 acres of land, adjoins three farms already owned by the firm which make up an area of something like 1,000 acres. Two of these farms are run on a normal self-supporting basis, while a third is equipped for experimental work with horses, cows and sheep, pigs and poultry. Thurgarton Priory itself has been equipped with veterinary, pathological, bio-chemical and bacteriological laboratories. The house, which is thus taken over for so useful a purpose, is an eighteenth-century construction occupying most of the site of a Benedictine priory founded about the middle of the twelfth century. A gentleman of Southwell called John Gilbert Cooper pulled down the old priory and built a brick house with a projecting pedimented three-bay centre here in 1777. The house became in time the residence of the first Bishop of Southwell. Part of it was built over the foundations of the south tower of the church, of which all that remains now is the battered fragment of a building of about 1230, but it is suggested that excavations, which could easily be carried out in the gardens of Thurgarton Priory house, would reveal the plan of the twelfth-century parts of what must have been originally a very large and imposing church. The main things to be noticed here now, in a remnant containing a Victorian timber roof and Victorian chancel, are the originally

Early English west portals, the middle one with nine columnettes on each side, and the north one with five, the north porch and doorway of the same type, and a fine and elaborate bracket and canopy of about 1330 on the east wall of the chancel. Finally, while at Thurgarton, our attention is drawn by Professor Pevsner to the railway station, which he describes as "a specially nice example of the early neo-Tudor stations on the Nottingham-Lincoln line".

That temporary diversion, on behalf of Boots, from Nottingham itself must not distract us from the job of recalling a few more of the industries on which the city's present prosperity is based. We obviously cannot enumerate them all but there are one or two, besides the hosiery and lace industries to which we have already paid our respects, which we cannot very well avoid noticing.

Perhaps you know—everybody seems to know—that Raleigh bicycles are made in Nottingham. But do you know why they are called Raleigh? It is rather a surprising story. It begins in 1887, just when the bicycle was about to begin its modern career. In that year the ordinary bicycle was still the iron-wheeled, front-wheel driven machine which we still know as the penny farthing, from the difference in size of the two wheels. But two years earlier J. K. Starley of Coventry had produced the first modern safety bicycle, rear driven, with power transmitted by a chain; and in 1888 a veterinary surgeon of the name of J. B. Dunlop was to "re-invent" and make a practical proposition of the pneumatic tyre which had been first conceived by Thompson in 1846, and thus permanently secured the position of the bicycle as a vehicle for transport and pleasure. Well, in 1887, the late Sir Frank Bowden, after fifteen years in Hong Kong, was forced to return to England because of ill health. He consulted specialists who told him that he had only a few months to live. However, a Harrogate doctor advised Bowden to take up the not yet fashionable exercise of cycling. He did so and within six months found himself completely fit again. Bowden was a practical and far-sighted man. Knowing of the rapid developments in the construction and comfort of the bicycle he saw that if properly handled its future possibilities were practically unlimited. So he set to work to trace the origin of the bicycle he had been using with such beneficial effects. His investigations led him to a small workshop where about a dozen men were turning out two or three machines a week; it was situated in Raleigh Street, Nottingham, which runs up from the Alfreton Road to the Arboretum. Within a short time Bowden had financed and taken control

102

The tomb of Thomas, Lord Scroope, at Langar, 1609

of the factory and formed the Raleigh Cycle Company, in good time for the extraordinary boom of the 1890's, when cycling was a craze and a fashion. To-day the thirty-acre Raleigh plant on Lenton Boulevard, which employs over 6,000 people, is the largest cycle factory in the world and is making bicycles at the rate of five a minute to be sent to nearly every country in the world. The number of components for each bicycle varies between 1,500 and 2,000, and, except for certain parts using rubber and leather, most of these components are made in the plant at Nottingham. The astounding thing about this industry is that production is more than seventy-five per cent greater than before the war. During the year 1949 the number of machines made for export exceeded the annual total of machines produced for the home and export markets combined in the years prior to 1939. Like every other Nottingham factory, during two wars, Raleigh Industries have had to make a break in the continuity of their development. During the first world war the plant was placed at the Government's disposal, which caused a four years' complete break in cycle production. Shortly after that war Raleigh began experiments with the motor cycle, and their first machine of this kind was put on the market in 1920. In 1933, however, the company decided to concentrate on bicycles and stopped making motor cycles. The second world war made necessary another complete reorganization of the factory in order to produce munitions. All the same, though ninety-five per cent of the factory was turned over to various Forces' requirements, nearly a quarter of a million bicycles were produced for the Services and a certain amount of experimental research was carried on.

Boots, Raleigh; and, of course, Players. Nottingham is one of the three largest centres of the tobacco industry in the country. It was in the year 1823 that the first business concerned with tobacco manufacturing was set up in the town. It was founded by a certain William Wright, and, although small, soon produced enough tobacco goods to supply all the local needs. In those days there were no proprietary names attached to the tobacco (it was long before cigarettes, of course) that you bought. You just asked for the type of tobacco, shag, cavendish, maybe, or thick twist, and it was weighed out for you over the counter. Cigarettes were popularized in England by soldiers returning from the Crimean War and the first English factory was set up, near London, in 1856. About 1866 the first ready-wrapped packet tobaccos began to be introduced. By this time Wright's Nottingham business was employing something like 150 workpeople. In 1877 the concern passed into the hands of Mr. John Player, who was the son of a

St. Mary's Church at Newark

solicitor of Saffron Walden, Essex. Player reorganized the business and quickly set up a packing department in which his products could be got ready for quick sale. Obviously to obtain the full value of this method it was essential that the Victorian customer should be able to identify the tobacco he wanted by the packing, and so came into being the trade mark of Players—which, if you look closely at them next time you have a packet in your pocket, have still a strangely mid-Victorian quality. The first Player trade mark, a drawing of Nottingham Castle, was registered in 1877, the year the business changed hands. A sailor's head was the next design, registered in 1883, a life-buoy with the words "Player's Navy Cut" superimposed in 1888, and the composite life-buoy trade mark, so well known to-day, with the sailor's head and two ships, was registered in 1891. These simple but effective symbols had their due effect and the business prospered. Player then bought a large site at Radford, which was then on the very edge of Nottingham, and the imposing façade of the Player factory on Radford Boulevard is now the most prominent feature of that quarter of the city. It is interesting that although Player straight away built three large blocks of this now, of course, much-expanded factory, only one of them was at first required, the other two being let as lace factories until the expansion of the tobacco business, which Player obviously foresaw, called for their incorporation. The first John Player did not, in fact, live long enough to see this come about. He died in 1884. But under his sons, John D. Player and William G. Player, the business continued to grow, and it was during the nineties that the Virginian cigarettes, until then regarded as a cheap and rather vulgar substitute for other forms of tobacco, first began to insinuate itself in fashionable taste. But throughout the remainder of the nineteenth century the only cigarettes accepted in polite society were Turkish or Egyptian. It really took the first world war to kill this taste and to bring the "gasper" into almost universal favour, but Player's cigarettes had been popular long before that. In fact, even prior to 1890 Player's "gold leaf navy cut" were well established: these were the forerunners of the famous "medium navy cut" which made their debut in 1900. In Edwardian times Player's cost 2½d. for ten. Before the turn of the century the demand for Player's products had increased so much that all John Player's three factories were absorbed and were employing 1,000 workers. One of the first events of the new century was the formation, in 1901, of the Imperial Tobacco Company, to protect the British trade from the attacks then being made on it by American manufacturers. Player's, which had become a private limited company in 1895, was one of the branches of the organization. Player's history since then has been one of continuous growth and expansion, of new factories and huge bonded warehouses built on the extended Radford site, in the 1920's and 30's, a factory built in Dublin, and the growth of the number of workers employed by Player's of Nottingham to more than 8,000 at the present time.

We obviously cannot go through, one by one, the scores of industries being carried on in the city and round it, but perhaps a naked list may serve to remind us of the kind of activity which, in all its variety, have given the English Midlands their importance. This list only includes, as it is, the more considerable trades, but I think it is striking enough—here it is then: motor body building, the industries allied to the manufacture of lace and hosiery, such as bleaching, dyeing, printing and dressing, gas meters, mechanical and electrical engineering, brickmaking from the county's valuable beds of clay, clothing, particularly that part of the industry known as "the making up", picture framing, timber, sweets and confectionery, brushes, cast-iron and concrete pipes, tanning and leather goods, beer, cardboard boxes, starch, pencils, printing (Nottingham has long been one of the most important centres of the letterpress and lithographic printing industry, and, incidentally, manufactures 1,000,000,000 railway and bus tickets every year), paper bags (something like twenty-five firms making these in the city), printing inks and printers' machinery, soap, electro-plating, sports goods (ever hear of a Gunn & Moore cricket bat?), thermometers, quilts, curled hair . . . no, one really can't go on like this. I will just pick out a couple more trades at random. Did you know, for instance, that the first British-made cash register machines were made in a factory at Beeston, breaking that monopoly of the trade hitherto held by the United States, to whom, before the war, Britain was paying about £5,000,000 a year for the importing of cash registers? Did you know that the idea of the pressure gauge was born in Nottingham, and that a firm here pioneered its manufacture? When steam power was in its infancy and its use was causing many accidents from the bursting of steam boilers, in a small workshop in Notintone Place, Sneinton, a certain Sidney Smith succeeded in producing a gauge to measure the pressure of steam and so reduce the danger of such accidents. His instrument won the approval of the great George Stephenson, the locomotive engineer, and its success was assured. Nottingham still provides gauges which are used wherever railway engines, ships or boilers are used and made.

It is now time to leave industry and, for our last subject before turning to the county outside its city, to consider a place where, for generations, the people of Nottingham have found relaxation from those very industrial activities. We have seen how lavishly sprinkled with green is the city's map, how well provided with parks and open spaces; we have looked at some, Wollaton and the university, in detail. Everyone knows of the existence of others, like Nottingham race-course, Trent Bridge Cricket Ground. Oldest among the parks we have so far omitted is the Arboretum, those delightful nineteen acres with their flowers and trees and shrubs, their lake and waterfowl, and aviaries of exotic birds. The Arboretum, which was one of the fruits of the Enclosure Act of 1845, was opened just a hundred years ago, on 11th May, 1852. Of the recreation grounds, as opposed to parks, the oldest is the great Forest Recreation Ground where, almost three-quarters of a century ago, the Nottingham Forest Football Club played its first matches, and where, as we have seen, the Goose Fair finds its modern home. But long before either of these green spaces— both so astonishingly close to the city's busy heart—were available to Nottingham people, they, or their ancestors, had been going to Clifton. We have heard of Clifton and its grove as the repeated, almost monotonous subject, of our local minor poets. The people of Nottingham have been making their excursions out to these beauty spots for two centuries and more. And if you should enquire why anyone should want to escape from a town such as pre-industrial Nottingham must have been, a place smokeless and clean, a place of red brick and old timber and green grass and trees, then study this account of the town just about 300 years ago: "The traveller, especially in winter, found the Trent lanes very dirty and after he had passed the Leen Bridge, the very foot of the town called the Bridge End, deep and miry. At this first entrance into the narrow passage which used to lead between two high precipices to the upper part of the town, he was from a parcel of little rock-houses (if the wind was northerly) saluted with a volley of suffocating smoke, caused by the burning of gorse and tanners knobs. Everybody knows the fragrancy and cleanliness of tanners, fellmongers and curriers, many of which were then dispersed all over the town; the greatest thoroughfare in the town, Bridlesmith Gate was then lined on both sides with the roughest kind of blacksmiths; the market place though spacious, yet was paved but on one side, and on the other called the Sands it was very miry. That place near St. Peter's church where the Monday Market was after projected, was not paved and part of it was so boggy that there was a bridge of planks laid across it with a single rail, till of late years, over which people did pass not without danger in the night time; all St. Peter's church-yard side was low and dirty, and from the rock of the churchyard to the Leen, was one continued swamp."

Not really an idyllic picture, is it? One may be all the more thankful for that present-day absence of smokiness which is so very noticeable considering the industrial circumstances of the city (and which is, in part at least, attributable to the fact that the highly specialized manufacture of patent furnaces and firebars for factories has long been carried out in the neighbourhood); thankful too that the tanners who, from the fourteenth century, had been grouped along the banks of the Leen, in the neighbour-hood of Narrow Marsh, and who, even in 1395, were a cause of offence for polluting the River Leen by soaking their skins in the water "to the great detriment of the whole people of the town", had so far diminished that by the early years of the eighteenth century the number of separate tan yards had dwindled to three and by the middle of the following century this industry in Nott-ingham had, temporarily, almost died out. Perhaps, then, in spite of the impending upsurge of the Industrial Revolution, Nottingham was a more pleasant place just two hundred years ago, in 1751, than it had been a century earlier when that account was written. Nevertheless, in the middle of the eighteenth century the habit of excursions into the immediate countryside was well established. A Nottingham doctor thus expresses the reasons, as he saw them in 1751, for making use of the rural amenities just outside the town: "Exercise is as necessary for the preservation of health, as food is for the support of life, it being impossible for a person long to enjoy an uninterrupted state of health, if the exercise he takes does not in a great measure counter-balance his way of living, I mean his eating and drinking: and it is observable that fewer people who have where-withal, eat to live, than live to eat. Persons therefore whose birth and fortune have exempted them from the busy part of life, or whose pro-fession or trade obliges them to sit much, require some other means to promote a due circulation of the juices, and thereby the necessary secretions and excretions, requisite to preserve the body in health and vigour; the principal of which are walking and riding."

For this purpose the doctor enumerates the various places that one could then go to. For instance, you could make the walk of only about a mile, a walk, "which is pleasant, the refresh-ment agreeable, and the usage obliging and reasonable", to St. Anne's Well which was frequented by many people as a cold bath and was reckoned the second coldest in England. Beside the well there used to stand a chapel dedicated to St. Anne, but the well was more popularly known as Robin Hood's Well. It might help to show how far from a merely modern phenomenon is the tourist racket if I quote you the doctor's description of local enterprise at this well: "The people who keep the green and the public house to promote a holiday trade, show an old wickered chair, which they call Robin Hood's chair, a bow, and an old cap, both these they affirm to have been this famous robber's property; this little artifice takes so well with the people in low life, that at Christmas, Easter and Whitsuntide, it procures them a great deal of business, for at those times great numbers of young men bring their sweethearts to this well, and give them a treat, and the girls think themselves ill-used, if they have not been saluted by their lovers in Robin Hood's chair." Blackner, who published a history of Nottingham in 1815, commented sarcastically and rather coarsely on this passage with the words "many a salute has been washed from the lips of the inamoratas with bumpers of the Woodward's nut-brown ale".

The surprising thing was that St. Anne's Well had been well equipped—and, from the sound of it, in a most delightful and highly sophisticated way—in the middle of the seventeenth century, judging by this account written in 1641: "At the well there is a dwelling house serving as an habitation for the woodward of those woods, being an officer of the Mayor. This house is likewise a victualling house, having adjoining to it fair summer houses, bowers or arbours covered by the plashing and interweaving of oak boughs for shade, in which are tables of large oak planks, and are seated about with banks of earth, fleightered and covered with green sods, like green carsie cushions. There is also a building containing two fair rooms, an upper and a lower, serving for such as repair thither to retire to in case of rain or bad weather. Thither do the townsmen resort by an ancient custom beyond memory. This well is all summer long much frequented, and there are but few fair days between March and October, in which some company or other of the town, such as use to consort there, use not to fetch a walk to this well, either to dine or sup, or both, some sending their provisions to be dressed, others bespeaking what they will have, and when any of the town have their friends come to them, they have given them no welcome, unless they entertain them at this well. Besides there are many other meetings of gentlemen, both from the town and the country, making choice of this place rather than the town for their rendezvous to recreate themselves at, by reason of the sweetness and openness of the air, where besides their artificial, they have natural music without charge; in the spring by the nightingale and in the autumn by the wood-lark, a bird whose notes for variety and sweetness are nothing inferior to the nightingale, and much in her tones, which filled with the voices of other birds like inward parts in song serve to double the melodious harmony of those sweet warbling trebles. Here are likewise many venison feasts, and such as have not the hap to feed the sense of taste with the flesh thereof when dead, may yet fill their sight with those creatures living which all summer long are picking up weeds in the corn-fields and closes, and in winter and hard weather, gathering sallets in the gardens of such houses as lie on the north side of the town."

Altogether, I think, one would have liked to have joined the people of Nottingham at St. Anne's on a fine summer evening, but this was not the only direction that you would find them walking. Are you fond of a game of bowls? If you are you could have gone on Tuesdays to Basford or on a Thursday to Holme Pierrepont, in both of which places you would find "good company and a plentiful ordinary; and the green of the latter is accounted as large and as fine as most bowling greens in England".

But you would note that " other persons of this town who cannot be spared so far from home, may have the opportunity of bowling in the town green any day in the week ". For people who liked "the wholesome exercise of hare hunting" there was a pack of hounds kept in the town of Nottingham by subscription; the Hon. Rothwell Willoughby, Esquire, kept a pack (his name is preserved in the handsome house of about 1730, called Willoughby House, in Low Pavement); and Lord Middleton's hounds were out, in the 1750's, several days in the week. If you were the kind of person who liked getting up early in the morning, you could, after breakfast, walk out by the fields to Sneinton Wood and work up an appetite for lunch by running in the Shepherd's Race on the part of Sneinton Common about a quarter of a mile east of St. Anne's Well. Sneinton Wood was not actually a wood even then. It was completely bare and had been handed over by the Pierrepont family as a common for the people of Sneinton. Here, cut out of the flat turf, was a sort of labyrinth which seems to have been called the Shepherd's Race because people who were looking after sheep on the common used to run in it to pass the time. There were various theories current about the origin of this labyrinth. It is rather surprising that even at this time, when antiquaries were suffering from an obsession about Roman Britain, that there was no suggestion that it was Roman. However, it was claimed to prove itself to date from

before the Reformation by virtue of the crosslets in the centres
of the four smaller rounds; and its reasonable antiquity seemed
further indicated by the fact that the trenches cut into the turf
had become so narrow that people could no longer run in them
but had to keep to the top of the turf banks. Anyway, nobody
knew when or by whom the labyrinth was first cut: a reasonable
conjecture was that it dated from the time of a monastic settlement round St. Anne's chapel, whose inhabitants being required
by their vows not to wander afield, thus provided themselves
with a means of exercise within sight and hearing of their chapel.

But perhaps running round a maze, even a monastic maze,
was not everybody's idea of how to pass the afternoon. Certainly
for the ladies "a concert of Aereal Musicians in Nottingham
Coppices" sounds more the thing, or, if they could not face
leaving the town itself, they could walk about in the green court
of the castle, and, if they liked a bit of a blow, in the paved yard
above. If you happened to be numbered among the acquain-
tances of Mr. Musters, the squire of Colwick, you might get from
him the key of the walled-in Colwick Hills, where, in the summer,
many young ladies used to enjoy the cool shade and the music
of the birds. You could walk, too, to Colwick Spring; also, "those
of the fair sex who like the water-side, have a very agreeable way
to it over Nottingham Meadows, where in summer evenings they
do not want conveniences at the Trent Bridge to bath themselves
unseen"; or, walk by the side of the Trent towards Beeston
Meadows and admire on your right the prospect of Wollaton Hall
in its park and on your left the hills of Clifton. Clifton is still,
in spite of its local fame and its nearness to the city, an unusually
delightful place to visit. It lies on the south side of the Trent,
more or less at right angles to the river with the hall at the top
of the village, and its lawns running down to the water's edge.
From here Clifton Grove follows the line of the river down towards the village of Wilford. Clifton village itself is elongated in
shape but has an ample green with a conspicuous brick dove-cote
on it, the largest in Nottinghamshire, with 2,300 nesting-places,
and probably dating from the early eighteenth century. The
pleasant group of the Well's almshouses, founded in 1709 and
adorned with two little detached gazebos, one on each side, adds
to the interest of the village, whose principal buildings are, of
course, the hall and the church.

St. Mary's church is a large, cruciform building, with a high
tower over the crossing, in the same manner as that of St. Mary's,
Nottingham. The oldest part of the church is the three-bayed
north arcade which contains the only Norman work to be found

here. The clerestory level is late fourteenth century and the enlargement of the chancel dates from the founding of a chantry college in 1476 by Sir Robert Clifton. His tomb, a brass, is one of the many which provide in this church an exceptional display of the continuity of a single family. One of the earliest is the alabaster figure of a knight of the late fourteenth century, and there is a lady of the same date, again in alabaster on her tomb-chest with rather expressionless features and her hair in a net, angels supporting her pillow and a lamb at her feet. As well as the brass of Sir Robert Clifton, who died in 1478, two other members of the family, Sir Gervase Clifton (died 1491) and George Clifton (died 1587) and his wife have surviving brass memorials. A second Sir Gervase, who also died in 1587, is celebrated by an alabaster effigy of himself in a ruff and Elizabethan armour. One on each side of him lie his two wives; and there are figures of children against the front of his tomb-chest. The carving of this monument clearly comes from the same workshop as that of the famous Sacheverell tombs at the nearby village of Ratcliffe-on-Soar. A third Sir Gervase, who is commemorated by a bust—not a very good one—in an oval niche between columns, had no fewer than seven wives, of whom the first three are collectively remembered in an austere tomb which is decorated chiefly with a gruesome carving of a charnel chamber filled with bones and skulls. Gervase, as you see, has been a common name in the Clifton family which, of course, takes its surname from the village where they are known to have been settled soon after the Norman Conquest. The family claims descent from an Alvaredus de Clifton who was warden of Nottingham Castle during the reign of William the Conqueror. According to the historian Thoroton, the manors of Clifton and Wilford were purchased from the family of de Rodes about the end of the reign of Henry III by an early Sir Gervase de Clifton, to whom the purchase was confirmed by King Edward I in 1281. The Clifton family history, quite apart from its remarkable continuity, is punctuated by several stirring episodes as well as by the steady tradition of marriage with distinguished and noble families, many of them within the county; the third Sir Gervase, in the 1340's, married a daughter of Sir Robert Pierrepont of Holme Pierrepont lower down the Trent; a Sir John (who is mentioned in Shakespeare's *King Henry IV* and was slain at the battle of Shrewsbury in 1403) married one of the Cresseys of Hodsock, where the Clifton family inherited a house and property, a sister of the Sir Robert who founded the chantry married a Byron, and in later centuries the Clifton, Byron and Pierrepont families were joined by marriage again. The families were not always on the same side in the various civil wars which divided England. A Sir Gervase of the 1491 brass, knight of Clifton and Hodsock as the family now was, who was quite an important person—Treasurer of Calais in 1482, esquire to the body of King Edward IV, high sheriff of Notts. and Derby and Receiver General of those counties, and Surveyor of the King's Works and Reparations in Nottingham Castle—was made a Knight of the Bath at the coronation of King Richard III, by whom he was granted lordships and manors in Nottinghamshire and three neighbouring counties. Then, when Sir Gervase had taken part with Richard III in the eventful Battle of Bosworth, he only managed to prevent the major parts of his estates being taken away from him through the intervention of his uncle, Sir John Byron, who was a Lancastrian. In the greater civil war of the mid-seventeenth century, however, Cliftons, Byrons and Pierreponts were all on the same side. The Lord Lieutenant of Nottinghamshire (later replaced by Parliament) was Henry Pierrepont, Lord Newark, the eldest son of the Earl of Kingston. The Byron Royalists included John Lord Byron, Gilbert Byron, who was Governor of Rutland Castle during the fighting, Sir Richard, who was Governor of Newark in 1642-4, Philip Byron, who was killed at York in June 1644, besides Sir Thomas Byron and Robert and William Byron, all of whom bore arms for the King. The Clifton of the time was the much-married Sir Gervase, the first baronet of Clifton and Hodsock, he of the seven wives. He had been made a Knight of the Bath at the coronation of King James I and later a baronet. He sat in Parliament up to the war and was Commissioner for the King at Newark and Oxford, being later fined by the Parliamentarians the very considerable sum of £7,650. Sir Gervase, who died in 1666, had children by the first, second and sixth of his wives, but not by the others. Having buried six of them he was only survived for a month or so by his seventh. He was the first baronet. The ninth and last was Sir Robert, who died in 1869, when the baronetcy became dormant and the estates devolved on a cousin of the name of Henry Markham and after him upon *his* second cousin Sir Harvey Bruce, a baronet who had twin sons, one of whom succeeded in the Bruce baronetcy and the other, changing his name to Clifton, inherited Clifton Hall and the Nottinghamshire property. The heir presumptive to the last baronet was his uncle who only predeceased him by a few days, dying in March 1869 in his ninety-ninth year. This Sir Arthur Clifton (he was a knight) was a general in the army and fought at Waterloo. It was he who opened the collieries at Clifton. The mansion of the Cliftons, Clifton Hall, is the largest Georgian house remaining in Nottinghamshire. It received its present form at the end of the eighteenth century, during the lifetime of the old soldier, Sir Arthur. It was designed by John Carr of York and is unusually plain and matter-of-fact, even for that unshowy architect. Carr's house incorporates fragments of an early seventeenth-century building. The most notable traces of this earlier house are the plaster ceiling and the imposing black-and-white marble chimney piece of the drawing-room on the first floor and the Painted Room adjoining it. This has a cornice decorated with strapwork, of an almost Elizabethan kind, above fluted pilasters; and the walls—hence its name—are panelled with an entertaining series of small Dutch paintings illustrating the handling of pike, musket and other weapons. There are in existence elaborate plans, either by Thorpe or Smythson (we have discussed them at length in connection with Wollaton) for a mansion of the time of the much-married Sir Gervase's youth. These drawings, which include a banqueting-house and stables, date from the first part of the seventeenth century and may either be a survey of an existing house or plans for a new one. Anyway, the drawing-room and the Painted Room can be associated with considerable building activities of this period. Other survivals from the pre-Carr house are a late seventeenth-century plaster ceiling in one of the upper rooms and the morning-room, of about 1720-30, with a fireplace surmounted by a marble overmantel in the manner of William Kent.

Carr's remodelling of Clifton Hall began in 1779. He gave the house an octagonal hall with its vault going right up to the level of the roof. He gave the south front of what had presumably been a rambling and rather shapeless building a regular appearance. The façade has two wings and a recessed centre with a one-storeyed colonnade of coupled Tuscan columns. The west front is given some shape by a semicircular bow window in the centre, but the other fronts were left irregular though they have a Georgian appearance now, further alterations having been made to the house about 1900. The most notable feature of the garden is an eighteenth-century curved double stairway with stone balustrade, vases and statuary. I am afraid I cannot enlarge upon the treasures of painting and furniture to be found in this home of an exceptionally interesting family, because I have never been inside it. There is, I believe, a notable Romney of Frances Clifton who married Robert Markham, a parson and later archdeacon of York, whose grandson was the Henry Markham who eventually succeeded to the estate after the death of the last baronet. It is, one gathers, full of treasure. Certainly, judging by the reality of the church, one can equally discount in this connection the remark on Clifton made by Horace Walpole when he was visiting the county. He said: "I was disappointed in the church; though there are many monuments their ruins are ruined, and their place no more. In the house there are about three pictures standing on the ground of which one is a very fine Van Dyck."

Chapter V

SOUTH OF THE TRENT

This account of Clifton has taken us, for the first time, on to the southern side of the River Trent which divides the county into two unequal halves. To this smaller half, to the green, low-lying and almost entirely agricultural area which lies to the south-east of the river, I shall devote the immediately following pages. It contains one town, and that an important though not a large one: Newark. It also contains a large number of attractive and in many cases surprisingly remote villages. The roads which traverse this area either cross it in the direction of Nottingham or radiate from Newark. Apart from these main roads it is a place of small and twisting byroads and lanes. The line of the Fosse Way on its way up from Leicester to Newark is about the only straight thing in this piece of country. The county is pretty sharply divided geologically, as well as by the river, into two halves and since the "beyond Trent" section roughly corresponds to one of these geological divisions it is worth making them clear at this stage. Within the county, apart from the citizens of Nottingham, most people are ready to say either that they belong to "the sand" or to "the clays", so sharply is the land divided between the Bunter sandstone of the western half and the Keuper marl of the east. We have already seen that the strip of limestone on the Derbyshire edge of the county provides it with its coal. The Bunter sandstone division, which stretches from Nottingham in the south to Bawtry in the extreme north and embraces Sherwood Forest and the Dukeries, provides Nottingham with its woods and with its towns, but is not particularly productive from an agricultural point of view. The district lying to the south, and to a lesser degree to the north, of Newark is purely agricultural. The soil, a rather heavy clay, is of the same sort as that found across the border in Lincolnshire. The main crop is wheat, and there is a fair acreage of beans, while a root crop which has become of great importance in England during the past quarter of a century has its centre in this county and a considerable part of the crop on which it depends is grown south of the Trent. There are still less than twenty factories in the whole of Britain for turning sugar beet into sugar and two of them are in Nottinghamshire. One is just outside the city boundary at Colwick and the other is just north of Newark, at Kelham. The Kelham factory, which was built in 1921, is credited with much of the pioneer work in accustoming farmers to growing what was at that time quite a new crop. This factory, by its practical experiments, proved that the making of home-grown sugar on this island was an economic proposition; and as a direct result, in 1924, the Government passed the Sugar Industry (Subsidy) Act which made considerable expansion possible. That same year the factory at Colwick was put up and has been producing vast quantities of white sugar for the past twenty-five years. Everybody realizes how very much worse off we should all have been if, during the last war, we had had no home-grown sugar, as was the case during the first war. It was the experience of World War I, when much of the large supply of sugar previously imported into the country was cut off, that showed that this industry, which had been established on the continent of Europe for fully a century (about half the world's sugar supply now comes from beet) before it was introduced here. Sugar beet, whose acreage in Nottinghamshire totals nearly 12,000, has done a good deal to improve arable farming in the county. The advocates of sugar beet claim that as well as getting a cash return for the roots themselves farmers that grow it get a good cleaning crop which also provides animal feeding stuffs in the form of dried sugar-beet pulp—which the beet growers get back on special terms—and also in the leaves and crowns. All the beet-sugar factories in Great Britain are now amalgamated into a single organization, and they produce annually enough sugar to provide eight ounces a week for everybody in the country. The Colwick factory, which employs about 500 people while the "campaign" is on, distributes sugar mainly in Nottinghamshire and the adjacent counties. The process of sugar manufacture is a continuous one and when the factory starts its season in September it continues working night and day, Christmas and Boxing Days included, until the crop— about 1,600 farmers grow beet for the Colwick factory alone— has been completely processed, which is usually early in January. After these four months the plant is overhauled ready for a programme of refining imported raw sugar, which usually exceeds in tonnage that from the home-grown beet. Then, once again, it gets ready for the produce of the Nottinghamshire fields. Kelham, by the way, is a place well worth going to whether you are interested in sugar processing or not. This village provides a bridge over the Trent on the road out of Newark into the rest of the county: you would have to pass through Kelham, for instance, if you were going to Southwell or up into Sherwood Forest and the Dukeries, and the Kelham Bridge provides one way into Nottingham. There are two things to look for in Kelham; one is the church and the other the hall. The two are, as usual, linked by the fact that we can find the tombs and monuments to the family that built the hall in the church. You have to go to Averham just on the other side of the river and about a mile upstream—we shall in a minute—to find the early monuments of the Sutton family. At Kelham they begin with the eighteenth-century Lexington chapel, added to the south of the chancel, with round-headed windows, and the tomb there to Robert Sutton, Lord Lexington, who died in 1723, and his wife who died twenty years earlier. They are shown, very capably carved in marble, back to back and half reclining above long and political rather than pious inscriptions. The church itself, to which this eighteenth-century chapel was added, in a somewhat noticeably contrasting stone, is mainly Perpendicular. It contains one other monument to a daughter of the seventh Earl of Scarbrough. This, by a fashionable Victorian monumental sculptor of the name of Gaffin, brings us, by its date and by the fact that it is in the revived Gothic style, to the subject of Kelham Hall. For though a house has stood on this site for many centuries it has not always been the same house. It is likely, however, that the Victorian Gothic structure which we see to-day is, architecturally, more interesting than its two and more predecessors. There seems no means of knowing what the house was, where, according to tradition, King Charles I was held prisoner after surrendering to the Scottish army. This, presumably an Elizabethan house, was burnt at the end of the seventeenth century. It was rebuilt; judging by its appearance, in eighteenth-century views it was a commodious but rather dull, barrack-like place redeemed by its pleasant situation on the river. And clearly some time during the eighteenth century the surrounding parkland had been laid out anew in the fashionably informal and still acceptable manner, incorporating, as part of the landscape, the handsome curve of the Trent. You can tell how keenly the eighteenth-century landscapers felt the need to mould the whole countryside into a properly tamed and obedient whole by the remarks of a draughtsman preparing, at the end of the eighteenth century, with a discreet lack of scruple, the surroundings ideal to the place. He says: " Kelham Hall is prettily shaded by some young, but spreading trees, whose foliage shows pleasing variety. Some offices, on the right, at this point of view, which at present are not screened sufficiently, are not indulgent to the roving eye. The wished-for effect, of a little thriving plantation before them, is visible. In the view I have shown what that may some time be, a complete screen."

But there is really no need to bother, now, about these careful proofs of eighteenth-century planning. The house was for a long time uninhabited (though rented, for a time, from Robert Sutton, by the Duke of Newcastle as a temporary residence) and in 1857 it, like its predecessor, was destroyed by fire. 1857. I stress the date because the disappearance of the old Kelham Hall coincided with a document that has close bearing on the appearance of the new mansion which now stands on the site. In 1857, George Gilbert Scott, later Sir Gilbert, who had behind him a successful career as a restorer of innumerable churches throughout the country and, among cathedrals those of Hereford, Lichfield, Salisbury and Ripon, published a book which, though coming late in the history of the Gothic revival, was destined to have a powerful effect on its later stages and remains, still, one of the most effective statements of the ideals that guided the movement. Gilbert Scott was not a medievalist or antiquarian like the people who had, in Strawberry Hill days, begun playing with the Gothic, nor was he a Catholic like the first important nineteenth-century apostle of the movement, Pugin (whose Catholic cathedral in Nottingham has already been mentioned). Scott's book, published in 1857, was called *Remarks on Secular and Domestic Architecture, present and future*. He argued that because people in the mid-nineteenth century had apparently lost the living style of good architecture they were at liberty to take their choice among the dead styles. He seems to have accepted the fact that a fully developed historical sense prevented nineteenth-century architects from ridding their minds of the styles of the past. What they had to do, then, was to choose that one of the old ways of building which seemed most closely allied to the facts of contemporary brick and stone, which was closest to nature—a matter the Victorians bothered about a lot—in decorative detail and was most in keeping with native traditions. It seemed obvious that one could find such qualities more in the Gothic tradition than in the offshoots of the Renaissance and the various classical revivals. Thus Scott urged the use of Gothic, but he qualified his insistence by saying that it could be used so freely that it could eventually become a completely separate and modern style. I have summarized Sir Gilbert Scott's teachings at this length because Nottingham, and Kelham, happens to contain one of his most ambitious essays in the designing of a country house in his new Gothic manner. Kelham Hall, mercifully, does not approach in size Scott's St.

St. Mary's, Newark: the new reredos by Sir Ninian Comper, 1937

Pancras Station and Hotel of 1865, but it bears out in every detail, and in a slightly Frenchified Gothic manner, the theories laid down in his *Remarks*. The architectural pundits consider Kelham Hall as of prime importance for an understanding of Scott's ideas on the use of Gothic forms in secular buildings. It cannot conceivably be called beautiful, but we are beginning to learn that what we think of as beauty was not necessarily what these Victorian Gothic architects, like Scott and Butterfield, aimed at; that there is a purpose of almost deliberate lack of visual appeal in the unattractive brick of which this carefully unsymmetrical and lofty building is constructed and in its nasty stone dressings. A contemporary critic, quoted by Professor Pevsner, describes the thirteenth and fourteenth-century ornamental motifs as " viewed on a broad basis, and freely admitting all which can be usefully learnt from the architecture, whether of England, France or Italy, though as Italy is the birthplace almost of modern domestic architecture (especially) many useful hints might be obtained from its productions ". You can see all of Scott's ideas worked out at Kelham. It is a modern—modern, that is, in the mid-nineteenth century—country house; in no way pretending to be anything else, either a Gothic castle or an Elizabethan mansion. There are Tudor chimneys and medieval machicolations and the surrounds of every window are duly and elaborately Gothic, though there was no nonsense about the casement openings being anything but sensibly rectangular. The whole effect, one can see, must have been completely and unmistakably up to date, just as to-day it is completely Victorian and is in no danger, as are the Gothicisms of twenty or thirty years earlier, of merging, even to the quite knowing eye, with medieval originals.

Stand outside and look at this important building. Ask, and you will probably be let in, because Kelham Hall is now a theological college. You will find that the state rooms inside are just as modernly but just as consistently Gothic. Their manner is a little earlier in origin than that of the outside, permitting the use of twelfth or thirteenth-century round arches. The hall, chapel and library are rib vaulted and their ceilings elaborately painted with rather more than Gothic arabesques. Great trouble has been taken over the carvings of the leaves on the somewhat florid capitals. You will find that the theological college which now occupies Kelham Hall is in the process of adding a new chapel of its own. It is in the Byzantine manner and designed by C. C. Thompson. It contains sculptures by C. S. Jagger.

Well, Sir Gilbert Scott seems to have brought us a long way from beet sugar, but while we have him here it might be as well

The Town Hall in the Market Place, Newark, by Carr of York, 1773

to make a note of what else in the county is to be put at his door.
I have already touched on his work within the city of Nottingham, the west front and the clerestory tracery of St. Mary's,
dating from 1843 and, in the same year, together with Moffatt,
the building of the church of St. John Baptist in Canal Street.
These earliest works of Scott's in the county were followed by
restoration at St. Edmund's, Mansfield Woodhouse, carefully
imitative of Nottingham tradition at St. Peter's, Gamston, in
1855; and at St. Giles', Costock, in 1863. Scott, who began as a
pupil of an arch-classic, Sir Robert Smirke—he built the British
Museum in London—turned to Gothic in about 1840 and by the
end of the sixties had, as Professor of Architecture at the Royal
Academy, more or less retired from active building. Thus, in a
rather scrappy and condensed way we can, in Nottinghamshire,
see samples of his style at most periods of his active life as an
architect. He died in 1878 and was, of course, the grandfather
of Sir Giles Gilbert Scott.

Suppose you are motoring to Nottingham, as you might well
do, from the south. You have come through Leicester, but don't
take the Fosse Way—the obvious way in by Six Hills (the
southernmost point of the county)—but go up through Loughborough and then trickle into the county by the King's Bridge
over the King's Brook just south of Rempstone. Rempstone is
not the point of this journey, but you will see there on the crossroads what is quite a rare object in Nottinghamshire, a village
church dating entire from the eighteenth century and with much
of its original furniture. The tower of this rectangular church,
covered with ivy, has classical windows but, all the same, battlements and pinnacles. Inside you can see the pulpit with the
reader's desk attached above the parson's pew, and the squire's
pew opposite it. But push on through Rempstone: certainly
don't bother to note, as I did, that a Robert Marsden was, for
forty-six years, rector here in the eighteenth century—before this
smart new church was built in 1771. Push on up through Costock. Note, of course, the work of Gilbert Scott in the church
here, already much restored, in the forties before he got to work
in the sixties. A manor house to see here if you have time, an
Elizabethan stone dwelling, one of the best in the county with a
jagged line of gables and mullioned windows. Costock Manor
has also a quite tidy eighteenth-century annexe.

But the purpose of this journey is not to linger at Costock, but
to move on up the road due north to the top of the hill whose
name heralds our destination. It is Bunny Hill, and, being a

hill, contradicts somewhat its own meaning. For Bunny, the name of the village which lies in the hollow beneath us, has nothing to do with rabbits, but with a marshy place. You sometimes see it spelt Boney. Bunny is a place to linger in and enjoy, because it is full of oddness and surprises and has great charm into the bargain. Pretty well everything that it contains, except its large fourteenth-century church, is there because of the enduring and, on the whole, philanthropic idiosyncrasies of one man who once lived here. Bunny really *is* Sir Thomas Parkyns; and I shall enjoy telling you about him.

First, however, stand at the little crossroads in the middle of the village and look around you. There is St. Mary's church. We shall go in there in a minute. Then picturesquely placed between church and the road, with steep-pitched roof, stone dressings, mullioned windows and rusticated door surround and looking entirely seventeenth century, there is the school which Sir Thomas Parkyns built in 1700. Along the string course which divides the ground floor from the first floor are the words (you must accept a bit of Latin here because Sir Thomas Parkyns won't let you escape it)—*Scientia non habet inimicum nisi ignorantem—Disce et Discede.—Nemo hinc egrediatur ignarus Arithmetices.* Elsewhere in the village—and you can survey the whole place pretty well at a glance—there are some attractive brick cottages, one of which has Parkyns' initial on it and the date 1739. You must, however, shut your eyes to some not so attractive new houses that have been built in recent years. The church, school, cottages—and the hall are what you come to Bunny to see.

It is not surprising that Bunny Hall is sometimes called Crazy Hall, because it is a most weird and unexpected place and shows what happens if the squire insists on being his own architect. You walk up to it from the road by a pleasantly untidy approach by way of farm buildings and brick arches. Hens and geese may accompany you and provide a chorus to your exclamations of astonishment. It is not like any other house that has ever been built. The front is tall and narrow and over the top of it is an elephantine semicircular pediment decorated with an incongruously large achievement of arms superimposed on a sort of chequer board of decorative brick and a lot of fussy stone dressing. Then, stuck on top of this pediment is a brick-and-stone tower ponderously castellated and looking very strange indeed. Set in the tower which, like the whole hall, is a monument, one would have thought to the individualism and intolerance of the restraints of formal discipline characteristic of the seventeenth century, are windows which speak of nothing but the eighteenth.

In fact, though he did not die until 1741, Parkyns was a completely seventeenth-century character. His house, whose last
owner was a Mrs. Cordaux, has now been sensibly divided up into
a number of roomy flats. The rooms in the strange tower are
hardly used. The whole place, in an unfussy, countrified way, is
well kept and one passes, through gates adorned with two pairs
of nice stone pineapples, into a garden, on the south side, that
gives every sign of being looked after with affection and pride.
We must pursue the character of Sir Thomas Parkyns and we
shall be best introduced to him, as he intended us to be, in the
church. His memorial is one of the strangest monuments in the
whole of England. It is a standing wall monument, and in the left-
hand half, Sir Thomas Parkyns stands, life-size, wearing breeches
and a simple coat and jerkin. He is a short thick-set man, with
a queer flat hat on his head. He is staring straight in front of
him with his forearms close to his sides and holding out his hands,
with outstretched fingers, palms inward, as though he were help-
ing someone to roll a ball of wool (and, indeed, when I was last
in Bunny church, its spiders had provided those waiting hands
with a skein of their own making). His knees are slightly bent.
The reason for this strange posture is that Sir Thomas Parkyns
was an enthusiastic amateur wrestler. Known usually as "The
Wrestling Baronet", he himself always preferred to be known as
"Thomas Luctator". While the baronet himself stands in the
left-hand bay ready to start a wrestling bout "in a bruising position, ever in an encounter with Master All-bones alias Death"
as he described it, in the other half of the monument a little
figure of a man—Sir Thomas, beaten at last?—is shown laid
out on a straw mat while an absurdly crude, winged figure of
Father Time stands over him. The monument is a mass of
inscriptions in Latin, Greek and English and this incident is
captioned:

> Though Time at length did throw him it is plain
> Who liv'd in hopes that he should rise again.

The monument, which Sir Thomas certainly designed for himself, is signed "*se ipse fecit*". Perhaps Sir Thomas did carve
some of it himself; he was quite capable of it, and one of his
hobbies was the collection of stone coffins. Alternatively, it is
said that the monument was carved by his chaplain. At any
rate either story can apply only to the little figures of Time
and the prostrate Sir Thomas, for the life-size effigy is clearly the
work of a professional sculptor who, it is suggested, may have

been Taylor of Nottingham who is credited with some competent work at about this period.

Sir Thomas Parkyns was the second baronet. The church contains the memorial, also, of the Richard Parkyns, who was Recorder of Nottingham, and the first of his family to come and reside in Bunny. He is shown kneeling and facing his wife, with the tiny figures of his eight children. Then there is Dame Anne Parkyns, the mother of The Wrestling Baronet, a local lady bountiful, who helped her son in his good works. She died in 1725 at the age of ninety-two, and she appears on her tomb as a most serene old lady with a sort of shawl round her head.

The Westling Baronet was educated, and planted in himself the seeds of a subsequent preoccupation with the classics, at Westminster School, where he studied under the celebrated Dr. Busby and his successor Dr. Knype. Thence he went to Trinity College, Cambridge, and to Gray's Inn. He remained at the study of Law for eight years until he succeeded his father in the baronetcy and the property at Bunny. He worked ardently, intelligently and progressively on his estates. He was a good magistrate and land owner, made improvements to the church, built the free school that I have described (now used as a village hall), a group of four almshouses, a new vicarage and a large number of farm-houses, besides adorning, in so personal a way, his own hall, round which he built a wall to enclose his park, which was three miles round and took three years to build and which is said to be the first wall in England built of arches. To these achievements can be added the afforestation of the hills on his estate. His interest in what happened inside his school was as persistent and practical as his care for its architectural appearance, and as well as being fond of displaying Latin and Greek quotations about his estate he compiled a Latin Grammar for his school's special use. He even took up the study of medicine so as to be of prompt use in dealing with the bodies as well as the minds of his tenants. But it is, of course, on his specific action in directing the bodies of his male tenants to energetic and self-preservative ends that he is most renowned. He instituted an athletic academy at Bunny, admitting only those who were "full-breasted, broad-shouldered, brawny-legged and -armed; but clean limbed". In 1712 he inaugurated an annual wrestling match at Bunny, under his own code of rules. The prize was a gold-laced hat. This match was maintained until just after the death of the last Parkyns baronet. It made its final appearance in 1810, and one wonders whether Lord Byron, who was always interested in pugilism, ever came down from Newstead to witness the match in its last years, for he was in residence there during 1809-10. Sir Thomas Parkyns always maintained a pair of wrestlers in the hall to train the young men of the village, and the baronet himself, on the slightest provocation, would unroll a carpet and have a go in his own dining-room.

His ideas on wrestling are perpetuated in a curious and valuable little book called *The Cornish Hugg* which he dedicated to King George I. I have never seen a copy of the first edition of the work, and I'm not sure where it was printed. If, as one can reasonably suppose, it was in Nottingham, it must have been a very early product of the presses of the town; for the second edition of *The Cornish Hugg*, which came out in 1714 with the imprint of "William Ayscough in Bridlesmithgate", was one of the first books to be produced by the father of Nottingham journalism. The third edition was published at Bunny itself by "Humphrey Wainwright at Bunny in Nottinghamshire". This rather surprising fact suggests that by 1727, when this edition appeared, the influence of Sir Thomas Parkyns was being felt to the extent of enlarging the activities of this, after all, very tiny village, to include publishing and perhaps printing. The book is a strange one and contains surprises from the very beginning; when, for instance, Sir Thomas recommends that rather than wrestle in what he calls "a pair of straight breeches" (which is certainly what one is accustomed to see in engravings of eighteenth-century pugilists) one should "choose rather to wrestle in a pair of linen drawers, wide at the knees, easie ty'd above the knees". He also recommends "narrow, low-heeled shoes". For a sample of the book's contents we might perhaps study the recipe for a typical Parkyns "hold". This one is called "The Flying Horse".

"Take him by the right hand with your left, your palm being upwards, as if you design'd only to shake him by the hand in a friendly manner at the beginning, and twist it outwards, and lift it upwards to make way for your head, and put your head under his right armpit, and hold his hand down to your left side, hold your head stiff backwards to hold him out of his strength, then put your right arm up to the shoulder betwixt his grainings, and let your hand appear behind past his breech without taking hold; but if you suspect that they'll cavil at that arm as a breeching, lay your same arm along his belly, and lift him up as high as your head and in either hold, when so high, lean backward and throw him over your head."

It will be observed that by modern standards of sporting ethics, Thomas Luctator veers towards gamesmanship rather than strict sportsmanship. It is not that in that phrase about the opening handclasp "as if you designed only to shake him by the hand in a friendly manner" that is contrary to the feel of all wrestling; but in the final instructions for the Flying Horse Parkyns shows clearly that he is on the side of the combatant, the wily combatant, *against* the opinions of "they"—the same "they" that Edward Lear uses so effectively and bitterly in his nonsense verses to represent all that is most rigid in public censure—who here represent the spectators and, presumably, the referee. You are to adopt, you notice, the alternative hold, the non-breech hold, only if "they" "cavil at" the other.

In contrast to what has already been said of Sir Thomas's seemingly advanced attitude towards his tenants, it ought to be remarked that Sir Thomas proposed a method for "hiring and recording of servants in Husbandry, Arts, Misteries, etc.", and that another of his written works, "On Subordination, or an Essay on Servants and their Wages", is described as a "somewhat belated echo of the policy so strenuously advocated by London writers such as Locke and Defoe, of increased severity to the poor".

There may seem to be something of a contradiction in these two varying aspects of Sir Thomas; but what one is left with is the impression of a man, something more than an eccentric—and certainly not a frenzied, heroic, crazy eccentric in the line of Squire Mytton—who *was* in advance of his time in his still rather feudal paternalism, who cannot but have been liked by his tenants and by all the people of Bunny. His obsession with wrestling must have been one of those "infernal nuisances" from which all localities suffer, a thorn in the flesh of all save the squire, but which, nevertheless, by its very notoriety and the attention it attracted outside the limits of the suffering community, must have become a pride, a local pride, against which, in time, one would not hear a word spoken without protest. Anyway, Thomas Luctator has got the immortality he deserved. As long as his monument remains in Bunny church and his house stands there, with its preposterous tower and coat of arms, no one in south Nottinghamshire is going to forget Sir Thomas Parkyns.

The name Parkyns continues to haunt us as we push on up the road past Bunny in the direction of Nottingham. The next village northward, a little over a mile on, is Bradmore. This, though it contains one brick house with mullioned windows which is probably mid-seventeenth century, was largely rebuilt by Sir Thomas, after a fire had destroyed the church and most of the village early in the eighteenth century. Of the church only the spire survives, a thirteenth-century ground floor and an upper floor dating from a century later. A small Victorian brick mission room has been built rather incongruously on to the church tower.

One village further on is Ruddington. This is a larger place, lying to the east of the road, a place of something over three thousand souls, where lace-making is combined, stickily, with the keeping of bees and the production of honey. The link with Sir Thomas Parkyns is more tenuous here, as we leave Bunny behind us, but at Ruddington was born, in 1823, Mansfield Parkyns whom we shall hear of in connection with the village of Woodborough, a village just about as far north-east of Nottingham as Ruddington is south, and to the same degree now encroached upon by the council housing of the city. For, out of Ruddington and over Wilford hill, which gives one of the best views of the approaching city, we are almost back where we began this excursion, on the banks of the Trent. Wilford itself, on the river, used to boast a ferry, the scene of an accident in the eighteenth century, when six people were drowned, and must, until recently, have been as pleasant a riverside village as Clifton is still. Here, in Victorian times, there was a popular tea-garden where, on Sunday afternoons and holidays in the fifties, the mechanics of Nottingham used to take their ladies in their Sunday finery to regale themselves on shrimps, gin and water, ale, bottled stout and bad cigars. The village still retains a fragment of itself and its character in a group of old buildings which includes the church, the Queen Anne brick rectory and its outbuildings, and the white-washed village inn; but on the other side of the river is the great mass of the Nottingham power station and the village does not well survive this propinquity. Anyway, there has been a great deal of newer building in what is now mainly a mining village. A group of houses on the village green were built by the first Lord Trent for veterans of the Crimean War and the Indian Mutiny. There are a couple of names to be remembered in Wilford. One is Gilbert Wakefield, scholar and controversialist, who was born at St. Nicholas' rectory in the city of Nottingham and came to the old school at Wilford to get his education; and there is Captain John Deane, who was one of those Englishmen who were attracted to Russia by the tsar, Peter the Great, when the reformer was trying to westernize his country. At the age of thirty-five, in 1714, John Deane was commanding a ship in the Russian navy that Peter created in the Baltic out of quite literally nothing—not even a rowing boat—and, after a later career as a British consul abroad, Captain Deane found his way to this so

very inland village of Wilford, died here in the year that
George III came to the throne and is buried in the churchyard, having built two houses in the village that are still known
by his name. The church is a very much restored dark grey
structure with fourteenth and fifteenth-century elements surviving. The north aisle was completely rebuilt in 1891. The thing
that people come, or came, to see here is the rather too brilliantly
coloured window, depicting the three magi, in memory of the
poet Kirk White, one of whose favourite haunts this was, but
who would hardly recognize the place now—except, perhaps
Wilford Hall, at the south end of the High Road, which had
been built a year or two before he was born and must still have
looked very new in its red-brick elegance when he used to come
to Wilford to admire the Trent and the scenery.

Only one more separate entity and we are in the city. Can
one still talk of West Bridgford as separate from Nottingham?
I think so, even though it has city buses running through many
of its streets, and has a population of something like thirteen
thousand. The hall, mid-eighteenth century, is now the Urban
District Council offices, and there is a brand new Shire Hall. A
couple of old houses, and a gabled cottage of Queen Anne's time,
in Church Drive, remain from earlier days. The church, to all
intents and purposes, does not, because, though it incorporates
the tower, the south aisle and nave of the medieval church, the
existing structure really dates from the early years of the present
century. In the new east chapel of the north aisle there is a very
much mutilated effigy of a cross-legged knight, who is supposed to
be a Sir Robert de Luttrell, of about 1298; for the distinguished
and ancient family of Luttrell of Dunster Castle in Somerset traces
its descent from a Geoffrey Luttrell who acquired lands here, at
West Bridgford, and at the adjacent village of Gamston, in the
latter part of the twelfth century. Geoffrey Luttrell took part
in the unsuccessful rebellion of John, Count of Mortain, against
his brother King Richard I. Luttrell was deprived of his lands,
but they were restored to him after the accession of King John, at
whose court he held many offices of importance. The present
Luttrell line springs from a grandson of this Geoffrey.

Gamston, by the way, a little place, has a high narrow church
with an unusually picturesque outline. It was restored by Sir
George Gilbert Scott, as I have already mentioned, in 1855. It
has an extremely low chancel, a short, tall nave with battlements,
and a west tower with more battlements and eight bold pinnacles.
At Gamston rectory was born Henry Fynes-Clinton, in 1781. His
father was the rector, and he himself was to become an eminent

classical scholar and the first of three generations of rectors of Cromwell, up in the centre of the county.

Let us, from West Bridgford, take a road southward again, one that runs for a time parallel with that which brought us up from Bunny. We go up Ludlow Hill into Edwalton. Here, under the shadow of the brick tower, ivy clad, of the church of the Holy Rood, is to be found in the churchyard the epitaph of Mrs. Rebecca Freeland, who was a considerable landowner in' these parts and died in 1741. It runs:

> She drank good ale, strong punch and wine
> And lived to the age of ninety-nine.

The next village is Plumtree, but there are no traces there of the family of Plumtre which plays so prominent a part in the county's history. The church is said to have been restored, in the 1870's, with stone from the old Trent Bridge. The building is remarkable for its large-scale Norman blank arcading and Norman characteristics in doorways and arches. The restoration was in the hands of G. F. Bodley (1827-1907) and Thomas Garner. These are two of the more remarkable Victorian architectural figures, who were responsible for the reredos and chancel screen in St. Mary's, Nottingham, the restoration of the church of All Saints at Coddington near Newark, and, above all, the building of the church at Clumber, of which we shall have occasion to speak later. Bodley had worked with the Scotts, father and son, but seems deliberately to have designed St. Michael's, Brighton, with an aggressively polychromatic interior to demonstrate his breaking away from the Scott technique of Victorian Gothic. Subsequently he built churches all over the country and abroad, notably, Washington Cathedral, and worked amicably with Thomas Garner until the latter seceded to the church of Rome. The two were responsible for the not-unattractive screen in Plumtree church.

Plumtree leads directly into one of the three places in the county with the name of Normanton. This is Normanton-on-the-Wolds (and it need not delay us), the others being Normanton-on-Soar and Normanton-on-Trent. At Stanton-on-the-Wolds, near by, the tiny church, owing to the depopulation of the village, has been left almost on its own, the exterior much overgrown but with Norman stonework still perceptible. From a house that used to stand close to the church Colonel Hutchinson made a spectacular escape in one episode of the Civil War. The house, the property of a William Needham, a Parliamentarian, was sacked by the Royalists. Needham, a Colonel in the Parliamentary forces, was Governor of Leicester.

Just up the road is Keyworth. An object of note here is the tower of the church of St. Mary the Virgin. This is something unique in the county, a curious sort of beacon tower, broad and square, and had originally larger ground-floor openings in the north and south walls which Pevsner suggests were either for processions or may have been occasioned by the existence of a right of way leading through the church. The tower has at the top a frieze with gargoyles and a solid parapet, and above it, set a long way inside the edges of the tower, rises a solid octagonal upper stage with a short spire. This rather startling object has, it is suggested, certain French affinities; nearer home, it can be compared with certain Hertfordshire spires like those of Baldock and Ashwell.

Two miles away is Widmerpool. Here there is a conspicuous nineteenth-century hall of stone, in a neo-Elizabethan manner, with towers, gables and terraces. The church is Victorian, too, built in the late eighties by Kimberley of Banbury, who left intact the pinnacled fourteenth-century tower of the earlier church. Inside is an Italian marble monument to Mrs. Robertson who died in 1891. Her effigy is shown recumbent on a pillow-strewn couch.

Down now into the curious little pocket of Nottinghamshire that juts into Leicester: almost the most southerly point of the county. Here is Willoughby-on-the-Wolds which, as containing in its church the magnificent early monuments of the Willoughby family, has already been discussed in connection with Wollaton.

A transverse road takes us to Upper Broughton—or Broughton Sulney to give it its alternative name—where there is a small church built of brown sandstone very badly weathered. The church has a classical entrance porch of 1733 built on to the thirteenth and fourteenth-century building, and in it are incorporated fragments of a quatrefoil frieze, and also a much dilapidated Norman tympanum with vertical stripes, vertical rows of diapers and a very crude figure in one corner. At the time that this eighteenth-century porch was built the south aisle of the church was pulled down; it was at a time of great poverty and depression in the wolds—much land was being enclosed and the medieval agricultural economy had disappeared, taking with it the excuse for these spacious wold churches. We are asked to admire here, in the churchyard, a number of slate headstones, dating from the early 1700's. Of about the same date, though they look earlier, are some timber-framed cottages in the village. Here, in the middle of that century, Charles Wildbore, a celebrated mathematician, lived.

Down the hill is Hickling. In the churchyard more of these slate tombstones, with an angel in shallow relief across the top, and good lettering. One of them, to John Smith who died in 1725, has as epitaph the lines:

> This world's a city full of crooked streets
> Death is the market-place where all men meets.
> If life were merchandise yt men could buy
> The rich would often live and poor men die.

It is suggested that Hickling was the home of the unknown engraver who executed these slate tombs—in a style of true folk art—which are to be found all the way up the Vale of Belvoir. The church at Hickling was restored in stages during the Victorian age, the chancel in 1845 and the tower in 1873, leaving the nave and the four-bay arcade to the north and south aisles, of the fourteenth century, more or less intact. The most interesting thing in the church is a Saxon coffin lid, decorated with a cross and rather violent interlacings and also with two heads of animals. It is perhaps mid tenth-century. (A musical side note. From Hickling came " Boomas Morice " who was authorized in 1664, in a document of the "Westminster Corporation", a musical body that came to an end in 1697, and signed by the Master of the King's Musick, " to use and exercise Musique on the Vyallin".)

Over the Grantham Canal and past the inn that stands beside it, to Kinoulton. Here is a brick church, of a singularly brilliant red colour, built in 1793 by the Earl of Gainsborough. It has three round-headed windows on each side and a west tower with a classical cornice below the roof. It has a gallery inside and is pleasantly, but very plainly panelled. The organ, which is Gothic in design, is probably contemporary with the church. Up on the hill, close to the Fosse Way, is the site of the church which the eighteenth-century St. Luke's replaced. Nothing is left of it "except", writes Professor Pevsner, "a few slate headstones, including one which is the finest in the county and ought to be preserved".

Close up to the Fosse Way is Owthorpe, where we have already been; on the other side is Clipston, a little place which must not be confused with Clipstone in Sherwood Forest. Tollerton, a mile or so away, is worth pausing at for two reasons—its church and its big house called Roclaveston Manor. This was the seat, for something like seven hundred years, of a Norman family of the name of Barry. The present manor house was built about 1675, considerably altered in the time of George II, and received its surviving external form in about 1790, when it was partially rebuilt by Pendock Barry who was the last of his line. He was also responsible for rebuilding, a little later, the church, a group of almshouses and a mausoleum in the church to his wife. The house, as he left it, has a heavily castellated front of stucco with a pointed central porch, a tower and a secondary turret on one side. A wing projects from the otherwise symmetrical front on the right side and is continued in a gallery leading to the church, and so forming a romantically picturesque group of buildings. (The house is now St. Hugh's Congregational College.) The church, which was rebuilt in 1812, still has some medieval features in the nave, though the outer walls and the tower, with its clearly revived Gothic windows, do not look anything but nineteenth century. Inside the church, separated from the south aisle by a neo-Greek iron gate, is a mausoleum that Pendock Barry built in memory of his wife Susannah who died in 1811. It has a glass ceiling supported on three semicircular arches, and niches containing obelisks and inscriptions. It is not really a very praiseworthy bit of work. Tollerton has nowadays a special meaning for Nottingham. It is only about three and a half miles from the city centre and in 1928 the City Council established an airport here. At the beginning of the war Tollerton airfield was taken over by the Air Ministry, and is listed by the Ministry of Civil Aviation for acquisition by the Government for the operation of scheduled airline services.

I should like now to turn to the extremely interesting southwest corner of the county, and would ask your indulgence in going back to Clifton as a starting point. If you take the road out of Clifton (leaving to the east the hamlet of Glapton, which contains a thatched, timber-framed cottage, with crucks at one end, dating from before the Reformation) you come soon into Barton-in-Fabis. Here is a fine fourteenth-century church notable for its monuments to members of the Sacheverell family. (The Barton estate passed to the Cliftons—by purchase—after the marriage of a daughter of Robert Sacheverell to the youngest son of the fourth baronet, Sir Gervase Clifton, in about 1715.) The most striking tomb is that of William Sacheverell, who died in 1616, and his wife Tabitha. It is of the local alabaster and comes, pretty obviously, from the same workshop as the contemporary monuments of the same family that we shall encounter in a moment at Ratcliffe-on-Soar. Of the Sacheverell manor house in

Barton nothing remains except one wall and an octagonal dove-
cote. In the neighbourhood was a Roman villa of which a
mosaic pavement was uncovered in 1856. By the way, beware of
thinking that the ferry marked on the map close to Barton is
more use than it actually is: it consists only of a rowing boat
and therefore can't manage cars! Thrumpton is the next place
down the road. Here, close beside an arm of the Trent, is
Thrumpton Hall which has belonged to several families—the
Powtrells, the Pigots, who built it in about 1610, the Emmertons
—before it came into the hands of the Byron family. It is a
brick house with stone dressings, built on a symmetrical H pattern
with gabled wings. Between the wings, on the garden side, is
a loggia consisting of two columns supporting three arches. In
the 1830's a similar loggia was added on the other side as
well. Inside the house the most conspicuous feature is a
very wide and very massively carved staircase dating from the
Restoration. The well of the staircase is square and the balustrade is carved all the way up with huge and florid scrolls of
foliage. I will quote a note on the staircase by Professor
Pevsner: "Mr. (Christopher) Hussey has drawn attention to its
similarity and that of a doorway with Thorpe near Peterborough,
ascribed to Inigo Jones's closest pupil, John Webb."

The church of All Saints at Thrumpton embodies the only work
of restoration in the county by one of the greatest Victorian
architects, George Edmund Street, best known for his Law Courts
at the Temple Bar. This great London building, the last secular
building of the Gothic Revival, although it was not begun to be
built until 1874—and completed ten years later—was already
occupying Street's mind in the year in which he was rebuilding
the church at Thrumpton—1872.

From Thrumpton we continue down to the very edge of the
county, to the interesting village of Ratcliffe-on-Soar (the two
Nottinghamshire places with this similar name, apart from being
differentiated by the rivers on which they stand, Soar and Trent
—the Soar, a tributary of the latter, forms the county boundary
with Leicestershire, from Stanford-upon-Soar up to the Soar's
junction with the Trent a mile or so upstream from Thrumpton
—are also, in this case, mercifully spelt differently, one with a D
and the other, this one, with a T in the middle). One comes
to Ratcliffe to look at the monuments in the church and to see
its thirteenth-century west tower. The Sacheverell manor house
is now traceable only in a farm-house, but the monuments are
some of the best in the county. The series begins with the tomb
of Ralph Sacheverell, who died in 1539, and his first wife, Ceceilia.

They are shown in medieval-style effigies, he in plate armour and wearing an SS collar, with his head on a helmet and his feet on a lion, lying on a tomb-chest placed in a niche which had a depressed arch and Gothic decoration. The tomb-chest itself is adorned with tracery and shields in panels. Next comes Sir Henry Sacheverell (died 1558), who lies again on a tomb-chest, rather stiffly, with his wife, and, round the walls of his tomb-chest, his seventeen children all holding shields. There are two other Henry Sacheverells—one who died in 1580, and the other who died in 1625. The difference between their two tombs is striking and instructive. The figures of the elder Henry, his wife and his six children are still medievally stiff, and though the decoration is of characteristically Elizabethan strapwork, contains little of the new Renaissance spirit. The tomb of the last Henry, however—he brought to an end this Ratcliffe-on-Soar branch of the Sacheverell family—in addition to the very conspicuous changes in fashions of the clothes displayed on the figures of his three (childless) wives who kneel, one behind the other, above their husband's tomb-chest, the little canopy or aedicule under which the three wives kneel has columns and a pediment in a manner that belongs firmly to the new age. It seems clear that these monuments of four generations were all produced in a single workshop, which was also responsible for other alabaster tombs in the neighbourhood, including the other Sacheverell monuments of the seventeenth century at Barton-in-Fabis.

Less than a mile from Ratcliffe is Kingston-on-Soar. Perhaps the first thing to be noticed is the large, but not very exciting, Kingston Hall, which was built in the middle of the last century, in the neo-Elizabethan manner, by the first Lord Belper. He was a grandson of the great industrial pioneer, Jedediah Strutt, who came from the mining and hosiery town of Belper seven or so miles north of Derby. The first Lord Belper, who died in 1880, included in the entrance hall of his noble seat some alabaster columns made from gypsum mined on the estate itself. In the village of Kingston he built a number of semi-detached, gabled, brick cottages which are discernible by their symmetrical grouping. His son, Frederick Strutt, who was a naturalist and archaeologist, died in 1909 and is buried in the churchyard. The church contains one of the county's most celebrated artistic possessions, which certainly makes a special visit to Kingston worth while. But the visitor is, I am afraid, apt to be put off by the dullness and unattractiveness of the church of St. Wilfred itself. The church dates, in its present form, from the year 1900, and it is from a floor of rather painful encaustic tiling, of the familiar red and russet colouring, that the church's one treasure, the Babington chantry arises. It is tiresomely and rather inappropriately placed, but it is possible to inspect it closely and to understand its celebrity among connoisseurs of decorative style of churches. The monument—which was originally placed elsewhere in the earlier church, and whose tomb-chest is now missing, consists of a canopy on four columns. The short, thick columns are entirely covered with a network of hexagonal panels in which shields, and Gothic tracery, trailing vines and small figures struggle to assert themselves. The figures are much damaged, but it is clear that one row was a dance of death and others contain saints and figures of people in mid-sixteenth-century attire. The chantry dates from about the year 1550. The very prominent capitals have on them a couple of hundred infants in barrels which, if you think for a moment, is a punning rebus of the Babington family name—babes, you see, in tuns; Babe-in-tun; Babington. Inside the canopy, on its east wall, is a somewhat better carving of the Last Judgment. This no doubt formed the reredos of the altar which used to be contained in the chantry. The enrichment of the chantry was probably due to Sir Anthony Babington; while another Anthony Babington, of a later generation—he was born in 1561—and who was a Roman Catholic, is said to have hidden on the top of this canopy when he was being sought for on account of his share in the plot in support of Mary Queen of Scots. For this he was beheaded at the age of twenty-five. But it is not so much the political as the stylistic history of the Babington chantry which makes it interesting. It certainly is an unexpected and rather foreign-looking object; and you can if you like take your cue from Mr. Sacheverell Sitwell who, from his great knowledge of the art and architecture of the Iberian peninsula, writes as follows of "Kingston-on-Soar and the chased and lozenged pillars of the chantry-chapel, suggestive of a temple of Golconda reported by mariners at second hand through the Portuguese, until we remember the century earlier Manoeline of Roslin Chapel, near Edinburgh. Persons familiar with Alcobaça or Belem will be unable to dismiss from their minds that there is somewhat of Portuguese-Indian influence in this church upon a tributary of the River Trent."

At Kingston-on-Soar, in 1716, was born John Berridge, a wealthy farmer's son, who became an evangelist and was much praised by John Wesley. The large manor farm, dating from the early eighteenth century, is worth a glance. And you will not fail to notice, as you move southward, the admirable buildings of what used to be called the Midland Agricultural College and

Victorian Baroque in Newark: the Corn Exchange, 1847

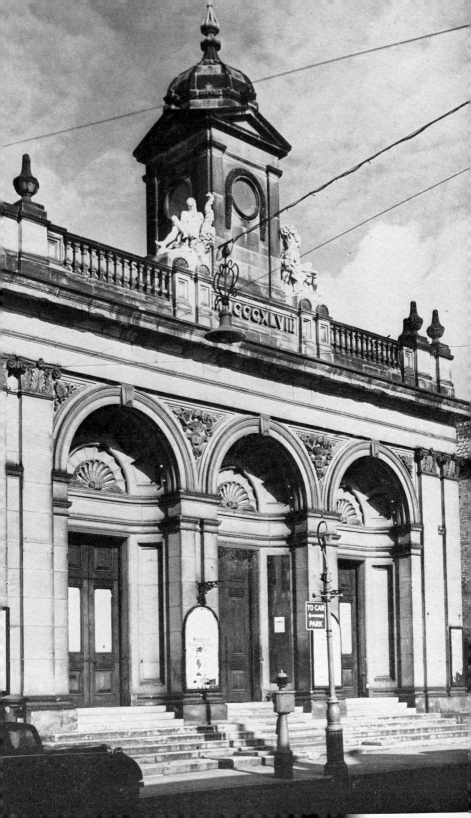

is now the Nottingham University School of Agriculture. This belongs as much to Sutton Bonington as to Ratcliffe. Sutton Bonington is the next place on our list, a charming village, many of whose houses and pubs are inhabited by teachers and students at the college which to some extent dominates the village. Of the two churches, one belongs to Sutton and is dedicated to St. Anne, the other, St. Michael's, being in the Bonington half. St. Michael's is the larger of the two, thirteenth, fourteenth and fifteenth century in date, with a spire 135 feet high. St. Anne's is smaller and lies on the hillside, back from the road. It has been much restored, but one can still see that the north arcade, which has both circular and octagonal piers, and the aisle belonging to it, are thirteenth century.

Two more villages and we are right down at the bottom of the county again: indeed I imagine that Stanford-upon-Soar is the most southerly community—though not the most southerly single habitation—within the borders. First, Normanton-upon-Soar. Here, the main interest is in the aisleless church, wholly dating from the thirteenth century, which has one of the only two towers in the county placed centrally at the crossing of the church. This tower, which has a spire, is also of thirteenth-century date, as is shown by the strong piers inside with fillets and moulded capitals. Two monuments in the church bring the name Willoughby back again. Here are Frances Willoughby, who died in 1606, and William Willoughby, who died thirty years later, with his wife. They both have kneeling figures. Elsewhere in Normanton are to be seen a much-titivated, late seventeenth-century brick manor house, a number of early eighteenth-century brick farm-houses and one good timber-framed cottage.

At Stanford we find another large house put to a modern use. Stanford Hall (which is in fact two miles north-east of the village) is now the Co-operative College. It is a brick mansion, built in the 1770's for Charles Vere Dashwood, whose family had succeeded those of Raynes and Lewes, in possession of the place. Later, in the nineteenth century, the village was largely rebuilt by the succeeding family of Ratcliffe. Stanford Hall, which has forward-curving wings at the entrance and a central feature composed of huge ionic pilasters and a pediment with a coat of arms, was considerably altered inside and given a rather incongruous cloister on the south-west by Sir Julien Cahn, to whom the county owes so much for his purchase and presentation to the city of Nottingham of the Newstead Estate.

Moving into Stanford village we find a very modest late-Georgian stucco manor house, and the houses built by the Rat-

The bridge over the River Devon at Newark, the spire of St. Mary's and the top of the Ossington Coffee Tavern

cliffes in the 1830's standing in little symmetrical gabled groups. One group bears the date 1836. The church (of St. John the Baptist) is a mixture of thirteenth and fourteenth-century work. It contains one brass, of about 1400, to the memory of a priest; one incised alabaster slab to a member of the Illingworth family and his wife, dating from 1488; the recumbent effigy of a man holding his heart in his hand (a feature which can be seen elsewhere in the county) of late fourteenth-century date; and a monument to a Thomas Lewes, who died in 1694, a frame decorated with the heads of putti.

In the preceding pages, by moving from village to village around the south-west corner of the county I feel that we have entitled ourselves to strike out, though still keeping south of the line of the Trent, in a different direction. This time we shall move eastwards and south-eastwards towards the Vale of Belvoir. The road which takes us out of Nottingham—it is the Grantham road—leads us once again through West Bridgford. A signpost, after a mile or two, directs us northwards to Holme Pierrepont. Here, silent, and rather dilapidated when I was last there, showing too obvious signs, then, of army occupation, with notices pinned to doors and the bases of Nissen huts disfiguring the garden, is the house which was long the home of the Pierreponts who became the Earls of Kingston. The hall was built early in the seventeenth century and some of its windows are still of that date. Towards the end of the eighteenth century it was very much enlarged, fitted with the fashionable castellations and faced with stucco. A little later part of the house was demolished and the rest restored. Apart from its modestly imposing battlemented front, perhaps the most attractive part of the house is the largish enclosed quadrangle or courtyard on the west side with Gothic french windows and a grassy centre. But, alas, it suffered sorely from time and the inappropriate uses of war. The creeper was pulled untidily away in the front, the stucco peeled and the bricks showed through it in a down-at-heel sort of way. The interior does not seem to have been elaborately decorated: there remains, conspicuously, from the earlier house a good seventeenth-century staircase with heavy scrollwork.

The hall at Holme Pierrepont stands some distance from the village with an unexpectedly open, unwalled and grassy approach to it. On the west side of the house, and very close to it, stands the church dedicated to St. Edmund. Architecturally it is a curious hybrid, for though the interior remains consistently Early English the outside dates from 1666, a time of non-Gothicizing.

But, though the church is more or less classical to look at—the porch has Tuscan columns and a cornice—it gives a faintly Gothic flavour all the same. Facing you, as you go in at the door, is the monument to a poet who, by virtue of patronage and of the fact that his death took place here, is regarded as a sort of honorary worthy of the county. The monument to John Oldham, who died in 1683, is a tablet with good white lettering (kept freshly painted) on black placed against one of the piers; but so well carved are the swags and wings and faces which surround it that it is suggested—for once—that it may be the work of Grinling Gibbons himself. Oldham's inscription is in Latin, but since it gives some of the facts of his life (with due prominence, naturally, to the patronage of William Earl of Kingston), we might recall this respected but not now much read poet, even before we examine the tombs of the family which gave him home and employment until his death in 1683. Oldham was something of a pioneer. At a time when so much verse was, in fact, a form of journalism, when writers like Marvell were treating the satirical form partly as the means of making speeches and partly, in an age virtually without newspapers, as a form of leading article, Oldham produced satire which in impulse and in value was purely literary. As he himself said, he wrote satire for satire's sake:

> Satyr's my only province of delight,
> For whose dear sake alone I've vowed to write:
> For this I seek occasions, court abuse,
> To show my parts and signalize my muse.

The son of a nonconformist minister, Oldham, as is duly recorded on his monument at Holme Pierrepont, was born at Shipton Moyne, near Tetbury in Gloucestershire, on the 9th August, 1653. His father subsequently moved to Newton, in Wiltshire, from which place he was ejected in 1662; thenceforward he remained as a dissenting minister at Wotton-under-Edge in the Cotswolds, outliving his poetic son by many years. The latter received his education at Tetbury Grammar School and was sent to St. Edmund's Hall at Oxford in 1672. He took his bachelor's degree in May 1674 and left the university to reside for about a year with his father. He was evidently without means; and he undertook the post of usher at Whitcliff's school at Croydon until 1678, following this by the more tolerable occupation of a private tutor, first to the grandsons of a judge, Sir Edward Thurland (not, I think, of our county in spite of the name) and, in 1681, to the son of a certain Sir William Hickes. This latter job brought him within reach of London and made possible an acquaintance with the literary men of the day to whom his poems were already known.

Oldham's *Satires upon the Jesuits,* which he had written in 1679, had been published in 1681, and remained the work on which his fame—and it was considerable throughout the next fifty years when nearly a dozen editions of his works appeared— was based. Lord Rochester and one or two other London men of letters had apparently gone to the trouble of visiting the young schoolmaster at Croydon on the strength of some of his compositions at that stage circulating in manuscript. Nothing, however, to Oldham's immediate advantage came from these encounters and the 1681 *Satires* bore no dedication. The next year, however, the newly succeeded Earl of Kingston rescued Oldham from the thraldom of schoolmastering, became his patron, offered him hospitality at Holme Pierrepont, and suggested, we are told, that he take Orders and become his chaplain. This was probably not seriously intended nor can it have been welcome. Oldham was an entirely secular and at times needlessly coarse poet. At any rate, we can well imagine that the sharp, amusing and decidedly satiric face which is shown in Oldham's portraits belonged to an agreeable companion for a youngish, intelligent nobleman of these Restoration years. Oldham, in addition, was bound to take what he could from his patron; in the seventeenth century it was virtually impossible to exist as a man of letters without inherited wealth or under conditions of complete dependence. We do not know what his relations with Lord Kingston were, but we can guess that he was anxious to escape from whatever degree of servility was involved because, quite soon, he decided to take up medicine for a livelihood and for a year studied in order to do so. But Oldham's health, though he was not yet thirty, was breaking down. He was said to have been consumptive. Then, when at Holme Pierrepont, on December 9th, 1683, he fell a victim to smallpox, and, as we have seen, is buried in the churchyard there. The greatest poet of Oldham's generation, John Dryden, thought sufficiently well of his young contemporary to write the opening tribute to him in Oldham's *Remains,* which were published in 1684. The publisher, who stresses the selective quality of his editing, recalled the dictum of Cowley (a poet who greatly influenced Oldham) that it is a mistake to think "a rude heap of ill-placed stones a better monument than a neat tomb of marble". Transferring the funerary figure from the metaphoric to the actual we might say that the extraordinarily neat but modest tablet which, presumably, Lord Kingston caused to be set up in

memory of his protégé in the church at Holme Pierrepont out-
shines, by its intrinsic excellence and the names it commemorates,
all the more costly and elaborate tombs of the family that gave
him encouragement and shelter.

Not that some of these monuments are not themselves interesting. A recumbent stone effigy, anonymous, of about 1300, and
the upper half only of an equally unknown knight are dull compared with several tombs of a little later. There is the late-
medieval Henry Pierrepont of 1499, a well-preserved alabaster
effigy, whose tomb-chest is adorned with shields in diamond-
shaped panels. The Elizabethan Sir Henry Pierrepont, in
alabaster again, has his wife and his seven children on his tomb-
chest with him. This was the Sir Henry who married Frances
Cavendish, the daughter of the famous Bess of Hardwick, and so
united two famous Nottinghamshire families. Sir Henry's son,
Robert, who became the first Earl of Kingston-on-Hull in 1628, is
the subject of a celebrated moral lesson derived from his reputed
experiences in the Civil War. He declared that if he ever joined
either side in the war he would offer a prayer that a cannon ball
would divide him between the parties. What happened was,
first, that one of his sons fought for Parliament and the other for
the King; while he himself, joining the King and being captured
by the Parliamentarians in the fighting at Gainsborough, was, by
a chance shot from his own side—mark the irony—cut neatly in
two. The severed halves of his body were united in the church
of the Sherwood village of Cuckney where they lie under a plain
worn stone. A later, celebrated, member of the Pierrepont family,
the seventeenth-century Countess of Kingston, known as Princess
Gertrude, who died in 1649, is commemorated by a massive urn.
Another draped urn on a plaque is to the memory of the second
and last Duke of Kingston, Sir Evelyn Pierrepont, who fought at
the battle of Culloden and is remembered, unfortunately, mainly
as one of the husbands of the notorious Elizabeth Chudleigh, who
was one of the less-respectable ladies of early eighteenth-century
society. Worth noticing, also, is a tomb signed by Flaxman,
depicting a woman, in profile, reading a book, which is in memory of a certain William Saltrem who, in 1811, was drowned
while skating on the lake at Thoresby Park. This incident serves
to remind us that Pierrepont is the family name of the Earls
Manvers of Thoresby; and, indeed, Holme Pierrepont was recently
still in the possession of the family, being the property of the
youngest daughter of the fourth Earl Manvers.

Apart from the massive tomb of a refugee from the French
Revolution I don't think there is much more to be seen here. It

is worth noting, though, that benefactions to the church have not come to an end and that the new electric blower of the organ was, in 1946, presented by Mr. and Mrs. Cursham.

If, leaving Holme Pierrepont and coming back to the Grantham road we were to go straight over the crossroads instead of turning left on our way to Bingham we should, passing through Cotgrave, a place with a church that has twelfth-century elements and where, in a pit close by, is found a suitable marl which is used here, and is also exported, for treating cricket pitches to bind and improve their turf, we find ourselves back in Owthorpe, where we have been before. So, in pursuing the road eastwards, we get to the other Radcliffe, the Radcliffe (with a D) on Trent. The church here is a rather grim and unsuitable product of the 1880's, with austere Early English detail and a tall tower. We are asked, however, to take note of the slate headstones in the churchyard by an artist of the name of James Sparrow, who lived and worked in Radcliffe during the eighteenth century.

We ought to leave the main road again here because, ahead, short of Bingham, there lies nothing much to comment on around Saxondale except a large airfield and the equally large Harlequin Asylum, before the line of the Fosse Way is crossed again. But southward are several places of interest. Cropwell Bishop and Cropwell Butler come first, close together. We have encountered these two small villages already, as being among the places near Nottingham which provided the plaster used in the construction of the town's houses many centuries ago, and have remarked on the things of interest to be found in them—a church with carved poppy-head benches, and a timber-framed cottage.

Through the Cropwells we come to Colston Bassett. This place is notable for containing the only piece of National Trust property in the county. I must confess that I find the market cross at Colston Bassett extraordinarily dull. The thing stands on the site of an older cross which was thought to have been put up by Ralph Bassett in 1257, when he got permission from Henry III to hold a market here. Of the existing, and second, cross only the fifteenth-century base remains. Both the shaft and the head have disappeared and what we look at now is an inoffensive but unremarkable classical column put up on the old base to commemorate, of all things, the coronation of King William IV. No doubt it is pleasant that this harmless object should not be swept away by road improvements, but I cannot altogether see why it should have been singled out for such conspicuous preservation. There are other things and places around the village of more interest. There is the hall, originally built in the early eighteenth century, but entirely converted in the middle of the last century to the Italian Renaissance style. I saw it at perhaps an unfortunate moment; though, in its desolation, with a fountain playing in its overgrown garden and only a few neglected flowers blooming in its unheated orangery, it had a certain macabre charm. After its rebuilding, it was the home of the family of Knowles, and it was Robert Millington Knowles who, in 1892, did away with the partly ruinous and depleted church in the village and built a brand new one on a new site, which still has all its newness about it. It was erected in memory of Knowles' son, and of his wife, Alice, who is commemorated by a large angel pointing to a cross. Knowles himself died in 1924 and the property passed to his son-in-law, Sir Edward le Marchant, who became the proprietor of Colston Bassett Hall and whose family pew is to be seen at the west end of the new church. The fifteenth-century tower and a good deal more, including a walled-up Norman arcade with scolloped capitals, remains of the old church. Its decay is not very dignified, being dependent wholly neither on man nor on time. Here is Pevsner's comment: "In 1892, the squire, to commemorate the death of his son and his wife, decided to build a new church close to the hall and unroofed the old one to convert it into a ruin."

The road north-eastwards out of Colston Bassett is one of the several means of access to an important place which lies a mile or so away—Langar. You will find the church at Langar mentioned in a number of works of reference because of the monuments it contains. It is a large church, with a tower over the central crossing, and is given an unusual appearance by the fact of its having a pew right across the west end of the church, but it has been heavily and not very subtly restored so that little of the original flavour of the stonework survives. The monuments in the church can be considered in three distinct sections. One, the tomb of Thomas Lord Scroope, has been described by an eminent authority as "almost the finest effigy in England". Scroope died in 1609, and with his wife, Philadelphia, under a four-poster canopy, his alabaster figure, the only example of a peer being shown in full garter robes, ear-rings and a hat, is certainly worth very special attention. Unfortunately one cannot normally get at close grips with the tomb, since the doors of the chapel are kept locked. The casual visitor has to content himself with looking down on the effigies from the top of a curious sort of stone balcony or stage. From here you do get quite a good view of the tomb. Note particularly the dwarf-like, bearded, kneeling figure of Emmanuel, the son of Lord Scroope, at his parents' feet.

There is something both moving and frightening about this little figure who, with his cloak and his armour, his long hair and his spade-shaped beard, seems so much older, in spite of his diminutive size, than either of his parents; she with her calm smooth face above her ruff, he, sleek and well fed and with a trim pointed beard. In any case, it was the son himself who erected the monument, so no doubt he was satisfied with his own portrait and with the way that he holds the book from which he is reading against his little armoured side. There are both earlier and later tombs than the Scroope monument. You go to the north transept for the earlier Chaworths and to the south transept for the later Howes. Both Sir John and Sir George Chaworth, of the middle and late sixteenth century, are of alabaster, but their workmanship is nothing like so good as that of Lord Scroope. The two Viscounts Howe, both of whose Christian names were Scroope, date from 1712 and 1734 and have classical busts on tapered shafts against the wall of the south transept. The famous Admiral Howe, of the glorious First of June, who died here in 1799, five years after that famous battle, and who had become the first Earl Howe, is commemorated by a plain tablet. The hall at Langar, the home of the Howes, has been replaced by a modern building. The residence, however, of the Chaworths survives in part up the road towards Bingham, at Wiverton. Wiverton Hall, with its battlements and turrets, and faced with stucco, was built in 1814; but at the back it incorporates the ground floor of the gatehouse of the Chaworths' mansion. This portion, dating from 1614, and built by Sir Thomas Chaworth, is all that remains of the older building. In the Civil War it was garrisoned by the Chaworths (a branch of the same family associated both with Colwick and Annesley) for the King; Queen Henrietta Maria passed a night here on her way to Ashby-de-la-Zouch. When Wiverton Hall surrendered in 1645 everything but the gatehouse was pulled down.

The tombs of the Chaworths and the Howes and the Scroopes provide one very good reason for coming to Langar, and the church which houses them, in spite of violent restorations in the nineteenth century, is still a stately and imposing building. Close beside it is the present red-brick Georgian rectory—spoilt, to my eye, by its too narrow windows—which is another and quite separate reason for many people's pilgrimage here. I suspect that the volume of these particular pilgrims will grow rather than diminish as time goes on, because Langar rectory was the birthplace of Samuel Butler, a writer whose proper place we cannot quite yet assess but whose reputation, surely, is not destined to decline. Langar is the "Battersby" of *The Way of All Flesh*, and the life of Battersby that is described in that book is the life of Langar as it was remembered by the observant and rebellious child who was born in the rectory in 1835. *The Way of All Flesh* was written between 1872 and 1885, but not published until 1903, the year after Butler's death. Butler's father, who has achieved an unenviable immortality as Theobald Pontifax in the novel, was the rector, the Rev. Thomas Butler; and his grandfather was an earlier Samuel Butler, headmaster of Shrewsbury School from 1798-1836 and afterwards Bishop of Lichfield. So Butler had plenty of inherited and personal knowledge of the Church of England to provide him with ammunition for his lifelong attacks on the conduct and hypocrisies of its ministers. We can only guess at the rigidity and repression that went on behind those narrow windows of Langar rectory in the 1840's, but that they were harsh and embittering is surely evident in the way—presumably following some thoughtless rejection of some gesture of the child's love in quite early years—it was turned to bitter, almost snarling hatred which Samuel Butler was prepared to express in such remarks as: "I said once when I wanted to be exceedingly proper without going beyond the truth, that I was sure no one could feel his father's death more than I did." Thomas Butler remained rector of Langar, which he had become the year before Samuel was born, until 1876. He was by that time a canon. Samuel, the second child of five (a sister married the brother of Robert Bridges, the late Poet Laureate), went from Langar to school at Shrewsbury and then on to St. John's College, Cambridge. He was prepared for ordination, but his doubts were too strong and, giving up the idea, went out to New Zealand and became a sheep farmer. *A First Year in Canterbury Settlement,* composed of his letters home, his first publication, appeared in 1863. But it was the great satire *Erewhon,* whose imaginary territory is set in the hinterland of a beautifully described, sheep-growing New Zealand, which was his first major work. It appeared in 1872, but the scenes of his birth and childhood were already being constantly turned over in his mind, for the writing of *The Way of All Flesh* was progressing, unknown to all except a single devoted friend, Miss Savage, and begun as early as 1873, before his father had left Langar. A glimpse of the relationship between father and son and brother and sisters is given in these acid notes written at the time of an illness of the rector of Langar a little later: "For the first few days there seemed no hope whatever, and my sisters were very civil, but as he gradually recovered they became ruder and ruder. It was in a high degree comic to see how when my father relapsed they became civil, and when he rallied, rude. . . . I went up to see my father. I found him, as I thought, very feeble. He took my going as he had taken my coming—as a matter of course. I said I was very glad he was so much better and hoped that he would now soon be well. He said with some difficulty, 'Yes, I'm better. Next time you come I hope you will have better weather.' I said, 'I should not have come if Dr. Burd had not sent for me.' He said more quickly, 'Did Dr. Burd send for you?' I said, 'Yes, and now he says I may go.' Then I said good-bye. He said good-bye and I left. I cannot say that I had a very pleasant journey home. All the time I was down my father was perfectly civil to me. He never even pretended to care two straws about me. He never said anything to me except the merest commonplaces; he does not care about my sisters; I think he likes me quite as well as he likes them, but he does not really like anybody or anything."

Before we leave Langar, a bit of rather earlier history to recall the great days of the now-vanished Langar Hall. The year 1754 was memorable for a momentous General Election. The Prime Minister, Henry Pelham, with the country on the verge of seven years war, had died that April. It was a moment when, in spite of the active presence of both the elder Pitt and of Henry Fox, later Lord Holland, the Whig grandees recommended to King George II, as his chief minister, the Duke of Newcastle. Here, in the Duke's own county, where he was usually able to secure—at very considerable expense—the return of his own candidates in four out of the eight seats available—that is one county member and one member for each of the boroughs of Newark, Nottingham and Retford—was suddenly challenged by his own protégé, John Plumptre, Junior, whose father had represented a county borough in Parliament for more than thirty years. The cause of young Plumptre, who had been a Whig, suddenly turning Tory, was a personal one: he had been asked to stand down in the election for his second cousin, Lord Howe of Langar. So, on one side were ranged the Duke of Newcastle himself and his nominee, Lord Howe, supported by the famous Nottingham banker, Abel Smith, and his two sons; and on the other the outraged and rebellious Plumptre, supported by the Earl of Middleton and others. What happened was a good example of election methods in those long pre-Reform times. Lord Howe entertained at Langar Hall, for a period of several whole months before the election, a number of important burgesses; there, securely ensconced in the hall, Lord Howe's hospitality reached a climax

in the days immediately preceding the poll and he regaled them
with such profusion that some of them died. But the method
was successful. The hospitality of Langar Hall justified itself.
Plumptre was beaten and Lord Howe got in.

I recommend that you go to have a look at Langar. It is full
of interesting history and memories. But go quickly for things
are happening there. Already the amenities of the rectory and
the church have been to some extent spoilt by the encroachment
of a new Council Estate whose houses, though they have the
decency to be of good red brick, are insipid and uninspiring to
the eye.

The road that leads away from the church and the hall and
the rectory, if pursued, leads through the hamlet of Barnston,
with its little church, under the railway, to Granby. It goes
without saying that the pub here is called the Marquis of Granby,
but there is no reason for thinking, I am afraid, that this carried
the original of that most famous among inn signs, which is to
be found far into the south of England and miles away from any
Manners estates. (There are, or were, well over twenty Marquis
of Granbys in London alone.) Why, one wonders, nearly two
centuries after the death of the Marquis in 1770, should his name
and his face be still one of the commonest signs over pub doors?
Most of the landlords who dispense refreshment under his portrait
have little idea who he was, and his survival is certainly a freak.
He was a soldier, son of the third Duke of Rutland. He was
appointed Colonel of the Royal Horse Guards in 1758 and was
present in the great action of Minden in the Seven Years War.
In 1776 he was appointed Commander-in-Chief of the British
Army, but he resigned his post at the end of three years owing to
ill health. The first Marquis of Granby sign is said to have been
hung out at Hounslow by one Sumpter, a discharged trooper of
the regiment of Horse Guards which the Marquis had commanded
as Colonel. Some explanation, obviously, is needed to explain
his reiterated popularity. He is said to have behaved with spirit
and personal courage everywhere, but his success on the signposts
of England had a lot to do, apparently, with a comparison generally made between him and his one-time commander, Lord George
Sackville, who was supposed not to have behaved so well in battle.
Another reason for his popularity as a sign may have been the
startling baldness of his head and the fact that he wore a short
haircut in the days when other people were much bewigged.
According to another account, at the Battle of Minden he "won
the battle but lost his wig". Anyway, he has lasted in a way
that few of his contemporaries besides George III (the most

popular of the King's Heads) and the occasional King of Prussia have.

The church at Granby is not very exciting. It is one of those south Nottinghamshire churches which were reduced in size after the Reformation. Its tower, at the west end, has Norman windows, and there are some thirteenth-century and later features, but the place was considerably messed about at the end of the eighteenth century.

On the way from Granby to Bingham it is worth pausing and turning up a side road to look at the outside of Whatton Manor. You may say that on the face of it there is nothing much to be admired about this neo-Elizabethan country house, but it is interesting because its date, the late 1830's, is a very early one for this particular revival. It belongs to just the same moment as the pioneering work of Anthony Salvin (he who built the new Thoresby) at Harlaxton Manor, near Grantham. Salvin was in his early twenties at this time, and he was able to show himself capable, thirty years later, of neo-Tudor at its most grandiose. Harlaxton, although monumental, is in a manner closer to the vernacular but less inventive, and there are certain similarities between this and Whatton. It would be pleasant to think, since, after all, Grantham is not far away, that Nottinghamshire included a sample of Salvin's early work as well as his mature and most elaborate structure. Otherwise, apart from Thoresby itself and its concommitant church at Perlethorpe, Salvin's only other work in the county seems to have been alterations, both inside and out, at Rufford Abbey, which he carried out during the precise years 1838-40 when Whatton Manor was building. Anthony Salvin, who lived from 1799-1881, was the son of a Durham General, spent his childhood in the shadow of Brancepeth Castle, and as a result was all his life fired by the romance and chivalry of the Middle Ages. In thought, as in his architecture, he was a romantic. He had his early professional training with George IV's favourite architect, John Nash, and in his office he came under the influence of a determined medievalist, the elder Pugin. Even from the beginning, though, Salvin showed a taste for the flamboyant and the grandiose, which he was prepared to indulge in styles quite other than Elizabethan or Gothic. Much of the remarkable effect created by Harlaxton is due to Salvin's uninhibited employment of a confident baroque style in the entrance pavilions and the gate piers to the west court of the manor. This baroque element in Salvin was later jettisoned when he became a thorough-going revivalist. The rebuilding of Whatton Manor was carried out for the then proprietor, Thomas

Dixon Hall. The house is now inhabited by a member of the Player family and, judging by the tidily raked drive and the trim surroundings of the house, it is lived in as a house should be lived in: which just goes to show that in comparison, say, with Holme Pierrepont, it fares better for a house to be re-made every century or so than to try to outlive the years in its original form.

At Whatton in the Vale—the village is less than a mile from Langar—the church has done less fortunately out of the activities of the Victorians. After rebuildings in both 1846 and 1870, practically nothing of the old church remains. This was one of the only two churches in the county with a central tower and spire over the crossing. T. D. Hall of Whatton Manor has left several traces in the church; a window to his memory recalls that he was born in 1808 and died in 1879, while, resting on the ledge of the front pew of the church, when I was last there, was still a Prayer Book inscribed "T. D. Hall. Whatton". The stained glass which fills, in a consistent and planned way, the majority, but not quite all, of the windows is worth looking at. That at the east end of the south aisle was designed by Sir Edward Burne-Jones and carried out by the firm of Morris & Co.; and the Christ who, with St. Peter and St. John, provides the figures for the three lights, with three stories underneath and three angels at the top, has a characteristically pre-Raphaelite look. Though noticeably inferior to the Morris work, the other windows of the church are also by well-known Victorian glass painters. A flat engraved alabaster tomb is that of the father of Thomas Cranmer, the martyred Archbishop of Canterbury. The father, also Thomas Cranmer, died in 1501. The Cranmers lived at the old manor house of the village adjacent to Whatton, Aslockton, where the future archbishop was born on 2nd July, 1489. No trace now remains of the house, but it is thought that it probably stood in a field where the path, called Cranmer's Walk, sets off beside the church for the village of Orston. One has pointed out to one in Aslockton an eminence called Cranmer's Mound, reputed to have been raised artificially by the archbishop in order that he might "sit and survey the face of the country, and listen to the tuneable bells of Whatton" across the River Smite which separates the two villages. Cranmer is one of the greatest of the county's worthies and the most eminent of its divines. It is impossible not to have a peculiar affection for Cranmer because of his many weaknesses which he managed to cancel out at the end by a final, and memorable, burst of courage. His career began by accident. As a professor of divinity at Jesus College, Cambridge, he happened, in order to avoid an outbreak of "sweating sickness" which was then raging throughout the country, gone to stay, in 1528, at Waltham with two of his pupils. Here he fell in with Bishop Fox, who had been the trusted adviser of Henry VII, and Stephen Gardiner, then secretary to Wolsey and enjoying the confidence of Henry VIII for having supported the King's matrimonial designs. Gardiner was sent to try to secure the Pope's consent to the divorce of Catharine of Aragon, and later was to conduct the case against the Queen. In conversation with Fox and Gardiner, Cranmer made a remark which was the cause of all his promotion—and his martyrdom— later on. He suggested that King Henry should have recourse to the canonists and the universities and not to the Pope. The King, hearing of it, promptly commanded Cranmer to write a treatise on the subject. Cranmer was later sent on embassies to Rome and to Germany and, during the latter sojourn, married the niece of the reformer, Ossiander, which was an uncanonical, but not illegal proceeding though not one to be expected of a man already high in the Church. His subsequent career is intimately tied up with the life of Henry VIII and with the progress of the Reformation, though he had little personally to do with the dissolution of the monasteries. His weaknesses, personal ambition high among them, had led him into too easy and unjustifiable compliance with the King's personal wishes, but he was a kind-hearted man and showed some courage in doing his best to save the lives of Anne Boleyn, Fisher and St. Thomas More. When Mary Tudor came to the throne Cranmer was brought to trial and deposed from the office of Archbishop. The Catholics persuaded him to recant. Then, at the moment when he should have publicly proclaimed his recantation, his frailty fell away, he restated his old position and deplored his past cowardice. With a courage that struck a powerful blow against the Catholics, who had hoped that Cranmer's recantation would make other Protestants fall away, he met his death on March 21st, 1556, putting first into the fire the hand which had signed his recantation.

Cranmer did not live at Aslockton, or pass any long periods here, after his fourteenth year. Besides his rather dubious "mound" there is little in the village to connect with him. The castle he would have known, for it was probably built in the twelfth century. Some thick walls, now part of a mission room, once belonged to an ancient chapel in existence in his day and which suffered desecration during the Reformation that he did so much to bring about. Otherwise there is little to see in Aslockton. The church of St. Thomas is an inappropriate structure built by Sir Arthur Blomfield in 1890. In 1893 an Anglo-Saxon warrior's grave was discovered in the barn field. There are three mud cottages surviving in Aslockton, about the only ones in the county.

The tiny village of Elton, with its inn on the crossroads, and church, manor house and few cottages set in a pleasant rectangular pattern, has even less to offer the visitor. The church of St. Michael is small and dates largely from a mid-Victorian restoration.

The centre piece of this Nottinghamshire part of the Vale of Belvoir is the little town of Bingham, an attractive place, built round three parallel streets, of which the centre one is the main road; motorists and passers-by are invitingly welcomed by a good pub called the Chesterfield Arms, which is approached through a drive gaily and, I think, fairly recently planted with roses. The centre of the town, the market-place, is dominated by a rather dreadful market cross of 1860, an octagonal affair, Gothic of a sort, with a lantern, which was put up by the friends and neighbours of someone called John Hassell of Shelford; and they saw fit to give him a strange and rather ambiguous epitaph: "To be Beloved is better than all Bargains." The church of All Saints is a large, rather dark, church, made impressive by the way it is lighted by the small lancet window at the west end set deep in the great thickness of the wall. It has a strong broad steeple with pairs of corner buttresses and an extra buttress in the middle of each side. The church is battlemented, and at the west end, instead of pinnacles, has two figures of bishops, recarved since medieval times. A broad, lowish spire with three tiers of windows gives a finish to the steeple. Buried in the church is Thomas de Rempstone (of a family which came from the place of that name higher up in the county), who helped to put King Henry IV on the throne and on whom was based the character in Shakespeare's *Richard II* who was misnamed Henry de Rempstone. The remains of engraved portraits to be seen on the flagstones of the chancel are said to be those of him and his wife. A badly preserved cross-legged knight of the first part of the fourteenth century is supposed to be a Sir Richard de Bingham. A more recent carving, with a more detailed and reliable history, but which perhaps emphasizes the continuity of the parish church as the repository of local sculpture, is an oak carving about eighteen inches high of an old lady sitting under an elaborate Gothic canopy of carved wood. She is wearing a bonnet and shawl and carries a stick and a large fish-basket; she was Ann Harrison, who lived just short of a hundred years, from 1829 to 1928, and gave the church a large share of what money she gained by going round with her basket of fish; her old arm-chair has also found a place in the church.

It is easy enough to guess that the road which you strike a little west of Bingham and which heads north-eastwards to Newark, is a Roman road. Its straightness—and the bit that covers seven or eight miles to the north of Bingham is as straight as any—tells you that at once. But it is perhaps worth pausing, for a moment, before proceeding along it to enquire its original purpose. All Roman roads were military roads, but the Fosse Way—so called from the fosse or ditch dug on either side of it to keep it drained and dry—differed from the majority of the other Roman roads in Britain in that it went across the line of the Roman advance through the island from the south-east corner and not on its axis. The building of the Fosse Way dates from the years immediately following the decision of the Emperor Claudius, in A.D. 43, to undertake the invasion of Britain. The southern part of the island, in the period that separated the arrival of the Claudian army from the armed reconnaissance of Julius Caesar nearly a century earlier, had become partly Romanized. Britain was no longer the outlandish place on the edge of civilization to which Julius Caesar had come. Already, under the ruling Belgic princes, gold and silver coins in imitation of Romano-Gaulish models were being struck in British mints. Colonies of Latin-speaking traders were settled in various towns and British exports of corn, minerals and slaves were bringing back wine, glass and amber from the Continent. The rulers of Britain spoke and wrote Latin; they drank Italian wine out of Italian or Gaulish glass-ware. The original of Shakespeare's Cymbeline (who reigned from A.D. 5 to after 40—to the very verge of the Claudian invasion) may well have been dressed in clothes of linen, silk and wool, imported perhaps from lands as distant as India. The invasion came when it did because, while the wealth of Britain was increasing, the disunion which followed Cymbeline's death removed the major obstacle to Roman conquest. Historians suggest that one can regard the activities of the Roman legions under Aulus Plautius in Britain in A.D. 43 rather as that of the liberators of the relatively sophisticated and cosmopolitan people of south-east Britain from the rule of unpopular chieftains than as the foreign conquerors of a native population. Though certain of Cymbeline's sons—Caractacus among them—resisted the Roman advance from the main landing at Richborough in Kent, at least one other had already appealed to Rome for help in the years preceding the invasion. The Emperor Claudius himself came to

The ruins of Newark Castle

the island shortly after the initial landing. He only spent a fortnight here, but in that time received the submission of sixteen kings. Thus began an occupation which was to last for 360 years—a period, as has been pointed out, as long as that which now separates us from the coming of the Spanish Armada. . . .

I have inflicted this history on you because I feel one cannot stand upon the stretch of Fosse Way—even though, at Saxondale, one's mind may be distracted by the modernity of the airfield— without being interested in knowing that it formed not only a road but a frontier, that it was built by Aulus Plautius' immediate successor in A.D. 47, at a moment when, the south-east conquered, attention was being directed to the fiercer people beyond. The line of the Fosse Way, beginning at Seaton on the Devon coast and then running north-east in an almost straight line to Bath (Aquae Sulis), Cirencester (Corinium), across the line of Watling Street near Rugby to Leicester (Ratae), through Newark to Lincoln (Lindum), was constructed through the territory of tribes who were already allies of the Romans. Beyond this line came the threat from the Welsh hills and the Pennines, from tribes alien in outlook and culture from the peoples of the south-east. So, standing on the Nottinghamshire section of this road, it is quite easy to visualize, particularly with the great obstacle of the Trent flowing so close, that this was the temporary edge of the whole Roman Empire, the edge of the civilized world. The Nottinghamshire stretch of the road, across the frontier, is specially privileged because there lies beside the road here the most substantial remains surviving of a frontier fort.

The site of the Roman village station of Margidunum, in the Barrow Fields south of East Bridgford, are conspicuous in a county curiously poor in both prehistoric and Roman monuments. The site was excavated during the 1930's by Dr. Felix Oswald. The place was older than the Romans. Relics unearthed by Dr. Oswald and deposited with the university of Nottingham show that it was important in both the Stone and the Bronze Ages. It also reflects, however, the flow of history in Roman times, for the rhomboidal area, of seven or eight acres extent, was encircled, presumably at the time the Fosse Way was being constructed under the direction of the legion which got to Lincoln in about A.D. 46, with a girdle of six ditches and an earth and timber rampart. As the Roman advances proceeded (within forty years of the Claudian conquest the legionaries had reached the extremities of both Wales and Scotland) these fortifications ceased to be useful and began to fall into

Southwell Minster from the east. The tower and the polygonal Chapter House

decay. However, when, in the fourth century, with Rome herself threatened by the final onslaughts of the Goths and Huns and Roman power in Britain running dry, the Roman control over the country, always weakly held and latterly with inferior troops, withdrew southward, a stone rampart eighteen feet high was constructed round the old fort. The history of the Roman withdrawal is confused, and its details obscure, but it may well be that the Fosse Way, or sections of it, became once again a frontier; certain that Margidunum was important again in that last phase. Portions of the stone rampart survived into the nineteenth century, but one cannot honestly say that there is much to look at at Margidunum to-day. So, returning to more familiar, and more visible periods, shall we move up the road into East Bridgford, which fills in the space, as it were, between the line of the Fosse Way and the bed of the Trent? Here again excavations have given a further quality of uniqueness to this little area of the county. For diggings under and around the church of St. Peter have brought to light the foundations of a cross-shaped Saxon church, the only positive evidence of Saxon architecture in the whole county. (The only other Saxon possibilities, even, are some work in the otherwise completely Early Norman tower and in a small window, of the church at Carleton-in-Lindrick; and certain remains that were uncovered in 1906 in the church tower at Plumtree.) The Saxon church was succeeded by a Norman one and of this the chancel still stands. The rest of the church is a distressing muddle, dating variously from the fourteenth, fifteenth and eighteenth centuries, especially from 1778 when the tower was rebuilt. Among the odds and ends in the church a small fragment of a Saxon shaft with interlaced decoration belongs to the period of the earliest church and the discreet late-Georgian pulpit to the time of later rebuilding. A tomb in the church gives hints of some local history. The monument of John Hacker, who died in 1616, and his wife, consists of the pair kneeling and looking at each other across a praying desk, with their children kneeling in a horizontal strip below. The Hackers lived from the end of the sixteenth century at the Old Hall which survives, with later additions and alterations. The Hackers, in the Civil War, were all Royalists except one, Francis Hacker (who married Isabella, the daughter of Gabriel Brunts of East Bridgford, whose tomb is also in the church). Francis Hacker was given custody of the King during his trial and was one of the people to whom the King's death warrant was addressed. Perhaps being an addressee might not be thought quite so bad in Royalist eyes as being one of the fifty-nine miscellaneous people who signed the warrant. After all, there were some of them, like Richard Ingoldsby, who managed to work their passage back to the favour of Charles II in spite of their signatures on his father's death warrant. But Francis Hacker led the procession of the King to the scaffold. He himself obviously thought that damning enough and on October 19th, 1660, five months after the restoration of Charles II, Hacker hanged himself. He is buried in St. Nicholas Cole Abbey in London. Francis Hacker's brother Thomas was killed in a skirmish at Colston Bassett against a Parliamentarian troop which included Francis Hacker. Another brother, Roland, lost his right arm in the defence of Newark but lived to buy back the East Bridgford estates of the family after their confiscation following Francis Hacker's death. Roland Hacker died in 1674. Fortunately for East Bridgford the road which leads to the bridge over the Trent here lies away, a little, to the south so that the pleasant village with its plentiful trees and its Georgian houses and cottages is left quiet and unencumbered by traffic. However, the main village street continues out to the river and joins up with the other road by the bridge. Just on the other side of the river there is an ugly white building, where boats can be hired, which serves excellent teas in a room overlooking the river, the bridge and the boats. The house is itself built on what seems to have been either the abortive beginning of another bridge or, more likely, the remains of an old one that has been replaced higher up the river. There is a similar portion of the bridge on the other side of the water.

What I propose to do now is to head up the Fosse Way to Newark, but, without straying over the Trent to the left or over the little River Devon to the right, to see if there are villages which demand our attention on either side of the road. Car Colston certainly does; it is an exceptionally charming village, with a large village green and pleasant houses and cottages. One specially worth looking at is an early eighteenth-century house with a shell-hooded doorway. (Incidentally, since it is the first time we have encountered it, note the word " Car ": particularly up in the north of the county they speak of swampy low-lying places as " car-land ".) Though the hall at Car Colston is neo-Elizabethan, there survive, at the northern end of the village, remains of a good-sized brick manor house of the seventeenth century, with contemporary panelling and a plaster overmantel decorated with cupids and fruit, known as Brunsell Hall. Dr. Brunsell, who lived there, was reputed to be a relation of Sir Christopher Wren. Perhaps he was; but what is certain in Car

Colston, and which gives it very great local fame, is that the county's first historian, Robert Thoroton, lived here, probably in a farm-house that survives just beyond the church, then called Moryn Hall. Thoroton's great work, *Antiquities of Nottinghamshire*, was published in 1677, the year before he died. Thoroton is buried in the churchyard of Car Colston's handsome church of St. Mary in his own very special stone coffin.

Thoroton was born just up the road at the almost adjoining village of Screveton; this was in 1623. The church here, dedicated to St. Wilfrid, in a charming green setting, has a fifteenth-century tower which is said to have been altered at a time when very little church building, or even restoring, was being done in the Elizabethan age. The most notable object in the church is the tomb of Sir Richard Whalley, of a family which lived at Kirketon Hall in the village, a house whose site is now partially occupied by the present rectory which is half-timbered and has the date, 1607, on a beam. Richard Whalley's tomb, originally in the chancel but now under the tower, shows him recumbent, in alabaster, in armour, with his long beard, and with his feet resting (a rebus) on whales. His three wives and his twenty-five children are ranged in three panels against the back wall. Richard Whalley, who died in 1583, was a courtier of Henry VIII; he played a leading part, a notorious part if you like, in the dissolution of the monasteries; we shall encounter his name again in the Dukeries, for as payment for his services he received the lands and buildings of Welbeck Abbey. However, he soon had to sell them in order to pay the fines imposed on him as a result of the parts he had played in the intrigues of the Protector Somerset, who was executed in 1552; hence, presumably, his return to the modest family property at Screveton and the presence of his tomb in its church. It is fascinating, but pointless, to wonder what would have been the history of Welbeck if this disaster had not overtaken Sir Richard Whalley. It was a family that was repeatedly involved in the most dangerous episodes in the country's political history, and we have, at Screveton, almost a repetition of the Hackers' story at East Bridgford. Edward Whalley, a century later than Sir Richard, was a cousin of Oliver Cromwell. Naturally he was a Roundhead. It fell to him to be the man who carried away " that bauble ", the mace, at the dissolution of the Long Parliament. He, at an earlier stage than Francis Hacker, had charge of the person of King Charles after his capture in 1647 and during his four months' confinement at Holdenby House in Northamptonshire. The end of Edward Whalley's story is, again, a version of Hacker's. After the Restoration he was stripped of his estates, but instead of suicide he chose flight. He went to America and died there.

A road whose position, between and parallel to a couple of tributaries of the River Devon, called Back Dyke and Car Dyke, reminds us that we are still in the southern Car lands, takes us up through Hawksworth to Sibthorpe. You can recognize Hawksworth because—quite a rarity in the county—its church has a brick tower. This tower is a survival of an earlier period than the rebuilding of the church in 1851. Over a doorway is an elaborate but clumsy piece of Norman carving of a cross, two figures and an inscription running over the lintel which tells of the founders of what was presumably the first Norman church— *Gauterus et uxor eius Cecilina fecerunt facere ecclesiam istam.* At Sibthorpe, in the church of St. Peter—which is the remains of a larger church, considerably altered in the eighteenth century —we encounter the first of those Easter sepulchres whose fame Nottinghamshire shares with adjoining Lincolnshire and which need a word of explanation. The Sibthorpe sepulchre is not so well known, so elaborate or so excellent as that at Hawton, but is of the same kind and they may as well be discussed genetically here.

What you see at Sibthorpe are the carved figures of sleeping soldiers in a niche and above it, in a tall, decorated canopy, the figure of Christ with two angels. These sepulchres are the remains of the elaborate dramatized service which used to be performed— that is the only word—in our churches on Easter morning. The term Easter sepulchre can be used for anything from a simple unadorned niche in the north wall of a church chancel to the elaborate Nottinghamshire structures. They provided each year the stage setting for the commemoration of the resurrection, whose story was told permanently in stone in the carvings with which the structure was adorned. On Good Friday the crucifix used to be removed from the high altar and placed within the niche of the sepulchre; from that time until Easter morning the sepulchre was attended by watchers, who were sometimes dressed up to impersonate Pilate's soldiers. When the third lesson of the Easter morning service had been read three priests approached the sepulchre swinging censers and wearing on their heads those square pieces of white linen, known as amices, which made them look like women. Then the priests, standing before the sepulchre, would intone the scriptural dialogue between the three women and the angel. It is worth noting that in these Nottinghamshire sepulchres, of the thirteenth and fourteenth centuries, the soldiers on guard over the tomb are represented as in a deep sleep while the resurrection takes place. In later representations of the event the soldiers are sometimes seen as starting up in amazement as the figure of Christ leaves the tomb. At Sibthorpe they sleep soundly. Also worth looking at in Sibthorpe church is a first-class alabaster tomb of the Elizabethan, Edward Burnell, which is dated "made anno domini 1590". The tomb, which is decorated with good carvings of shields, wreaths and putti, was erected by Edward Burnell's widow, Barbara. She was the third of the three wives represented on the tomb of Richard Whalley at Screveton and she was responsible for putting up that tomb too. An eminent eighteenth-century divine was a native of Sibthorpe —Thomas Secker, who was the Archbishop of Canterbury who officiated at the coronation of King George III in 1760.

It is time we made our way back to the Fosse Way; and we can do so by going through the village of Flintham, where hall and church lie side by side at the end of the village. The hall dates from the last years of the eighteenth century and is a square white-washed building with some additions made by one of the lesser-known bearers of the great architectural name of Wyatt, in 1829. He, Lewis Wyatt, also carried out the enlargement of Stoke Hall at East Stoke, just the other side of the Fosse Way. Flintham Hall had added to it, in the 1850's, a rather unseemly tower, a tall brick palm house with a semicircular glass roof and some decoration to the east, south and west fronts. The architect of these last works was apparently one Thomas Hine of Nottingham. St. Augustine's church dates in its present form from 1828.

A sudden rise in the ground, which goes by the name of Trent Hills, gives character to the stretch of country that separates the Fosse Way and the Trent between the uneventful villages of Kneeton and East Stoke.

We are in the Darwin country, and at Elston, in the church, otherwise uninteresting, there are a number of monuments to the Darwins who lived at Elston Hall. The most attractive are those to three Darwin children who died at the ages of thirteen, fourteen and fifteen in the years 1835-38. Elston Hall, a long grey house, with an early eighteenth-century centre and later additions, was the home of the Darwins from the seventeenth century, when a William Darwin moved here from Lincolnshire. The family's scientific interests seem to have manifested themselves first in William's son Robert. Robert Darwin had two sons one of whom, another Robert, was the author of an eighteenth-century *Principia Botanica*; and the other the famous Erasmus Darwin, grandfather of the still greater Charles Darwin, author of the *Origin of Species*.

Erasmus Darwin was born at Elston Hall on December 12th, 1731. Would he, one wonders, be remembered at all now if he had not been the grandfather of one of the greatest of Victorians? Certainly one cannot take him seriously as a poet, though the science which he combined and incorporated in his verse appears to have been original and to some degree pioneering. He seems to have been well versed in physics, with a special aptitude for the choice and demonstration of natural analogies; as well as being an enthusiastic botanist, some of his ideas on evolution foreshadowed the work of his grandson. Unfortunately it was the very genuineness of his scientific knowledge and interest which robs his verse of its quality. His subjects just were not suitable to the eighteenth-century couplet which he wielded in a painfully artificial and stilted way. *The Botanic Garden* and, above all, *The Loves of the Plants* are literally ludicrous; they provoke laughter and ridicule and have brought many parodies upon themselves, including a famous one by Canning. It is only for reasons unconnected with poetry that anybody, nowadays, hacks their way through the pomposities of *The Loves of the Plants*— as, for instance, to find those lines in which Darwin predicted the development of steam locomotion and foresaw the aeroplane, albeit powered by steam:

> Soon shall thy arm, Unconquered Steam, afar
> Drag the slow barge or drive the rapid car;
> Or on wide waving wings expanded there
> The flying chariot through the fields of air.

Erasmus Darwin, being the second son, did not, after his education at St. John's College, Cambridge, and at Edinburgh University, where he took his degree in medicine, live at Elston Hall. He settled as a doctor at Lichfield and from there won a high professional reputation. At one stage he was offered the appointment of physician to King George III, but he declined it. He was a man, for his times, of unusually temperate habits, the advantages of which he was for ever pointing out to anyone he came into contact with; by his temperance propaganda he rendered good service to the poor people of Lichfield. Whatever we may think of old Dr. Darwin's didactic poetry now it did not lack admirers in his own century. William Cowper called his verses "strong, learned and sweet"; and Horace Walpole called them at different times "sublime", "charming", "enchanting", "gorgeous", "beautiful" and "most poetic"—"the *Loves of the Plants*", he said, was "the most delicious poem upon earth: I defy you to discover three bad verses in the whole stack ". The decline of Darwin's reputation as a poet began with the equivalent rise of romanticism with Coleridge and Wordsworth, and the famous parody called *The Loves of Triangles*, the work of Canning, Frere and Ellis appeared in the famous Tory paper *The Anti-Jacobin* in the year 1798. I fancy that if we could encounter Dr. Darwin somewhere on the Fosse Way we should find it an awe-inspiring and perhaps rather exhausting experience; he would walk us fast, because he seems to have been to the end of his life an athletic sort of person; he would tell us a great deal about the virtues of temperance; and if, as he might well do, as we walked up the road from Elston Hall to East Stoke, he quoted long passages to us we should find that we listened, as well as to learned information on scientific subjects, to the doings of sylphs and nereids, various gnomes and Spenserian personifications of abstract subjects. If he took us for a tour of the immediate neighbourhood of Elston he would have to show us, as well as the church of All Saints, whose tall, slim thirteenth-century tower is all that now remains of the church of his day, a chapel out in the fields towards Stoke Field, where some Norman masonry and fourteenth-century windows were, of course, there then. But the interior as we now see it, with a gallery and deal box-pews, hat pegs along the walls, commodious squire's pew, pulpit and reader's desk, dates from after Erasmus Darwin's time. It is the fitting of a rather impecunious church of Regency times and is almost untouched. Opposite the village church—as opposed to the chapel—Darwin might show us, finally, the almshouses that were built when he was thirteen.

We should have to take leave of Darwin as we got up to the crossroads at East Stoke, because this is no longer, historically, Darwin territory. Here, set among trees north-west of the little village, are hall and church side by side. The house is a modest brick building of Elizabethan date that was much enlarged in 1821 by the Lewis Wyatt already mentioned. Further extensive alterations were made about a quarter of a century ago. The church is small and mostly seventeenth century, with round-headed windows. Stoke Hall was bought, in the mid-eighteenth century, by the Nottingham banker, Abel Smith (the fine set of plate in the church of 1769, was given by the Smiths) and remained until quite recently the home of descendants of the Smiths, the families of Bromley and Pauncefote. In the church is buried a diplomat who became the first Lord Pauncefote. After a legal career during which, in 1865, he was Attorney General, and later Chief Justice of the Leeward Islands, he was appointed British Minister in Washington and, in 1893, became the first British Ambassador to the United States. Pauncefote negotiated a general arbitration treaty between Great Britain and the United States and his diplomatic ability did much to further cordial relations between the two countries. He died in 1902.

East Stoke is a little place, but its position on Fosse Way at a crossroads which led to a crossing over the Trent close at hand, by ferry or by bridge at different dates, has given it a long and varied history. In Roman times a settlement, civil, probably, rather than military, called Ad Pontem, lay half a mile north of the village. There was a medieval village, clustering round the church and now marked only by mounds, while the modern village has moved on to the road. It was East Stoke beside the Trent (and not, as you might gather from many history books, at Stoke-on-Trent in Staffordshire) that the defeat of the Yorkists took place during the uprising against King Henry VII in 1487 in which the impostor, Lambert Simnel, was put forward in the pretence of being Earl of Warwick. An armed force from Ireland (where Lambert Simnel was "crowned" in Dublin Cathedral) had landed in Lancashire and met the Royal army near East Stoke on June 16th, 1487. The Royalists were victorious and both Lambert Simnel and the Oxford priest, Richard Symonds, whose tool in the uprising Simnel had been, were taken prisoner. Lambert Simnel was contemptuously pardoned by Henry VII and, tradition says, was given a job in the royal kitchens. In the battle, the Yorkists were driven down from the crossroads to the steep track beyond the hall and the church on the way to Fiskerton Ferry which is still called Red Gutter, and large numbers of their dead were buried beside the Fosse Way in what are known as Dead Man's Fields.

159

CHAPTER VI

NEWARK AND SOUTHWELL

WE are fast approaching Newark now; but a few places deserve mention before we arrive. The only village to the left, between the Fosse Way and the Trent, is the sizeable place called Farndon, where there are some pleasant Georgian brick houses and a very much restored church with some early Norman herringbone masonry. On the other side of the Fosse Way there is Thorpe, a little place with a church rebuilt in 1873; and two other villages whose churches contain sculpture of special interest, in one case known far beyond the borders of the county. First, Cotham: there is not much here besides the church and about even it, as a building, not much to comment on, as it was much altered, and considerably reduced in size, in both the eighteenth and nineteenth centuries; but the church contains some monuments of the family of Markham, who used to live at the now-vanished hall. Far the most striking of these is the wall tablet to Ann Markham, who died on 17th November, 1601. She, as her inscription tells us, was the daughter of John Warburton of Cheshire, knight, and wife to Robert Markham of Cotham. She is shown in relief kneeling under a curious thing like a tent tied with a bow at the top, with her three sons and her four daughters kneeling in front and behind her. The frame which surrounds the relief is a fine example of quite early English Renaissance classicism. It consists of fluted Corinthian columns and a pediment, very correct, very elegant and well carried out. At Hawton there is much more to see. The chancel of the church of All Saints at Hawton is regarded as one of the most notable pieces of architecture in the county. It was built by Sir Robert de Compton, who died in 1330. (No trace remains of the home of the Comptons and, later, of the Molyneux, both of whom contributed greatly to the church.) Sir Robert de Compton is buried in his chancel which is lit by large windows with elaborate and flowing tracery. The founder's tomb is in a recess on the north side of the chancel and beside it is the famous Easter sepulchre, the best Nottinghamshire example of these rare church features, whose origin and function have already been described.

The Hawton sepulchre is infinitely richer in its carving and general effect than that at Sibthorpe; indeed its work can be compared only with that of the screen in Southwell Minster, which, it is likely, was made by the same craftsman. The sepulchre is divided into three parts, with a main canopy separated by knobbly pinnacles from side pieces containing small ogee arches surmounted by diagonal struts, like flying buttresses in relief. Running the whole length of the sepulchre is the niche where the recumbent image of Christ was placed at the Easter celebrations. The sleeping soldiers, four of them, are in relief at the foot of the sepulchre. The badly mutilated scene, also in relief, of the Ascension of Christ, occupies the back wall of the main niche. Above and around the canopy the Apostles are shown gazing upwards at Christ. Only His feet appear through the topmost carving. The whole monument is close-packed with decoration —flowers, rosettes, leaves and crockets against an elaborately patterned background. What gives an especially sumptuous appearance to the chancel is that, facing the sepulchre, on the south side, the three seats for the priests are again a mass of patterned decoration with more leaves, figures and playful capitals —a pelican and two boys picking grapes. The Compton legacy to Hawton is something to be remembered and revisited. As imposing, in a different way, is the west tower of the church that was built in 1482 by Sir Thomas Molyneux of Hawton; it has no fewer than eight pinnacles. How close we are to Newark is indicated by the fact that at Hawton can be seen an earthwork, the largest in the county, which provided the south-west end of the defences of Newark in the Civil War. It consists of a rectangular mound with projecting bastions and a deep moat. Unlike so many of its kind it is clearly defined and easy to visualize as a defensive work.

Much of the country to the south-east of Hawton, between the River Devon and the county boundary, has provided space for an airfield. At the top of this area is the largish village of Balderton now, more or less, a suburb of Newark. The thin sharp spire, of the same shape as Newark's own famous needle, surmounts a rather dark church whose most interesting feature is the Norman doorway which now forms the entrance to the porch. This has a pattern of beakheads—that fascinating but, if you look at it for long, rather grim and unpleasant Norman motif—all round the arch and borders of decorated coronets and scolloped capitals outside them. The church contains a number of interesting, but minor pieces of medieval sculpture and some scraps of earlyish stained glass. Through Balderton runs the road which connects

Newark with Grantham and which bears the number A1. A mile or so up through New Balderton and we arrive in Newark itself.

I could imagine that if you took visitors from the Continent straight to Newark from their arrival, shall we say at Dover, without letting them find it as, presumably, most do find it, after visits to places still more celebrated, and then were to send them away back to their homes, they would carry away from their day or two in this single township quite a good picture of an English "historic" town. For there is a bit of everything at Newark and I cannot think of any passage in England's story which cannot be connected with some corner of the place. Saxon, Medieval, Tudor, Stuart, Georgian, Victorian; no epoch passed Newark by and there is none but that has left its mark on this varied and fascinating town.

It seems generally agreed that a place on this site, or perhaps on the River Trent itself, taking a slightly different course from now and not, as at present, on the canalized River Devon, must have existed in Roman times. But no authentic record of its history exists until Anglo-Saxon times. There are two possible interpretations of its name—New Work—either that its newness refers simply to new fortifications of a river ford as against older, Roman, fords either at the bridge of Ad Pontem (East Stoke) or at Margidunum; alternatively the newness may refer to the reconstruction of the walls of Newark after its destruction by the Danes during the reign of Edward the Confessor, 1042-66. The Danes sacked the town, slew its defenders and carried out a systematic destruction of its fortifications. The name of "the key of the north" was given to Newark very early, by the Saxons when they rebuilt it after this destruction by the Northmen. Communications have been its making, and not only its position on and between rivers. In Roman times the main road towards the northern frontiers of Britain had gone by way of Lincoln, through Littleborough to Doncaster. When this was given up a route was developed on the gravel spit approaching the Trent and this, in time, became the Great North Road. In medieval times and up to the Elizabethan age Newark was almost as large as Nottingham. While Newark had about 2,000 inhabitants in 1377 and 3,000 in 1600, Nottingham had 3,000 at the first date and only 500 more at the second. The figures crept away from each other steadily in subsequent centuries and now stand at about 23,000 for Newark and for Nottingham about 300,000.

For the earlier part of Newark's history there remain two buildings, one perfect and one a ruin which help to underline these bare figures of the city's growth. One is the church and the other the castle. The castle was the expression of the power and importance, in the Middle Ages, of Newark's Lord of the Manor, who, with only brief interruptions, was the Bishop of Lincoln. The castle was his residence and fortress and his church was Lincoln Cathedral. St. Mary's, Newark, on the other hand, was the church of the town, which became rich because of the individual wealth of its wool merchants, who acted as middlemen between the sheep breeders of the Midlands and the Flemish clothiers. Though there is nothing now to be seen of the masonry of his time, Newark Castle was almost entirely reconstructed, if not built initially, in 1125, by Alexander, Bishop of Lincoln, who was called "the Magnificent" because of his "vast pomp, boldness and audacity". It was Alexander who completed the superb west front of Lincoln Cathedral, and he also built castles at Sleaford and at Banbury. The earliest surviving section of Newark Castle, its north gateway, the largest and most elaborate of the sort in the country, together with the chapel on the first floor, dates from the brief period, after 1139, during which it was surrendered to the Crown. So were a number of other castles that had been erected by prelates during the disturbed part of the reign of King Stephen. These architectural survivals were probably carried out when the castle was the residence of Henry II's illegitimate son, Geoffrey Plantagenet, Bishop of Lincoln. Other twelfth-century remains are the tower at the south-west corner of the building and the eight-bayed crypt which lies below ground level under part of the west wing. Newark Castle was often the residence of King John both before and after he came to the throne. During the struggle which culminated in the granting of Magna Carta in 1215 Newark Castle was seized by the barons. However, after 1215, it was the King's again and was available for him the very next year, 1216, to become the scene of his death. In his final journeyings through England he had crossed the Wash from Norfolk into Lincolnshire and had lost his baggage train, with the crown of England and the great treasure and costly equipment which accompanied a medieval monarch on any journey, in the treacherous sands covered by advancing tide. Many of his troops had been drowned, and he himself had barely escaped with his life. The first night after the disaster was passed at the abbey of Swineshead in Lincolnshire. In an attempt to console himself John settled down to an evening of copious feasting which, followed by peaches washed down with wine and fresh cider, brought on a dysentery which was too much for the constitution of a weakened and shaken man. He travelled the next day on his palfrey to Sleaford Castle; from there, however, too ill to ride, he was borne on a litter to Newark Castle. There, on the night of 18th October, 1216, John died. There is no need to take too seriously any local indication of precisely the chamber in which John breathed his last.

During the next few centuries the castle continued important and was repeatedly altered and added to. The surviving wall of the west wing and its hexagonal north-western and central towers belong to the later thirteenth century. During the Wars of the Roses, in the second half of the fifteenth century, the castle was the scene of several martial incidents. On one occasion Edward IV was there with his army and at least twice the Lancastrians were in the town. All the same, some of the more civilized and gentler structural alterations were done after the beginning of the Wars of the Roses. The Bishop of Rotherham, for instance, between 1470 and 1480, heightened and shortened the hall and added the attractive oriel window. During Tudor times, though it was honoured with a visit by Cardinal Wolsey, who stayed here on his way to Southwell, the castle became dilapidated. It had reverted to the Crown in 1547 and in 1581 it was described as "in great decay and ruin". A few years later the Earl of Rutland, who then owned it, had it put back into repair and built the square-headed windows on the river front. Newark Castle's moment of greatest fame was, of course, still to come. When the Civil War began the townspeople of Newark declared in favour of the King and the old castle was once again, and for the last time, fortified. The King himself was at Newark in 1642 about a month before the raising of his standard at Nottingham. It was, of course, a progaganda visit and what he is reported to have said to the populace has in it many of the elements of flattery: "I go to other places to confirm and undeceive my subjects, but I am come here only to thank and encourage you." The events of the succeeding weeks were vital to the part that the county was to play during the war. The King was once more in the county and on July 21st arrived in Nottingham with eight hundred horse. Both King and town were well aware of the strains existing in this already predominently Parliamentarian place. The King was welcomed by the corporation in a formal manner though the mayor fully expected to receive a rebuff. The King, however, accepted the mace from the mayor; but it was noticed that he did not give him his hand to kiss. The King remained several days. In the first week of August Henry Pierrepont, Lord Newark, arrived in Nottingham with Sir John Digby of Mansfield Wood-house and tried to gain possession of the magazine in the castle which held the county's supplies of gunpowder. They were resisted by Colonel Hutchinson who threatened bloodshed. Lord Newark withdrew; but the incident had the effect of making quite clear that Hutchinson was going to be the centre of hostility to the King.

The early seizure by the Royalists of Newark Castle was a matter of considerable strategic importance for the war. It both commanded the lowest bridge over the Trent and stood on the main road from the south; it was the funnel through which any invasion from the north would have to pass. It remained through-out the Civil War the single large-scale Royalist fortress in a neighbourhood otherwise dominated by the Roundheads centred on Nottingham Castle. It withstood three separate sieges and underwent horrors of famine, disease and slaughter.

By a curious chance King Charles was once again in the immedi-ate vicinity when the Civil War ended, just as he had been at its outset. The action which ended the first, and main, Civil War took place on 6th May, 1646. Just previously, as the Roundheads finally closed in on the Royalist stronghold at Oxford, the King had escaped, dressed as a servant. He reached the camp of the Scots army—whose long billeting on the countryside had been very unpopular in Nottinghamshire—under Alexander Leslie, first Earl of Leven, at Southwell. He surrendered himself to the Scots and gave orders that Newark should at last surrender. Among those Nottinghamshire landowners who also surrendered their estates after the fall of Newark were Lord Bellasis, the Governor of the castle, and his son; Lord Chaworth; Lord Lexing-ton; and Sir Richard Byron.

The fall of Newark in 1646 was all but the end of the Civil War for the county. Newark Castle was destroyed after its sur-render and has remained ever since an interesting and picturesque ruin. The high walls and towers of what must have been an exceedingly imposing building in five storeys, are now no more than a shell with gardens and flower-beds within as well as out-side the castle. Besides certain architectural features already mentioned, the shape of the great hall can be visualized going through the ground floor and the first floor. It must have been about 130 feet long and 22 feet wide and its window openings are still there, but not their tracery. The castle, fortunately for the tourist, is not without two features considered necessary to a castle of any date. The north-west tower contains cannons, cannon balls and other objects connected with the defence of the castle; while in the thickness of the north wall is the entrance to the dungeons. One of these is pointed out with special awe. It is a chamber of beehive shape, ten feet in diameter and seventeen deep, sunk low in the rock. The best view of the castle is from the promenade along the river's edge.

But there are a multitude of other things to look at in Newark besides the castle. Close at hand, just at the end of the bridge and opposite the castle, is a building whose appearance seems remote both from its date and its history; this is the Ossington Coffee Tavern or Coffee Palace, an example of late Victorian romantic Tudor revivalism. It is a violently picturesque red cum black-and-white affair, carefully non-symmetrical, its upper floors jutting—and then re-jutting with oriel windows—over an arcade. The oriel windows, heavily leaded, repeated over and over again, comprise the whole of the exterior of the first floor. Above are gables and Tudor chimneys and latticed dormer windows. It is a highly romantic reconstruction of Merrie England; and it is interesting that in their design for it the well-known firm of London architects, Ernest George and Peto, peopled the scene with quite un-Victorian figures, obviously ghosts from a simpler, if perhaps merrier, age. But the purpose of the building was not merry in the generally accepted sense, in spite of the fact that an armorial inn sign under a coronet hung on a handsome wrought-iron bracket against the wall of the tavern and that a further sign, on an ornate post of its own, advertised skittles. I have examined the drawing carefully, but I cannot be sure in my own mind whether, under the name "The Ossington", the sign goes on to announce "Good *beds*, etc." or "Good *beer*, etc.". If it is the latter then Messrs. Ernest George and Peto were playing an un-seemly joke (the careful illegibility of the last two letters, imply-ing deliberate equivocation, suggests that it may be so) on the noble lady who commissioned the work. She was Viscountess Ossington, daughter of the fourth Duke of Portland, and her pur-pose in putting up this expensive structure was "the earnest desire to promote the cause of temperance" and to uphold the—in the eighties—not particularly popular banner of coffee. What is so curious about the Ossington Coffee Tavern is that although designed with a precisely opposite intention it incorporates, in advance, as it were, all the details of ye oldeishness and sham medievalism associated with a style of public house design which it so long anticipated—the "Brewer's Tudor" of the 1920's. The original purposes of the Coffee Tavern (which cost, in the eighties, £20,000, which must signify something like £100,000 now) does not seem to have survived the Victorian age, for the Ossington Coffee Tavern is now a hotel; though, so far as I knew, not licensed.

The Norman nave of Southwell Minster, early twelfth century

Castle Gate, the street at one end of which the Ossington Coffee Tavern and the castle stand, contains a number of admirable Georgian brick houses, in some cases close beside, or facing, earlier buildings of half-timbering.

A building opposite the end of Stodman Street, the Corn Exchange, is worth a glance for its confident and lively baroque quality at a date, 1847, generally inimical to the manner. The architect was Dewsbury and the large Italianate sculpture is by J. Bell. (At the entrance to Stodman Street, incidentally, is the house where the Governor of Newark Castle lived during the Civil War. It has three tiers of vaulted timbering overlooking the street and it is recorded that, during the Governor's occupation at the time of the siege, Prince Rupert stayed in the house after his quarrel with the King, on October 19th, 1645.)

The exciting and still busy market-place reminds us, with the size and proliferation of its inns, of the importance of Newark as a stopping place on the Great North Road. Newark is a great place for inns and many of them are clustered round the market-place, so let us consider them first. By far the oldest, though it is not a hotel now but a drapers' shop called Bainbridge, is the White Hart Inn, one of the most important examples of four-teenth-century, timber-framed, domestic architecture in England. Its ground floor is quite modern, but the two upper storeys which form, at one end, an archway which provides one of the entrances to the market-place, are worth careful study. The front consists of two sets of twenty-four upright posts placed close together and adorned with plaster figures of angels and saints. Windows, obviously altered since the house was built in, say, 1350, or so, lie between these two rows of functional decorations. On the same side, the south side, of the market-place are two big inns which still fulfil their functions. The Saracen's Head has been an inn since 1341. Charles I stayed there; and Sir Walter Scott, who often did the same, makes it Jeanie Deans' stopping place in his *Heart of Midlothian*.

The present Saracen's Head, like the Old Town Hall on the opposite side of the market-place, dates from the first decade of the eighteenth century. It is made of brick, with stone dressings and dormer windows in the roof. It stands on a plain colonnade of Tuscan columns. The hotel next door has the same colonnade or loggia in front of it but it was given adornments of rustication in the columns and windows around, and Palladian pediments to the main windows, in the mid-eighteenth century. This hotel is now called the Clinton Arms and was formerly the Kingston Arms. One of the most important hostelries in the Midlands, it

Leaves in the Chapter House at Southwell

had, in 1800, accommodation for ninety horses. It was here that Lord Byron stayed when he was supervising the publication of his first book of poems which was published anonymously in 1806 under the title of *Fugitive Pieces*. It was printed and published in Newark, as were both of his next books, *Poems on Various Occasions* and *Hours of Idleness*, each of which is dated 1807. The printers, S. and J. Ridge, had their business at the Bridge Street corner of the market-place. These books, especially the first, are now, of course, exceedingly scarce and valuable. It was also from a window of the Clinton Arms that W. E. Gladstone made one of his first public political speeches; the window was shattered when a stone was hurled at him by someone in the crowd below. At the Ram Inn near the castle George Eliot stayed in 1868 "enjoying some charming, quiet landscapes on the Trent". An inn which, so far as I know has not survived, is the Talbot Inn, which was the setting of what might have been an important event in the Civil War. After the first clash at Edgehill, the Royalist John Digby (who, with Lord Newark, had made an earlier attempt to seize the Nottingham magazine) summoned all the justices of Nottinghamshire, one December day in 1642, to the Talbot at Newark. Among those invited were Colonel Hutchinson and the Parliamentarian, Francis Pierrepont. Digby planned to seize them, take Nottingham and secure the county for the King. Colonel Hutchinson obviously got wind of the plot because his own action was to surround himself with a body of seven hundred men headed by his brother.

From inns to schools. In Appleton Gate, a pleasant spot which forms a kind of close behind the church, is the small sixteenth-century stone building of the old Grammar School. Not far off, to the south of the church, is the stuccoed front of the Mount School of 1838. The most celebrated name in Newark education is that of Magnus. The Magnus Grammar School dates from 1238, but as it was endowed about 1530 by Archdeacon Magnus, a friend of Cardinal Wolsey, it acquired and retained his name.

Among those who were educated at the Magnus Grammar School were several who attained fame in the wider world. For instance, the musician John Blow, who was eventually organist of Westminster Abbey, an appointment which he received at the age of nineteen in 1668. He had been born at the village of North Collingham, one of a pair on the edge of the county north of Newark. North Collingham contains a church with both Norman and Early English remains, the dull remnants of a village cross and some interesting timber-framed and brick houses of the sixteenth, seventeenth and eighteenth centuries. A celebrity of the eighteenth century, whose alleged schooling at Magnus Grammar School does not seem to be substantiated by his most recent biographer, is the eminent antiquary William Stukeley. Whether or no he was acquainted with Newark as a child he certainly got to know the town later, in the course of his archaeological travels through Eastern England, and his papers contain many references to Roman and other specimens found at Newark and places in the vicinity. Magnus Grammar School also claims credit for the education of one of the most celebrated of the critics and editors of the poet Alexander Pope—his contemporary and admirer, William Warburton, later Bishop of Gloucester.

The Magnus Grammar School, one part of which is now used as a museum and contains a collection of prints, paintings, books and coins concerned with the history of Newark, is by its position connected with the church. And it is time that we brought ourselves to do more than stand in awe of its tremendous spire.

The church of St. Mary Magdalen is one of the major parish churches of the country. If you were to take it out into a field and turn it on end you would discover that its spire was 30 feet longer than the length of the church—252 feet against 222. As it stands, close to the market-place, the tower and its octagon spire seem almost uncomfortably high and hardly suggest so close a relation with the body of the church. The lower part of the tower is Early English of the thirteenth century and the upper part, together with the needle-sharp spire with its four tiers of dormer windows—which form a landmark for miles around—is of the fourteenth century.

The general impression of the church is that of a Perpendicular building of the fifteenth century, but the great nave, although its details and general impression are of that period, dates from the time of the erection of a great church, a frequent event in towns like these, in the time of Edward II. Such churches are characterized by their wide naves, divided from the aisles by slender piers and by their long ranges of windows. The nave of Newark was begun about 1390 after the disaster of the Black Death had ended work on the south aisle, which dates from an earlier period. The oldest parts of the church are the four central piers and the unfinished crypt. The church, almost as we see it now, including nave, transepts, north aisle, and chancel, were all built and completed by the year 1500. The nave has its particular and wide-spaced sense of control over vacancy. But it is in the transepts, the latest parts of the building, that the boldest exercise in the control of space is to be found. The north and south windows of the transepts, with their seven lights, are as large as they could possibly be made. They give the effect of a display of glass which drowns the very existence of the stone which frames it. "Nothing like it was tried again until the time of the Crystal Palace." Whether or no one could not make that claim for a great many other churches of the Perpendicular period in Eastern England, it is certainly applicable to these glass transepts at Newark.

When one's eyes descend from the magnificence of the church itself they receive a rude shock in the gilt, blue and white reredos at the back of the altar which dates from 1937. The rood screen, of about 1500, is worth looking at and so are the choir stalls of approximately the same date. They have twenty-six of those easing, tip-up seats called misericords. Carvings on them, rich, as so often, in the strangest and most revealing of medieval sculpture on a small scale, include various angels, an elegant owl, an eagle, a man on a lion attacking with a lance an arbitrary monster, a more specific dragon, and a variety of naturalistic foliage. The church has two chantry chapels. One is to a certain Thomas Meyring who died in 1500. His chapel is placed between the choir and the north choir aisle. The money to provide it was obtained, we are told, by the sudden sale of his whole stock—he was a wool merchant—of his clipped wool and his whole flock of sheep. The second chantry chapel, of much the same kind and dating from only a few years later, contains two panels of a rather crudely painted rendering of the popular Dance of Death.

These are all part of the structure of the church, but the most important monument is one which you cannot see unless you pay special attention to it. It is the brass—one of the largest brasses in England—to Alan Fleming, a merchant of Newark. It is placed on the wall of the south transept of the church and is more than nine feet long and over five feet broad. Learned opinion has decided that it is almost certainly of foreign—either North German or Flemish—origin. On it the incised figure of Alan Fleming is surrounded by broad piers each with several rows of double niches containing figures; and there is another row of small figures above his head. The widow of Alan Fleming, who is thus so nobly commemorated, Dame Alice Fleming, erected a Chantry House which stood beside the old Grammar School in Appleton Gate until it was pulled down in 1919.

Beside St. Mary's any other church in Newark pales. Christ Church, Lombard Street, ought to be mentioned for its rendering, in the year of Queen Victoria's accession, of the Early English style. It has three galleries inside.

One or two other things before we go. Look at Wilson Street, with its sixteen severe and identical brick houses. This was begun in 1766 and was the product of the somewhat dubious wealth of Bernard Wilson, who was Vicar of St. Mary's, and a pluralist, whose activities outside the church gave rise to some suspicion.

Outside the town some works of engineering, of different sorts, deserve to be looked at. One is to the north. It consists of the arches, dating from 1770 and built by Smeaton, which carry the Great North Road out of the town. The other is at the southern end of Newark, approached by way of Mill Gate. These are what are called the Sconce Hills. They are not hills at all but are what remain of the finest surviving earthwork fortifications of the Civil War period. The King's Sconce has disappeared. But the Queen's Sconce remains, for the moment, quite clear to see— a four-pointed star, built out of the soil, with gun positions at each corner, and on the straight bits between the corners remains of the breastwork for musketeers. Recent visitors suggest that, although the outline is still clear and the ditch still deep, if the Queen's Sconce is to survive any longer it will need nursing and preservation.

I am not able to raise any enthusiasm about a Newark monument which, for some reason, is pointed out to all visitors. This is the Beaumont Cross at the south end of Carter Gate, where that street joins Lombard Street and three others. It is a late Gothic shaft—no cross survives—of the fifteenth century. It used to bear a plate stating, correctly or incorrectly, that it was "erected in the reign of Edward IV". The plate has gone; what remains of the cross was very heavily repaired in 1778 and again in 1801. It consists now of a very slender, slightly tapering, fluted shaft with a niche for the Holy Sacrament at the bottom.

The other Newark monument which I have left until last is the Town Hall in the market-place. This prominent and admirable building occupies the centre of the western side. It was built in 1773 of Mansfield stone by the famous Carr of York, one of whose most important buildings it is. All along the bottom there are arched windows behind rustications. The next two floors have as their centre piece a Palladian loggia with four Tuscan columns and a pediment. Inside is an imposing assembly hall with large corinthian columns, two of which form the frontis-piece to an apsidal end to the room.

Of the immediate environs of Newark, on the Trent side we have already discussed Kelham, its house and its new industries. If you travel up the eastern side of the river, by a number of very sharp bends, the next place you get to, close to the water and providing a ferry, is Holme. This is not Holme Pierrepont. It could be called Holme Barton, because its history is linked with that of the Barton family which used to live in the hall whose site is now occupied by a creepered farm-house. The Bartons were Newark business people concerned with the wool trade with France, and it was a John Barton who employed his affluence in rebuilding the church of St. Giles at Holme. He died in 1491 and he lies buried with his wife between the chancel of the church which he renovated and the south chancel chapel which he built anew. The tomb of this business man, this wool merchant—in a window of whose house at Holme there was said to read an inscription:

> I thank God and ever shall
> It's the sheepe hath payed for all—

consists of two tiers, with a rotting corpse underneath and two carved effigies above. The east window of the church was formerly filled with glass that commemorated the generosity of John Barton, and recent meticulous piecing together of these early fragments, with others from different sources, make the window bright and interesting in a kaleidoscopic sort of way. It was a girl of the Barton family who married the brother of that Lord Bellasis who has already entered into this account as the Governor of Newark Castle at its surrender. The son of this defiant Royalist married Mary, the daughter of Oliver Cromwell. Where Lord Bellasis lived at Holme is not quite certain. It was either at the Old Hall or in an earlier house on the site of the present red-brick Holme Hall. Old John Barton has left a most valuable record in the church that he rebuilt. Its entire interior, including most of the fittings, dates from his early Tudor ordering. Above the porch of the church one is rather apt to be shown what is known as "Nanny Scott's Chamber"; she, apparently, was an elderly dame who took up her refuge here during the plague of 1666. Disease was raging in the village and, having carefully laid in a stock of provisions, she took up her abode over the church door and watched from a safe distance the constant funerals of her friends. When forced to descend for further supplies of food she was horrified to find only one inhabitant of Holme still alive. She returned to her refuge over the church door and there expired.

The Fosse Way ends its sojourn in our county after only a few miles north-east of Newark; it leaves on its way the villages of Winthorpe and Langford and Brough (where remains of Roman dwellings have been found, belonging to the station called Crocolana) and then goes over the county boundary on its way to Lincoln. A smaller twisting road leads due east to Sleaford. It takes us to Coddington, where the newest fashions in ecclesiology would have us go to look at the decorations in the church of All Saints. Here, in the 1860's, G. F. Bodley, who restored the old church, ordered from the firm of Morris & Co. the decorations and furnishings of the interior. They consist of a curved ceiling, stencilled patterns on the walls, two windows filled with characteristic early Morris glass, transparent and full of brightness; and also, instead of the conventional seats for the priests, an object whose name and somewhat massive appearance has become the hallmark of William Morris' efforts to return to the forthright medieval manners of furnishing—a settle. This high-backed and uncomfortable object has been used, with exquisite effect, by Sir Max Beerbohm, in affectionate ridicule of Morris' good intentions. Take note of the settle in Coddington Church. It is something of a museum piece on a par with those preserved in Morris' own home at Kelmscott Manor.

Through Coddington, and we are almost out of the county again. Right on the edge is Barnby in the Willows, sitting beside the River Witham which, for a short distance, divides us from Lincolnshire.

If we pursue our journey northward from Holme we come soon to the Collinghams, North and South. South Collingham, beside the river, has the tall steeple of its church as its main feature. North Collingham boasts, in addition, the remains of a village cross and a number of interesting houses, including some good Georgian ones within their walled gardens, and a timber-framed cottage in Low Street dating from the sixteenth century. North of the Collinghams, in the narrow area of the county east of the Trent, South Scarle draws attention to itself because of the magnificent Norman features of its pinnacled and battlemented church. Through the tiny hamlet of Girton to another pair of villages, confusingly duplicating a familiar Nottingham name— Clifton North and South. The two villages lie a mile apart and their church of St. George lies on its own between them. Out to the east is Harby. It is a little place, with not much to look at (the church is unexciting Victorian). But Harby has a place in medieval history because it was here in 1290 that there died Eleanor of Castile, the Queen of King Edward I. It was the journey of her body from here to London which was commemorated by her devout and sorrowing husband with the famous Eleanor Crosses, of which Charing Cross—though it is, of course,

not original—is the most famous. The only three which survive
of Edward I's devotion, with statues of the lovely Queen whose
appearance is also indicated by her effigy, cast by William Torel
in Westminster Abbey, are at Hardingstone and Giddington in
Northamptonshire and at Waltham Cross in Hertfordshire.

Beyond the villages of Newton, with its white windmill, and
Thorney, which has an unexpected neo-Norman church designed
in 1849-50 by the Victorian theorist and writer on medieval
architecture, L. Cottingham, the east side of the Trent ceases to
interest us because from here, northwards, it forms the county
boundary.

We have traversed in detail what might be called the village
area of the county. The green and fertile vale is richer than all
the rest in the casual beauty of these clusters of dwellings which
contain, so often, unexpected excitement and wealth. It is time
for us to cross the Trent and to explore the fringes of what will
require a different sort of study—areas which can be thought of
as cohesive wholes—Sherwood Forest, the Dukeries, and the
colliery area, which, though separate, belongs in part to both.
But first there is a place which must be considered on its own;
and I am going to make Lord Byron, whose appearance in this
account cannot be confined only to the discussion of Newstead,
provide, with his own vigour of expression, an introduction to
Southwell.

It was in 1804 that Mrs. Byron moved from Nottingham to
Southwell. Byron was at school at Harrow and, on holiday in
Southwell, he formed a friendship with Miss Elizabeth Bridge
Pigot with whom, and with whose intelligent mother and brother,
John, he found sympathy and a certain degree of gaiety. Miss
Pigot, who lived until 1866, remembered Byron in his Southwell
days as "a fat, bashful boy, with hair combed straight over his
forehead". When he went up to Cambridge in 1815 it was to
the Pigots' house on Burgage Green at Southwell that he most
often wrote back during his first year at the university. The
Byrons had rented a neighbouring house on the green, a modest
Georgian residence called Burgage Manor (it is still there, an un-
impressive white residence with a portico, on the west side of the
green which lies between the railway station and the little town:
recently it has been used as a hostel). The Pigots sympathized
with Byron in his frequent quarrels with his mother, and they
must have been exceptionally unprovincial if they appreciated
the young man's opinions of her and of the little town they
lived in, opinions which he freely committed to paper in such a
letter as this:

"Seriously, your mother has laid me under great obligations, and you with the rest of your family, merit my warmest thanks for your kind connivance at my escape from 'Mrs. Byron *furiosa*' . . . All Southwell, without doubt, is involved in amazement. *Apropos*, how does my blue-eyed nun, the fair ——? Is she 'robed in sable garb of woe'? My lodgings must be kept secret from Mrs. B. . . . I have taken measures to retreat immediately to Portsmouth, on the first intimation of her removal from Southwell . . . Without doubt the dames of Southwell reprobate the pernicious example I have shown, and tremble lest their babes should disobey their mandates, and quit, in dudgeon, their mamas on any grievance. . . ."

One wonders what can really have been the emotions of these tolerant people at receiving from this conceited and bumptious youth the sort of comments on their home which were contained in his letters. To Miss Pigot he writes from Cambridge in June 1807: "I care not if the whole race were consigned to the Pit of Acheron, which I would visit in person rather than contaminate my sandals with the polluted dust of Southwell. Seriously, unless obliged by the emptiness of my purse to re-visit Mrs. B., you will see me no more. To forget and be forgotten by the people of Southwell is all I aspire to." He writes again, still from Cambridge: "*I hate Southwell* . . . Stay in town a month, perhaps six weeks, trip into Essex, and then, as a favour, irradiate Southwell for three days with the light of my countenance; but nothing shall ever make me reside there again. . . . Oh! Southwell, Southwell, how I rejoice I have left thee, and how I curse the heavy hours I dragged along, for so many months, among the Mohawks who inhabit your kraals!"

He was not, you see, a bit polite. "Southwell," he says a bit later, "was a detestable residence. Thanks St. Dominica, I have done with it: I have been twice within eight miles of it, but could not prevail on myself to suffocate in its heavy atmosphere. This place (Cambridge) is wretched enough—a villainous chaos of din and drunkenness, nothing but hazard and burgundy, hunting, mathematics and Newmarket, riot and racing. Yet it is a paradise compared with the eternal dullness of Southwell."

It is characteristic of the worst side of Byron's nature, the arrogant, rude, rather vulgar part of him (though one must not forget that he was an undergraduate of barely twenty when he wrote these letters) that such comments on Southwell should have been addressed to residents of that place who had made, by their kindness and sympathy, his life there far more endurable for him than it would otherwise have been. There is a complete lack of grace and sensitiveness about these remarks. Hardly more tolerable is the remark he made to his friend John Hanson, writing from Southwell early in 1807. "You speak of the Charms of Southwell: the place I abhor. The fact is I remain here because I can appear nowhere else, being completely done up. Wine and women have dished your humble servant; not a sou to be had; all over; condemned to exist (I cannot say live) at this Crater of Dullness till my Lease of Infancy expires."

Surely, it can't have been quite as bad as that; but there is, to this day, something indeterminate about Southwell which gives meaning, still, to the remark made of it in 1789: "A well built clean town, such a one as a quiet distressed family ought to retire to."

Since Byron's attitude to Southwell was hardly one likely to provoke a mood of fine poetry you will not expect from him any sort of an ode to the place. Indeed, so far as I know, Southwell provoked only a single rather foolish jeu d'esprit. Since, however, it is included in the canon of Byron's work it ought to find a place here. It is the epitaph, written in September 1807 on " John Adams of Southwell, who died of drunkenness:

> John Adams lies here, of the parish of Southwell,
> A Carrier who carried his can to his mouth well;
> He carried so much, and he carried so fast,
> He could carry no more—so was carried at last;
> For, the liquor he drank, being too much for one,
> He could not carry off—so he's now carri-on."

On Burgage Green, not far from the house that Mrs. Byron inhabited, you may notice a severe rustic gateway, dating from the same year as that "poem", 1807. It led to the former House of Correction for which Southwell was, in earlier days, famous or infamous. It is hard, now, to associate this gentle and friendly place with the existence of a violent and morose semi-criminal population, but the Southwell House of Correction for vagabonds and vagrants operated for the whole county. It was established in 1611, and here vagrants were to be whipped by the master according to the direction of the justices and set to work on spinning, the weaving of haircloth and sackcloth, jersey woollen or linen yarns and knocking hemp. The instructions issued to the master forbade him ever to let anyone out of the house on any pretext except by a warrant from a justice, and he was not to release any of his prisoners except by the direction of two justices. The Southwell House of Correction was not a source of pride to the county at any period in its history. In 1653 the sum of £200 was levied on the county for the erection of a new house; but it must have been a very poor building as it was constantly having to undergo repairs—four times before the end of the seventeenth century and constantly during the eighteenth. It cannot have been a pleasant neighbour for the dignified residents of the Georgian houses of Burgage Green—though, indeed, many of them may have thought the Byron ménage even more unseemly for, during the year 1806-7, when Byron was living with his mother, her foul temper and his aggravating ways caused constant scenes and uproars. After one specially bad quarrel, both mother and son are said to have slipped out, one after the other, to the neighbouring chemist to ask him not to supply the other with poison. But what went on in Burgage Manor was nothing compared with the scenes of squalor and misery within the House of Correction. Presumably neither Byron nor his mother ever set foot inside it or, one would guess, any of the respectable townspeople of Southwell, whose attitude to rumours about it must have been much the same as those of the Germans, recently, who happened to live near Belsen. Anyway, in the first years of the nineteenth century a visitor did get in and thus describes part of it: " In the floor of one room is a trap door, from which ten steps lead down into a loathsome hole or dungeon measuring 13 feet by 10 feet and 7 feet high. In it were three wooden bedsteads on which lay some short dirty straw. The only ventilation is through an iron grating measuring 2 ft. 10 by 8 ins. and on a level with the courtyard outside. In this loathsome hole seven persons, heavily ironed, sleep every night. The House of Correction has no infirmary, no bath, not even an oven. Some of the prisoners are employed on cutting pegs for twopence a thousand which the master sells at fourpence a hundred. Nothing," this visitor adds, " can exceed the squalid wretchedness and filth and severity which are everywhere presented."

A large square-built house called Elmfield, on the opposite side of the green to the Manor House, and a little nearer the station, was the home of a Miss Glaister, authoress of one of the more readable of Nottinghamshire's local novels, *The Markhams of Ollerton,* a story of the Civil War.

To move out of Burgage Green is to discover, in Southwell, a little town entirely dominated by its great church. It is not a cathedral town, although it contains the cathedral of the diocese of Southwell. It is one of the most recent of the English sees, having been created in 1884 and comprising the counties of Nottingham and Derby, the former having been previously within the diocese of Lincoln, and the latter of Lichfield (the only other nineteenth-century sees are Ripon, of 1836, and St. Albans, of 1878. Southwark alone, of 1905, is later than Southwell). In 1927 the see was divided and Derby was made the centre of a new one. Apart from the cathedral and the buildings immediately around it, which we come to in a moment, there is little of note. The centre of the town is the crossroads where the main street meets that which skirts the cathedral yard. On the crossing is the Saracen's Head Hotel, a coaching inn with a long unassuming front which includes, as part of the hotel, an assembly room built in the first decade of the nineteenth century. The history of the Saracen's Head can be traced back to the reign of Richard II, but the inn's rendezvous with history was reserved for the times of the Civil War. Charles I stayed here more than once in the course of the conflict and Cromwell is also said to have lodged here during one of his marches. The King ate his last meal as a free man in the present coffee room of the hotel. When he had finished that meal he surrendered himself to the Scotch Commissioners, and began three years of varied confinement which was to end only with his execution. A room in the hotel is pointed out as the one in which the King slept.

The town—this is the odd thing about it—consists of five quite separate clumps of buildings with open spaces in between them, so that although it houses only 3,000 people it covers quite a considerable area. The part that is known as High Town is Southwell proper and, beside the little River Greet, which used to be noted for its abundant population of trout, there has been a settlement since very early times. The town is probably now a good deal smaller than it was a couple of centuries ago. Its early history is a bit obscure, but it seems that it was fairly certainly the site of a Roman encampment and a legend maintains —not with a very great deal of authority—that Paulinus, the founder of the sees of York and Lincoln, established a church in Southwell when he was baptizing the people of this district in the Trent about the year 630. Somewhere about that time, in any case, there did come into being here a collegiate church. (Such a foundation was for a collective body of priests called "secular clergy" as distinguished from the "regular clergy" who lived together in monasteries. These latter were celibates and monks. The "seculars", on the other hand, lived normally in houses of their own and were not prohibited by any vows from holding property. They were much, in fact, like modern clergymen and fulfilled many of the functions of the parish priest. The college at Southwell was dissolved by Act of Parliament in 1848.)

The next stage in Southwell's history—still largely legendary—was early in the eighth century when a certain Eadburh, who was Abbess of the monastery of Repton, near Derby, and the daughter of Aldwulf, King of East Anglia, migrated to Southwell. She is said to have founded here an early school of Christianity, or monastery of men and women, similar to one at Repton. She died at Southwell and was buried there, so Southwell became the shrine of an Anglo-Saxon saint and a place of pilgrimage. The first date which can be accepted with any confidence for the history of the minster is 956, when the manor of Southwell and a lot of land around it was granted by King Edgar to Oskatel, Archbishop of York, and for nearly a thousand years it was ruled from York. It was never monastic but early in the Middle Ages it had already become one of the major churches in the province of York. It was, however, except for occasional visitation, almost entirely independent of York. It owned or controlled something like a quarter of the whole county of Nottinghamshire and had obviously just as much local importance as a true cathedral.

Work on the building of the church began about 1108 under Archbishop Thomas of York. The parts which survive of this first period of building, which went on until 1150, are the transepts and nave. They are enough to make Southwell one of the best examples in the country of a great Norman church of the middle of the twelfth century. The nave is tremendously impressive; it gives an impression of great majesty and confidence. The nave has seven bays, and the circular stone columns, six on each side, are 4½ feet thick and only 9 feet high. Yet, in spite of these short thick piers there is no feeling of heaviness; the two ranks of the arcade above them are so skilfully proportioned that it gives no effect of weight or ponderousness or of bearing down too heavily on the piers. Instead it gives a feeling of springing movement running the length of the church. If you look up through the arches of the triforium you will see the remarkable and unexpected range of circular windows in the clerestory. The circular oak roof is modern, having replaced the lower flat ceiling in the restorations carried out in 1881.

The church is pretty well unique in this country in retaining all three of its Norman towers, and the fact that the two western towers have not lost their pyramidal roofs gives the church a slightly Continental appearance, because we are so accustomed in England to seeing flat tops given to Norman churches all over the country. It is in many ways remarkable that the two Southwell west towers have got these tops at all. Their history is, apparently, something like this. They were "probably a little steeper than they originally were. (They were rebuilt in 1880 on the pattern which they had when taken down in 1802, which in its turn was not original either, but a copy from the presumably medieval pattern in existence until a fire of 1711.)" It is possible, certainly, to feel sore about the insertion, in the fifteenth century, of a huge seven-light Perpendicular window at the west end of the church in between the two Norman towers. To do this, pretty well the whole of the Norman west front was knocked out. Certainly the west window floods the Norman interior with a brilliant light, but it sorely disrupts the unity of the Norman church.

If the Perpendicular of the fifteenth century has to some extent spoilt the Norman of the twelfth, the Early English of the thirteenth century has given Southwell two benefits; one, a tactfully inserted chancel and lady chapel, and the other an independent chapter house which has no equal for the delights of its decoration. The old Norman east end of the church had a straight-ending chancel, not an apse. In 1234 Walter de Grey, Archbishop of York, pulled down the Norman east end. He lengthened the chancel by four bays, added a new lady chapel and a pair of transepts. We are told that a special indulgence of thirty days was offered to all contributors to its building fund. The brass lectern and candlesticks, made about 1500, which stand in the chancel, are the subject of a picturesque legend. They belonged to Newstead Abbey and, according to the story, when the dissolution took place in 1539 the monks hid their ancient charters and deeds in the hollow ball on which the eagle of the lectern stands, hoping that they could be recovered when the monks returned to the monastery. They then threw it into the piece of water which is now known as the Eagle Pond. For three hundred years they remained in the water, a very deep pond with a perpendicular stone wall all around it and steps leading to the bottom at each corner (these facts suggest that it was used by the monks as a bath). In the middle of the eighteenth century, in the time of the "wicked" fifth Lord Byron, the lectern and candlesticks were discovered. In the interior of the lectern boss were found a large number of parchment deeds and grants of the reigns of Edward III, Henry V and Henry VIII, to some of which the great Seal of England is attached, all relating to the Abbey of Newstead and its rights and privileges. The lectern and candlesticks were bought from Lord Byron by Sir Robert Kaye, who was rector of Kirkby in Ashfield and prebendary of Southwell. In a letter to the third Duke of Portland, dated 12th December, 1775, Kaye wrote: "I have bought Lord Byron's strong beer for my parish and his brass eagle for Southwell, at very good bargains." He presented them to Southwell, where they still remain. Legend also records that, at the time of the eagle's recovery, two very large and heavy chests were found in the mud at the bottom of the lake. Owing, however, to peremptory orders from the "wicked" lord to refill the lake at once as he was coming to Newstead with a party of friends, they had to be left in the water. Sixty or seventy years later Colonel Wildman, who had bought Newstead from the poet, tried to locate the chests soon after he took possession of the abbey. But one of the searchers was suffocated in the mud and the attempt was abandoned.

The glass in the lower part of the Early English east window at Southwell also has a curious history, but this time has nothing to do with the county. The glass, sixteenth-century work, was originally in the Temple, the chapel of the Knights Templars in Paris—the church in which Queen Marie Antoinette was imprisoned. The glass was bought at a pawnbroker's shop in Paris, for a trifling sum, in 1815, where it had presumably lain since its removal from the church during the secularization by the Revolutionary Government. It consists of a series of large figures against an architectural background. The subject of the first light is the Baptism of Christ. The second light depicts the Raising of Lazarus. One of the figures in it is Francis I of France in a crimson cap. The third light shows Christ entering Jerusalem. Close to the Saviour's side is shown the figure of Luther; Louis XI is there in a blue hat and the Duke of Orleans in a yellow cap. The subject of the fourth light is the mocking of Christ, into which a full-face portrayal of Dante is introduced. These windows bear the legend "Venzicus Gally. Knight Arm. Anno Dom 1818 D.D."

Near the east end of the choir is the kneeling effigy in bronze of the first Bishop of Southwell, the Right Reverend George Ridding—"Ruler: Scholar: Divine" as his monument describes him —who died in 1904. There is something rather moving about this handsome Victorian prelate, on his knees as he is portrayed in the sculptured figure by F. W. Pomeroy (1907), with his hands outstretched in an attitude of supplication. It is hardly likely that in his lifetime Bishop Ridding—who was for nearly twenty years headmaster of Winchester College—would have allowed himself to be discovered in so humble a posture.

The only other pieces of sculpture for which Southwell is noted are very different from each other. One is situated over the door leading to the belfry. It is generally accepted as late Anglo-Saxon and as such would be one of the oldest sculptures in the

Midlands. It represents St. Michael—who is equipped with a very handsome pair of wings—and an extremely scaly and coiled dragon. Certain other beasts, a lamb and below it a lion, out of whose mouth a kneeling man is apparently removing something, enter into the design. It is a most vigorous piece of carving and the pattern made by the dragon in fitting his length of body and tails into the space imposed by the shape above the door lintel has something quite oriental about it, while the saint's wings, too, remind one of sculptures familiar in Eastern Byzantium rather than in the West. It certainly gives a Saxon effect, of not later than the eleventh century; but scholars point out its resemblance to the carvings on the capitals on the east side of the crossing in the nave—rude and slapdash renderings of the Annunciation, the Adoration of the Shepherds, The Last Supper, Christ washing Peter's feet, and the entry into Jerusalem—and suggest that the possibility of this carving being of the same date as these, as late as 1120, should be reconsidered. The second notable sculpture in the body of the church is the tomb of Archbishop Sandys, who died in 1588. This conventional but exceptionally well executed piece of Elizabethan alabaster work shows the Archbishop—the head, one guesses, is an excellent portrait—lying in his episcopal robes with four small angels at his head and feet on a richly carved sarcophagus in the front panel of which his widow and his eight children are kneeling. This Archbishop of York was one of Southwell's major benefactors.

A church, then, a cathedral, with plenty to admire in it—the great Norman nave, the Early English chancel, and some varied specimens of sculpture. But the reason why, to-day, a great many of the people who visit Southwell have made their journey thither at all is to look at the Leaves. In about 1290, when the new chancel had been built, but when the nave was still darkish and the west front had still its small Norman windows, the Archbishop of York of the time decided to build on the north side of the minster, connected with the chancel by a corridor—which now has glazing in the openings—giving on to a little courtyard. The various components of this admirable Early English addition to the cathedral, the doorway that leads from the chancel, the corridor, the entrance to the chapter house and the chapter house itself, make up the greatest glory of Southwell. For, not only is the chapter house itself given a quality of lightness and airiness by the fact that, exceptionally, it is built without a centrally supporting pier which was found to be a necessary structural feature of the majority of other polygonal English chapter houses; but from the moment you pass through the doorway from the chancel

One of the Southwell Chapter House Capitals

you come into a world in which the artist has, perhaps more lovingly than anywhere else in the country, reproduced nature in stone.

You might think that to have the motif of leaves repeated over and over again on the doorways, round the windows, above the seats that surround the chapter house would, in time, become boring and give a monotonous and mechanical feeling. It probably would at any other moment than this, when the clarity and restraint of the Early English style had reached perfection and was about to break out into the relative excesses of the Decorated. Such a wholesale commitment to a single theme would certainly have become mechanical in Victorian hands. But the delight of the Southwell chapter house and its surroundings is that never is there any actual repetition, never, although the carving, almost exclusively of foliage, is intended to copy and to emulate nature, do you lose contact, as you look at it with the emotions of the sculptors who have always, miraculously, avoided mere imitation. This imaginative realism was something that came from France late in the thirteenth century; and one can guess that the inspiration of the carving was about equally divided between living leaves brought in from the forests round Southwell and from sketches made during journeys, or apprenticeships, in France. The result of the combination of a rigorous and almost inspired single control over the general design with the discreet freedom of the individual craftsman is to bring taste and execution together to produce an artistic achievement of the highest level. While the repeated pattern of the leaves themselves is decoration almost in the abstract, the human element of fun and curiosity is never quite suppressed and peeps out just often enough from among the constantly changing pattern of the leaves. For beyond the unity imposed by the single theme of foliage, no single carving is the same as any other. No two capitals or bosses or spandrels, however hard you look, can you declare to be alike. The variety of different species of leaves interpreted in this subtle and delicate way is not in itself sufficient to provide the constant change. Admittedly, naturalists have studied the forms and have made a startlingly long list of the plants found in the chapter house. Chief among them are oak, maple, vine, hop, ivy, rose, whitethorn, hawthorn, ranunculus and potentilla. But the fluency and freedom of the carving is such that if you stand in the doorway of the chapter house and look around its eight sides, set with small columns and above them the trefoils and decorated triangles above the seats and, higher still, the great windows in groups of three lights surmounted by three circles containing

Southwell: the seventeenth-century front of the
Saracen's Head Inn

trefoils, you can sense, though you are not within eyes' range
of the details of any but a few of the carvings, that they *are* all
different, and that the gesture and curl of each leaf will be as
separate from its neighbour's as in nature itself. It is as though
the essence of Sherwood Forest had come into this clear and brilliantly lighted room bringing with it something of the mystery
of woodland. If in the clear light the leaves live, twitch
and rustle with sunny friendliness, there is in the creatures
and little faces that peer out from among the leaves a hint of
the strangeness, comedy and surprise inseparable from forest
lore.

Growing out of the leaves, as it were, there is indeed a curious
Robin Hood-like person whose face has something of a wink
to suggest his private uncertainty about his own existence.
In his case the leaves spring from his ears. There are heads, in
the spandrels above the stalls, with branches issuing from their
mouths. Other spandrels have birds or lizard-like monsters.
Among the capitals a man reclines beneath a tree, blowing a horn.
A goat is shown gnawing the leaves, or a bird pecking the berries,
or a pair of pigs grubbing up acorns. Elsewhere a brace of
hounds is seen in the act of grabbing a hare. Within the chapter
house, all the incidental anecdotes to the foliage decoration are
concerned with the forest and its life. Out in the corridor, between chancel and chapter house, rather more domestic matters
are incorporated, as in a boss on the west side, near the door,
which bears the representation of a "secular" cleric on the top
of a "regular" monk, pulling both his ears (Southwell, you
may remember, was founded as a collegiate church for "secular"
clergy).

Not very much remains of the living quarters of the medieval
inhabitants of Southwell, but from a variety of different dates the
minster surroundings provide an attractive and quite sizeable
close. The group of houses built for the Vicars Choral, who did
the work of the non-resident canons, which was rebuilt in 1780
consists of five charming red-brick, rather severe houses, placed
in a U-shape with one now occupied by the Provost at the end,
between the arms, and giving pattern to the whole with a modest
portico.

On the south side of the minster is the Bishop's Palace. At a
quick glance you see only a large, forty-year-old, roughcast house
(already too large, one gathers, for the bishop because part of it
is flats), but in fact it joins up with and incorporates the remains
of what was the exceedingly large and splendid residence of the
Archbishops of York. The old palace was rectangular, covering

a space of about one and a half acres. The building of it was begun in about 1360 by Archbishop Thoresby, on the site of an earlier mansion. Shortly afterwards a second great hall was added to the initial structure. Its main buildings were ranged around a quadrangle, with hall and chapel to the north, state apartments to the east, living quarters to the south, and domestic offices to the west. It received its final shape under Archbishop Kemp in about 1440. From his time dates the appearance of the great hall on the first floor—the sort of hall to be found in an Oxford or Cambridge college. Kemp enriched the hall and state apartments with traceried windows, sculptured fireplaces and ornamental chimney shafts. In the reign of Henry VIII, when Southwell was one of the northern manors of Cardinal Wolsey, considerable sums were spent in ornamenting and repairing the structure. It seems likely that the work was carried out by a certain John Forman who was master mason at York Minster between 1523 and 1558. It would have been he who would supervise repairs and extensions at places like Southwell and Scrooby in the period before the Cardinal's downfall; Forman was one of the many servants to whom sums of money—considerable for the time— were due when Wolsey's end came. Forman was owed £58. It is possible, even from the scanty survivals, parts of the east and south walls with some windows, a fireplace, an arch or two and a corbelled-out turret in an angle, to imagine how luxurious a palace it was under the Archbishops of York. Like so many buildings in southern Nottinghamshire, it met its fate in the Civil War. The Scotch Commissioners, as we have had occasion to observe already, sited their headquarters in Southwell and the reason that it was at the Saracen's Head Inn that King Charles had to reside when he came to surrender himself may well have been because of the state which the old palace had already got into after a few years of war. The soldiers attending the Scotch Commissioners had apparently already stripped the roof of its lead and sold it before they left the town. The interior had been looted and practically gutted and after the Civil War it was allowed to slide into complete ruination. Descriptions of it in the eighteenth century indicate that there was not much more of it then than there is now. In 1882 the then suffragan Bishop of Nottingham Dr. Trollope, undertook the restoration of a portion of it. The work was continued by the second Bishop of Southwell who, between 1907 and 1909, had the new bishop's palace, to the design of Caroe, put up in its present form.

I hope I have said enough about this unexpected and unusual little town to persuade you that, even if you agree with Byron, that to live here would be going too far, it is a place one ought to add to the list of those that one knows. It incorporates a great deal of Nottinghamshire history and it is something to be said for the town itself that there is so little of it. It is a restful and satisfactory place to visit because the things to see are few, compact, but of superlative quality. In spite of its reduction in size and a curious lack of reasonableness in the relation of a mere village to one of the country's twenty-seven great cathedrals, it is not a sad or depressing place, nor unduly peopled by ghosts. The medieval craftsmen of the chapter house have instilled so much life, and love of life, into their work as to make Southwell and its leaves seem a place of constant growth where the sap continues to rise. Only in one way is the place a sad one. It cannot escape the shadow of King Charles; and a story which is still told here brings out the loneliness of the King's last journey as a free man. They say that the day after his arrival in Southwell he walked by himself through the town, not known to anyone; he entered a shop of a shoemaker of the name of Lee, a man who had some local reputation as a fanatic and seer. The King, after some conversation with this man, asked him to measure him for a pair of shoes. Lee took the King's foot in his hand and then, having looked at him earnestly for some time, refused to proceed. The King was astonished but politely asked him to do what he requested. Lee refused again saying that he could recognize a customer he had been warned of in a dream the previous night, in which he learnt of the King's doomed destruction and that those who worked for him would never thrive; and then, continues the traditional account, " the forlorn monarch, whose misfortunes had opened his mind to the impression of superstition, uttered a sigh expressive of his resignation to the will of providence and returned to the place of his abode ".

I have said how Southwell, although a single place, is divided into several parts which think of themselves as more or less separate. The area of the minster, the palace and the Saracen's Head Inn lies about half-way between two extremities, Westhorpe and Easthorpe. I am sure that many important things have happened in Westhorpe and that many important people have lived and died there; but somehow the inhabitants of Westhorpe seem to keep quiet about it. In Easthorpe, on the other hand, there is a celebrity whom you will be certain to hear about. In Easthorpe, over a hundred years ago, Mr. Bramley lived. He had an apple tree which had been raised from seed in a plant pot. The tree produced such exceptional fruit that cuttings of it were dispatched all over England. The apples they produced became known as Bramley's Seedlings and the name of the famous cooking apple was established. At the Easthorpe end of Southwell they will still show you a tree which they say is the original one, belonging to Mr. Bramley, where it all began.

187

NEWARK AND SOUTHWELL

CHAPTER VII

ROAD AND RIVER

IN considering the villages of south Nottinghamshire we have so far confined our attention to those south and east of the River Trent. Apart from the city of Nottingham itself and such villages as for reasons connected with the city's growth were introduced to the account of it, the only place to the north of the river so far described has been Southwell.

Out of Newark two roads lead northward, each of them crossing the Trent within a mile or so. One of them is the Great North Road. Its course through Tuxford and East Retford, by Barnby Moor and Scrooby and out through the northern limits of the county at Bawtry we shall come to later, for the Great North Road is so important a feature that it ought to be thought of in one piece. For the moment, let us take the other road branching off westwards from Newark once the line of the railway is passed. It goes up to the Trent and it crosses it at Kelham, whose hall and church have already been described. Three or so miles further north a side road takes us—no inconvenient detour back to the main road—into a little place called Caunton. It is a charming place with a stream and a footbridge, a church with a Norman arcade and an old brick manor house that has a much newer stone portico. Caunton is a very quiet and retiring little place, but it comes into the history of England all the same. King Henry VI, who reigned from 1421 to 1471, had the reputation of performing miracles, and the wonders that were performed by him either in person or by proxy were recounted by monastic chroniclers. In one case the witness of a miracle tells how a certain William Bartram, " being struck in his most sensitive parts by the foot of one who played with him, sustained long and intolerable pain; but, having seen in a dream the glorious King Henry, suddenly received the benefit of health ". This miracle took place at Caunton. Very well, you may say, what of it? I would ask you to note, in reply, the fact that William Bartram was struck in his most sensitive parts " by the *foot* of one who played with him ". The implications of this are explained in a note, some reflections about the incident, which the monk who wrote the narrative, added to it. He said: "The game at which they had met for common recreation is called by some the football-game. It is one in which young men, in country sport, propel a huge ball, not by throwing it into the air but by striking and rolling it along the ground and that not with their hands but with their feet. A game, I say, abominable enough, and, in my judgment at least, more common, undignified, and worthless than any other kind of game, rarely ending without some loss, accident, or disadvantage to the players themselves." The fifteenth-century monk who expressed these admirable sentiments went on to describe the particular incident at Caunton—it, as you will now have gathered, is one of the earliest detailed references to a game which seems to have been known in England earlier than any surviving sport—which gave King Henry VI an opportunity of manifesting royal interest in what would now be called "this great British sport". After his general description the monk goes on: "What then? The boundaries had been marked and the game had started; and, when they were striving manfully, kicking in opposite directions, and our hero had thrown himself into the midst of the fray, one of his fellows whose name I know not, came up against him from in front and kicked him by misadventure, missing his aim at the ball."

It is an incident which must have been repeated many times subsequently, even at Caunton itself, but there seem to be no further records of miracles on the football field. As you probably know, football is a game which subsequently came under royal disapproval, and twenty or so years after King Henry's miracle a proclamation against the sport was made. But, particularly in the Midlands, in Nottinghamshire and Derbyshire especially, football was by no means stopped by these prohibitions and was growing in popularity in Elizabethan times. One cannot altogether blame the authorities for their disapproval because there were no set rules for the conduct of the game and no referees or umpires; consequently the number of accidents at football was large and some of them fatal. In the reign of James I who brought with him from Scotland a tradition of violent hostility to sports (the Scottish James III had ordered that "football and golfe be utterly cryed down and not to be used") two Nottinghamshire footballers got themselves into trouble with the law. This was at Sturton-le-Steeple up in the north. In 1623 William Barnbye and John Bingham were hauled up for playing football in the churchyard. They denied it, claiming, when evidence was produced of the damage caused to each other, that "Bingham's nose fell a-bleeding of its own accord" . . . yes, altogether, Caunton as an early hotbed of the sport has a lot to answer for. In Caunton Manor, by the way, long the home of the family of Hole, there lived Dean Hole of Rochester who was a famous rose-grower and a friend of the famous Punch artist John Leech. Between Caunton and Maplebeck lies the late Georgian mansion, of Elizabethan origins, called Beesthorpe Hall, the seat of the ancient family of Bristowe who have been settled at Maplebeck and Beesthorpe since at least the fourteenth century. Until the beginning of the eighteenth century an ancient chapel stood beside the house but the William Bristowe of the time destroyed it in order to enlarge a bowling green. There is not much to see at Maplebeck along the road. Winkburn is a different matter. This tiny place which lies, as it should, beside a stream with the delightful name of The Wink, contains, set in a surprisingly large park, a big house and a church side by side, with an inn and a few cottages at the end of the drive. The church, dedicated to St. John of Jerusalem, has an almost complete Norman tower; apart from that it consists only of nave and chancel. The family of Burnell, the owners of Winkburn Hall, have left some attractive monuments in the church. One, William Burnell, who died in 1609, kneels, lifesize, between columns. He is wearing armour and it was he who received the grant of the Winkburn Manor from King Edward VI. The other, much later, commemorates the last of the direct line of Burnells, D'Arcy Burnell, who died in 1774. His handsome marble tomb shows a youthful Death, holding a reversed torch, and Fame, who displays a profile portrait of D'Arcy Burnell, on each side of a pedestalled urn.

The house of the Burnells (D'Arcy Burnell's heirs-at-law assumed the name) is large and dates mainly from the early eighteenth century, with a later top storey. A four-columned porch stands before the door and the staircase is adorned with florid carving and there are carved panels over the doors of the central hall showing scenes from Aesop's fables.

Of the villages which lie on the various roads which radiate from Southwell neither Hockerton nor Kirklington have a great deal to offer except, in the latter, a large, battlemented, late Georgian mansion with Victorian neo-Elizabethan additions; and in the former a church with Norman elements and what appears to be a rudimentary Easter sepulchre.

From Kirklington the twisting roads lead through Edingley, through Halam down to the road which connects Southwell with Nottingham. Here we soon strike Oxton. Here is one of the quieter but most pleasant of Nottinghamshire houses, Oxton Hall. The Oxton estate has long been in the possession of the

The Trent from Gunthorpe Bridge
The Trent at Stoke Bardolph

family of Sherbrooke. But recently, a hero of the late war, Captain St. Vincent Sherbrooke, of the Royal Navy, who was awarded a Victoria Cross for his defence of a North Russian convoy in 1942, put the house into the market. The house has thirty rooms and, round it, sixteen acres of ground with a lake and a water garden. The purchaser was also offered the option of shooting over about two thousand acres. Captain Sherbrooke had not lived at Oxton Hall for many years, occupying, instead, a smaller house on the estate. In Oxton Hall there resided until recently, at any rate, an uncle of the proprietor of Welbeck Abbey, Lord Charles Cavendish-Bentinck. Oxton is a pleasant, not over tidy late Georgian building, with a porch of four Tuscan columns. Its outbuildings are showing, inevitably, signs of the times in neglect and dilapidation. At Oxton we are beginning to come into the higher ground and are already within sight and sense of the collieries. Indeed, the place closest to Oxton, just to the south, is Calverton. The name may be familiar as the presumed birthplace of the Rev. William Lee who invented the stocking frame. But this village, set in pleasant rolling country, has a great deal more to it than merely that memory. Not far from the groups of old stocking knitters' cottages, that we have already had occasion to refer to, are clusters of modern brick buildings of the last fifteen years. They comprise some admirable miners' housing and the buildings of Calverton colliery itself, the work of G. A. Jellicoe.

Whether Lee was or was not born here (Woodborough is the alternative suggestion for his birthplace) there is no reason to doubt that he was curate here in the year 1589 when he achieved his great invention. He would not, however, recognize the church of Calverton as the one which he attended in Queen Elizabeth's reign. To be sure there are some Norman elements inside St. Wilfrid's. Up in the tower, for instance, are a number of Norman panels which represent various occupations for the different months of the year—a reaper, for instance, for August, a huntsman for February—but as a whole Calverton church is a Georgian building, having been reduced in size and rebuilt in 1763.

Calverton has always moved with the times. It seems to have provided, for each phase of Nottingham's industrial development, indication of exceptional enterprise. In Elizabethan times Lee and his stocking frame; in the eighteenth century Calverton had one of the county's larger ironworks; and recently Calverton, the colliery Calverton of to-day, has been in the news again as the scene of another extraordinary piece of mechanical ingenuity. Recently a new experiment was carried out here. Underneath

At Newstead Abbey
Bilsthorpe Colliery

Calverton and its surrounding country lies a mass of virgin coal which, it is estimated, will yield a million tons a year for at least a century. But to get at this hidden wealth any new shaft has to pass through the strata of the porous bunter sandstone which forms an underground watershed from which the city of Nottingham and the surrounding towns draw much of their water supply. If pits had been sunk in the ordinary way the result—apart from impossible conditions of mining, involving the pumping away from the workings of water that would be seeping in at the rate of over a thousand gallons an hour—would have been a serious loss to the local water supply. For this reason the seams have been hitherto regarded as inaccessible.

But the rich veins were opened up and both these obstacles were averted by a spectacular feat of engineering. A man-made ice pillar—consisting of the earth's surface frozen to a depth of some 410 feet—was created. It was achieved by means of a giant replica of the domestic refrigerator, the principle being the evaporation of ammonia. The first step was to encircle the site of the proposed shaft with a ring of pipes passing through and below the stratum of porous sandstone. The pit shaft itself was to be about 20 feet in diameter, but round a circumference some $17\frac{1}{2}$ feet from the centre the engineers who came to Calverton drove 25 bore holes at 4-foot intervals to a depth, as I have said, of rather over 400 feet. These bore holes contained closed tubes. Inside these were narrower tubes through which the freezing mixture—a brine solution—was pumped from a refrigerating plant on the surface. Three compressors were kept at work continuously, and condensers and a water-cooling tower were erected near the shaft.

Let us follow the process step by step. The cold brine went down at minus two degrees fahrenheit and returned to the surface at plus eight degrees fahrenheit. The freezing of the earth extended by about one foot a week, gradually solidifying the immediate pit site into a solid pillar. Within two months an adequate collar of ice was formed and within this barrier normal excavation could proceed. As the freezing advanced towards the centre, the expanding ice forced the surplus water up an overflow bore hole. When the freezing operation was completed the water which would otherwise have been seeping steadily into the workings was icebound and was kept, like a block of ice-cream in the family fridge until the winding gear—including a 1,750 horsepower electric plant for bringing excavated rock to the surface, and other new head stocks—were in place.

Then, as the twenty-foot shaft descended through the porous

layer, collars of cast iron were fitted round its inner circumference, supported at intervals by "cribs" or ledges driven into the shaft wall. When the complete shaft wall was in position, cement was pumped into the crevices behind. Thus, when the earth was finally unfrozen and the refrigerating plant moved from Calverton for similar work elsewhere, the shaft, like a huge cemented iron drain pipe, continued to hold back the surrounding water. The shaft goes down, of course, much deeper than the water-bearing strata, but the lower formations are non-porous, so that the actual mine working will have a solid roof of rock dividing it from what one can regard as a sort of "cistern" above.

(One ought to add that although Calverton was the first place in the county where this fascinating process was carried out, large-scale earth freezing is not in fact a new procedure. It was first applied in South Wales as long ago as 1862—only at shallow depths but with some success. The process was subsequently patented by German engineers in 1883. Its real possibilities, however, were not fully exploited until, shortly before the last war, it was used to a depth of more than thirteen hundred feet in the Campine coalfield in north-east Belgium.)

Thus Calverton, in the twentieth century, remains as much ahead of its times as it was in the sixteenth. Calverton has a late Georgian manor house, a rectory with a fine circular staircase and, half a mile to the south, at Foxwood, the remains of an oval hill fortress. Past Foxwood House we come to Woodborough, a village where the special cottages of the stocking knitters are even more conspicuous than at Calverton, each to be recognized by the single wide upper window behind which the frame stood, and here built in terraces, evidently as a single piece of speculative building. You could, until recently, hear an occasional hand frame at work in a cottage. Small though it is, Woodborough has numbered some celebrities among its residents. Here, for instance, in 1769, was born a character of the name of George Brown. The son of a stocking knitter, he became eminent locally as a gospeller and gained himself the name of The Walking Concordance. He died, still in Woodborough, in 1833. We may be thankful that he was before our time.

In Woodborough Hall there lived at the end of the nineteenth century Mansfield Parkyns who had been born in 1823 at Ruddington, south of Nottingham, and after being sent down from Cambridge went to the Middle East. After three years in Abyssinia he was found in Khartoum living as a native. He subsequently became a diplomat and was at the British Embassy in Constantinople. He wrote a book on his experiences in Abyssinia and in later life amused himself with wood carving, of which some specimens can be seen in the church at Woodborough. Woodborough was earlier one of the manors of the Strelleys of Strelley and the most interesting part of the church is the chancel built about 1356 by Richard de Strelley. This is lighted by a large east window filled with elaborate tracery and by smaller windows on either side of it. Among the names which appear on brasses and monuments in the church are those of Lacock and Bainbrigge.

A lady of this latter name, resident in Woodborough in the last years of the eighteenth century, caused Throsby, the otherwise unemotional editor of Thoroton, to go off suddenly and without explanation, in a paroxysm of eulogy of this Mrs. Bainbrigge. He wrote: "The lady lives in an old hall house; built in a plain style. She is the most extraordinary character, for benevolence, that I have ever heard of: it will be an agreeable task for her biographer to enumerate her extensive charities when the world shall be deprived, by her death, of these beneficent acts which are now the theme and praise of every social and good mind: To attempt here to particularize those merciful and pious deeds, which have made her name dear to all who know her, would be a task of difficulty, and might offend the serenity of that happy disposition which every one who knows would surely study not to offend: may her years be long! Happiness she must possess in superlative degree: may her death be like the setting sun, in a bright and calm evening when his rays, on leaving us, form a splendid and magnificent scene." Throsby inserts that passage abruptly among his usual austere retailing of facts. One wonders what is behind it. It can hardly have been the tender emotion: Throsby seems to accept Mrs. Bainbrigge's death as imminent. He implies that she was an aged lady. What benefit had she bestowed, or might she still bestow, on Throsby?

Epperstone is the nearest village east of Woodborough. It is an attractive place, which has a church mainly of the thirteenth century. Close by are Gonalston and Lowdham lying on parallel roads divided by the course of the Dover Beck. The church at Gonalston was rebuilt in 1853. It is clear, from eighteenth-century accounts of the place, that having been a large church in the Middle Ages it has been much reduced in size. Something of its condition then can be guessed from a contemporary remark: "The chancel appears, at first sight, to have been painted green; dampness has made the walls completely of that colour." As it happens, the old chancel walls, now no longer green, were incorporated in the existing building. The church contains three

monuments to members of the family of Heriz, who occupied the
manor of Gonalston from the time of Henry I. Two of the
monuments are of knights, cross-legged, wearing chain mail over
their heads and short swords at their sides. They are in poor
condition, but the third monument, of a lady wearing a wimple,
is much better preserved. Over her head—as though she were
not lying flat but standing upright—there is carved a trefoil arch
decorated with leaves. Just south of the village, which contains
several nice houses, seventeenth- and eighteenth-century, there
is a factory, a manufactory of the late eighteenth century. It lies
close to the Dover Beck and is thought to be the one described
in a book well known in these parts, *The Memoir of Robert
Blincoe*. Blincoe described the gruesome sufferings of a party of
eighty children from St. Pancras Workhouse in London. They
were sent to work in the mill at Gonalston, many of them of an
extremely tender age, and were apprenticed here until they were
twenty-one. They underwent appalling hardships and many of
them were dead long before this. Lowdham has less to offer than
Gonalston, though Lowdham Grange was converted, in 1930, into
an experimental Borstal Institute. The church here lies outside
the village across a stream. There is thirteenth-century work
here, as well as a fifteenth-century spire of the same kind as at
St. Peter's, Nottingham, and a chancel that was rebuilt at the end
of the last century. The font at Lowdham is considered one of
the best of its date in the country. It is octagonal, made in about
1300, with decorated gables issuing from human faces or the
bodies of animals. It is suggested that it was probably carved
by a mason, if only a minor one, of the group engaged in
the carving of the chapter house at Southwell. The house at
Lowdham, Lowdham Hall, or otherwise known as Broughton
Hall, is a gabled building of the late sixteenth or early seventeenth century, half timbered and plastered over. The family of
Broughton was formerly prominent in the village. The last
member seems to have died in 1777 and Throsby, twenty years
later, was remarking " the mansion which was formerly occupied
by this family is now the abode of a shoemaker". From Lowdham the road down to Hoveringham leads us to a ferry that
crosses the river opposite an inn at the bend of the road, and we
are on the Trent again looking over to Kneeton and behind it
the line of the Fosse Way.

The Trent. We have not yet paused long enough to think of
the Trent as a whole; as a whole, that is, that portion of it which
flows through our county. It never seems a bad plan when an
English river is under discussion to turn up old Drayton and

see what he has made of it. Do you know Michael Drayton's
Poly-Olbion? People do not read Michael Drayton very much
nowadays, but in his own time his work was greatly admired
and *Poly-Olbion*, which is a sort of poetical guide-book to
England, has much in it that can still instruct and, in modera-
tion, entertain. Drayton saw himself almost as much as a historian as a topographer, and his journey through the English
countryside, starting in the Channel Islands and ending in West-
morland, is just as full of legends of the past as of descriptions of
the existing natural scene. As he goes—and there is no saying
quite how much of the country he travelled himself in preparing
the poem—he describes the flora and fauna of England, its mountain ranges and its towns, and he pays special attention to its
rivers. Drayton's rhyming couplets of twelve syllabled lines do
become a little monotonous. But it is a capacious metre and
Drayton had a great deal to say. Drayton will be called to our aid
again to give his summary of the Robin Hood legends of Sherwood. Let us hear him now on the third river of England, on
the one hundred and seventy miles that divides the source of the
Trent in Staffordshire from the point where it joins the Ouse to
form the Humber. Drayton, and it was one of his ways of holding the interest of his contemporaries, almost always personified
his natural phenomena, and his rivers talk, argue, even marry
among themselves. So, inevitably, the Trent speaks to us with
a voice of her own. Apparently we take her a little unawares:

> looking wide, as one that newly waked had been,
> Saluted from the north, with Nottingham's proud height,
> So strongly is surprised, and taken with the sight,
> That she from running wild but hardly can refrain,
> To view in how great state, as she along doth strain,
> That brave exalted seat, beholdeth her in pride,
> As how the large spread meads upon the other side,
> All flourishing in flowers, and rich embroideries dressed,
> In which she sees herself above her neighbours blessed.

And so the Trent:

> As wrapt with the delights, that her this prospect brings,
> In her peculiar praise, low thus the river sings:
> "What should I care at all, from what my name I take,
> That thirty doth import, that thirty rivers make;
> My greatness what it is, or thirty abbeys great,
> That on my fruitful banks times formerly did seat:
> Or thirty kinds of fish that in my streams do live,
> To me this name of Trent did from that number give."

What reck I, the Trent asks, about my own etymology? Let Thames
and Severn boast their descent from Thame and the maid Sabrin:

> Let these imperious floods draw down their long descent
> From these so famous stocks, and only say of Trent,
> That moorlands barren earth me first to light did bring.

Then our Nottinghamshire river goes on:

> And of the British floods, though but the third I be,
> Yet Thames and Severn both in this come short of me,
> For that I am the mere of England, that divides
> The north part from the south, on my so either sides,
> That reckoning how these tracks in compass be extent,
> Men bound them on the north, or on the south of Trent.

(Nearly three and a half centuries later this observation of Trent's
still, to a great extent, holds good.) Finally the Trent embarks on
a list of the fishes to be found in her waters:

> My silver scaled skulls about my streams do sweep,
> Now in the shallow fords, now in the falling deep,
> So that of every kind, the new spawned numerous fry
> Seem in me as the sands that on my shore do lie.
> The barbel, than which fish a braver does not swim,
> Nor greater for the ford within my spacious brim,
> Nor (newly taken) more the curious taste does please;
> The greyling, whose great spawn is big as any peas;
> The perch with pricking fins, against the pike prepared,
> As nature had thereon bestowed this stronger guard,
> His daintiness to keep (each curious palates proof)
> From his vile ravenous foe: next him I name the ruffe,
> His very near ally, and both for scale and fin,
> In taste, and for his bait (indeed) his next of kin,
> The pretty slender dare, of many called the dace,
> Within my liquid glass, when Phoebus looks his face,
> Oft swiftly as he swims, his silver belly shows,
> But with such nimble flight, that ere he can disclose
> His shape, out of your sight like lightning he is shot.
> The trout by nature marked with many a crimson spot,
> As though she curious were in him above the rest,
> And of fresh water fish, did note him for the best;
> The roach, whose common kind to every flood doth fall:
> The chubb (whose neater name) which some a chevin call,
> Food to the tyrant pike (most being in his power)
> Who for their numerous store he most doth them devour;

The lusty salmon then, from Neptune's watery realm,
When as his season serves, stemming my tideful stream;
And Humber, to whose waste I pay my watery store,
Me of her sturgeons sends, that I thereby the more
Should have my beauty's grace with something from him sent:
Not Ancum's silvered eel excelleth that of Trent;
Though the sweet smelling smelt be more in Thames than me,
The lamprey and his less in Severn general be;
The flounder smooth and flat, in other rivers caught,
Perhaps in greater store, yet better are not thought:
The dainty gudgeon, loach, the minnow, and the bleak,
Since they but little are, I little need to speak
Of them, nor doth it fit me much of those to reck,
Which everywhere are found in every little beck;
Nor of the crayfish here, which creeps amongst my stones,
From all the rest alone, whose shell is all his bones:
For carp, the tench and bream, my other store among,
To lakes and standing pools, that chiefly do belong,
Here scouring in my fords, feed in my waters clear,
Are muddy fish in ponds to that which they are here.

With those words the River Trent ends her song. Out of the
list of her finny population only one or two items are perhaps
not entirely relevant even to the Nottinghamshire stretches of
the river. Is the cucumber-like odour of "the sweet smelling
smelt" familiar between Long Eaton and Gainsborough? Is
"the flounder smooth and flat" caught up here; and are there
really sturgeon in the Trent? But otherwise this list of about
1600—barbel, greyling, perch, pike, ruffe, dace, trout, roach,
chubb, salmon, eel, lampern and lamprey, gudgeon, loach, minnow, bleak, crayfish, carp, tench, bream—seems both reasonable
and comprehensive. Indeed, if one were to try to add to that
list to-day one would, in suggesting the miller's thumb or bullhead
and the three- and ten-spined sticklebacks be offending against
Trent's refusal

to reck
Which everywhere are found in every little beck.

However, if one was being fussy and natural-historical, one might
insist, as established Nottinghamshire fauna, on the turbot, the
rudd, the white bream, the spiked loach and the shad. As Drayton continues, rather majestically I consider, having given special
praise to "the lovely Soar, gentle Soar", he watches the river
flow out of the county in the enumeration of some of the Trent's
tributaries and affluents:

Open-cast mining at Gilt Hill

From Nottingham, near which this river first begun
This song, she the meanwhile by Newark having run,
Receiving little Smyte, from Belvoir's battening grounds,
At Gainsborough goes out, where the Lincolnian bounds.
Yet Sherwood all this while not satisfied to show
Her love to princely Trent, as downward she doth flow,
To Meden and her Man, she down from Mansfield sends
To Idle for her aid. . . .

O

Rufford Abbey in 1951

CHAPTER VIII

COUNTRY OF TWO WRITERS (I)

I T is an odd and somehow very satisfying coincidence that the same stretch of country, not much more than ten miles square, should, for posterity, enshrine the memory of two great writers whose lives were separated by almost exactly a hundred years. To be sure, only one of them was born here; but both spent their young manhood within, so to say, walking distance of each other —though in what extraordinarily different social circumstances! —and for both, though each travelled very widely and each died on the shores of the Mediterranean, it is not forcing the issue to claim that for ever the stretch of country between Nottingham and Mansfield contains the souls of Lord Byron and D. H. Lawrence.

To claim any literary affinity between the two would be grotesque. We have, as a matter of fact, woken up in recent years to the fact that Byron's greatest work was the slapdash, arrogant, take-it-or-leave-it versification of *Don Juan*. We are going, I fancy, to wake up soon to Lawrence's more delicate, more careful excellencies as a writer of what I suppose one must call *vers libre*. Personally, if I were to be permitted on my shelves only one volume of Lawrence's works I would hug in preference to all others the volume of his collected poems which contains that incomparable sequence called *Birds, Beasts and Flowers*. If Byron were able to pass judgment on Lawrence's writings I suspect that over most of them he would be bewildered and scathing; he would think *Lady Chatterley's Lover*, for instance, ludicrously sentimental; which indeed it is. I doubt whether he would be bothered with the involved interpretation of reptiles and insects and fruits which are to us the interest of *Birds, Beasts and Flowers*. But I suggest that Byron would, if not admire, at least have a fellow-feeling for those cross, outrageous firecrackers that Lawrence let off between the feet of the British bourgeoisie and which he made into the two volumes called *Nettles* and *Pansies*. Many of these tiny satirical poems are silly; many are badly written. But Byron was often silly, particularly when he was angry about British public opinion; and he descended to many stylistic horrors when the stanzas of *Don Juan* were being thrown off at speed. Yes, I think Byron would have known what Lawrence's feelings were, though perhaps a meeting between the two of them in the Elysian fields would be a chilly and embarrassed affair, each conscious of the other's differences of outlook, each scornful of the other's self-dramatized personality. But there is one thing they certainly had in common. Byron was perhaps the best letter writer in the English language. This is no place to argue about the epistolary style; but of its own kind, its intimate yet detached, selfish yet self-mocking kind, Byron's is pre-eminent. And as for Lawrence, well, if I were allowed it, there would stand beside *Birds, Beasts and Flowers* that volume of D. H. Lawrence's letters that Aldous Huxley edited so brilliantly before the war. In that, it seems to me, Lawrence is shown as coming within hailing distance of Byron. All in all, in the freedom and ease of their verse and in the wonderfully direct use they made of prose, there is a connection between the two.

The two of them have, so far as the Nottinghamshire setting of their lives is concerned, to be discussed quite separately. To try to squeeze them into the same bed would be ridiculous. I am going to begin by pulling together, now, around Newstead, all that I think should further be said about Byron and the county, his life at Newstead as opposed to the brief uneasy sojourn at Southwell that we have already heard of, and outside, again, his incursions into the political and industrial life of Nottingham. And with Newstead and Colwick must come a brief word about Byron's ancestry. Byron first, then; but before we go to Newstead I want, as it were, to take one glimpse at the country which separates Newstead and Nottingham, looking at it from that mining village about eight miles from Nottingham and one mile from the small stream, the Erewash, which divides Nottinghamshire from Derbyshire. "It is hilly country, looking west to Crich and towards Matlock, sixteen miles away, and east and north-east towards Mansfield and the Sherwood Forest district. To me it seemed, and still seems, an extremely beautiful countryside, just between the red sandstone and the oak trees of Nottinghamshire, and the cold limestone, the ash trees, the stone fences of Derbyshire. To me, as a child and a young man, it was still the old England of the forest and agricultural past; the mines were, in a sense, an accident in the landscape, and Robin Hood and his merry men were not very far away."

I shall use Lawrence's eyes again later, when we have made our pilgrimage to Newstead, but I would prefer to quote here and now—partly because Byron's descriptions of "his" country are so much less specific—that deservedly famous passage from a letter which Lawrence wrote in 1926, three years before he died. "How well I can see Hucknall Torkard and the miners! Didn't you go into the church to see the tablet, where Byron's heart is buried? My father used to sing in the Newstead Abbey choir, as a boy. But I've gone many times down Hucknall Long Lane to Watnall—and I like Watnall Park—it's a great Sunday morning walk. Some of my happiest days I've spent haymaking in the fields just opposite the S. side of Greasley church—bottom of Watnall Hill—adjoining the vicarage: Miriam's father hired those fields. If you're in those parts again, go to Eastwood, where I was born, and lived for my first 21 years. Go to Walker St—and stand in front of the third house—and look across at Crich on the left, Underwood in front—High Park woods and Annesley on the right: I lived in that house from the age of 6 to 18, and I know that view better than any in the world. Then walk down the fields to the Breach, and in the corner house facing the stile I lived from 1 to 6. And walk up Engine Lane, over the level-crossing at Moorgreen pit, along till you come to the highway (the Alfreton Rd)—turn to the left, towards Underwood, and go till you come to the lodge gate by the reservoir—go through the gate and up the drive to the next gate, and continue on the footpath just below the drive on the left—or through the wood to Felley Mill (the *White Peacock* farm). When you've crossed the brook, turn to the right through Felley Mill gate, and go up the footpath to Annesley. Or better still, turn to the right, up-hill, before you descend to the brook, and go on uphill, up the rough deserted pasture—on past Annesley Kennels—long empty—on to Annesley again. That's the country of my heart."

And, to some extent, of Byron's heart too. Let us leap backwards, without more ado, to the year 1811. Byron had been abroad for the whole of the first half of that year, but he was intermittently in residence at Newstead from the beginning of August until mid-October. Nevertheless, although he wrote from Cambridge on 22nd October, 1811, that "Newstead is my regular address" he does not seem to have been installed there for any length of time until October 1813, when he wrote to Lady Melbourne "from the melancholy mansion of my fathers, where I am dull as the longest decease of my progenitors . . ."; which gives us our cue to go right back to the beginning, to Newstead before those "progenitors" possessed it. Newstead (which simply means "new place" and which in old deeds is called "Novo Loco in Sherwode") was never an abbey. It was founded between 1165 and 1173 by King Henry II as a priory of Augustinian canons.

Its foundation—as was that of other monasteries—was partly a penance for the death of St. Thomas à Becket, brought about by the King's anger. The community that occupied the monastery were "regular" canons of St. Augustine, the ones commonly called, from the sombre hue of their habit, black friars. The King bestowed on the monastery the church and town of Papplewick and other endowments and Newstead grew rich, acquiring under successive kings new lands and tenements in Bulwell Wood, Edwinstowe, Hucknall and Nottingham. On their journeys through the kingdom successive monarchs were entertained by the abbots of Newstead. King John was there in 1201, Edward I in 1290 and again the following year, and was followed by Edward III, Edward IV and Henry VII; while Cardinal Wolsey slept a night at Newstead during his last sad journey from York to Leicester in 1530.

Less than ten years later, on July 1, 1539, Newstead was surrendered to King Henry VIII. The following year the site and the lands were granted to Sir John Byron, Knight, commonly called Sir John Byron The Little With The Great Beard. He died in 1567 and his alabaster tomb-chest (now—to anticipate—removed to Newstead) was to be seen in the church at Colwick, the former seat of the Byrons, together with memorials to his wives.

The Byrons were an ancient and warlike family. They were originally Norman, and the founder of the line, Ralph de Burun, apparently *did* come over with the Conqueror and was given lands in what are now the counties of Nottingham and Derby. Byrons—John and Richard seemed to have been the most common names for the eldest sons—fought in England's wars abroad, at Cressey and Calais, at Antioch and Ascalon, and later, in their own shires, at Bosworth Field, at Edgehill—where no fewer than six Byrons fought—and at Marston Moor. The Byrons were Royalists in the Civil War, and for distinguished services to King Charles I, Sir John Byron, the seventeenth of the line since the Conquest, and the fifth since the acquisition of Newstead, was created Baron Byron of Rochdale in the county of Lancashire.

The first Lord Byron suffered bitterly for his attachment to the King: his estates were sequestered by Parliament and he died in exile, and in poverty, in France in 1652. However, the estates were restored to the family at the Restoration and Charles II himself visited Newstead and was magnificently entertained.

The Byron title occurs once more, before we get to the poet, in national or at any rate local history. With the doings and misdoings of William, the fifth peer, known as the "wicked Lord

Byron ", whose exploits were the terror of the neighbourhood. A younger brother was Admiral John Byron, the poet's grandfather. He was a popular sailor but was known as "foul weather Jack". Although the sailors liked him there was a superstition among them that the Admiral always ran into storms. The fifth lord led, in his younger days, a riotous and extravagant life, and in his maturity was generally supposed to be mad. He enjoyed such pastimes as flinging his wife into the lake, killing all the deer in the park and cutting down all the trees, and converting the best rooms in the abbey into stables and lumber rooms. In the summer of 1760, in the fifth lord's time, Horace Walpole visited Newstead. He reported that "the great east window of the church is still untouched, though connected with the house, the hall entire, the refectory entire, the cloister untouched". Admirable though the creator of Strawberry found these authentic Gothic survivals, and impressed though he must have been by the fifth lord's Folly Castle in the grounds, a sham Gothic structure, now demolished, built in 1749 before Walpole began Gothicizing Strawberry Hill, yet he found much to disapprove of in Lord Byron's activities. "The present Lord," Walpole wrote, "has lost large sums and paid part in old oaks, £5,000 worth of which have been cut near the house. In recompense he has built two baby forts, to pay his country in castles for the damage done to the Navy, and planted a handful of Scotch firs that look like ploughboys dressed in old family liveries for a public day." These two castellated forts on the upper lake opposite the front of the abbey are still there to be seen: one near the Victorian stables and the second on the other side of the water. In addition the fifth lord who in his early days had been in the Navy like his brother, is said to have kept a twenty-gun ship afloat on the lake.

But these architectural eccentricities were spoilt by the wicked lord's ill-doings. Since the incident, distressing though it was, played so large a part in county history, in bringing together, in such unpleasant circumstances, two of its most famous families, the duel between the wicked lord and William Chaworth ought to be described in detail. Apparently Lord Byron and Chaworth were not only neighbours and cousins but close friends as well. There was a club in London, composed exclusively of Nottinghamshire gentlemen, of which both were members. The club held its meetings at the Star and Garter Tavern in Pall Mall. One of these meetings was in progress on 17th January, 1765, at which ten gentlemen were present. After dinner, while all were sitting over their wine, a conversation arose about the game laws. Lord Byron and Chaworth held different views on the subject,

Chaworth insisting that poachers should be treated with severity, while Byron maintained that the best way to preserve game was to take no care of it at all. The argument became quite heated. Chaworth asserted that he had more game on five acres than Lord Byron had on all his manors. Byron bet one hundred guineas that this was not the case. The bet, however, was not accepted and the rest of the company, sensing that matters were going a little too far, interfered and good humouredly tried to put an end to the subject.

For a time they were successful, but the argument between Chaworth and Byron broke out again, the former asserting that if it were not for his, Chaworth's, care and that of Sir Charles Sedley, another Nottinghamshire landlord, Lord Byron would not have a single hare on his estate. Byron asked with a smile which Sir Charles Sedley's manors were. Chaworth answered, Nuthall and Bulwell. Byron did not dispute Nuthall, but said Bulwell was his. Chaworth, rather heatedly, replied, "If you want information with respect to Sir Charles Sedley's manors, he lives at Mr. Cooper's in Dean Street, and I doubt not will be ready to give you satisfaction; and as to myself, your lordship knows where to find me in Berkeley Row . . ." or words to that effect. This speech of Chaworth's put an end to the discussion and the company chatted among themselves until, as was his habit, Chaworth called for the bill. Byron followed Chaworth out of the room and caught up with him on the stairs. It was never clear whether Byron challenged Chaworth or Chaworth Byron, but both went up to the landing and told a waiter to show them an empty room, which he did. Having opened the door himself and put a small tallow candle which he had in his hand on the table, he withdrew when the two gentlemen went in and closed the door behind them.

After a very few moments the bell was rung (again, it is uncertain who rang it). The waiter went up, looked into the room, ran downstairs again in a state of alarm and went to the landlord. He went upstairs and found the two combatants standing close together. Chaworth had his sword in his left hand and Lord Byron his in his right. Byron's left hand was round Chaworth's neck and Chaworth's right hand was round Byron's shoulders. Chaworth told the landlord to take his sword and Byron handed him his at the same time. One or both of them called to the landlord to get some help and in a few moments a doctor had arrived.

Chaworth was able to give his account of what had happened. He said that he and Byron entered the room together, Byron leading the way. While Byron was saying something about their previous argument Chaworth closed the door. When he turned round from doing this he saw Byron with his sword drawn or nearly so, and instantly drew his own. He made a thrust which he thought had wounded or even killed the other man, and then, seeing Byron shorten his sword to return the thrust, he tried to parry it with his left hand. He remembered looking twice at his hand thinking it had been cut in the attempt. Then he felt Byron's sword enter his body and go deep into his back. He struggled with Byron and being, in spite of the wound, the stronger man, he disarmed him, expressing the fear, at the same time, that he had mortally wounded him. Byron said much the same thing to Chaworth, adding at the same time that he hoped now he would allow him to be as brave a man as any in the kingdom. Shortly after this Chaworth died.

The sequel to the duel took place some three months later when, on 16th April, 1765, Lord Byron surrendered himself to be tried by his peers and at about half-past nine that morning drove to Westminster. Escorted by parties of the Horse and Foot Guards, and attended by the Lieutenant Governor and Constable of the Tower, he travelled by coach to Westminster Hall. The trial lasted two days, after which the peers adjourned to the House of Lords where they deliberated on their verdict. They found Byron guilty of manslaughter; but by an old statute that " peers are in all cases, where clergy is allowed, to be dismissed without burning in the hand, loss of inheritance or corruption of blood ", Lord Byron was immediately dismissed on a payment of his fees.

These costs must have been considerable, for it is said that to defray the expenses of the trial Byron was obliged to mortgage Hucknall for £30,000. The mortgage was never redeemed and so the manor in which the family burial place of the Byron's is situated, and where, in time, the poet's own ashes were to lie, passed out of the family and were never in the possession of the poet.

From that time on he lived in sombre and savage seclusion. He retired to Newstead and acquired a legendary reputation for unbelievable wickedness. He occasionally wandered afield under false names but most of his time was spent at Newstead, where he was believed locally to be waited on by devils and to spend his time drilling battalions of crickets, whipping them when necessary with straw, to such effect that on his death they marched out of the abbey in close formation. Rumour had it that having shot his coachman he drove Lady Byron about with the dead man sitting beside her in the coach. Most of this was nonsense. All the same the fifth lord seems to have had, in his later years, a fixed determination to wreck Newstead, so that when it passed to his son, whom he hated, it would be in a completely dilapidated condition. He did his malevolent work thoroughly. He died, almost alone and unattended, in literally the only room in the abbey which did not admit the wind and the rain. The whole mansion was rotten, decayed and neglected. Resolved, apparently, that not a single deer should remain in the park, the herds had been slaughtered and out of the thousands that had roamed there previously not a single animal remained alive. Venison, we are told, hung plentifully in the shambles at Mansfield and was sold for practically nothing.

For some reason the fifth lord considered that he had been wronged by his son. Certainly the boy had married contrary to his father's wishes, though not without his reluctant consent. However the son died soon after his marriage and his issue, a son, was killed in Corsica. Thus it was that the title and property came to the young son of the wicked lord's nephew, John Byron, or "mad Jack" Byron as he was called. He was an officer in the Guards, a profligate and unsatisfactory fellow. He was gay and handsome, however, and had seduced Amelia D'Arcy, Marchioness of Caernarvon, daughter of the Earl of Holderness and Countess Conyers in her own right. She was divorced by the marquess, and John Byron married her. They had two daughters, only one of whom, Augusta, survived. On his first wife's death, John Byron persuaded an Aberdeenshire heiress, Catherine Gordon of Gight, a member of the ducal house of Gordon, to marry him. The £20,000 of her fortune was soon spent; and shortly after the birth, at 16 Holles Street, London, on 23rd January, 1788, of a son who was named George Gordon Byron, the child's father had to flee from his creditors in London. The future poet and his mother went to live in Aberdeen. There, for a time, John Byron lived with them; but he soon moved to France, where, at Valenciennes, "penniless, poxed and unrepentant", as a modern biographer described it, he died in 1791.

Neither circumstances nor John Byron had been kind to the poet's mother. Nevertheless her misfortunes do not excuse her deplorable shortcomings as the parent of a sensitive only child. "My poor mother," Byron told Lady Blessington, "was generally in a rage every day, and used to render me sometimes frantic: particularly when, in her passion, she reproached me with my personal deformity." Catherine Byron was absurdly proud of her ancestral connection. "My mother," Byron wrote, "who was as

207

haughty as Lucifer with her descent from the Stewarts, and her right line from the *old Gordons, not the Seyton Gordons,* as she disdainfully termed the ducal branch, was always reminding me how superior her Gordons were to the southern Byrons." With her, Byron's childhood was violent and unhappy. He defied her in her tantrums, and shouted back at her, even when she had been drinking. Sometimes the scene was different: weeping, she would clasp him to her fleshy self and smother him with sentimentality.

When Byron was ten years old the fifth lord died. The poet and his grand-uncle had never met, and the old lord referred to him as "that brat in Aberdeen". The new peer was made a Ward in Chancery; and selling her possessions in Aberdeen for a paltry £74 17s. 4d., Lord Byron's excited mama, with the boy in tow, inflated with her new grandeur, hastened south to Newstead. They took with them only one nursemaid.

By 1798, when Byron first saw it, Newstead was a wreck, but it is the moment, perhaps, to consider the history of the building, as it was in monastic days, as it was when he first saw it, and as one sees it to-day. The way one usually comes to the abbey—or priory to be more correct—is from the gate on the Mansfield road, guarded by the Pilgrim Oak, from which a winding drive brings you to the west front of the building. Facing you is the ruined west wall of the priory church and beside it the front of the house. The west front dates from the latest period of medieval work at Newstead, and is a specially fine example of late thirteenth-century church front. The front is divided into three parts with narrow buttresses between, as though there had stood behind it a church with two aisles. In fact there never was an aisle on the south side, and that portion of the façade is therefore a sham. (Professor Pevsner refers to this as a "remarkably early instance of preference given to aesthetic over functional considerations".) Actually the south end of the front merely screens the buildings—originally the north end of the block that included the prior's lodging and hall—which stood at the north-west angle of the cloister lying along the south side of the church.

In spite of its sightless eyes and the palpable blankness and emptiness behind it, the west front remains an object of great beauty, and a superb specimen of an Early English façade. The ground-floor level is taken up with tall, rather narrow ranges of blank arcading with hardly any ornamentation beyond cusps in the wider arches, capitals carved with the formalized leaves, the so-called "stiff leaf" of the Early English period which preceded the naturalistic foliage sculpture of which the chapter house at Southwell provides the supreme example. Certain of the Newstead capitals, presumably those carved last, display some naturalistic vine leaves with grapes. Over the finely moulded central portal, which is divided in two by a mullion, is carved a seated figure of Christ. The first-floor level consists of three huge windows of equal height, of which those on the flanks are blank—the tracery of four-light windows being over stone work and not glass—while that in the centre had six genuine lights, and must have brought brilliant illumination into the church. Its tracery has vanished except for a few small fragments. The façade is crowned by a gable containing a niche in which—astonishingly, and no doubt due to its inaccessible height—a figure of the Virgin still survives. Beneath this niche, and filling up most of the remainder of the triangular gable, a not altogether satisfactory six-fold window was cut, in the late fourteenth or early fifteenth century.

Behind the west front of the church there lies merely an empty space. The remains of the church were evidently used as a quarry for the alterations that were carried out when Sir John Byron, son of Henry VIII's grantee, converted the domestic buildings of the monastery into a residence for himself. The alterations carried out by the Byrons in the early period of their occupation did not involve large structural changes or the disappearance of the monastic character of the building. The prior's lodging and hall, the dining-hall or refectory with its vaulted under-croft, the complete quadrangle of the cloister (originally unglazed; the date when glass was first put in is unknown), with fountain and, presumably, fish pond in the centre, the parlour, rectangular chapter house and dormitory, with warming house below it—all these were incorporated with the minimum of fuss or search for comfort into the mansion which the poet eventually inherited. Minor alterations were made during the sixteenth, seventeenth and eighteenth centuries.

Certain overmantels survive, one in the prior's parlour, dated 1556. The ceiling of the great hall was remade in 1633 with plaster panels of vases; but, after the severe dilapidations which took place during the ownership of the " wicked " lord, the place must have presented an appearance, yet, of a decayed monastery rather than of a nobleman's residence. The rooms which Byron occupied himself were still, literally, the only ones habitable, and there is some excuse for the rather violent methods he employed to keep himself and his guests cheerful and warm in the lack of comfort or even of the amenities of a normal house. To-day one is apt to feel that the dressing up as monks and the drinking out of skulls that Byron and his guests indulged in are unnecessarily "romantic", even for Newstead. But the Newstead which we see to-day is very far from the tumbledown, draughty, echoing ruin that he knew.

Its present appearance is almost entirely due to Colonel Wildman and his architect, John Shaw, of whose almost entirely praiseworthy contributions to the preservation of Newstead we shall come in a moment.

Meanwhile we may permit ourselves a few glimpses of Byron in residence and of some of his reactions in verse to the place as he knew it. His first views of Newstead seem to have affected him deeply, and he was constantly returning in his poetical work to the sense of desolation which the place produced in him. He wrote later of his accession to the title:

> Newstead! what saddening change of scene is thine?
> The yawning arch betokens slow decay!
> The last and youngest of a noble line
> Now holds thy mouldering turrets in his sway.
>
> Deserted now, he scans thy grey walled towers!
> Thy vaults, where dead of feudal ages sleep;
> Thy cloisters pervious to the wintry showers;
> These he views, and views them but to weep.

Right at the end of his life, in writing what were destined to be the final cantos of his unfinished masterpiece *Don Juan*, he returned, from his Italian exile, to the vision of the house and the church façade lying calm and ancient between its woods and its lake.

> A glorious remnant of the Gothic pile
> (While yet the church was Rome's) stood half apart
> In a grand arch, which once screen'd many an aisle.
> These last had disappear'd—a loss to art:
> The first yet frowned superbly o'er the soil,
> And kindled feelings in the roughest heart,
> Which mourn'd the power of time's or tempest's march,
> In gazing on that venerable arch.
>
> A mighty window, hollow in the centre,
> Shorn of its glass of thousand colourings,
> Through which the deepen'd glories once could enter,
> Streaming from off the sun like seraph's wings,

Now yawns all desolate: now loud, now fainter,
The gale sweeps through its fretwork, and oft sings
The owl his anthem, where the silenced quire
Lie with their hallelujahs quench'd like fire.

Here are two more passages, the first dealing with the garden as
well as the house:

Through thy battlements, Newstead, the hollow winds whistle;
Thou, the hall of my fathers, art gone to decay;
In thy once smiling garden, the hemlock and thistle
Have chok'd up the rose which late bloom'd in the way.

and the second the building alone, with a reference to the circumstances of its foundation:

Newstead! fast-falling, once-resplendent dome!
Religion's shrine! repentant Henry's pride!
Of warriors, monks, and dames the cloister's tomb,
Whose pensive shades around thy ruins glide,
Hail to thy pile! more honour'd in thy fall
Than modern mansions in their pillar's state;
Proudly majestic frowns thy vaulted hall,
Scowling defiance on the blasts of fate.

In 1798, even though the fifth lord may have died there, residence
at Newstead was impossible for the sixth and his mother. Having
looked at Newstead, they moved into rooms in Nottingham.
Schooldays at Dulwich and then at Harrow followed. Mrs. Byron
had got a pension of £300 a year from the King and could live
in rooms in London. In 1800 Byron made his "first dash into
poetry".

In 1803, while Byron was in his third year at Harrow, Newstead was let for a mere £100 a year to Lord Grey de Ruthyn, a
young man of twenty-three. During his tenancy he wrote and
asked Byron to stay with him at Newstead, a suggestion which
outraged Mrs. Byron but which her son accepted.

At Newstead Byron met and fell in love with the heiress of
Annesley, Mary Ann Chaworth. She was at that time a graceful
and charming girl of about seventeen, much more experienced in
the world and its ways than the impressionable Byron, who was
then a fattish, limping and rather ungainly schoolboy of not quite
sixteen. She accepted his companionship: after all, in spite of
the fifth Lord Byron's duel with Mary Ann's great-uncle, the

friendship of centuries' duration survived between the two neighbouring families. But she was cold and patronizing in the face
of his undoubted, if adolescent, passion. She is supposed to have
remarked within Byron's hearing to a maid or a friend: "Do
you think I could care for that lame boy?" To do her justice
she was, at that age, already bethrothed—and deeply attached—
to the Jack Musters whom, to her eventual unhappiness, she was
soon to marry.

It was Byron's first serious passion for a woman. He had had,
at the age of eight, a strong attachment to a little cousin in Scotland, Mary Duff—an affair whose precocity, as were the early
physical developments of Byron's amorous propensities, was a
cause of astonishment, in later life, even to the poet himself. At
Harrow he had had sentimental friendships, hovering on the
brink of passion, with other boys, chief among them Lord Clare,
who warmly reciprocated Byron's affection (towards the end of
his life Byron wrote: "I never hear the word 'Clare' without
a beating of the heart even now."). But his passion for Mary
Chaworth—which was also never to leave him—was perhaps the
only deeply felt and lasting love for a woman he would ever
experience. Juvenile though it was, this love affair must have
been impossible for those around him not to take with some
measure of seriousness, because even his mother was obliged to
write of him, this year, 1803: "He has no indisposition that
I know of, but love, desperate love, the worst of all maladies
in my opinion." The poem containing the most striking impression of this love affair was composed at the Villa Diodati,
near Geneva, in July 1816, shortly after Byron had made
his dramatic, and final, departure from England. It is called
The Dream; and it includes this description of the hills of
Annesley:

> I saw two beings in the hues of youth
> Standing upon a hill, a gentle hill,
> Green and of mild declivity, the last
> As 'twere the cape of a long ridge of such,
> Save that there was no sea to lave its base,
> But a most living landscape, and the wave
> Of woods and cornfields, and the abodes of men
> Scattered at intervals, and wreathing smoke
> Arising from such rustic roofs;—the hill
> Was crown'd with a peculiar diadem
> Of trees, in circular array, so fix'd,
> Not by the sport of nature, but of man.

As a footnote to this passage from *The Dream* it is perhaps worth drawing attention to a letter which is preserved at New-stead Abbey in the Roe-Byron collection. It dates from November 1831, seven years after Byron's death. It is a letter from Byron's half-sister, Mrs. Augusta Leigh. She is writing to a Miss Cursham, who was the author of a romantic novel called *Norman Abbey*, based on the history of Newstead and of the Byrons. Mrs. Leigh thanks Miss Cursham for the details she has supplied of the fate of poor Mrs. Musters, the former Mary Ann Chaworth, who died of exposure and exhaustion after her husband's house, Colwick Hall, had been attacked by Reform Bill rioters on the same night that Nottingham Castle was fired. "The devastation," she writes, "seems to have been dreadful." Then she adds: "Oh! the Diadem. You do not really mean that it has been cut down!" Certainly the "hill crowned with a peculiar diadem of trees" has long been bereft of the wooded circle that Byron knew, and where he took his leave of Mary Ann. There was a legend that Musters had the trees cut down out of spite and jealousy of Byron. The fact is, apparently, that the soil is very sandy and the trees fell down out of exhaustion, though Musters may have cut down some of the last survivors, when he found they were in danger, to prevent them causing mischief. Byron's description of the Annesley Hills is well known, from the fragment of rather amateurish verse, scribbled in pencil on a piece of notepaper, which used to be preserved at Annesley:

> Hills of Annesley! bleak and barren,
> Where my thoughtless childhood strayed;
> How the northern tempests, warring,
> Howl about thy tufted shade.
>
> Now no more the hours beguiling,
> Former favourite haunts I see;
> Now no more my Mary smiling
> Makes ye seem a heaven to me.

"Bleak and barren" the Annesley Hills may have been in Byron's time, but of recent years good work has been done by the Forestry Commission in planting on the hills on to which the windows of Annesley Hall look out. Alas, the pleasant group of buildings formed, on the bend of the road, within a bowl of hills by Annesley Hall and its adjoining old church of All Saints is now sadly spoilt by the derelict condition of the church, which seems to be going the way of the already roofless church beside the

Musters' old house, Colwick Hall. Annesley Hall which, until the nineteenth century, presented a picturesque, if irregular and rather haphazard mass of partly medieval masonry—house and long outbuildings close round the church—was given symmetrical form in early Victorian times; some gables of the sixteenth and seventeenth century, incorporated in the rebuilding, can be detected. Restored à la Elizabethan, it retained some of its original atmosphere, being built in a square with a courtyard in the middle. The main house occupied one side, stables on another, and the remaining two given up to domestic apartments.

The present colliery village of New Annesley lies a mile or so further north and with the other settlements of Annesley Grove and Annesley Woodhouse it shares the new church of All Saints, built in 1874, as a substitute and ultimate replacement for the old one beside the hall. The architect of the new church was that remarkable man Thomas Graham Jackson, whose only building in the county this is. Jackson, who died in 1924 a baronet and Royal Academician, was the designer of the Examination Schools in the High Street in Oxford with which, by winning the competition for the design, two years after the building of the church at Annesley, he introduced a particularly elaborate and confident style of revived Jacobean architecture which is known familiarly as "Anglo-Jackson". Jackson was born in 1835 and after being educated at Oxford studied architecture in the office of Gilbert Scott. It was in Oxford that Jackson did his most important work, and it is a pity that one cannot, at Annesley, apart from an attractive wooden porch, see the church as he left it. Unfortunately it had to be partly rebuilt after a fire in 1908. The church contained an alabaster monument of the sixteenth century. It is the figure of an unknown man lying down swathed in a voluminous shroud. The lines of the dead face and the deep folds of the drapery—through which the form of the body's knees and legs are skilfully suggested—makes it a sombre and impressive piece of sculpture.

1803 was the year of Byron's love affair with Mary Ann Chaworth. Two years later she had married Jack Musters, Byron had quarrelled with Grey de Ruthyn and so paid no more visits to Newstead during his tenancy, and Mrs. Byron had moved from Nottingham to Southwell. His attitudes during this period we have already touched on, but the poet's brief but important Newstead period was beginning to take shape while he was still corresponding with his friends there. Early in 1808 he wrote from London to the Rev. John Becher, a Southwell friend and an intimate of the Pigot family who, you may remember, was Byron's

In the oilfield at Eakring

main support against the boredom of Southwell. To Becher he wrote: "I hear Lord Ruthyn leaves Newstead in April. As soon as he quits it for ever, I wish much you would take a ride over, survey the mansion, and give me your candid opinion on the most advisable mode of proceeding with regard to the house. *Entre nous*, I am cursedly dipped; my debts, every thing inclusive, will be nine or ten thousand before I am twenty-one. But I have reason to think my property will turn out better than general expectation may conceive. Of Newstead I have little hope or care; but Hanson, my agent, intimated my Lancashire property was worth three Newsteads. I believe we have it hollow; though the defendants are protracting the surrender, if possible, till after my majority, for the purpose of forming some arrangement with me, thinking I shall probably prefer a sum in hand to a reversion. Newstead I may sell;—perhaps I will not,—though of that more anon. . . ."

But this mood soon changed: or, perhaps, does that letter in fact conceal the affection which Byron was developing for "the hall of my fathers"? Now it is 1809 again—the year in which we first encountered Byron in these pages, the year in which he came of age, took his seat in the House of Lords and made his speech on the Luddite Riots. That year he writes to his mother: "Come what may, Newstead and I stand or fall together. I have now lived in the spot, I have fixed my heart upon it, and no pressure, present or future, shall induce me to barter the last vestige of our inheritance. I have that pride within me which will enable me to support difficulties. I can endure privations; but could I obtain in exchange for Newstead Abbey the first fortune in the country, I would reject the proposition. Set your mind at ease on that score; Mr. Hanson talks like a man of business on the subject,—I feel like a man of honour, and I will not sell Newstead."

Of course, Newstead *was* sold, nine years later, but circumstances had by that time so changed for Byron that he can hardly be thought of as the same person. He was then famous; he had been courted; he had been married—and ostracized; and he had gone abroad. To him, in 1809, still obscure, the acquisition of Newstead was the first exciting event of his life.

But now he wrote to a friend: "If my resources are not adequate to the supply I must sell, but not Newstead." He was by now installed there and his personal connection with the place had by that time been cemented in a curious way. The same day that he wrote the sentence quoted above he wrote to inform a friend: "Boatswain is dead, he expired in a state of madness

Open field cultivation at Laxton

on the tenth after suffering much, yet retaining all the gentleness of his nature to the last, never attempting to do the least injury to anyone near him. I have now lost everything except old Murray. . . ." He adds later: "Boatswain is to be buried in a vault awaiting for myself. I have also written an epitaph which I would send were it not for two reasons: one is, it is too long for a letter; and the other, that I hope you will some day read it on the spot where it will be engraved."

We can do that in the gardens of Newstead to-day, even though the epitaph, still legible, remains too long even for a book. The monument, which lies at the extremity of the ruins of the old church, consists of a rather over-large octagonal pedestal, panelled with white marble and surmounted by an ornately carved urn. It stands on a circular base consisting of six steps some of which gape apart in an odd way, due, it is said, to an earthquake. Above the long verse epitaph it bears the following inscription: "Near this spot Are deposited the Remains of one Who possessed Beauty without Vanity, Strength without Insolence, Courage without Ferocity, and all the Virtues of Man without his Vices. This praise, which would be unmeaning Flattery If inscribed over human ashes, Is but a just tribute to the memory of BOATSWAIN, a Dog, Who was born at Newfoundland, May, 1803, And died at Newstead Abbey, Nov. 18, 1808." The twenty-six lines of the epitaph which follow consist, mainly, of an attack upon the pretensions and degradations of mankind in contrast to the humility, in life as in death, of the faithful dog. It ends:

> Ye! who perchance behold this simple urn,
> Pass on—it honours none you wish to mourn;
> To mark a friend's remains these stones arise;
> I never knew but one,—and here he lies.

When Byron wrote that Boatswain (who was a black-and-white Newfoundland) was to be buried "in a vault waiting for myself", he seems to have meant it. In his will, which was executed three years after Boatswain's death, in 1811, he left directions to have his body laid beside that of his faithful hound, in a vault constructed underneath the monument. He was "to be buried without any ceremony or burial service whatever, or any inscription, save his name and age. His dog not to be removed from the said vault". He apparently never repented this wish, and expressed his regret when, in 1817, the abbey was sold, he would be deprived of his desired resting place. Byron also intended that his servant, old Joe Murray, who, in his youth, had been a "sailor boy" on

the "wicked" lord's boats, should share the vault with himself
and Boatswain. But this too was frustrated and Murray lies close
to his master in Hucknall church. His portrait is still to be seen
in the abbey, however, as is that of Boatswain.

Byron believed that the spot he chose for Boatswain's tomb
was the site of the high altar of the priory church which, if so,
must have been of very great length. But modern authorities
considered that Byron's bit of blasphemy was several feet out.
It may possibly cover the line of the east wall, but even that is
open to serious doubt. Between the tomb and the west wall of
the church is now only a stretch of green turf.

Presumably Boatswain's tomb was in the course of construction
when Byron came of age on 22nd January, 1809. He was not
actually at Newstead. While the event was being duly celebrated
on the estate, he himself was dining frugally in London on bacon
and eggs and a bottle of ale. But before he departed for his first
journey abroad—he set out in June for that trip which was to
take him, via Portugal and Spain and Malta, to Greece and
Turkey and to lay the foundations of *Childe Harold's* and his
own fame—he gave the first of the Newstead parties or revels
which have become part of local history. Recent biographers of
Byron have warned us against regarding these gatherings as anything much more than just "buffooning all around the house",
which is Byron's own phrase. Certainly, they were the merest
undergraduate high jinks compared with the Hellfire Club's
revels at Medmenham half a century earlier; all the same, I have
suggested reasons why they might not have been a sort of self-
defence against the enveloping, chilling, even depressing environment of the abbey in its pre-Wildman state. A letter from Byron,
written from Ravenna in 1821, to John Murray, his publisher,
gives the fullest account we have of the Newstead party of 1809.
The junketings do not even sound unduly sinful. There was
certainly the trappings of mild blasphemy and, no doubt, the
housemaids of the abbey obliged the revellers, but their Dashwood preceptors would, no doubt, have laughed at them.

Byron says that he and his friend Matthews went down to Newstead together, "where I had got a famous cellar", and they hired
some monks' dresses from a masquerade warehouse. They were
a party of seven or eight, with an occasional neighbour or so for
visitors, and they used to sit up late at night in their friars'
habits, drinking burgundy and claret and champagne and what
not, and "buffooning all around the house" in their conventual
garments. The skull cup from which toasts were drunk, an
elegantly mounted and polished object, said to be made of the

cranium of a long-deceased friar, is to be seen at Newstead still. I notice, though, that in late Victorian times, when the house was the property of William Frederick Webb, a description of the abbey states that there was in the saloon or grand drawing-room "a splendid cabinet of tortoiseshell and silver, once the depository of the celebrated skull cup", but adds, "with characteristic good taste this unseemly object is not shown to visitors".

Byron says that his friend, Charles Skinner Matthews (who was shortly, in 1811, to be drowned when bathing in the Cam), always denominated his host "the abbot"—"and never," says Byron, "called me by any other name in his good humours, to the day of his death". Byron recalls how, during this gathering, Matthews and John Cam Hobhouse, the future Lord Broughton, who was to be Byron's travelling companion in his first journeys abroad the same year, and was also to arrange the burial of his body when it was brought back from Greece in 1823, became involved in a quarrel. Matthews threatened to throw Hobhouse out of the window. Hobhouse, who was pretty well humourless and, in later life, was to develop into something of a prig, came to see Byron about it and said that "his respect and his regard for his host would not permit him to call out any of the guests, and that he would go to town the next morning". This he did, Byron adds, in spite of the host's vain representations that the window in question was far from high and the turf under it particularly soft. "Away he went," says Byron. But he seems to have come back, for Byron also tells us that "when the Newstead party broke up, Hobhouse and Matthews, who were the greatest friends possible, agreed, for a whim, to walk together to town". (Newstead is something like a hundred and twenty miles from London as the crow flies.) But the two quarrelled again on the way and actually walked the latter part of the journey, occasionally passing and re-passing, without speaking. Apparently when Matthews had got as far as Highgate he had spent all his money except $3\frac{1}{2}$d. He decided to spend this on a pint of beer in a public house and was sitting on a bench in front of the pub drinking it when Hobhouse passed him, still without speaking, for the last time. The anecdote ends by assuring us that the two were reconciled once more in London.

On his return to England in 1811, Byron, as we have already seen in our first meeting with him, did his best to recreate the atmosphere of 1809 at Newstead. But there was sadness and disorganization in the air. He had come back to find his mother dead. Matthews was drowned. And Bryon wrote: "Some curse hangs over me and mine. My mother lies a corpse in this house;

one of my best friends is drowned in a ditch." Sitting disconso-
lately in his room at Newstead he appealed for companionship to
another, very frivolous, Cambridge friend, Scrope Davies. "Come
to me, Scrope, I am almost desolate—left almost alone in the
world . . . write or come, but come if you can, or one or both."
Davies made the journey to Newstead, but before he arrived
Byron wrote to John Cam Hobhouse: "In the room where I now
write (flanked by the skulls you have seen so often) did you and
Matthews and myself pass some joyous unprofitable evenings, and
here we will drink to his memory, which though it cannot reach
the dead, will soothe the survivors, and to them only death can
be an evil. I can neither receive nor administer consolation;
time will do it for us; in the interim let me see or hear from you,
if possible both. I am very lonely, and should think myself
miserable were it not for a kind of hysterical merriment, which
I can neither account for nor conquer; but strange as it is, I do
laugh, and heartily, wondering at myself while I sustain it. I
have tried reading, and boxing, and swimming, and wine, with a
number of ineffectual remedies, and here I am, wretched, but
not ' melancholy or gentleman-like '." He continued to use the
Newstead skulls as the text of his epistolary sermons. Two days
later, asking his friend to write to him, "on any subject—but
death" he said: "I am already too familiar with the dead. It is
strange that I look on the skulls which stand beside me (I have
always had four in my study) without emotion, but I cannot strip
the features of those I have known of their fleshly covering, even
in idea, without a hideous sensation; but the worms are less
ceremonious." A visit from the bibulous Scrope Davies revived
him a bit, but when he was gone Byron again described himself
as "solitary and sullen".

But the year 1811 was drawing to a close. Arrangements were
made for a visit by Augusta—a visit which did not take place,
although Byron wrote: "My house here is large enough for us
all, and we should go on very well." However, the first two
cantos of *Childe Harold* were in the press and the Years of
Fame were close ahead. Throughout 1812 and 1813 Byron spent
an increasing amount of time in London, basking in the admiration which society lavished on him, but he paid repeated visits
to Newstead. From the already quoted remark to Lady Melbourne ("I write to you from the melancholy mansion of my
fathers, where I am dull as the longest deceased of my progenitors"), he was, by the end of 1813, regarding the place with less
and less favour. That October we get another, curiously undergraduate, glimpse of the skull cup. He writes from Newstead:

" My dear Lady M.—The whole party are here—and now to my narrative. But first I must tell you that I am rather unwell, owing to a folly of last night. About midnight, after deep and drowsy potations, I took it into my head to empty my skull cup, which holds rather better than a bottle of claret, at one draught, and nearly died the death of Alexander—which I shall be content to do when I have achieved his conquests. I had just enough sense left to feel that I was not fit to join the ladies, and went to bed, where, my valet tells me, that I was first convulsed, and afterwards so motionless, that he thought, ' Good night to Marmion '; but I believe my guests were boasting, and ' company, villainous company, hath been the spoil of me '. I detest drinking in general, and beg your pardon for this excess. I can't do so any more."

Early the next year Newstead saw first the visit by Augusta Leigh. On the 12th January, 1814, Byron wrote to Augusta: " On Sunday or Monday next, with leave of your lord and president, you will be well and ready to accompany me to Newstead, which you should see, and I will endeavour to render as comfortable as I can, for both our sakes." This visit seems to have been a period of calm and quiet pleasure, an island of ease and, literally, of family life, amid the tempest of romantic gloom, against which Byron more or less self-consciously was at that time battling. Augusta was pregnant (Medora Leigh, who was to be such a scandalous nuisance in later life, was born that April) but her general mood can be regarded as one of contentment and gaiety.

Together they wandered over the old house and no doubt Byron and she talked of their ancestry and of the mansion's historic and personal associations. Though it was not in fact by any means his own last appearance at Newstead, this visit shared with Augusta can, for our purposes, be regarded as a farewell. Later that year Byron became engaged to Annabella Milbanke, he was married in January 1815 and, little more than a year later, with his marriage shattered, he had left England for ever. By the time the sale of Newstead actually took place in 1817 it seems fair to say, as does a recent biographer, that " his affection for the place, or for anything immovably English, had evaporated altogether ". That is quite possible. Byron's feelings for England and things English were very bitter by 1816, when he left. The earlier part of his sojourn abroad was complicated by financial worries; and when the sale was accomplished Byron was, for the first time, able to live in a truly gentlemanly style.

The impoverished condition of the Newstead estate had reduced the annual income which Byron drew from it, large though it was, to only about £1,300 a year. It is consequently not easy to understand the motives of Colonel Thomas Wildman who bought it. He had been a friend and former Harrow school-fellow of the poet's and one wonders whether he was perhaps a little under the Byronic spell. Though the "improvements" which he wrought at Newstead may seem a little heavy handed at a time when there was still a light, gay version of the Gothic accessible to the gentleman who wished to remodel his house in one of the alternative fashions of the Regency, yet the present-day visitor undoubtedly owes to Wildman the survival of the fabric. One cannot, however, insist too forcibly on the rather remote connection between the present domestic buildings and those which Byron knew.

Colonel Wildman paid £94,500 in November 1817. This was after several ineffective and abortive negotiations with other parties. Wildman must have been an exceedingly wealthy man for the fortune that was laid out on the restoration and adorn-ment of the abbey was little short of princely. It is unreasonable, I think, to express too much regret that he and his architect, John Shaw of London (who designed St. Dunstan's in the West and many country houses), should have gone to such lengths to give the new building an individual character, because externally the front, which lies alongside the remains of the church, does look remarkably like what old drawings and engravings tell us of its former appearance. The exception, of course, is the so-called "Sussex Tower" in the south-west corner which Shaw put up for Wildman—one presumes at enormous cost—as an entirely new pivot for the whole architectural composition. In a sense, a historical sense, it was an error; for there was formerly no roofline in the whole group as high as that of the old church, which was allowed to dominate unchallenged. The Sussex Tower is in the Norman style and has some elements of an original Norman doorway incorporated on the ground floor. (The name is in honour of George IV's brother, the Duke of Sussex, to whom Wildman, having been aide-de-camp to Lord Uxbridge at the Battle of Waterloo, served as equerry.) Apart from the Sussex Tower, Shaw, whose work at Newstead did not begin until ten years after Wildman had bought it—his plans for restorations and additions, still preserved at the abbey, are dated 1829-30— improved the west front by placing the entrance on the ground floor instead of the first floor and by adding an extra bay window to the two which existed already with a semicircular bay enclosing the staircase. The low arcades, however, on ground-floor level are a pre-eighteenth-century feature.

The visitor enters the house by the main door on the west side. He finds himself in a vaulted crypt, which has been used to house the tombs of the Byrons that were in the now-ruined church at Colwick. These consist of the monument to the Sir John who died in 1567, consisting of an alabaster tomb-chest with small figures kneeling against its walls; to a second Sir John, who died in 1604, and his wife, whose effigies lie prone between alabaster columns (this monument is adorned with obelisks and has an achievement of arms on the top); and a composite monument to two Sir John Byrons who followed each other from this world in 1624 and 1625. They and their wives are shown, all kneeling and facing each other, one generation above the other. A doorway at the north-east end of the crypt leads into the cloisters which, apart from the glazed windows and the flat ceilings—which have the effect of cutting off the mouldings of the heads of some of the door-ways—are presumably much as they were when reconstructed, to-wards the end of the monastic period, about 1450. A door at the north-east corner of the cloisters leads into a modern room which was originally the south transept of the priory church. Byron also constructed, off one arm of the cloisters, a bath for his special use. It is said to have been formerly the room where the abbey choir practised. Further south is the doorway into the present chapel, which was formerly the chapter house of the priory, a rectangular chamber on the east side of the cloisters with a roof of six ribbed vaults on slender moulded and carved shafts. On the same east wall of the cloisters, near the south-east angle, is placed a tablet bearing the names of the priors of Newstead from the foundation of the monastic house until its dissolution.

Moving round to the south cloister we find an opening which leads to a spiral stone staircase, replacing an ancient stairway that led up to the dorter or dormitory on the floor above. Some authorities say that the west cloister was that reserved for the senior canons, whose prerogative it was to use it for their private peram-bulations. Other theories are that, as in certain other priories, the west cloister was set aside for the teaching of novices, while the senior canons used the north walk. The fountain in the middle of the cloister garth is not the one, or at any rate in this position, as that which Byron described in the thirteenth canto of *Don Juan*:

> Amidst the court a Gothic fountain play'd,
> Symmetrical, but deck'd with carvings quaint—
> Strange faces, like to men in masquerade,
> And here perhaps a monster, there a saint:

> The spring gush'd through grim mouths of granite made,
> And sparkled into basins, where it spent
> Its little torrent in a thousand bubbles,
> Like man's vain glory, and his vainer troubles.

In fact, the present fountain was quite probably on the cloister green in the seventeenth century, but it was moved by one of the Byrons to the front of the house and was restored to its present position by Colonel Wildman. It appears in its temporary position in the front of the house in a number of old views of Newstead. The conduit of this fountain is inscribed W.B. 1720.

Above the cloisters, on the first floor, are long galleries or corridors. Each gallery except that on the north side contains doorways, on the side opposite the cloister windows, leading to rooms of various sizes. On the west side is the great dining-room, which is thought to have been the guestern, the room in which important guests were entertained by the prior, whose private dining-room communicates with it. The roof of the dining-room or hall is thought to be, at least in part, original work. It is of oak, as is the quarter panelling of the hall, all of which—the total length of the room is sixty-five feet, and it is twenty-four feet broad—is said to have been cut entirely from one single oak which grew in Hardwick Park. At the end of the room is a richly carved oak screen, by no means original—it is dated 1820 but, all the same, is a remarkably competent piece of wood carving in what one is tempted to call Gothic survival rather than Gothic revival. Pevsner suggests that it might be by the same hand that carved the crocketed, neo-Decorated pulpit which was in South-well Minster and was moved, about 1900, to the little church at Blidworth, high up in Sherwood Forest. The chimney piece in the hall is expensive, nineteenth-century, porcelain stone. In the adjacent prior's parlour, however, there is a carved overmantel dated 1556, which is reputed to have been brought by Sir John Byron from Colwick Hall. By the way, the prior's parlour was used by the poet as a dining-room and by Victorian owners of the abbey as a breakfast-room. Its ceiling is decorated in blue and gold. The overmantel is worth a second glance. It has the armorial bearings of the Byrons in the centre with various figures carved in relief including the projecting heads of a Christian lady, a crusader, a knight and a Moor. The theme suggested by these four figures recurs in carvings elsewhere in the house and has naturally given rise to suggestions as to its meaning and reason. That sentimental American, Washington Irving, who spent some nights at Newstead during one of his visits to England was, as one would expect of him, filled with romantic speculations and conjectures. "As I lay in bed at night," he wrote, "and gazed at the mysterious panel work where Gothic knight, and Christian dame, and Paynim lover gazed upon me in effigy, I used to weave a thousand fancies concerning them." (Washington Irving, in fact, slept in what is known as the Duke of Sussex bedroom where there is another representation of this theme.)

Above the prior's parlour, and reached by a spiral staircase from the north end of the west gallery are the poet's bedroom and dressing-room and a small empty room, reputedly haunted, which is given the name of the prior's oratory. It has a window that looks out on to what was the nave of the ruined church. There is no reason to doubt that the poet's bedroom *is*, as is claimed, left pretty well exactly as it was during his occupation. Although the poet had six years still to live when Wildman bought the house, he was already a legend and it is perfectly reasonable to think that the preservation of his relics should have begun from the very time that he abandoned them. No doubt, too, Wildman, his old school friend, made him an open invitation to come and sleep at Newstead whenever he wanted to. He could not know, any more than Byron himself knew, that he would never see England again. In the circumstances Byron's bedroom makes a more convincing shrine than such collections of relics usually do. Though the house, particularly in the show cases displayed in one of the galleries, contain great numbers of miscellaneous objects connected with the poet which have been gathered painstakingly, from many different sources, and which had probably never been seen at Newstead in Byron's lifetime, the same does not, I feel, apply to the chairs, tables, dressing-table, looking-glass, toilet utensils and bed which we are shown as being the poet's. Of course, there are certainly objects in the room that are later than Byron's time and the room itself has been redecorated. The bed itself is what one would expect—over-baronial—a gilt and much betasselled four-poster surmounted by many large carved coronets, quite incongruous in its very modest surroundings. On the walls of the bedroom hang views of Cambridge and Harrow and also a portrait of his faithful servant, Old Murray. Murray is represented with pipe in hand; it is said that when Byron asked Murray what he thought of his portrait the old man replied: "It can't be a good likeness without my pipe", on which Byron at once desired the painter to introduce the long clay object. Here is also to be seen a portrait of the well-known pugilist "Gentleman Jackson" from whom Byron learnt boxing and with whom he continued to spar, from time to time, whenever he went to London.

Byron was superstitious as well as sentimental, or at any rate pretended to be, and took much pleasure in the legend of the ghost in the " oratory " close by his bedroom which was affirmed to be that of a guardian monk, whose spirit remained to keep possession of the abbey,

> For he is yet the church's heir,
> Who ever may be the lay.

Byron was wont to declare that he had seen the reverent ghost on more than one occasion. The ghost, it was alleged, would walk through the abbey at times when misfortune hung over the Byrons. But with the Byrons he departed and has never been heard of since. He appears, however, in the thirteenth canto of *Don Juan*.

The passage over the north side of the cloister consists of a long narrow gallery which was, in Victorian times, the library. On the east side, which, in monastic times, was the canon's dormitory, are the various royal bedrooms—the Charles II room, the Edward III room (very improbable!), the Henry VII room and the Duke of Sussex room—so called because these various royal personages are reputed to have slept in them. Over the south arm of the cloister is the saloon, in monastic times probably the canons' refectory and in the post-Reformation period the great drawing-room. This is now fitted with bookcases and vitrines in which are housed the extensive Roe-Byron collection of Byron manuscripts, first editions, paintings, prints and relics. This remarkable assemblage, much of which is original and in some cases unpublished material, was bequeathed to the city of Nottingham by the late Herbert Charles Roe in 1937.

I think it is quite right that Byronic enthusiasm within the county has not resulted in the narrowing down of the mansion's furnishings to those that could be traced back to the poet and his family. The house, with its accomplished and, on the whole, tactful Regency and Victorian restorations and additions would be dreary indeed to visit if the pictures and furnishings provided for it by Wildman and his successors had been entirely removed. It is perhaps a little unfortunate that there seem to be no traces of any of the family portraits or the furniture which the poet must have inherited with the house. The bed and the other odds and ends in Byron's bedroom seem to have been the only things which Wildman took over. The rest were presumably sold elsewhere. Consequently, on the main staircase and in most of the larger rooms the paintings, though they have nothing to do with Byron, have to do with the continued history of the house in the hands of owners who did a great deal more for it than did the later members of the Byron family.

Colonel Thomas Wildman, who had bought the abbey in 1817, and whose major alterations cannot have been complete until well after 1830, was lucky enough to enjoy the fruits of the money he had lavished on the house, for forty-two years in all, until his death in 1859. The next year, 1860, the estate was bought by William Frederick Webb, one of whose first acts—which seems to suggest that the mansion imposes a sense of continuity on its owners—was to restore the former chapter house and redecorate it in the Early English manner and incorporating a stained-glass window—illustrating, for some reason, an allegorical theme woven round King Solomon's temple and put up to the memory of Colonel Wildman. Webb, who must have been another wealthy man, had spent two years hunting big game in South Africa, where he had become friendly with Livingstone. This journey brought to Newstead in the sixties and seventies a large number of souvenirs, living and dead. The most remarkable of these was a living one, David Livingstone himself, who came to Newstead for a prolonged visit to the Webbs in 1865-6. The great explorer was given a room in the Sussex Tower where he worked on the proofs of his second book, *The Zambesi and its Tributaries.* The following year he returned to Africa where he was to die, without coming home again, and having undergone the ordeal of being "found" by H. M. Stanley, in 1873. In late Victorian times the memory of Livingstone assumed great importance at Newstead: the table on which he wrote about the Zambesi took on a certain rivalry with that on which Byron wrote *English Bards and Scotch Reviewers,* while Livingstone's cap, found beside him when he died, and his Consular sword (he was, for his last journey, appointed unpaid Consul to Central Africa) vied with the less-heroic relics of a poet who would have little in common with Livingstone, particularly in the matter of big game.

Even before his own residence, during the period of Lord Grey de Ruthyn's tenancy, his rooms at Newstead, in their dilapidated state, had been occupied, as well by the noble tenant as by his hounds and numbers of jackdaws, swallows, starlings and other wild life. Later Byron himself had brought hither from Cambridge a detachment of such animals as already formed part of his personal entourage. Though these were prosaic compared with the beasts that were later to frequent his apartments in Italy— the crane, the monkeys, the fox, the mastiff Mutz, besides a badger, a falcon, a tame crow and a civet cat that ran away—their behaviour formed a striking feature of a visit to Newstead. There were bloodhounds and there was also a bear and a wolf. It was of the bear that Byron, when asked at Cambridge what he meant to do with it, replied that he was bringing it up for a degree. As well as this near insult to a sensitive university, he had not endeared himself to the Cambridge authorities by naming each of his bloodhounds after some prominent senior member of the university. At Newstead the wolf and the bear lived chained up on each side of the front door of that vaulted hall in which the modern visitor still makes his first introduction to the house. In the year following Byron's first journey abroad, the representatives of the local wild life which had been pulled in under Newstead's roof to comfort its lord in his loneliness—they included a hedgehog and a badger—had been joined by some Athenian tortoises. Livingstone, seated at his table in the Sussex Tower, must, if he knew of this, have thought it absurd: his friendship with Webb brought dead, not living, fauna into the abbey.

(A word, in parenthesis, about the man who gave his name to the " Sussex Tower ". Augustus Frederick, Duke of Sussex, was the sixth son and ninth child of George III. A chronic asthmatic, he was in many ways the most likeable and worthy, and certainly the most progressive and liberal minded of all George IV's brothers. At the time of the Reform Bill, after its third reading, the few Whig peers made a valiant effort to speak in the face of an immense Tory majority. The Duke of Sussex, the King's brother, was shouted down by the Tory Lords, but he managed to say: " I know the people better than many of your Lordships do. My situation, my habits of life, my connection with many charitable institutions and other circumstances on which I do not now wish to enter my nuclei, give me the means of knowing them . . ." and the Duke added: " I have gone to the ' Mechanics' Societies ', I have visited their institutions and seen their libraries. At Nottingham they have a library that would do credit to the house of any nobleman." The Duke of Sussex was well qualified to discuss libraries by virtue of having an admirable one of his own in which he spent a great deal of his time and, as he read, sketching in ink an elaborate hand pointing to any passage he thought memorable or with which he disagreed, and whose volumes to this day with their fine armorial bookplate, ducal coronets stamped on the binding, and watered silk end papers, still sometimes come into the sale rooms. This Duke, when he visited the artisan library at Nottingham was as like as not on his way to or from Newstead. Colonel Wildman, who had been his equerry, was a close friend and the Duke made long and repeated visits to his house.)

If W. F. Webb brought Livingstone back in triumph from Africa, he also filled Newstead with other tropical objects. Descriptions of the house suggest that it contained a positive menagerie of dead animals which would have seemed surprising to Byron who was both sentimental and personal about animals and liked to surround himself with live ones. The walls of the great hall were hung with African trophies and its stone floor was strewn with the skins of wild beasts, the victims of Mr. Webb's prowess. Webb also introduced into the house the huge painting on the staircase which represented himself, leaning on his horse, surveying a huge lion (which could be seen in all but life, stuffed, in the hall) which his African servant is in the act of skinning. Beside him is seated his brother-in-law, who accompanied him on his travels. The painting is the work of Alfred Corbould. The structural additions made during Webb's time were not of major importance, consisting of a new piece at the eastern end of the south side of the house where there had been a conservatory, and a bay on the ground floor at the northern end of the east side. This means that no alteration was made to the familiar western aspect, only to that which looks out, southwards, over the garden lake and eastwards across terraces.

W. F. Webb died in 1899 and he left the Newstead property first to his second surviving daughter, Lady Chermside, who died without leaving issue in 1910; secondly to his third daughter, Ethel Webb, who died in 1915; thirdly to trustees for the benefit of his son who died on active service in 1916; and finally to his eldest daughter, Mrs. Fraser, of Reelig, Invernesshire, who died in 1925. The estate then passed to her son, Mr. Charles Ian Fraser.

In 1931, Sir Julien Cahn, who had purchased the historic and, at that time, uninhabited portions of the abbey, presented them to Nottingham Corporation. At the same time, valuable Byron furniture and relics contained within the house were presented to the city by the former owner, Mr. Fraser, who has subsequently made additional gifts in connection with the abbey. It is to him that is due the continued existence at Newstead of the portrait of Lord Byron, by Thomas Phillips, which is hung in the room that Lord Byron used as a dining-room, of a picture of the dog Boatswain, and of the furniture and odds and ends in Byron's bedroom and dressing-room. In June 1932 Mr. Fraser gave to the city the so-called Hutt Entrance Lodge, together with the celebrated

Pilgrim Oak, and the land in which it stands, an area of land in the park comprising seventy-five thousand acres, the six-acre wood known as the Poet's Corner, and the two leaden figures of satyrs which give the Devil's Garden, or Devil's Wood, on the eastern edge of the Newstead grounds, its name.

It was an admirable thought which brought on 16th July, 1931, to Newstead the then Greek Prime Minister Eleutherios Venizelos, who came on the occasion of the handing over of the property to the city of Nottingham, to pay his respects to the memory of one whom he described as " the immortal champion of the liberty of Greece ". One suspects that Byron would have seen in this bold and fiery Cretan some of those qualities which he felt ought to belong to the Greeks, on whose behalf he made the magnificent if futile gesture that was to cost him his life.

Thus, this most worthwhile literary shrine has been given, by means of personal generosity, a reasonable assurance of surviving as long as Byron's name survives. Apart from the monastic portions, and the rooms which are shown to the public, parts of it, at any rate until recently, have remained in use as a private residence. It is only nine miles out of the city of Nottingham and the care and attention which, since Wildman's time, have been lavished on the garden and grounds are now available, as the most delightful of their parks, to the people of the city and its surroundings.

The existence of a park as part of the Newstead property—that which suffered such depredations in the time of the "wicked lord"—only dates from its conversion into a mansion under the Byrons. During the centuries when Newstead was an Augustinian priory the park that surrounded it was considerably smaller. The foundation charter of Henry II granted the canons a considerable part of the untamed Forest of Sherwood, but to begin with only the land in the immediate vicinity of the priory was enclosed. Some fencing and cultivation was carried out during succeeding centuries; but long after the Byrons had taken possession a great deal of the land within the old boundary wall (the line of which can still be traced) remained uncultivated.

One of the traditional signs or emblems of Sherwood Forest stands just outside the abbey gate. This is the huge oak tree, the Pilgrim or Gospel Oak, which may well have been standing before the canons were driven from the priory. Its name, common enough elsewhere, is an indication of the popular belief that pilgrims coming to the priory used to hear the gospel under its shade. It acquired, in later times, secular associations. Washington Irving, whose stay at Newstead as Wildman's guest in the

1830's has already been remarked on, wrote of the Gospel Oak that "under its shade, the rustics of the neighbourhood have been accustomed to assemble on certain holidays and celebrate their rural festivals. This custom has been handed down from father to son for several generations, until the oak has acquired a kind of sacred character." Tradition also has it that the tree was among the timber marked for destruction by the "wicked lord", but that the thought so roused the indignation of the neighbouring gentry that they combined to purchase it to save it from the axe. Anyway, there it still is, saved again by Mr. Fraser's gift.

The hotel called the Hutt, on the opposite side of the road, had already been an inn for some time before the poet's ownership of Newstead. Later in the nineteenth century it became for a period the residence of the abbey chaplain.

The motor buses that travel between Nottingham and Mansfield pass the crossroads on which the Hutt and the Pilgrim Oak stand, and the visitor's approach to Newstead is more likely to be from this eastward direction than from Annesley or Hucknall Torkard. A long winding drive leads up to the house. It is flanked by rhododendron bushes, planted in the time of the Webbs (rhododendrons only became widely popular in England after the discoveries made in the Eastern Himalayas by Sir Joseph Hooker in the mid-nineteenth century). They have now reached full maturity and are of towering height. Beyond stretches an expanse of open moorland covered with bracken and ling or bell heather. Another local tale here! It is said that the local people laid heaps of this bell heather on a boat that was being conveyed through the park for use on the lake by the exceedingly unpopular "wicked lord" whose nautical eccentricities we have already heard of. The purpose of this curious gesture is said to have been to fulfil a prophecy, attributed to Mother Shipton, that when a boat laden with ling should cross Sherwood Forest, Newstead would pass away from the Byrons. Which just goes to show the versatility of Mother Shipton's repertoire. Such trees and small plantations that are to be seen are of fairly recent planting, for the "wicked lord's" slaughtering of timber was carried out so efficiently that in 1809 one of Byron's friends wrote of Newstead that it was "surrounded with bleak and barren hills, with scarce a tree to be seen for miles, except a solitary clump or two".

The surroundings of the abbey owe a great deal of character to their water. Some, at least, of the lakes and ponds that surround it existed in the Middle Ages, for it is known that there was a dam on the west side of the priory. The larger lakes are fed by the little River Leen (which used to be noted for its excellent

The Duchess of Newcastle's Mausoleum near Markham Clinton, 1822-33

trout and crayfish) which rises a mile or so away to the north. It flows right through the park of Newstead on its way south to Nottingham where it formerly ran past the castle and into the Trent but now merges with the canal at Lenton.

It is easy enough to imagine the successive scenes which the upper lake has witnessed. First, in the "wicked lord's" time, the mimic naval warfare in which the armament of his twenty-gun ship and of the two little forts, which still survive, one on each side of the lake, took part. Secondly, those afternoons of deceptive placidity when the poet would go boating, drifting about, reading, with Boatswain by his side. Suddenly he would precipitate himself into the water to give Boatswain the chance of effecting a heroic but quite unnecessary rescue. It is sad that the "wicked lord's" Folly Castle, that piece of early Gothic revival, of 1749, should have been demolished. The local and more or less official reasons for its disappearance are given in these terms: " It was the scene of many concerts and gay parties that tradition has naturally translated into unspeakable orgies, and in later times was believed to be haunted. In fact, even after it had long been used as a school, its sinister reputation was so strong that it was thought advisable to demolish it." This will hardly be accepted as sufficient reason by amateurs of architecture.

Close beside one of the forts is the carefully romantic group, belfry and arches and wall, of the Victorian stables which were put up by Webb. As a matter of fact they are by no means an unworthy addition to the composition as a whole. A path to the right of the stables leads to a smaller lake sometimes known as the Reed Pond. At the opposite corner of the upper lake is a waterfall from which the Leen descends to widen out again and form the garden lake or middle lake facing the south front of the abbey. This secondary piece of water was created in Colonel Wildman's time. Here, on a smooth lawn that slopes down almost to the water's edge, is to be seen the stump of an old tree smothered in ivy. This is the remains of the oak that was planted by the poet on his first arrival at Newstead in 1798, as a boy of ten. About it he wrote a not specially commendable copy of verses, the manuscript of which, in the Roe-Byron collection, is exhibited in the salon whose windows overlook the lawn in which the tree was planted. Four lines will be enough:

Young oak! when I planted thee deep in the ground,
I hoped that thy days would be longer than mine;
That thy dark-waving branches would flourish around,
And ivy thy trunk with its mantle entwine.

All Saints Church, Markham Clinton

We are told that because of the complete unsuitability of the soil for trees, the unfortunate oak had a desperate struggle for existence. It was carefully nursed by Colonel Wildman and the Webbs who took particular pride in it ("this vigorous and flourishing tree has become as famous as Pope's willow or Shakespeare's mulberry and promises to become one of the most remarkable and best known trees in the universe," announces a Victorian guide-book); but it succumbed some time in this century.

The path between this lawn and the abbey passes an octagonal structure which one might think was or had been—apart from its position—a chapter house. In fact it is the old kitchen of the house and is believed to occupy the site of the original monastic cookhouse. The remaining pieces of water are the monastic Stew Pond on the other side of Byron's oak from the garden lake; and the Eagle Pond whose existence has already been described in connection with Southwell.

The monks' Stew Pond, where Newstead canons bred fat carp for their Friday meals, is bordered by a dark avenue of overhanging yew trees, which are said to be as much as eight hundred years old. At the northern end of the pond there rises out of the sandy rock a well of clear cold water of singular purity and sweetness. It is known as The Wishing Well and has a high local reputation for efficacy in this capacity. Between the Stew Pond and the Eagle Pond lies the sheltered tropical garden where palms and other southern plants have been planted, the egress from which in the direction of the Eagle Pond is by a narrow tunnel. The Eagle Pond lies midway between the formal gardens stretching northwards from the remains of the church, and the so-called Devil's Wood which occupies the north-east corner of the gardens. These parts of the grounds have changed least since the early days of Byron ownership. Before that it was certainly within the precincts of the priory, as is indicated by the fact that the wall along the north of the garden is supported on the park side by fourteenth-century buttresses. Some part of it is likely to have been cultivated as a garden for nearly seven hundred years. The record of the visitation of the priory by its archbishop in 1261 gives instructions about the particular lay servant who had the care of the gardens. Certainly, to make the monastery self supporting, extensive vegetable gardens must have been maintained, for the production of vegetables and medicinal herbs, perhaps where the present kitchen garden lies, beyond the tropical gardens and due east of the Stew Pond. But we can imagine that flowers, for decorating the church, would also have been wanted. The eastern end of the garden, though it has lost its wild and forest-like appearance, is still adorned by the statues of a male satyr and of a female satyr with her child, that were bought by the fifth Lord Byron in 1784. This part of the garden is now open and planted, at wide intervals, with youthful yew trees. But it used to be a somewhat untidy and rather gloomy place in which the presence of the statues provided sufficient reason for calling it the Devil's Wood. It was in this grove that there grew the twin trees, interwoven with each other in a way which Byron liked to think symbolized the separate, but united, fortunes of himself and his half-sister, Augusta Leigh. Washington Irving's description of the trees is: "An elm of peculiar form having two trunks, which sprang from the same root, and, after growing side by side, mingled their branches together." On the visit which the poet and Augusta spent together at Newstead, Byron carved his name and that of his sister on this double tree. The tree's subsequent history was encouragingly dramatic. One half of the tree remained strong and vigorous while the other drooped and was sickly; later on, soon after Webb's purchase of Newstead, the whole tree began to decay. Webb had the portion of the trunk bearing the two names cut out, and put, to preserve it, in a glass case. It is still to be seen in the house.

The whole grove was cut down in the present century and now the terrace, where the two lead statues stand on their pedestals among lavender bushes and Siberian crab-apple trees, is one of the most cheerful parts of the whole grounds. In Victorian times, besides an "American Garden", there used to be a part which went by the name of Venetia's Garden. It was a tamely wild place with a winding stream running through it. The name and the idea of it apparently came from the reading of Benjamin Disraeli's novel *Venetia* whose heroine constructs, in the book, just such a wild garden. Here the pleasant Victorian picture of usefully idle mornings at Webb's Newstead are suggested by the contemporary words: "Additions are being constantly made by Mrs. Webb and the Misses Webb, who all take a peculiarly strong interest, which indeed was originally suggested by Miss Caroline Webb, and since carried out by Mr. Belliss. . . ." Nor is it remarkable that the Misses Webb should have read, at Newstead, or taken "a peculiarly strong interest" in Benjamin Disraeli's seventh novel *Venetia*. This book dates from 1837 and is regarded as merely a topsy-turvydom of literary portraiture and reminiscence. It has, however, the special appeal of containing a brilliant portrait of the man who can hardly have failed to have been the romantic Disraeli's principal literary hero. Byron appears not under his own name but that of Cadurcis. The portrait of Byron is derived no doubt from the recollections of the novelist's father, Isaac Disraeli, whose literary work Byron admired and whose acquaintance he sought. (Near the end of his life Byron wrote to the elder Disraeli a moving, but very friendly, letter about his own life and character; also about that burnt volume of memories, in which he says to Disraeli: " In it I have told what, as far as I know, is the *truth*—*not* the *whole* truth—for if I had done so I must have involved much private and some dissipated history. . . .") Disraeli introduced into *Venetia* a number of rather feeble lyrics attributed to the pen of the Byron-Cadurcis character. So, altogether, *Venetia* had every claim to an important place on the tables, with their tasselled and fringed cloths, in Miss Geraldine Webb's boudoir at Newstead in the 1860's.

Disraeli, in choosing the name Cadurcis for his version of Byron, gives us our cue for leaving Newstead, this time in the opposite direction from that in which we approached it, taking a road that does not lead, like the other, into more or less unspoilt stretches of forest but across the railway and across the Nottingham-Mansfield road on the western side to Annesley again and thence to Hucknall Torkald. Annesley, because of the connection between the name Chaworth and the Cadurcis of *Venetia*. The Chaworths were an ancient family who had come, in Norman times, to England and had their origin in Brittany. The name Chaworth has assumed its present form by some of those changes which I am not philologist enough to explain, through the Norman-French of the conquered island, from an original with which Disraeli graced his Byronic figure—de Cadurcis. The lands of Wiverton were granted, at the Conquest, to a certain Engelremus de Cadurcis, who, we are told, was a close favourite of King William. The family's name seems to have assumed its present form at any rate by the early seventeenth century for, by that time intermarried with many noble families, it was a Sir George Chaworth who, in 1621, was raised by King Charles I to the peerage. . . . Well, our emergence from Newstead in the Annesley-Hucknall direction brings before our eyes some of the most important, if least lovely, spectacles in the county. Even in Victorian times the contrasts were conspicuous. Here is a Victorian picture of the industrial age, half pleased at the material progress, half poetically sentimental: " The road to Annesley passes right through parts of Sherwood Forest which are fast being cleared up to make way for the collieries, which are springing up in all directions, and which promise ere long to make Nottinghamshire one of the most thickly populated counties in England, as it certainly is one of the richest in mineral wealth. The first sight one gets of Annesley is the block of miners' houses, built on the brow of the hill, and which have a clean, tidy and comfortable appearance. Around are all the evidences of mining upon an extensive scale, trucks laden with coal, wagons being shunted, waiting to be filled with the fuel which is one of the main elements in England's greatness, and the whole scene busy and animated in the extreme. To the poetic visitor," the mid-Victorian account continues, " this must be a rather rude shock as an introduction to a spot around which hangs a halo of sublime poetry: between the swarthy, honest faces of the colliers, and the sylvan deities with which the groves and dells of Annesley are filled in the imagination of a votary of Byron. . . ."

Perhaps; but we have already considered New Annesley in its relation to the hall and its park. Between two and three miles to the south is the remaining spot to be connected, and that finally, with Byron's life—and death.

Byron died at Missolonghi in Greece on 19th April, 1824. " Something tells me," he had said gloomily to Lady Blessington in Genoa, before he set sail, " that I shall never return again from Greece." On his last birthday, on January 22nd, 1824, he clearly envisages the likelihood of his surrendering his life to the cause of Greek independence:

> Seek out—less often sought than found—
> A soldier's grave, for thee the best,
> Then look around, and choose thy ground,
>   And take thy rest.

Byron, of course, succumbed to no wounds. His last illness was brought on by a cold, caught by keeping on wet clothes too long. His last words were " Now I shall go to sleep", and he fell into a deep slumber which lasted for twenty-four hours. When, eventually, he opened his eyes he was raised in bed by his faithful valet, Fletcher, and died in his arms, calmly, at six o'clock on Easter Sunday morning.

The news of his death caused a profound sensation throughout Europe and in America, but especially in Greece and England. In Greece, the provisional Government decreed a national mourning for three successive days. A magnificent military funeral service was held in the church of St. Nicholas at Missolonghi and an eloquent funeral oration was pronounced by a young Greek nobleman named Spiridion Tricoupi. In England, to Jane Welch Carlyle, for instance, the news of his death " made an awful and dreary blank in the creation". The young Tennyson (he was fifteen) found "the whole world seemed to be darkened" and, half stupefied by the news, scratched upon the sandstone slabs of a deserted quarry "Byron is dead . . . Byron is dead". But it was not only poets who felt the loss. "Gentlemen, Lord Byron is dead!" the Duke of Rutland announced to a gathering of local foxhunters: and, we are told, "the country gentlemen abandoned their banquet and silently, unquestioningly trooped home".

Byron had left no directions, finally, as to where he was to be buried though he had, from time to time, dropped some intermittent and sometimes contradictory hints. In a lucid interval during his last delirium he had said: "Let not my body be hacked or be sent to England . . . lay me in the first corner without pomp or nonsense." As it was, after being embalmed, his body was sent to Zante where, after various consultations, it was decided to convey it to England with the idea that it would be found a resting place in Westminster Abbey. Accordingly the body was placed in an oblong wooden case bound with hoops and perforated all over; and this container was in turn placed in a cask holding one hundred and eighty gallons of spirit. The body, thus preserved, was taken on board a ship of the name of *The Florida* which arrived at the Nore on 1st July, 1824. There it was met by Byron's two executors, John Cam Hobhouse and the solicitor John Hanson. It was taken to a house in Great George Street, Westminster, where it lay in state for two days, during which time a vast concourse of people filed past it to pay their respects to the dead poet. Those who inspected the body noted that, in spite of the efforts to preserve it, by the time it reached England the face was much decayed.

It seems quite appropriate that it should have been, not the widow, Lady Byron, but his half-sister Augusta who made arrangements for the poet to be buried at Hucknall Torkard, and who afterwards erected the tablet in the church. While the body was still lying in state just around the corner from Westmnister Abbey, an intimation was received from the abbey authorities that should application be made to have Byron's remains buried in the Poet's Corner a decided refusal would be given. Consequently, although no Nottinghamshire estates remained in the hands of the Byron family and although, as we have already seen, Hucknall Torkard had never been included in them during the poet's lifetime, Augusta made it quite clear that it was there she wanted him to lie.

The body had been placed in a coffin of polished oak covered with costly Genoa velvet. On it a silver plate bore the following inscription: "The Right Hon. George Gordon Noel Byron, Lord Byron of Rochdale, Born in London, January 22, 1788: Died at Missolonghi, in Western Greece, April 19th, 1824." Accompanying the coffin was an urn on which it was stated: "Within this urn are deposited the heart, brain, etc., of the deceased Lord Byron." (His lungs in a canopic jar had been deposited in the church of St. Spiridione at Missolonghi.)

At eleven o'clock on Monday, 12th July, 1824, the long funeral procession left the house in Westminster. The hearse was followed by thirty-five carriages of family and noble mourners and the streets through which the procession passed were thronged with people. Hats were everywhere removed as the cortège passed slowly by. The route lay by way of Parliament Street, up Whitehall, through the Haymarket, along Regent Street (then called Prince's Street) and thence by Oxford Street and the Tottenham Court Road to St. Pancras church. Most of the shops along the route were closed and many houses put out signs of mourning. Three poets, Tom Moore, Samuel Rogers and Thomas Campbell followed the coffin. At St. Pancras church the procession halted and the carriages and most of them who had followed on foot returned to town. The remainder of the cortège then set out for Nottingham. As it moved slowly up Highgate Hill the widows of Shelley and of Edward Williams, who had been drowned with him, and both of whose bodies Byron had watched burning two years earlier, stood in a window to see it go by.

The body arrived in Nottingham early on the Friday morning. There, after a rest, the funeral procession assembled at the Blacka-moor's Head Inn for the journey to Hucknall. The composition of the funeral procession, so different in its formality from what we are now accustomed to, is perhaps worth briefly describing. First went two constables on horseback, followed by two bailiffs similarly mounted. Behind them rode the undertaker, alone. Next came a local gentleman and twenty-six tenants, on horse-back, riding two and two. Two mutes on horseback were next in order, followed by a large plume of black feathers, carried on a man's head, with two supporters on foot. Four cloaked men, on horseback, two and two, preceded the richly caprisoned state horse which was led by two pages. Its rider carried in his arms Byron's baronial coronet on a crimson velvet cushion, ornamented with gold tassels and fringe. The hearse, with all its sombre trappings, containing the body, now appeared, followed by a mourning coach and six with the urn containing the heart. Behind this another similar coach bore the chief mourners, Byron's brother-in-law (his half-sister's husband, that is), Colonel Leigh; Colonel Wildman, whom we know well; John Cam Hobhouse and the lawyer John Hanson. The remainder of the procession consisted of coaches, carriages and chaises, the first of which bore the Mayor of Nottingham, Aldermen, Sheriff and Under-Sheriff, the Town Clerk and other dignitaries and servants of the town. Behind the last vehicle rode about forty gentlemen on horseback in pairs. This was the route of the procession—along Smithy Row and Long Row, along the top of the market-place, up Chapel Bar and round into Upper Parliament Street, thence along Milton Street and into the Mansfield Road. At the seventh milestone it turned off for Hucknall by way of Papplewick. A celebrated incident which occurred while the procession was still moving through the streets of Nottingham has always seemed to me rather surprising in view of the great crowds present in the streets and, one would have thought, of universal local knowledge of the day's events. Anyway, on the morning of the funeral we are told that Mrs. Musters, the former Mary Chaworth, drove into the town from her house at Colwick. Observing the closed shops, the silent crowds, and the general indications of mourning, she stopped her carriage, by a singular coincidence, just opposite a building in Pelham Street which had long been the Nottingham town house of the Byrons. Enquiring what was to do and informed that it was Lord Byron's funeral she is described as turning deadly pale and bursting into tears. The procession then wound its way past her carriage in which she sat with the blinds drawn. Thus, then, did Mary Chaworth and Byron meet again for the last time.

Hucknall Torkard is far from an attractive place to-day, and the large church which stands in the otherwise featureless and uninspiring market square was a great deal smaller in 1824 than it is now. It consisted only of a tower, nave, chancel and north aisle. It was described, rather earlier than this, as being a neat and clean church, serving a village of about two hundred dwellings, disposed chiefly in a single long street at the top of which the church stood. It contained already a mural monument commemorating Richard Lord Byron who, with his seven brothers, served King Charles I in the Civil War and lost their fortunes in his cause, "yet," the inscription adds, "it pleased God so to bless the honest endeavours of the said Richard Lord Byron that he re-purchased part of their ancient inheritance, which he left to his posterity, with a laudable memory for his great piety and charity". He died in October 1679. The present south aisle

of the church was added in 1872 and the two exceptionally long
transepts fifteen years later. During the same period the old
part of the church was so restored as to give the whole an
almost uniformly Victorian appearance. This is not to say that
there are no recognizable medieval portions. The west tower
is clearly original Early English and the south porch is a worthy
piece of fourteenth-century timber work. Present-day fashions
in ecclesiology, however, tend to focus our attention not on these
survivals or on Byron's tomb but on the twenty-five stained-glass
windows by the Victorian glass painter Kempe, whose work is to
be seen elsewhere in the county in the church at Clumber, at
Clayworth, at East Retford parish church, at Saundby and at
Trowell. The experts say, however, that "if you want to study
late Victorian stained glass at its most competent (not the
genius, the innovations, the aesthetic purity of Morris, but the
accepted high church medium) Hucknall is one of the best places
to go to". These Kempe windows at Hucknall are described
as "of his best, early period, beginning with the east window
of 1883, and then mostly 1888-90, with his dark blues and
brownish reds, his plenty of vegetation, and his unmistakable
faces". The church also contains a painting—of Christ and
the woman taken in adultery—by Daniel Maclise, a somewhat
pretentious but, in his lifetime, much-lauded painter of whom
Ruskin said he had "every fault usually attributed to the pre-
Raphaelites without one of their excellences". The painting at
Hucknall dates from 1869, from the year before Maclise's death.

But all these adornments were still in the future when the
body of Byron was brought to Hucknall. Between the burial of
Byron's body on the south side of the chancel, adjacent to the
grave of his mother, and the restorations which have so altered
the character of the church, one other tablet was to appear to
accompany that plain one of white marble which Augusta Leigh
put up. This other tablet is in memory of Byron's only legitimate
offspring and, indeed, apart from the unhappy Allegra, his
daughter by Clare Clairmont, who died in 1822, when she was
five, his only child. This tablet reads: "The Right Honourable
Augusta Ada, wife of William, Earl of Lovelace, and only
daughter of George Gordon Noel, Lord Byron, born 10th December, 1815, died 27th November, 1852."

Of all the many visitors to Hucknall Torkard and to Newstead
in the years immediately following Byron's death, among whom
were Tom Moore and Washington Irving, there was none who
has better claim to close this account than Teresa Guiccioli.

In 1832 the woman with whom Byron had found, in so far as he was capable, happiness in the last years of his life, made what she called a "pilgrimage" to England and particularly to Newstead Abbey. This short, sentimental, romantic and rather unstable little person, whose out-of-date corkscrew curls became objects of ridicule when she visited England later, came for her first journey here accompanied by her brother Vincenzo. Byron had been dead eight years. His publisher, John Murray, provided the Countess Guiccioli with books and theatre tickets, took her to dinner parties and to Regent's Park and, more important, provided her with introductions to Augusta Leigh, to Dr. Drury at Harrow, Byron's tutor, to the Pigot family at Southwell, and particularly to Dr. John Pigot, the brother of Byron's friend Elizabeth; and, above all, to Colonel Wildman. To the introduction provided by John Murray she added one supplied by the amiable Lady Blessington, who had enjoyed including Byron's famous and still young and attractive mistress among the curiosities of her salon in London. She appears to have received every kindness from the proprietor at Newstead. On her return, she wrote to Murray: "I cannot express to you how much gratified I have been with Colonel Wildman's reception, and with all the kind attentions he has bestowed upon me. He is a very amiable and gallant man—and I cannot express how extremely glad I have been to see this interesting spot in the hands of a person who is so very sincerely attached to the memory of Lord Byron. In all the improvements he has done and is doing to the building (which are considerable and of a very refined taste) he seems rather to consult the intentions of the last possessor of the abbey than his own. The arms of Lord Byron, his likenesses, his very name engraved on a beech tree—together with that of his sister— are shown by the Colonel to the visitors to the abbey with a kind of religious feeling, which you may imagine what sincere though melancholy pleasure has given to me!" Before leaving Newstead in that summer of 1832, the Countess Guiccioli collected some souvenirs: a rose, an acorn, a branch from the tree on which Byron's and Augusta's names were carved, and a piece of the silk of Byron's bed curtains. These, when she got back to Italy, she placed in the carved mahogany casket which already contained his portraits and her other relics of Byron—the locket containing some of his hair which he gave her when he sailed for Greece, a piece of the wall hangings of the room in the Italian palazzo where Byron used to visit her, his handkerchief and a fragment of one of his shirts. And in that mahogany box, the property to-day of the Countess Guiccioli's great-nephew, they still lie.

Chapter IX

COUNTRY OF TWO WRITERS (II)

"The scene of my Nottinghamshire-Derby novels all centres round Eastwood, where I was born: and whoever stands on Walker Street, Eastwood, will see the whole landscape of *Sons and Lovers* before him: Underwood in front, the hills of Derbyshire on the left, the woods and hills of Annesley on the right. The road from Nottingham, Moorgreen up to Underwood and by Watnall on to Annesley—gives you all the landscape of *The White Peacock*, Miriam's farm in *Sons and Lovers*, and the home of the Crich family, and Willey Water in *Women in Love*. *The Rainbow* is Ilkeston and Cossall moving to Eastwood. And Hermione in *Women in Love* is supposed to live not far from Cromford. *The Lost Girl* begins in Eastwood—the cinematograph show being in Langley Mill." That is perhaps D. H. Lawrence's most detailed expression of the ties which bound him and his most important early novels to the country which climbs north-eastwards away from Nottingham into Derbyshire.

It is worth adding, perhaps, that when, at the outset of his career, he and "Miriam" (Jessie Chambers, that is, or E.T.) were sending Lawrence's first poems to London they asked that if they were published it should be under the pseudonym of "Richard Greasley". Lawrence, he tells us himself, used to be very happy working in the hay fields at Greasley that were rented by the parents of "Miriam", about four miles from their farm. But Lawrence's most recent biographer surely has our sympathy in expressing relief that this pseudonym was, in fact, never adopted. "Greasley," he says, "was the name of a village they liked; still what a beastly name for a poet!"

The recent publication of a hitherto unrecorded work by Lawrence reveals the fact that his first published writing appeared in the *Nottingham Guardian* of December 7th, 1907, when he was twenty-two. The newspaper had offered a prize for a story on the theme of "The most enjoyable Christmas the writer remembers or has ever heard of"; and the story called "A prelude to a Happy Christmas" was the winning entry. The pen name Lawrence adopted was "Rosalind" and the name and address

241

of the author was given as "Miss Jessie Chambers, Hagg's Farm, Underwood, Jackdale, Nottingham".

Jessie Chambers was, of course, "Miriam" and Hagg's Farm was the "Willey Farm " of *Sons and Lovers*. (Besides " A Prelude" Lawrence submitted in the competition two other stories, both of superior literary quality to that of the sentimental prize-winning piece. One was sent in under his own name and the second under that of another friend. Each of them was given special mention. These, each based on a concrete symbol which had touched Lawrence's imagination—a piece of coloured glass he had picked up, a white stocking which figured in one of his mother's anecdotes about her youth, became, when carefully re-written, respectively " A Fragment of Stained Glass " and " The White Stocking ", one first published in 1911 and the other in 1914 and both now to be found in Lawrence's *Collected Tales*.) It has been suggested that the painfully over-sentimental "Prelude" may have been a purposely sugary version of the Christmas scene later described in *Sons and Lovers*; and that in the same book the prize-winning success—though there it is a picture that wins, not a story—was based on the same episode.

We have already heard, in Lawrence's own words, the matter-of-fact, though slightly nostalgic, expressions of his lifelong identification with the scenes of his birth. In the letter written in 1926, from Italy, already quoted, he permitted himself almost a touch of emotion: " How well I can see Hucknall Torkard and the miners! My father used to sing in the Newstead Abbey choir as a boy. I've gone many times down Hucknall Long Lane to Watnall—and I like Watnall Park: it's a great Sunday morning walk." Then he voices the recollections we have already noted: " Some of my happiest days I've spent haymaking in the fields just opposite the south side of Greasley church—bottom of Watnall hill—adjoining the vicarage: Miriam's father hired those fields." And indeed it is a placid and entirely rustic scene to this day, although so close to Nottingham and in the middle of the colliery area. The field that falls steeply below the churchyard was under potatoes when I passed it. There is a fine view of green country all round from the church's eminence, and the vicarage is a pleasant enough spot. The church of St. Mary has a tall, solid, fifteenth-century tower which, by its position, serves as a landmark for miles around. The remainder of the church is late Victorian, but inside it a monument to a member of the Rolleston family, who died in 1685, helps to recall its earlier state; and the slate commandment boards remind us that the county's slate districts reach up as far north as Greasley. Here also are the remains of the fortified manor of the Cantilupe family which boasts the name of Greasley Castle, still detectable in part of the moat and a few bits of walling as part of a farm-house. The building, which dated from the middle of the fourteenth century and for the fortification of which Nicholas de Cantilupe had permission from Edward III, has been a total ruin for many hundreds of years. Excavations which were carried out at the beginning of the present century suggest that it was a square castle with angle towers. In the eighteenth century Greasley had the reputation of being a larger parish than any other in the county with the living extremely inadequate to its duties.

"That's the country of my heart." We have heard that phrase and it is worth pursuing Lawrence for a moment, him and his forebears, beyond Eastwood into Nottingham itself and its other suburbs. Some new light on Lawrence's ancestry was recently shed by Mr. Harry T. Moore, whose biography of Lawrence appeared in the year 1951. Moore draws attention to the fact that almost nothing has, in the past, been known of Lawrence's antecedents; information has been more or less limited to hints about his parents' background given by Lawrence in the autobiographical first section of *Sons and Lovers*. For instance, Lawrence's mother's maiden name has been known to have been Lydia Beardsall and all readers of Lawrence have been made very conscious of how different and how superior she felt herself to be to her miner husband. But it has not been appreciated that she was already related, by marriage, to Lawrence's father, Arthur, before they met. For Arthur Lawrence's aunt, his mother's sister, had married Lydia Beardsall's uncle, her mother's brother. It was, we are now told, at the house of this uncle that Lydia met Arthur Lawrence in 1874 or 1875. The home of Lydia's Uncle John and Arthur's Aunt Alice was in Basford—the colliery suburb closer in to Nottingham than Eastwood. Arthur Lawrence had come over from Eastwood, or, more probably, from the Brinsley Pit where he worked, to help sink a new pit at Clifton, south-west of the town; and in the evenings he used to walk right through Nottingham to visit his aunt. When Lydia came to see her uncle she also had to cross the town, but from the south-eastern corner, where most of the large Beardsall family lived. Moore, in his article, quotes D. H. Lawrence's elder brother George as declaring that Arthur Lawrence's father (D.H.L.'s grandfather) came from Nottingham, too, though the general impression has been that he came from the south of England. It seems to be now established that he went from Nottingham to become tailor at Brinsley colliery in the days when the mine owners supplied the men with the clothes they wore in the pits, thick flannel singlets and moleskin trousers lined at the top with flannel. His grandchildren, of D. H. Lawrence's generation, remembered his shop with its great rolls of flannel for thick vests, "and the strange old sewing machine, like nothing else on earth, which sewed the massive pit trousers".

The old man was remembered by his grandchildren, when he was in his eighties, as "a big, shambling, generous-hearted man whose waistcoat front was always powdered with snuff". His wife used the front room of their cottage as a shop, in which she supplied odds and ends of drapery to the miners' wives of Brins-ley. It had once been quite a flourishing little business but was, obviously, declining in the 1890's, when the Lawrence children used to walk due northwards across the fields from Eastwood to Brinsley to see their grandparents. The old tailor's wife had been Sarah Parsons, daughter of a man once prominent in the stocking and silk industry in Nottingham. The John Lawrence whom she married was, in his youth, quite a well-known character in the town for his sporting prowess—a cheerful and strongly built young man, who rode and swam in the Trent and was a noted boxer. It is remembered of him that he had huge hands (it is surprising, perhaps, that he followed the delicate trade he did, albeit an outsize and gigantic version of it); and his son used to say that once, in an informal match, John Lawrence defeated the English champion, Ben Caunt.

Those were D. H. Lawrence's paternal grandparents. His own father, John Arthur Lawrence, had been working in the pits since the age of ten, belonging, as his son pointed out, to the last generation of Englishmen who escaped compulsory state educa-tion. To the end of his life he could barely sign his name and could only painfully read the daily newspaper. His life and his attitude to life was primitive, and almost entirely animal, yet the artist's temperament that D. H. Lawrence inherited came from him and not from his wife, for all her better education, her nag-ging sense of superiority and her resentment at Arthur Lawrence's refusal to be tamed by her. As a young man he had been a very good dancer ("Father," D.H.L. once said, "says one ought to be able to dance on a threepenny bit") and had at one stage even run a dancing class. But this was only an expression of the almost completely physical life that he lived, the underground existence in the mines alternated with drinking and talking on the surface and going for long walks into the country. His inter-ests, as well as the need to earn, centred his life round the pit head, but he enjoyed the early morning walks through the fields to the mine and, like his son, understood animals and could tell vivid stories about them. In appearance he apparently looked strikingly virile with hugely developed arm muscles, thick black hair and bushy beard. His position in the pit was that of a "butty" which at that time meant a kind of foreman or liaison man between the company and the other miners; it was a responsible and, in good times, well enough paid job. Arthur Lawrence had a theory that he was only partly English and that his grandfather had been a Frenchman. By temperament, he was indifferent to what other people thought of himself, his habits, or his opinions, taking life as it came and extracting from it the greatest possible amount of enjoyment.

This was the young man who, at a party in Nottingham, met a girl named Lydia Beardsall. She was an entirely different sort of person, both in character and in background. Being so unlike, each held for the other a certain sense of mystery and strangeness. For him, the miner, she was that fascinating thing, "a lady". She, in turn, knowing nothing of a miner's life, was attracted by the virility of the young man who, rough as he was, danced so well. Lydia Beardsall believed herself to be "of a good old burgher family who had fought in the Civil War with Colonel Hutchinson and who had remained stout congregationalists". Whether this was so or not, Lydia's father had been an engineer foreman at Sheerness dockyard and had paid for her to be educated at a small private school where she later became an assistant teacher; and, certainly, on both her father's and mother's side are to be found connections with the religious life of Victorian Nottingham, which explains why Lawrence's mother "read a good deal and wrote poetry . . . loved ideas, and was considered very intellectual. What she liked most of all was an argument on religion or philosophy or politics with some educated man." Her own dissimilarity from the sensuous, unthinking life of the miner she married can, in the first place, be traced to her father, the engineer, who, as "George Coppard" in *Sons and Lovers,* is described by his grandson as "proud in his bearing, handsome and rather bitter; who preferred theology in reading, and who drew near in sympathy only to one man, the Apostle Paul; who was harsh in government, and in familiarity ironic; who ignored all sensuous pleasure—he was very different from the miner". Lawrence also spoke of his grandfather in relation to Jesse Boot, later Lord Trent, and said that the two "quarrelled and had a long war as to which of them should govern the chapel at Sneinton, in Nottingham. My grandfather won." Lawrence also

said that George Beardsall "was the earliest friend and collaborator of William Booth, and that he broke off with the 'General'
over their joint plans for the formation of what turned into the
Salvation Army". This preaching, hymn-singing grandfather
came from a family that had lost its money in the collapse of the
hosiery industry in the 1830's.

But there is a further reason why Protestant hymns should have
played so large if almost unconscious a part in Lawrence's
imagination. George Beardsall had married Lydia Newton,
daughter of a certain John Newton who lived from 1802 to 1886,
who was most of his adult life a lace-maker, a twist hand, but was
also a noted choir master. The most famous surviving hymn of
this John Newton (who is not, of course, to be confused with
John Newton, 1725-1807, the earlier hymn writer and collaborator
of Cowper) is one called "Sovereignty", which is still sung in
chapels. Once, in order to pay for a book of his hymns, with the
title of *The Pilgrim*, Newton walked from town to town getting
subscribers and giving concerts.

To the miner who, when he came out of the dark mine, wished
to continue, in talking and in drinking, the intimacy with his
mates he found below, and the woman horrified at the miner's
life from the moment when she first realized that he came home
unwashed to the house, who felt that she had married beneath
her, and found herself committed to a life of nagging about the
facts and necessities of life, five children were born, three sons
and two daughters, of whom David Herbert Lawrence was the
fourth. Their early childhood was made terrible by the scenes
of anger and recrimination which took place between this ill-
matched couple. Outside the cottage in Walker Street, Eastwood,
where the young children would lie in bed waiting for their
father's return, stood a great ash tree which Lawrence described
as shrieking in the night gales and mingling with the angry voices
of the quarrelling parents: "Having such a great space in front
of the house gave the children a feeling of night, of vastness,
and of terror." This terror came in from the shrieking of the tree
and the anguish of the home discord.

Often he would wake up, having been asleep a long time,
aware of thuds downstairs. Instantly, he says, he was wide awake.
He heard the booming shouts of his father, come home nearly
drunk, the sharp replies of his mother, then the bang, bang,
of his father's fist on the table, and the nasty snarling shout as
the man's voice got higher. And then the whole was drowned
in a piercing medley of shrieks and cries from the great, wind-
swept ash tree. The children lay silent in suspense, waiting for

The Norman font at Markham Clinton
In Sherwood Forest near Edwinstowe

a lull in the wind, to hear what their father was doing. He might hit their mother again. There was a feeling of horror, a kind of bristling in the darkness, and a sense of blood. They lay with their hearts in the grip of what he calls an intense anguish.

Lawrence's overpowering love for his mother and the fact that during his childhood he almost certainly felt himself to be wholly on " her side " in his attitude to these quarrels did not prevent him, in later life, from writing with extraordinary understanding and tenderness about the kind of miner that his father was. The passage I quote also serves to emphasize the continued rurality of the Nottingham to Annesley country that Lawrence has described.

" There was a big discrepancy, when I was a boy, between the collier who saw, at the best, only a brief few hours of daylight —often no daylight at all during the winter weeks—and the collier's wife, who had all the day to herself when the man was down pit. The collier fled out of the house as soon as he could, away from the nagging materialism of the woman. With the women it was always: This is broken, now you've got to mend it! or else: We want this, that and the other, and where is the money coming from? The collier didn't know and didn't care very deeply—his life was otherwise. So he escaped. He roved the countryside with his dog, prowling for a rabbit, for nests, for mushrooms, anything. He loved the countryside, just the indiscriminating feel of it. Or he loved just to sit on his heels and watch—anything or nothing. He was not intellectually interested. Life for him did not consist in facts, but in a flow. Very often, he loved his garden. And very often he had a genuine love of the beauty of flowers."

Before we take the bus from the market-place out to Eastwood we ought to remind ourselves of Lawrence's very close associations with Nottingham itself. The city is more than merely the background of *Sons and Lovers,* it is one of the leading characters of the novel. Certain incidents in it are inseparable, to those who know the place at all, from their setting. The book contains a hint of what the market-place must have seemed like to a Nottingham boy at the beginning of the century, when it was still filled with stalls. You may perhaps remember the incident when Paul Morel and his mother travel in from Eastwood (which is called Bestwood in the book) to hunt for a job for him. Lawrence describes how the mother and son walked down Station Street " feeling the excitement of lovers having adventure together ". (They have arrived by train at Nottingham station.) They turn right out of Station Street and go up Carrington Street. Soon

Sherwood Forest: the Major Oak
Cuckney: " The Greendale Oak"

they cross the Nottingham canal and they stop and hang over the parapet and look at the barges below. "'It's just like Venice,' he said, seeing sunshine on the water that lay between high factory walls." It was in this part of the town that was situated the factory in which both Paul Morel and D. H. Lawrence (for *Sons and Lovers* is almost wholly autobiographical) found a job as an office boy. Lawrence's elder brother, William Ernest, who was a clerk in London, had been called in by D.H.L. to help him, in secret, to look for a job. Every day Lawrence had gone to the newspaper room of the local public library to look through the situations vacant advertisements and his brother wrote out in orthodox business phraseology a letter of application. Oddly enough this letter survives and it mentions the applicant had just turned sixteen. The letter served its purpose and brought him a job almost at once.

So, a month or so after his birthday, in September 1901, he entered the service of Messrs. Hayward of Nottingham, makers of surgical and orthopaedic instruments. As in *Sons and Lovers*, there was an interview between the employer and the mother and son, and he was taken on as an office boy at a salary of eight shillings a week. In the novel Lawrence describes how the pair of them walk up, after the interview was over, to the market-place: "it was very sunny. There was the big desolate space of the market-place, the blue sky shimmered, and the granite cobbles of the paving glistened. Shops down the Long Row were deep in obscurity, and the shadow was full of colour. Just where the horse trams trundled across the market was a row of fruit stalls, with fruit blazing in the sun—apples and piles of reddish oranges, small greengage plums and bananas. There was a warm scent of fruit as mother and son passed."

To switch back from fiction to fact, I said that brother Ernest's letter written for D.H.L. to Messrs. Hayward had survived. Well here, as a curiosity, it is: "Gentlemen,—In reply to your ad, in to-day's G (this is how the brothers referred to the *Nottingham Guardian*) for a Junior Clerk, I beg to place my services at your disposal. I am sixteen years of age and have just completed three years course at the Nottingham High School. Although I have not had any business experience in accounts yet, I studied book-keeping and obtained two prizes for mathematics, as well as one for French and German. If desired, I shall be pleased to furnish you with the highest references as to character and ability, both from my late masters and the minister in this town. Should you favour me with the appointment I would always endeavour to merit the confidence you place in me. Trusting to receive your favourable reply,—I beg to remain, gentlemen, Yours obediently, D. H. Lawrence."

As it turned out, Lawrence's career as a Nottingham clerk was a good deal briefer than most people realize. But two events combined to cause the short period of employment with Messrs. Hayward to be a memorable and distressing one in the life of the Lawrence family. After he had been at the factory for only a few weeks his energetic and successful brother, William Ernest, whose job in a London shipping office at £120 a year seemed a justification of their mother's ambition for them both, suddenly developed pneumonia, complicated by erysipelas, and died, with his mother beside him in his London lodging house. Then, a few days before Christmas, when the mother was still brooding over her loss and her disappointed ambition, D.H.L. came home from Nottingham one cold night stricken with pneumonia. That winter of 1901-2 Lawrence lay very near to death, experiencing, as he himself described, during the crisis of the illness, " the ghastly sickly feeling of dissolution, when all the cells in the body seemed in intense irritability to be breaking down, and consciousness makes a last flare of struggle like madness ". At any rate, even when convalescence became possible, any continuation of his bare three months' employment at the factory was out of the question; and in a sense the illness was a blessing to the career of the future writer, for not only did it take Lawrence out of Nottingham and out of the business world (his next step was to go back to Eastwood to take a post as pupil teacher in the British school there) but it also gave him an opportunity of extending his friendship with the kindly parents of Jessie Chambers ("Miriam") at The Hagg's Farm, which was so great an influence on the development of his personality. Of the Haggs we shall hear more in a moment.

Lawrence's two years at University College, Nottingham, certainly played a powerful part in shaping Lawrence's future life because it was there that he met Frieda von Richthofen, who was to become his wife and was at that time the wife of his instructor in French at the university, Professor Ernest Weekley; but the period did not greatly affect his writing, nor his academic instruction his career. He entered Nottingham University in 1906, when he was twenty-one. He was to take a two years' training course in the Normal Department where he began reading for an arts degree, getting extra tuition in Latin from a congregational clergyman at Eastwood and from one of the professors of the university. This project was dropped, but he was successful in his final examination, winning six distinctions, including French and Botany—but not English. His own opinion seems to have been that the two years at the university were wasted years.

Certainly, from a topographical point of view, his university period left little mark on a writer, who, in spite of his intense inner individuality, was quick to absorb impressions from outside; and the Nottingham memories in *Sons and Lovers* are mainly derived from the recollections of childhood. The castle has its due place in the remembered urban landscape and dominates the second half of the novel where the scene is Nottingham itself, just as Eastwood was the setting for the first half. Paul Morel takes up with a girl who works at lace spinning at home when he first meets her and later comes to work at the surgical appliance factory where he is. There is an effective description of the two of them going up to the castle together in the dinner hour. They look down upon the town from the Castle Rock and observe the pigeons preening themselves in their holes in the sandstone, the trees below looking tiny in pools of their own shadow, and the people in the streets scurrying about like so many tadpoles. This second half of the book takes us into many different sections of Nottingham. We are shown Paul and Clara travelling by tram through the city, down the Wilford Road and out past the dreary Wilford churchyard. We see Paul going to Clara's home in the grim unloveliness of Sneinton nearly half a century ago. Then, on the other hand, we are shown St. Mary's church, and the people coming out after evening service with the sound of the organ audible from the darkness outside, and the stained-glass windows glowing in the night making the church seem like a great lantern.

To get to Eastwood easily you can take a bus from the market-place in Nottingham. It takes you through the suburb of Basford, past the shameful remains of Nuthall Temple, with a petrol station beside the dismantled gate, and only an untidy fragment and the overgrown drive to remind one of Sir Charles Sedley's Palladian extravaganza. So completely does the village of Eastwood appear to belong to the acute industrialism of late nineteenth and of the present century that one might perhaps imagine that no inhabited place existed there before those times. Its history is indeed older than that but has been connected with coal for a surprisingly long time. A description of the village at the end of the eighteenth century observes: " In it are extensive coal mines; coals are found here at the depth of five yards, and at fifty. The village has many scattered dwellings seated on swells and declivities of the earth." An early and at the time astonishing symptom in coal-mining areas, which has since become commonplace, is reported in an old history. " A remarkable circumstance happened here, about eleven years since, by the sinking of an old coal mine. A farmer, refreshing himself in a room of a public house, ordered the landlord to fill him a cup of ale; but, to the surprise of the host, when he returned, he found the farmer lying on his back, with his arms extended, holding his knife and fork in his hands, and the table overthrown, both jumbled together in a sunken part of the floor, and he expecting every moment to be swallowed up by an earthquake." Even at this time there seems to have existed no church earlier than about 1740, St. Mary's, a building mostly of brick, with a tower. So Eastwood, in spite of being a manor of the greatest antiquity, may be regarded as having its origin as a sizeable village mainly in the discovery of coal in these parts. The Brinsley Collieries, discovered on the estate of the Duke of Newcastle, have likewise been worked for several centuries. Eastwood to-day is an ugly and a poor place, but it is not dirty or squalid in the way that urban slums are squalid. For one thing it has views. It is built on quite a high, windy ridge. It is possible to see the country around—which, as Lawrence insisted, is still country—consisting of fields and smallholdings, isolated trees, copses and the promise of forest woodland beyond the horizon, by peering, in either direction, behind the screen of red-brick houses and shops that line the main street of the village. It is not a compact village but long and straggling, based on the road that goes on to Heanor. Compared with most of the suburban overflow and the mining areas passed during the half-hour journey from the centre of Nottingham on the Midland General Bus or the A.1 trolley bus which passes through Eastwood on its way to Ripley, it is relatively rural. But it is not anything but ugly; and one remembers what Lawrence said: "These mining villages *might* have been like the lovely hill towns of Italy, shapely and fascinating."

There would surely be quite a lot of shops that Lawrence would recognize to-day. Hunter's Tea Stores and the Nottingham Trustee Savings Bank next door: they must have been there in Lawrence's time. So, too, the pubs, the Wellington in the main street and the Ram that Lawrence's father patronized. And at the end of the village, where the main street joins the road to Annesley, the village's single more pretentious inn, the Sun Hotel, which describes itself as " Birthplace of the Midland Railway". Part of the reason why the shopping face of Eastwood would still be recognizable to Lawrence is that the shops, unlike those in industrial suburbs generally, are still "village" shops; hardly any chain stores seem to have thought it worth their while to establish outposts here. The absence of their slick newness makes the place seem all the poorer.

The house in Victoria Street where Lawrence was born in 1885 is very small, has a little shop window (Mrs. Lawrence, in her early married life had tried to sell lace caps and aprons and linen to help the family budget, but had not prospered) and a gate-entrance at the side leading to a back court. The outdoor privies of the houses are ranged against a wall at the far end of the little strips of vegetable garden. When Lawrence was a year old his parents moved to a house in The Breach, "a corner house. A field path came down under a great hawthorn hedge. On the other side was the brook with the old sheep bridge going over into the meadows. . . ." The corner house is still occupied by the same sort of people, in the same sort of mining village. The way to The Breach and the High Street, for all the country beyond it, is through miserable side streets with dustbins and washing lines and the harsh red brick which Lawrence has described so well.

The Lawrences moved again, when D.H.L. was six. They went to live in one of the four stark blocks of miners' houses in Walker Street, red-brick terrace houses cut with tunnels that led to the yards at the back. The yard is mostly paved with brick and is barely ten feet long. The house has a bay window and three steps up to the front door. The Lawrence children were happy living here, with a view of Brinsley, Underwood, Moorgreen and the woods of High Park in the distance; and immediately in front were the fields that stretched to The Breach, where every sort of game could be played by the children. The ash tree outside the house which so scared the children has gone. From Walker Street there was one more move while Lawrence remained in Eastwood. They went to a house just round the corner, to Lynncroft. This move took place when Lawrence was sixteen, when he had become intimate with Jessie Chambers. She had known him first when they were living in Walker Street and, in contrast to the more spacious, rural farm dwelling at The Haggs, the Lawrence house for all its three floors (one of them an attic with only a tiny window) must have seemed cramped. The children, however, thought the Walker Street cottage "nice", and the kitchen "homelike", with its arm-chair for their father, their mother's rocking chair, sofa covered with red chintz and cushions to match, dresser, bookcase and some "quite decorative oleographs". There were more oleographs, heavily framed in gilt, in the parlour and mahogany and horsehair furniture. Exactly like any other respectable working-class home: but the Lawrence children felt there was something about it which made their house different from those of their neighbours, and Jessie Chambers herself, highly critical and intelligent as she was, says that the Lawrence household had "a curious atmosphere" which she felt whenever and immediately she entered the house. There was, she said, a tightness in the air as if something unusual might happen at any moment which was exciting but made her feel, she says, "a little sick". When the Lawrences moved to Lynncroft, Lawrence showed Miriam over the new house, we are told, "with quiet pride". It had a little entrance hall, with the stairs and the doors to the other rooms opening out from it. There was a cooking range in the scullery as well as in the living-room and a cupboard under the side window where the school books were kept. From the big window of the living-room there was a view over the roofs of Eastwood to the square church tower standing high above. The house had a pleasant garden adjoining a field. This last Eastwood house was the scene of two crises in Lawrence's life, first, the nightmare of his mother's long-drawn-out death from cancer during the autumn and winter months of 1910, and secondly—what was Jessie Chambers' tragedy rather than Lawrence's—the defeating of "Miriam's" love for him by a combination of Mrs. Lawrence's disapproval and the inescapable fact which Lawrence rather callously expressed later, that she was not physically attractive to him and that in his view no amount of sympathy, spiritual affinity or friendship could make a successful marriage if there was no physical attraction as well. Anyway, Lawrence's ambition centred on getting away from Eastwood— that above all things, for he was not, like his mother, concerned primarily with worldly success; and marriage, he felt, would have doubled the chances against his getting away.

Lawrence had, in fact, by 1910, sucked out of Eastwood, out of the Annesley countryside, out of The Hagg's Farm, all that they had to give him, and his future already lay elsewhere. Physically, of course, he had by this time made his first move away. After his two years at University College, Nottingham, he went off to London, as a fully qualified teacher, to a post in the Davidson Road Schools at Croydon. It was, by a cynical twist of fate, Jessie Chambers herself who had given Lawrence his first taste of appreciation and encouragement, who was, after he had already made clear that he needed from her no more than intellectual companionship, responsible for opening the literary world to him and so ensuring that he left Eastwood, and her, for ever. In the spring of 1908, more than two years before his mother died, Lawrence told Jessie Chambers that a parcel of his manuscripts had been returned, apparently unread, by an author whom he had asked for criticism. He was very discouraged. At the end of that year Lawrence came home to Eastwood on his first Christmas holiday from the Croydon School, and he brought with him a copy of a new magazine, *English Review*, edited by Ford Madox Hueffer (later Ford). It is an indication of the exceptional intellectual curiosity of the Chambers family at The Haggs that they were sufficiently interested in the new periodical to take out a subscription. After reading a few numbers Jessie was convinced that the paper would consider Lawrence's work and she pleaded with him to allow her to send in some of his verses. He was reluctant but eventually gave in, saying: "Give me a *nom de plume* though; I don't want folk in Croydon to know I write poetry." So Jessie Chambers copied out several of his poems and sent them to Hueffer with a letter explaining Lawrence's situation as a schoolmaster and asking that if the poems were published it should be under the pseudonym of Richard Greasley! Hueffer wrote back an encouraging letter suggesting that Lawrence should come and see him. Jessie replied that Lawrence would call after school reopened, but she kept the letter to herself until he returned to Eastwood. One gets, within the space of a very few words, the essence of the conflict between Jessie and Lawrence's mother in the way the former describes the subsequent scene:

"'Oh, I've got a letter for you.'

"He looked at me quickly, then his eyes narrowed.

"'From the *English*? About the poems? Show it me.'

"I gave him the letter, and his face became tense.

"'You are my luck,' he murmured. Then he said with suppressed excitement, 'Let me take it to show mother.' And I never saw it again."

Hueffer published in the *English Review* during 1909 and 1910 about a dozen poems and two short stories by Lawrence. After reading the novel, *The White Peacock*, he gave Lawrence a warm letter of recommendation to Heinemann, the publisher, and began asking him to meals and parties at his own house. The novel was accepted by Heinemann and the literary people Lawrence met at Hueffer's lunches took him seriously as a writer of promise. Hueffer himself told Lawrence "you've got genius".

So Lawrence's career began, and the building of the Lawrence myth in places so very different and so very far away from Eastwood. The county of his birth scarcely enters into the story again after his mother's death, except—and how vividly—in written recollections. In 1912 came the virtual capture of Frieda

Weekley from her husband at Nottingham University; and in later years Lawrence paid visits to his sisters at Middleton-by-Worksworth and at Ripley over the Derbyshire border. That is about all. Of Jessie Chambers, Lawrence's own, rather heartless, laconic remark brings to an end her story so far as he was concerned, and begins his own, which has no more place in this account: "The girl had launched me, so easily, on my literary career like a princess cutting a thread, launching a ship."

CHAPTER X

THE DUKERIES AND THE FOREST

THIS must necessarily be a rather sombre chapter. Exhilarating though its subject would have been to write about fifty years ago it is one in which the changes wrought by the passing of time, in this case almost wholly disadvantageous, seem to be brought under a magnifying glass or shown speeded up, as if in a nature film. The Dukeries. What a magnificent expression that is! It contains wit, admiration, a sneaking affection for the grandiose, with a salutary sense of the preposterousness of the very grand. With its immediate analogy of Rookeries, it treats the whole thought of a gaggle of Dukes nesting among the oaks of Sherwood Forest as something quite absurd; and yet, in a way to be admired, something to be proud of. To be sure, the word in the singular, a Dukery, was an old synonym for a Dukedom; but it had ceased to be used by the end of the sixteenth century. Its revival, in the plural, with its special Nottinghamshire association, dates from just about the time of Queen Victoria's accession and in the phrase, if it were broken down and analysed, would be found overtones and subtleties which crystallize the general attitude of nineteenth and early twentieth-century England to its landed aristocracy, and perhaps helps to explain why the English Revolution has been so gradual and conservative. But if any foreigner should doubt that there had been a revolution, then let him go immediately to the Dukeries and look around and he will question no longer.

It is possible, certainly, to find some satisfaction, in comparing this microcosm, this museum of English, indeed European, aristocratic history, in the fact that the inevitable—but not yet by any means complete—abandonment of the Dukeries by their traditional owners has been brought about not by bloodshed or burning or force of arms but a just as irresistible economic revolution, an altered way of living and a changed relation between land and ownership. Great mansions, it is true, have been razed to the ground; but any revolutionary fervour that stimulated the blows of the housebreaker's axe were private and personal and had nothing to do with the planned and peaceful demolition of an outdated symbol. Better this, perhaps, than the blackened empty shells to be seen, shall we say, in Ireland. But the effect, the disappearance of huge slabs of history and—sometimes—of art, is none the less to be regretted and any account of what survives of the Dukeries must necessarily have a touch of regret, if not of bitterness in it.

There is another grim aspect of any survey of country houses in England to-day which, because its effects are the more conspicuous the larger the building, brings itself to a head in the Dukeries. Perhaps by the time this book is read the traces of wartime handling of country houses will have been obliterated—most likely, one guesses, by the demolishing of buildings so severely handled as to be incapable of restoration. Large or small, a country house suffers, I would claim, far more sorely from the effects of mishandling—for which "requisitioning" is virtually a synonym—than does a town house. In a town, the fact of being constantly under view, the comparison with the state of adjacent houses, civic pride, commercial or speculative concern, combine to make the chances of speedy restoration of a house that has gone downhill through no fault of its own, probable and desirable by all. A country house lives on its own, out of sight; it lets no one down but itself by its decayed appearance. There is nothing but its own pride to insist on its pulling itself together. Moreover, in the case of a town house, a lick of paint over the single front that it presents to the street, some new panes of glass, a touch of polish on the door knocker and the place is respectable again, whatever horrors may still lurk within and behind. A country house stands foursquare to the world, and it grows out of the soil and not out of the pavements. Vegetation is ever lurking in readiness to take command. A town house may lie empty and ownerless for years on end and all that happens is that its windows become dirtier and dirtier. Leave a country house abandoned for a year and nature will see to it that it looks derelict. As a man, however new, clean or well pressed his clothes, will look seedy and ill kempt if he has stubble on his cheeks and chin, so will the ministrations of painters and builders and bricklayers on a country house be of no avail if there are no hands to shave the lawns and weed the paths.

Now our county of Nottingham has probably not suffered from the material effects of wartime military requisitioning as much as did, say, the seaside townships of the south and east which lay within the prohibited zones and from which a degree of evacuation was compulsory. Inland counties like ours were spared the steady deterioration of whole streets of modest houses that came from the continuous, but changing, occupation by one or other of the armed forces. Counties such as this, though well stocked with those sizeable country mansions which are the inevitable targets of requisitioning authorities, suffered as hardly if in a more dispersed and less conspicuous manner from the war's secondary destruction. One had only to wander through Nottinghamshire during the five years following the war to become aware of the grievous burden that it bore.

As we shall see, the circumstances that caused, in the Dukeries, the interior of Rufford Abbey to emerge from the war in the pitiful state that it did, were in part special ones, and the vandalism (the word, in this context, needs doubling back on its own history, because it was Latins who committed the outrage) was here deliberate. But, distressing as are the results of military occupation, I am inclined myself to think that they are generally unavoidable. I believe that if one accepts the much-quoted Le Corbusier definition of a house as having been well understood by architects and builders for at least three hundred years, then the disparity between the careful balance of that machine—designed for just so many, for just such a manner of living—and its treatment under billeting conditions becomes plain, and its sufferings the more understandable. (I write as one who, when in charge of billeted detachments, always tried, to the extent of causing murmurings, to prevent " damage to civilian property ".) It is a matter of the constant equilibrium between use and the sensitive adjustment and frail material out of which the small things of a house are constructed. It is a matter of how often a door handle is turned in the course of a day—not how roughly; of how often a window is opened and shut, of how many of those little, unavoidable, domestic blows that wainscoat, banister, window-frame and light switch receives. Strangely, the extent of internal cleaning—particularly scrubbing—affects the balance adversely: the more, the worse. That has a hard sound, and I am sure it is true. One can generalize and say that a house, on an average, is designed for occupation by as many people as there are rooms in it. It cannot long survive the activities, however disciplined, of more. A house built for ten cannot stand up to, as it was often asked to, fairly rough handling by a hundred.

It is at Rufford Abbey, more than anywhere else in the county, that the weight of the Army's destructive capacity was shown, in the years after the war, at its most oppressive; and since I have referred, rather misleadingly, to Rufford as in the Dukeries, I ought to place them, first, squarely on the map and in history. The district known as the Dukeries has served one exceedingly valuable purpose. It has preserved (what, if it had not been for the Dukes, would probably not have been preserved) a part of Sherwood Forest. The lordly parks include what is undoubtedly the finest portion of the surviving forest. The title, which I prefer to look upon as an affectionate nickname, is derived from the fact that within the limits of this single unbroken area were situated, at one time, the princely mansions of the Dukes of Portland, Newcastle, Norfolk, Leeds and Kingston. To-day, the Dukes of Norfolk and Leeds have long parted with their property in this county; the Duke of Newcastle has, in more recent times, disposed of his; there is no Duke of Kingston to-day, but Earl Manvers, the representative of the Pierreponts, the family of the Dukes of Kingston, maintains lordly traditions at Thoresby; Welbeck is still the seat, though not the normal residence of the Duke of Portland —of the recent uses to which it has been put we shall hear in a moment. Rufford Abbey, which is usually included in the Dukeries though not within the actual boundary, was the seat of the Lords Savile from the early seventeenth century until just before the late war. It is that no longer.

There is one sense in which the present-day visitor has an advantage over anyone who, in the more orderly days between the wars, wished to acquaint himself with the mansions and domains of the Dukeries. Suppose at some time after the first war you had established yourself at a point convenient for excursions into Sherwood Forest. You could stay, as you can still stay, at the Lion or the Royal at Worksop, or at that favourite forest inn The Hop Pole, at Ollerton. (You can probably do the same now again, but there was a time, a few years ago, when a changed ownership at The Hop Pole and the sale of its well-remembered curious contents—it caused quite a local stir—was made the occasion for so complete a repairing and redoing of the inn that for a while you would do no more than have a drink in the bar there, not eat, let alone stay.) You are, let us presume, an "ordinary" person who has come without having elaborately prepared the ground by means of letters of introduction to the local magnates. You wish to visit the houses? That was normally impossible. Clumber, admittedly, was still—until 1937—standing but its interior was not shown to the public. The best you could do, at one stage, was to look at the Duke of Newcastle's pictures which were on loan to the Nottingham Castle museum. You could, however, by application to the Newcastle Estate Office in Worksop, receive permission to visit Clumber church. There was no admission to Thoresby. At Welbeck, the privilege that had been enjoyed before the first war of visiting parts of the outbuildings, the riding school and other adjuncts, upon payment of a shilling had been withdrawn; and the house itself had never been "a show place". Worksop Manor was not shown to the public. To the inside of Rufford alone could you normally gain access by making application in Newark to the Rufford Estate Office.

Now for the parks. The first thing that you would discover was that, at any rate until very late in the inter-war period, it was no use taking your motor car. You *could* get into the parks of Clumber and Thoresby (which latter is, by common consent, the best of all in the Dukeries, as well as being the largest, and also had a good claim to be the finest deer park in the whole country), but it had to be a Monday or a Thursday or a Saturday and no cars were allowed. You could go on foot or you could go on a horse, or in a horse-drawn vehicle. That, so far as I know, was the position in, say, the 1920's.

What was the position after the war? The parks were to some extent spoiled. They were strewn with the—in two senses—endless Nissen-style arched hiding places of military ammunition. The Dukeries were the site of one of the biggest dumps in the country. Clumber Park, incidentally, was, in 1947, the scene of what must have been one of the noisiest incidents in the history of the Dukeries. There was still much ammunition about and on a day and a night during that summer there was to be seen the spectacle, among the glades in which Robin Hood did, or did not, ride, of steel-helmeted firemen, together with hundreds of troops and German prisoners of war, lying face downwards full length in the bracken while red-hot steel splinters whizzed over them. In this fire, which lasted for more than twenty-four hours, over a square mile of Clumber Park was devastated. Yes, the brief, corrugated tunnels which shared with the trees of Sherwood Forest the domination of the Dukeries' landscape—they were everywhere and inescapable—made the Dukeries seriously different from before the war; moreover new and sternly practical concrete and asphalt roadways had been driven through parts of the forest where previously only the traveller on foot could penetrate. (These, beguiling you into the thickest parts of the forest and then ending, meaninglessly in nothing, were extremely misleading if you were trying to find your way about by means of a map.) However, these lasting disadvantages were almost outweighed by the, perhaps, temporary blessing that you could, in the post-war years, move about pretty well where you liked. There were a few new obstacles. You might find a road, marked as a thoroughfare on the map, blocked suddenly by the entrance gates of a prisoner-of-war camp. You might pass, in the length of the lime and chestnut avenues, an odd military sentry; but he would not necessarily stop you.

The parks, then, survive, though having lost much of the look of the primeval woodland and the sacrosanct game reserve that once they had. The houses have not fared even so well as this. Clumber has disappeared. Welbeck remains, but is put to strange uses. Rufford has only survived by the skin of its teeth. The remains of Worksop Manor (and its diminution is no recent story) are still inhabited. But only from the steep, fantastic roof line of Thoresby does the proud standard of Earl Manvers tell of a mansion still occupied by its noble owner.

I do not know which direction is considered the best to approach the Dukeries from. I have always gone into the area from the south and for the present purposes will follow that. It provides us with quite a convenient sequence: dealing, initially, with Rufford, not really part of the Dukeries at all, and then, crossing the railway line and the River Maun which form the southern boundaries of the area, plunging, after a glance at Ollerton, Edwinstowe and Clipstone, the three villages at the bottom end of the Dukeries, into the finest of the parks; so from Thoresby with its dependants, Budby and Perlethorpe, passing into Clumber, thence to the climax of the Dukeries, to Welbeck, and out into Worksop. That is the itinerary and we begin with Rufford Abbey.

Rufford Abbey stood empty and idle when I was last there some years ago. Its recent history has been so confused and so disputed that its fate, even at the time of writing, did not seem absolutely certain. There appeared little chance that it could be saved from demolition. It had been sold by Lord Savile just before the war to Sir Alfred Ball, a Lancashire magnate. With the coming of war it was requisitioned and its fate, after the army evacuated it, hung for many years in the balance. There were proposals, at one stage, to use it as a film studio, which would presumably have involved some extraordinary process of disembowelling, of de-flooring—in spite of the great height of some of the rooms—in order to turn it into an enormous stone hangar. But this came to nothing. Rumours of impending demolition had been in the air for a long time, but opposition to the project was strong and the Nottinghamshire County Council issued a preservation order protecting the abbey. This, however, was ultimately cancelled and a notice issued to the final owner of the abbey, Mr. Henry Talbot de Vere Clifton (not, so to speak, one of *our* Cliftons, though of equally ancient lineage) consenting to the demolition of the building. The campaign for its preservation had been strengthened by the fact that the Minister of Town and Country Planning (it was at a time when such a person existed) had listed the property as a building of historical interest and had issued a provisional order fully protecting it. It certainly *was* of interest and, into the bargain, it had a charm, even in neglect, a dignity and complete lack of ostentation or vulgarity, which made it in many ways more attractive than the far "greater" houses of the Dukeries proper. All the same, having seen it soon after de-requisitioning I feel considerable sympathy for the owner's agent who, observing that the mansion had been bought from Lord Savile in 1938, complained: "But the Army Authorities took it over during the war years and left it in a deplorable state." This spokesman added that the mansion had been offered as offices to the National Coal Board and as a hospital to the Ministry of Health, and that when they rejected it, the owner had no option but to start demolition. It was said, by the way, at one time that the house alone could be bought for as little as £5,000. The only proviso made by the Nottinghamshire County Council in granting permission to pull Rufford down was that the portion of the abbey known as the Crypt was to be retained.

The entrance to Rufford was by a massive gateway which was put up by the eighth Earl of Scarbrough, and the approach to the house was through an avenue of lime, beech and elm trees. There seem never to have been any elaborate gardens as at Welbeck, and the park came quite close up to the house. To the north-east is a handsome lake of considerable size.

The relevant history of the place that was earlier called Rumforde began soon after the Norman Conquest. Possession passed from the Saxon owner to Gilbert de Gaunt, a nephew of William the Conqueror. His eldest son became Earl of Lincoln and made the place the site of a Cistercian abbey, founded in 1148. The monastic buildings have disappeared much more completely than at Newstead though perhaps less utterly than at Welbeck. The only visible remains are a single large room, now sub-divided, which is groin vaulted and has three octagonal piers. This is the crypt which the County Council wanted preserved. At the dissolution the property went to the Earl of Shrewsbury, who was the father of Bess of Hardwick's fourth and last husband. The famous Bess is supposed to have been responsible for the late Elizabethan or Jacobean parts of the building as we have known it. It was at Rufford that Bess brought about the marriage of her daughter Elizabeth with the brother of Darnley, the husband of

Victorian magnificence in the Dukeries: Thoresby, by Anthony Salvin, 1864-75

Mary Queen of Scots, an alliance which deeply offended Queen Elizabeth. An issue of this marriage was the unfortunate Arabella Stuart who, when her cousin James I was on the throne, married without his permission. Both she and her husband were immediately imprisoned and from her weary incarceration in the Tower she was only released by her death, insane, in 1615. It was a granddaughter of Bess of Hardwick who brought Rufford to the Saviles.

Though there is nothing complicated about its shape—basically, a single elongated rectangle—it is stylistically confusing and has little or no formal pattern. The nucleus of the building is the entrance with its barley-sugar columns and the large mullioned Elizabethan window to the left of it.

A certain vagueness prevails about the architectural history of Rufford. That there is a late fifteenth-century or early sixteenth-century part is obvious enough. There is also an evidently Georgian block whose roof has sloping ends. The eighteenth century exerts its influence largely over the appearance of the north side of the building, while the south side retains its Jacobean look. No architect or details of building seem to be recorded for these earlier periods; and it is interesting that a late eighteenth-century observer remarked of Rufford as a dwelling that it " has neither enough of religious antiquity remaining to attract, or splendour as a seat to arrest the stranger's travel ". He admits, however, that " it is seated pleasantly, and is of sufficient magnitude for the residents of family and fortune ". A view of the lake, with the house in the distance, accompanying this description, indicates that the Georgian extension was by that time already presenting its north face to the water. In early Victorian times, Anthony Salvin who, a quarter of a century later was to come back to the Dukeries to create a new Thoresby and its accompanying church at Perlethorpe, carried out, between 1838 and 1840, some neo-Jacobean alterations at Rufford. Subsequent nineteenth-century work seems to have been largely concentrated on the inside of the house.

One can say that it is the sanitation at Rufford which marks most clearly the period at which its greatness ended. In the north end of the house, the Georgian part, a suite of rooms was set aside for the use of King Edward VII who frequently visited the abbey and was the last of a considerable series of monarchs to be entertained there. (The Stuarts came, and so did George IV when Prince Regent: on this latter occasion the elder Charles Dibdin, the author of the famous song, " Tom Bowling ", was engaged as master of ceremonies, and it was through seeing an aged woodman

The Great Hall at Thoresby

fell one of the ancient oaks in the park at Rufford that he was moved to write his equally popular piece, "The Woodsman's Stroke", that affecting piece of Sherwood Forest literature.) One can presume, surely, that the apartments in which Edward VII resided must, in their own day, have represented the height of luxury. But when I was last there, the elaborate arm-chair commode which stood in the window of the King's narrow bathroom had clearly been discovered by marauding and unconstipated soldiery, and had become an unpleasing object. Even its tight-fitting wicker lid could not dim the buzzing of flies and blue-bottles. It was unfortunately typical of the condition of Rufford after the war.

Evidence of the over-habitation, in spite of its size, that I have already dwelt on, was immediately noticeable in the most cele-brated portion of the house, the Brick Hall, a stately apartment in the Elizabethan style, whose chimney piece and screen were restored in mid-Victorian times. It was the usual lofty rectangu-lar affair, with a dais at one end. It has a high open roof, and the carved-oak screen was inscribed with the words *Murus oenus conscientia sana,* which I take to mean that the possession of a sound conscience is as good as a wall of brass. The hall's most remarkable feature was its polished red-brick floor. This appeared not to have been protected during the period of military occupation. The effective but very friable material of which it was made had been sadly worn down by the necessary but constant passage over it (I stick to my thesis) not of the timid heels of an occasional flitting housemaid, or of the heavier but still discreet footfall of butler or flunkey, but of the searing edges of many hob-nailed boots. The Rufford floor was an excellent object lesson in the good sense of the Moslems, who, because the floors of their mosques were of brick or tiles, forbade, as a religious precept, the wearing of shoes within their walls; or of those curators of historic monuments in many countries—Russia is among them—who provide visitors, compulsorily, with soft leather over-slippers in which to glide innocuously over polished floors and pavements. At Rufford, anyway, the decorative pattern of the brick floor had all but disappeared, and the surface of the square tiles were roughened and grey. Seeing the hall only in its scarred and un-happy state one could still feel that the chamber emerged from Victorian times as something much more than a fairly convincing restoration. Was it beautiful? Less so I should guess than the handsome saloon which led from it, its long windows giving on to the garden and its walls hung with rather stained but still effective ivory-coloured damask. There are certain other rooms in the upper parts of the house, reached by the imposing central staircase, which deserve mention.

There was the Prince of Wales' bedchamber—the Prince in this case was George IV—and there was the Yellow Room on the first floor. Its walls were adorned with hangings of brilliant golden silk, and it is here, in these upstairs rooms, that Rufford's saddest damage was suffered; all the sadder because it was truly unnecessary. During the war there were, of course, huts in the grounds of Rufford Abbey. There were a lot of them, stretching away from the stables at the south-west end of the house, up through the orchards towards the Ollerton road. British soldiers occupied them first, soldiers who washed down and maintained, endlessly, their vehicles in the modest, untidy, yet charming stable courtyards of this very old-fashioned and workaday end of the house. But when the soldiers had gone they were replaced in the huts by Italian prisoners of war. It was these people, one is told, who inflicted upon Rufford the only truly wanton damage it suffered. The Italian prisoners were not billeted in the abbey itself. But somehow they got in. They got upstairs and tore down, systematically, the wall coverings of any rooms, including the Yellow Room, that were fitted with fabric hangings. I understood from people on the spot (and it sounds perfectly plausible, for the Italians are still an industrious and inventive people, as skilled in the applied arts as they are dexterous in impromptu mechanics) that this organized vandalism had the object of sewing the strips of fine damask up into handbags which were sold or perhaps remitted to the women of the neighbouring villages.

At two stages in the abbey's history as a residence attention had been paid to the fitting up of a surviving chapel. During the reign of Charles II, an admirable period for English woodwork, the chapel on the ground floor, rather low-lying, on the garden side of the house, by the flight of exterior steps, was provided with new seats, with carved fineals, the walls of the gallery were covered with embossed leather and other walls provided with tapestries. In the late 1880's a new chapel was built in, opposite the surviving monastic room, where old woodwork was made use of.

I find it hard to make up my mind whether I think the disappearance of Rufford would have been an outrage or just a regrettable indication of our changing times. I rather incline to the latter. History had already flown from it when the war began. It was an empty shell, even then. Admirable, of course, if to serve some useful purpose it could have been saved. But its justification for continued existence would have to have been entirely architectural and, in spite of the interesting mixture it presented, like a long brick of Neapolitan ice, of the work of several centuries, I have my doubts whether it really rates very high. Although the conventional preservers of ancient monuments seized upon the existence of something medieval, however secondary, in its crypt as a reason for raising a shout, and although it embodied the work of so many periods, I have a suspicion that, resentful though posterity may be about our letting it go, they would feel even more strongly if it had been Welbeck, with its unique, freakish singularity, or Thoresby, that superb specimen of Victorian romantic assurance.

A word or two about the villages on the southern edge of the Dukeries. Closer to Rufford is Eakring, which has two quite separate reasons for fame. First of all, in recent times, Eakring has become England's only oil field that can possibly be called by that name. It is no toy oil field; in the ten years between 1939 and 1949 the wells produced well over ten million gallons and by the end of that period the daily output was over one hundred and fifty tons. Even so, if you go to Eakring you must not be disappointed if it does not look *quite* like the great oil fields abroad that one knows from photographs. The wells are there all right, marked Well Three or Well Four, whatever they may be and the pumps, with their birdlike heads, looking rather like those toys that, for a brief season, drank mysteriously and—until they stopped—everlastingly, raising and lowering their heads, in every public house in England; and there are ranges of elaborate piping and cylindrical containers for the oil, both slender and squat. But somehow it doesn't look the least foreign or romantic. The apparatus gives the impression of being slightly surprised to find itself in such very ordinary English fields and in so unimpressed and rather unsuitable a landscape.

Of course there are collieries just over the rise, so perhaps the countryside has become used to this kind of intruder and that is why it seems so bored by it. (Looking even odder and more unexpected are the smaller wells in the fields near Kelham.) Eakring's industry and its importance to the country is very genuine; and the name of this otherwise not startling place, which boasts a goodish small church, much restored in the 1880's, and a disused circular windmill at one end of the village, has the ring of authority and newness about it. But it had its status, demure and unassertive, in history, long before people began to bore holes in its fields. For nearly forty years it had as its rector a man who was certainly a hero and very nearly a saint. For thirty-eight years

William Mompesson lived and ministered at Eakring, dying in 1708, and his life there was interrupted by few adventures.

But before he came to Eakring he had undergone enough to last him a lifetime. The story of what happened at his previous living at the little village of Eyam in the Derbyshire hills is pretty well known; and you may be aware why it was that, when William Mompesson first came to Eakring in 1669, the local people were so afraid of him that he was forced to live for a time as a sort of involuntary hermit in a hut in Rufford Park. But it is a great story and Mompesson's nearly forty years at Eakring demand that it be told again. (The Nottingham writers, William and Mary Howitt, are among those who have perpetuated the little epic in verse.) The inhabitants of the village of Eyam numbered about three hundred and sixty people, and William Mompesson was their rector, in 1665, the year of the plague. The disease was quite unknown in this isolated, out-of-the-way place, but it arrived in the latter half of September that year, the instrument of its conveyance being a box containing tailors' samples and some second-hand clothes dispatched from London to Edward Cooper, the village outfitter. The box was opened by Cooper's servant and, since the contents were damp, he put them in front of the fire to dry. Within three days an unmistakable plague spot had appeared on his chest and three days later he was dead. There was no doctor in the village, no squire, only two people to take command, Mompesson, the very young rector and an older parson, Thomas Stanley, who had been ejected from the living but had remained in Eyam.

The development of the outbreak was gradual. Cooper, the tailor, soon followed his servant to the grave. There were four more victims that month and twenty-two in October. Then a lull came during the winter frosts. But in the next spring and summer it raged unchecked through the village, fifty-six people dying in the month of July alone. The remaining inhabitants, panic stricken, were on the point of scattering, but Mompesson, realizing what this would mean, succeeded in inspiring them with his own courage. A circle was drawn round the village and its inhabitants, with selfless heroism, undertook never to cross it. The next month, August, seventy-eight men and women of Eyam, including Mompesson's wife, died. Twenty-four more died in September and fourteen in October. The population was reduced to thirty-three. Eight out of every nine people who had remained in Eyam after the first outbreak died, but there was no serious spreading of the plague in the neighbourhood. Perhaps it is hardly surprising that when, three years later, Mompesson came to Eakring, his parishioners were still frightened of infection. During his period in his hut he held weekly services under an ash tree, the site of which is now marked by a stone cross.

Over the hill to the south-west of Eakring is Bilsthorpe, Old and New, with its colliery, and beyond is Kirklington with its church of St. Swithin, which has a seventeenth-century brick tower. Here, too, is a battlemented eighteenth-century hall with octagonal wings and Victorian neo-Elizabethan porch.

Striking out from Eakring in the opposite direction, north-eastwards, one soon hits Kneesall which has a church built about 1425 with an elaborate west tower whose battlements are decorated with gables and tracery and has angel figures instead of gargoyles. At Kneesall, also, is Hall Farm, which is said to be one of the earliest brick houses in the county, dating from, perhaps, the last part of the sixteenth century. It has been a good deal altered. Beyond Kneesall, in the northerly direction, is Laxton, and though this is no very large place it has a unique interest and we must stop there a moment.

The shape and internal pattern of every village we have described—and that would go equally for every village in every other county of England—has been dictated by the enclosing of common land which went on throughout the country from medieval times almost up to our own century. The principal disadvantage of maintaining all the cattle of a parish on common ground for a large part of the year was that only so much ground was kept under meadow as would produce hay to feed the cattle during the winter. The result was that arable land was not well cultivated and there was no one who would undertake the responsibility of draining the common, of clearing it of wood or of manuring its fields. There was perfectly good sense behind the bulk of the enclosing, particularly in Tudor and immediately subsequent times. To put a permanent hedge round waste or forest ground to turn it into agricultural land was reasonable. So was the enclosure of open field strips into a smaller number of hedged fields to make better individual tillage possible. These could hardly cause dissatisfaction. In spite of the good reasons given, however, the enclosure of village commons and the enclosure of arable land for pasture was bound to produce discontent; and our county is one of those which suffered greatly from the acceleration and altered character of enclosure in the eighteenth century. In the early histories of the county which consider the area parish by parish there is an undercurrent of resentment in the repeated phrases: " Here the land was enclosed about fourteen years since ", or "This lordship was enclosed about the year 1780 ". Almost alone under the heading of Laxton does one read, after learning that the "lands are owned, chiefly, by Mr. Savile and Mr. Pierrepont", the sentence which, uniquely and astonishingly, still holds good: " It is a large open field lordship." Its present-day implications we shall discuss in a moment.

I referred to differences of character and increased rates of enclosure. During the period of the later Stuarts and first Hanoverians, the enclosure of open fields, common and waste, had been a matter of agreement between the parties concerned or by purchase. Enclosing was carried out, locally, as and how the occasion demanded. It was not a matter which yet concerned the government or parliament. But from about 1740 onwards the work of enclosure was carried on in a quite different and more wholesale way. Private Acts of Parliament were introduced and passed which gave rights over the individual proprietors of small areas of land and over common ground, comparable to the compulsory alteration in the status of land in contemporary town and country planning. The Parliamentary Commissioners had the force of law attached to the decisions they made and the small farmer had to be content with what land he was granted or the money compensation he was awarded. These private acts were rushed, in large numbers, through every parliament during the reign of George III, and the accelerated pace can be seen from the fact that from about two hundred and eighty of such acts passed between 1702 and 1760, the number rose to over four thousand in the period of only twenty years between 1760 and 1780. It is estimated that something like two million acres were taken into consideration. There is no doubt that in a period when the methods and science of agriculture were taking huge steps forward, the general effect upon English farming as a whole was to the good. But when the process was over, the magnates of the realm owned a far larger percentage of the acreage of England than they had before and, particularly in a midland county like ours, in the heart of the open field system, the number of small landowners considerably, and regrettably, diminished.

Within the whole county only at Laxton has the open field system of farming survived pretty well unchanged, at any rate in its essentials, since times long before the Norman Conquest. It is a survival of a method of rural existence which was general, although already here and there threatened, in medieval days. Laxton itself, even before you come to it, gives an impression, in spite of Eakring and its oil wells so close, of being shut away from the modern world. The lanes leading to it from Boughton, from Egmanton, from Ossington and from Kneesall, are all narrow and twisting and it lies just about as far as it could from any of the county's main axes. And when you get to Laxton you see at once that there is something odd about it. You pass, as you come in to it by any of its four roads, none of the usual farmsteads with their complex of outbuildings; instead the farm buildings—each farm-house usually having its haystack attached to it—of the Laxton area are concentrated in the long village street and behind them, on every side, the huge open fields, without permanent hedges, stretch away across the gentle hills. "Laxton: Lands are owned chiefly by Mr. Savile and Mr. Pierrepont. It is a large open field lordship." The eighteenth-century description holds good to-day on more than one point. Not only does the open-field system prevail but the land is still owned chiefly by the head of the Pierrepont family, Earl Manvers. And, perhaps, before we go any further it is worth making the point that the existence of open-field farming does not imply anything communal or co-operative about the character of the use of the fields. All the land is part of the Manvers estate and the people who have holdings in the open fields are tenants just as they are on any other property. The difference lies principally in the fact that no farmer has his land all in one piece. The ploughland of the area is divided into three very large open fields of about three hundred acres each, and each year two of the three fields are cultivated while the third remains fallow. Of the two that are cultivated, one is planted with wheat, and the other with some form of spring corn which may be barley, oats, peas or beans. Following the medieval system, a tenant has his land allotted to him in ten strips which may be scattered anywhere in the two fields under cultivation that year. The original idea of allotting the land in this dispersed way was to ensure that the tenants shared among themselves the poor land as well as the good. One visual effect of this system is, of course, that an enormous number of men—working for different farmers—are to be seen at the appropriate seasonal employment—ploughing or whatever it may be—at the same moment. They do not, however, get in each other's way, nor are any arguments possible, because each strip is separated from its neighbour by a grass track which must not be ploughed up even if a tenant has strips which lie side by side. These grass tracks are called "sykes" and each one, running the length of the big field, has got its own name, such as Roebuck Syke or Sidelings Syke. At haymaking time there is an auction for the right to cut hay from them. By a local custom the highest bidder for each syke puts a shilling in the pool and the sum raised is subsequently spent, for the good of all, on beer and cheese. At harvesting time, when the work on all the strips has been completed a day is fixed on which the livestock of the whole village can be turned loose to graze on the stubble of the complete six hundred or so acres. At other times animals that have strayed are rounded up by a man who still has the title of an old manorial office, the pinder, and put into the stone-walled pound or pinfold. The owner has to pay a fine of fourpence to get them out.

The Laxton open-field system is controlled by a body called the Court of the Manor, which meets twice a year. The bailiff summons the farmers to the court by ringing a bell, and anyone who fails to attend is fined twopence. A jury of twelve men is elected and they allot the strips and decide when the fields shall be declared open for grazing. In December the jury goes out to the fields to see that all the farmers have looked after their strips properly. Those who have not kept their ditches clean or who have left soil on common grass are fined. (As you will observe, a good deal of fining goes on, though the sums involved are trifling in terms of modern inflation.) Half the fines go to Earl Manvers as lord of the manor, and the other half is, very reasonably, spent on beer for the jury. A mildly complicated situation is produced when, as once happened, Lord Manvers was himself fined for leaving a heap of soil on common grass.

Such is an outline of the characteristic of Laxton, which makes it a sort of living history lesson, a working museum, and a place in which any alteration at this late stage would surely be deeply regretted. Its agricultural peculiarities give it, anyway, a special appearance, but there are other things to see in Laxton besides the farm-houses in the village street. The place contains also an imposing earthwork which is described as the largest and best-preserved Norman motte-and-bailey castle in the county. (The motte is the broad low mound, curved or forming an angle and often leading, at one end, up to the circular castle itself, which was typical of Norman and post-Norman fortification. The bailey was the open space or court within the mound.) Here, at Laxton, the castle mound has a circumference of more than eight hundred feet and has a smaller mound, about one hundred and fifty feet round, on top of it. And there is also the church. Here is another of those Nottinghamshire Easter sepulchres, a very small one this time, consisting of an upright niche with flowing tracery, and on the other side of the chancel a row of gabled and decorated sedilia. The most impressive part of the structure of the large church itself, from the outside, is the clerestory level of the nave which has five large windows placed extremely close to each other, decorated battlements and pinnacles. This addition was made to the church by Archbishop Rotherham, who was lord of the manor about 1490. The church contains a number of exceedingly battered monuments of the de Everingham family, of various dates in the thirteenth and fourteenth centuries. Adam de Everingham, who is commemorated by a stone effigy, awarded his first wife one of the same material, but the figure of his second wife is made of oak and is the only wooden medieval effigy in the county to survive.

We get an unexpected, and uncomfortably graphic view of a neglected parish church in the eighteenth century from the pen of a writer who had come to Laxton to make drawings of these various tombs in the revolutionary times of 1790. He describes, with great indignation, the part of the church where these tombs were placed, in these terms:

"I will attempt a description of it without the smallest exaggeration. The floor and old stones are completely covered with coals, coal-slack, cinders, fire-wood, straw, lime, broken bricks and stone, hassocks and floor-mats torn in pieces, ladders, an old sieve, broken scuttles, and spades; brushes without handles, and handles without brushes, mortar boards and mortar, reeds, tiles, soot, broken glass, dog's dung . . . Under the arch, that leads into this place of filth, stands an old tomb almost 6 feet high, on which lie three figures, seemingly a knight and his two wives; but so covered with dust, that I find it difficult to sketch them. While I viewed with indignation the insulting devastations around me, the deeds of the modern Goths and Vandals, in France, rushed, like a rapid stream, into my mind: in idea, I saw the atrocious, if not similar, destruction of the arts in the churches of that once fair country. How has it happened that not one fostering hand has been found in Laxton or its neighbourhood to shelter these monuments of our forefathers from the most shameful abuse? Could not their uplifted hands, and their prostrate bodies in the solemn acts of prayer for mercy, command respect or pity? Is it left for the present age to despise, condemn, or neglect, the memorials of the pious, the charitable, and the good; the founders of our holy sanctuaries, the munificent patrons of religious establishments, whose zeal for the service of God was ever marked with dutifulness and obedience?"

Perhaps one could, with some justification, have piped a thin echo of this complaint, a few years ago, on the subject of the old church of All Saints at Markham Clinton, just north of Tuxford. The trouble here was that the fourth Duke of Newcastle, after the death of his Duchess in 1822, commissioned Sir Robert Smirke, the architect of the British Museum, that monumental parade of the Ionic order, to build a classical mausoleum to contain her tomb and also to act as a new church in substitution for the, presumably, already rather decaying All Saints. As it turns out the Duke's action has left Markham Clinton with neither church in proper condition. The Smirke building, which lies quite by itself in a field nearer the hamlet of Milton than the triangular village of Markham Clinton, belongs to a well-defined class of " sepulchral churches" that was very popular with the great land-owners at this period. It was finished in 1833 and is a combination of church and mausoleum. It is cruciform in plan; an octagonal lantern of two stages rises from what appears to be the crossing of a church containing nave, two transepts and a chancel. There is a four-columned Doric portico at the east end with only pilasters at the other three extremities. The door at the west end leads into the church portion which is seen, inside, to consist only of the nave and to end, with an Ionic reredos, short of the crossing. The eastern portico gives access to the mausoleum part, comprising a circular vestibule under the tower with oblong tomb-chambers (the apparent transepts) leading out of it. There are, in fact, monuments only in the southern burial chapel. They are of the Duchess by Westmacott—a reclining marble figure, two nestling children and an allegorical figure in relief at the back; and to the Duke himself, who died in 1851—two sentimental medieval pages and a Gothic arch, all in wood, and described by a recent authority as " a perfect example of the taste of the 1851 Exhibition at its chastest". The detail throughout the building, with the exception of the external dome, is severely Greek, and its construction is very solidly carried out in stone. Unfortunately, quite apart from the oddness of this very urban bit of Attic classicism stuck quite by itself in a field on a windy ridge, circumstances and time have combined to make it a rather miserable and depressing object. It clearly has no relationship to the life and traditions of the little red-brick village at the foot of the hill; the meagrely populated churchyard which surrounds it is overgrown and unkempt.

Inside it has a shoddy look. The distempered walls are blotched and peeling, the ceiling is filthy, and the rather cheap appearance of the pews does nothing to add to the dignity of an unsightly interior. It is a sad memorial for the fourth Duke of Newcastle, who was at least a man of spirit, and a great landowner in the old style. He was thoroughly anti-reform and also anti-Gladstone, although it was at the instance of the Duke that Gladstone first went to Parliament in 1832 as one of the members for Newark. After the burning of Nottingham Castle, which belonged to him, by the Reform Bill rioters in 1831, the Duke of Newcastle fortified both Clumber and his town house. As a result of this, the question of his conduct was raised in the House of Lords and in 1839 he was dismissed from the Lord Lieutenancy. His Duchess, Georgina Elizabeth, who lies on her marble mattress in Smirke's mausoleum, was only thirty-three when she sacrificed her life for the two infants who are carved beside her figure.

Meanwhile, the old church down at the crossroads, quite a tiny building with a half-timbered porch and a weather-boarded turret, was allowed to fall into decay. It has been very much tidied up quite recently, but until then must have acted as a very dubious lesson on the state of the Church of England to the scholars of the village school that lies just across the road. In the years just after the war its interior looked like that of a church that had lain in the path of an invading army; it had its few old pews of natural oak, but also some school benches with their blotched inkwell holes. The Norman font with its crudely carved figures under arcades was there; an old wooden poor box; and a rough stone altar had been newly made, with a bronze cross on it. The broken floor was inches deep in rubble, the plaster had broken away from the walls in huge patches and in one corner a medieval carved stone figure lay like a bomb casualty on a stretcher. It was a gloomy spectacle; but the appeal for funds to make it decent apparently had effect and it is much better now.

One of the few other classical churches in the area is to be found at Ossington which is slightly further on the southern side of Tuxford than Markham Clinton and Milton are on the north. The church of the Holy Rood at Ossington lies close to the large eighteenth-century brick hall, surrounded by its grounds, lake and park. The church was built, of buff-coloured stone, in 1782. Its west tower is surmounted by a dome enclosed in a square screen of coupled columns, with a smaller dome on the top of it. The body of the church is low and rectangular. Within, besides tombs that must have originally been in the previous church (to sixteenth-century Peckhams, and to seventeenth and eighteenth-century Cartwrights—the family of Edmund, the inventor of the power loom—who rebuilt Ossington Hall), there are some interesting monuments to the family of Denison, wool merchants from Leeds, who bought the manor of Ossington from the Cartwrights in 1753. His great-nephew was an eminent Speaker of the House of Commons who married a daughter of the fourth Duke of Portland and was created Viscount Ossington on his retirement from the House. It was his widow who erected the astonishing Ossington Coffee Palace opposite the castle at Newark. The Denison monuments in the church include statues by Nollekens to the original William Denison who first came here from Leeds and died in 1782, and his brother Robert who died the following year. The base of the statue of William, who is holding a large inscribed sheet of paper, contains a relief which commemorates the fact that the disastrous earthquake at Lisbon in 1755 greatly added to the family's wealth. One of the Denison's ships happened to arrive there just after the disaster, and it is shown unloading in Lisbon harbour with men taking off the bales of merchandise. In a corner the wool-bearing sheep are shown grazing.

Tuxford is on the Great North Road. Its dignified Newcastle Arms Hotel is perhaps all that the majority of travellers bother about, but it has also an eighteenth-century hall, a late seventeenth-century grammar school and a medieval church with monuments to many generations of Whites, lords of the manor here; from seventeenth-century ladies and gentlemen in ruffs to a White who was killed at Salamanca in 1814. These tombs are in a chapel on the north side of the church which also contains the Tuxford war memorial. It is a reredos with paintings of the Last Supper and it is not an addition that I can admire. There are two disused windmills on the edge of the town; but you must not look here for many pre-eighteenth-century buildings because a fire in 1702 destroyed most of the town. The Georgian Newcastle Arms on the main crossroads was presumably built soon after the fire. The road leading west out of Tuxford takes us by way of Kirton and Boughton to Ollerton, whose Hop Pole Hotel we have already mentioned. It is another of these largish eighteenth-century hostelries. The hall at Ollerton, built on the site of an Elizabethan house belonging to the Markhams, the last of whom died after the Civil War, is a handsome red-brick mansion in the late Restoration manner with projecting wings and a doorway made prominent by large stone pilasters and pediment. The church at Ollerton is a very plain place, dating from the early nineteenth century, with a west tower modelled, without much inspiration, on local medieval patterns.

Ollerton is one of the three gateways into the Dukeries. The others are Edwinstowe and Clipstone. At Edwinstowe, in the church, one need not bother about the tradition that Robin Hood married Maid Marian here. It is better merely to note that, although its prevailing stamp is that of the late twelfth century, the church has Norman decorated and Perpendicular elements as well as the mausoleum of the Ward family, of about 1830, attached to the north aisle. At Edwinstowe, also, is buried Dr. Brewster, the editor of a famous dictionary of Phrase and Fable. (He died here when living with his daughter at the vicarage.) There is no church at Clipstone but, instead, there is, near by, a ruin that goes by the name of King John's Palace. It consists of no more than an obviously ancient wall behind a corrugated-iron chapel. It is all that is left of the royal hunting lodge for Sherwood Forest with which many kings were more closely associated than King John. Henry II spent a lot of money on it and in 1180 enclosed it within a park. Richard I is said to have visited the palace and tradition, presumably as the result of the description of the scene in Sir Walter Scott's *Ivanhoe,* has decided that it was here that King Richard had his meeting with Robin Hood. But apparently Richard did really meet, on his return from the Crusades, the Scottish William the Lion here. Edward I was often at Clipstone and held a parliament in the hunting lodge in 1290. It was here that his Consort, Queen Eleanor, in the same year, was first seized with her fatal illness. Edward II made Clipstone a favourite retreat during his reign and under him and Edward III the lodge took on the size and dignity of a royal palace.

After the Plantagenet dynasty came to an end the status of Clipstone declined and it was granted by successive monarchs to a large number of different noblemen, including the Earl of March in Henry IV's reign, the Duke of Norfolk in Henry VIII's, down to the Earl of Shrewsbury in James I's. It afterwards passed into the possession of the Newcastle family and of the Dukes of Portland. The wall that remains is supposed to be a portion of the hall. One other object in the neighbourhood of Clipstone demands notice. It is the Duke's Archway or The Duke's Folly, which stands in a grassy drive less than a mile north of the village. This structure is a literal imitation of the priory gateway at Worksop and was built for the fourth Duke of Portland in 1842-4. It is decorated with figures of Richard I, Robin Hood, Little John, Friar Tuck, Allan-a-Dale and Maid Marian, has a schoolroom above the gateway and living accommodation on the two sides. The Duke of Portland is supposed to have intended a turf ride that he envisaged stretching all the way from Welbeck to Nottingham to pass through the archway. Modern Clipstone has some architecture of merit to subscribe to earlier accretions in the place —the good pithead baths and the colliery housing dating from the later 1930's.

Either from Clipstone, then, or from Edwinstowe, can one make one's entry into the forest—an experience which, in the light of the aura of its name and of the various spoliations of which warning has already been given, should be a disappointment. But somehow, in spite of decay and disfigurement, the majesty of the forest is still sufficient to impress even the best forewarned of visitors. You must not, of course, expect the whole thing to be composed of a sort of stockade of enormous oaks. A great deal of the forest is grassy clearings; the bulk of the thickly wooded part consists of quite young trees. The isolated giants are not so much objects of beauty as of curiosity, sometimes pathetic and even hideous. But the sum of the varied elements which make up this surviving remnant of the old forest, and—for this island—its considerable extent, can still cause surprise and admiration.

The forest once covered an area of some two hundred square miles and stretched away to the north of Nottingham as far as Worksop and inclusive of the then forest town of Mansfield. It was, of course, a royal forest, and "King John's Castle", the Plantagenet hunting box, was to it what the ducal seats were afterwards to become. Welbeck was the principal monastic centre within the area, with Newstead, Rufford and Worksop as others. The royal forest had its forest courts or eyres in which cases of poaching (Pleas of Venison) and of illicit felling of trees (Pleas of Verte) were heard. One green oak was valued at sixpence. These courts were held regularly until the end of the thirteenth century and then became much rarer. The monastic communities had special rights in the forest for the felling of trees and timber was also presented by the King, on certain occasions, to churches at quite distant parts of the kingdom, besides being used for the construction of royal palaces and chapels, for ships, machinery and so on. The forest was administered by a warden or steward and policed by foresters at fee. (In several churches in the forest area there are monuments to these medieval forest officials: at Papplewick one is distinguished by his sling, bow and arrow, and another by his knife, while at Skegby, west of Mansfield, there is a well-preserved carving of a forester whose long robe-like garment has the horn of his office slung over it.) The question of the medieval inhabitants of the forest and particularly the matter of policing, with its implications of clashes in the glades between officials and various forms of poacher and robber, brings us at once up against the matter of Robin Hood. There is no purpose, and no advantage to be gained, when a legend has taken deep root, in adopting an exclusively rational or scientific attitude towards the legend itself or to the multitudinous accessories and dependencies of the legend. It is, no doubt, irritating to be told that such and such a place is Robin Hood's larder when you are quite positive in your own mind that it is nothing of the kind. It is tiresome to be informed flatly that Robin Hood married Maid Marian in Edwinstowe church when you are sure that neither of them ever existed. But it is too late to do anything about it. Robin Hood is a national possession, our principal specimen of folk legend; he is more than that, he is a valuable export and we must not touch him. The student of his territory has therefore to study his exploits with a purposeful dicotomy of mind. On the one hand he is at liberty to study, in an attitude discreetly scientific, the origins of the legend. But when retailing the names of places and objects associated with the legend he must, since he has no alternative title or fancy to put in their places, pass them on at their face value.

My own personal favourite among the many industrious historians and researchers who have tried to get Robin Hood straight, to pin him down, like a butterfly in a case, is that magnificent, intuitive, unreliable antiquary of the early eighteenth century, William Stukeley. He, in the course of a long and acrimonious pamphlet warfare about a hole which was discovered underneath a building in the Hertfordshire town of Royston, which he insisted was a hermitage made for a semi-mythical character to whom he gave the name of Lady Roisia de Vere, produced a complete pedigree of Robin Hood. He was, according to Stukeley, " Robert Fitzooth, commonly called Robin Hood ", was the grandson of Ralph Fitzooth or Fitz-othes, a Norman companion of William the Conqueror, grandson, also, of Geoffrey de Mandeville and descended from Lady Roisia. Until the last century one could, with complete equanimity, accept Robin Hood as a real, if somewhat mysterious person. Though a certain degree of scepticism can be detected even in the sixteenth century (as in the saying "a tale of Robin Hood", meaning a fabulous story) the early historians had all taken him seriously, Major, Grafton, Holinshed, Stow, Leland and Fuller. For a sample of the blithe or verdant period of Robin Hood studies we might do worse than look at what Fuller says of Robin Hood under the heading of Memorable Persons for our county in his *Worthies of England*: " Robert Hood was (if not by birth) by his chiefest abode this countryman. Camden calls him *praedonem mitissimum*, the gentlest thief that ever was; and know, reader, he is entered into our catalogue, not for his thievery but for his gentleness. Take the character of his (though not good) less bad behaviour from the pen of our poet Drayton:

278

In the Dukeries: Thoresby Park

" From wealthy abbots' chests, and churls' abundant store,
What oftentimes he took, he shar'd amongst the poor:
No lordly bishop came in lusty Robin's way,
To him before he went, but for his pass must pay:
The widow in distress he graciously reliev'd,
And remedied the wrongs of many a virgin griev'd.

" But who made him a judge? or gave him a commission to take where it might best be spared, and give where it was most wanted. His principal residence was in Shirewood Forest in this county, though he had another haunt (he is no fox that hath but one hole) near the sea in the North-riding in Yorkshire, where Robin's Hood Bay still retaineth his name: not that he was any pirat, but a land-thief, who retreated to those unexpected parts for his security. One may wonder how he escaped the hand of justice, dying in his bed, for ought is found to the contrary: but it was because he was rather a merry than a mischievous thief, (complementing passengers out of their purses) never murdering any but deer, and this popular robber feasted the vicinage with his venison. He played his pranks in the reign of King Richard the First, about the year of our Lord 1100."

There, you see, there is no questioning the assumption which underlies everything that has been built upon the legend—that Robin Hood really did exist and that the names of the other personages in the story are also of real people. Even now it is hard to find anyone who is prepared to commit himself positively to the statement that there is no historical basis whatever for Robin's existence. Matter-of-fact historians will suggest to you that the name Robin Hood originally belonged to a mythical forest elf. Robin is a familiar diminutive of Robert and is found in the same sort of context in Robin Goodfellow; while everybody knows that elves wear hoods—or alternatively hood may be a corruption of "O' the Wood" as in the name of the similar French figure, Robin du Bois. Such an elf, who has a corollary in the Irish Rory of the Hills, lent his name to the ballad writers of the northern and midland counties from the twelfth century onwards to be built up into a full-blown and detailed piece of folklore. A contributory element was probably the ancient figure of Woden, or Odin who, during the twelfth century, as the English written and spoken languages developed, was gradually metamorphosed into the attractive figure of Robin Hood. It was in the fourteenth century, and the first half of the succeeding one, that the figure of the outlaw takes final shape. Robin Hood becomes the typical hero of English popular romance: " Open-

Castle William at Budby near Thoresby

handed, brave, merciful, given to archery and venery, good humoured, popular, loyal, woman-protecting, priestcraft-hating, Mary-loving, God-fearing, somewhat rough withal, caring little for the refinements of life, and fond of a fight above all things." Perhaps in these varied qualities one can detect a mingling of Norman and English characteristics which helped to make medieval England the "merry England" that we believe it to have been. A political element in the development of the story was the outbreak of lawlessness consequent upon the dislocation of life in town and country following the ravages of the Black Death. This disease at its height caused the death of one out of every two people in London and of two out of every three in certain parts of the country and led to an inevitable relaxation of current laws and conduct, and was a direct cause of the Peasant's Revolt in 1381. Labour troubles and repressive counter action sent outlaws into the forests and helped to make Robin Hood, in the ballads that grew up around his name, emblematic of the spirit of revolt against lordly tyranny and of the free open life of the greenwood.

He becomes a combination of Hereward the Wake and a somewhat proletarianized version of the knightly figure of Arthurian legend. He appears in something like forty early ballads and makes his debut in conscious literature in *Piers Plowman,* the allegorical poem attributed to William Langland and written about the year 1377. Rather more than a hundred years later his exploits were first set up in type. Caxton's disciple and successor, Wynken de Worde, printed, about 1495, *A lytel Geste of Robyn Hood,* in which the hero, among other things, kills a swan for the sheriff of Nottingham. He had also about this time become a familiar figure in carnivals and in those semi-dramatic performances which were the ancestors of English comedy. He entered into the dances on May Day and his adventures were sometimes performed then. In one of the famous Paston letters, Sir John Paston complains, in 1473, about the defection of one of his household: "W. Woode, wyche promysed . . . he wolde never goo ffro me; and ther uppon I have kepyd him thys iiij yer to pleye Seynt Jorge and Robyn Hod and the Sheryff of Nottyngham; and now, when I wolde have good horse, he is goon into Berynsdale, and I without a keeper."

Before we leave the realm of history for the details of the legend it is necessary to note a very curious and fairly recent discovery, which may be the merest coincidence. In 1936, Professor L. V. D. Owen called attention to an item in the Pipe Roll of 14 Henry III—the year 1230—which he translates to read: "The Sheriff (of Yorkshire) owes 32s. and 6d. in the matter of the chattels of Robert Hood, fugitive." This might conceivably be a reference to the famous outlaw, and although it appears in records relating to the West Riding of Yorkshire this does not invalidate such a theory, for the activities of such an outlaw might quite possibly have extended over Barnsdale as well as Sherwood. Incidentally, Sherwood Forest does not make its appearance as the setting for the story until some of the later ballads, in the sixteenth century and subsequently, by which time Robin Hood was represented as of noble descent and had been raised to the peerage, for no known reason, as Earl of Huntingdon. (In historical fact this title was borne by the Scottish kings from David I in the eleventh century until they lost their English possessions under Edward I at the beginning of the fourteenth—covering the whole of the period possible for the existence of a real Robin Hood.) The name of Robin Hood was not itself an uncommon one in medieval times and is to be found in many records that cannot, with all the will in the world, be connected with the legend. Professor Owen's is the most convincing discovery in this field so far. One other such reference is worth mentioning. A Victorian scholar tried to show that Robin Hood belonged to the time of Edward II, was an adherent of Thomas, Earl of Lancaster (who was executed after leading an insurrection in 1322) and afterwards served in the King's household. Certainly a " porteur Robyn Hode "—who was a " vadlet " or " porteur du chambre "—received payment in the household of Edward II (who, by the way, made a progress through Nottinghamshire in the autumn of 1323) between 24th March and 22nd November, 1324. The entry reads: "Robyn Hode, jadys a des porters, pour cas qu'il ne poait pluis travailler. 5s."

But I insist that if one is truly to enjoy the county, to enjoy Sherwood Forest, one must take the names that are connected with the legend, from Hodsock down to all the Robin Hood's wells, stables, larders and the rest of them, as though one believed the whole thing to be true. So, adding together all the most reasonable versions of the tale, one arrives at some such biography as this: Robin was born at Loxley in Nottinghamshire (a village of which no trace remains to-day). The date of his birth was about 1160. His extraction was noble. His true name, (Stukeley, whom I referred to, took it from legend) Robert Fitzooth, was easily corrupted, in vulgar pronunciation, into Robin Hood. He was styled, or had pretensions to being, Earl of Huntingdon. In his youth he was wild and extravagant so that his inheritance, being consumed or forfeited by his excesses, and his person outlawed for debt, either from necessity or choice, he sought an asylum in the woods and forest, which then covered enormous tracts of the northern part of the kingdom. He chiefly haunted Barnsdale in Yorkshire, Sherwood in Nottinghamshire, and, according to some, Plompton Park in Cumberland. He gradually gathered around himself a band of kindred spirits, a hundred or so of them, of whom the principal was known as Little John, on account of his great size, and others were Will Scarlet, George à Green, Much the miller's son, and a monk called Friar Tuck. There was also Maid Marian (who makes her first appearance in literature in about 1500 in *The Ship of Fools*, by Alexander Barclay, who wrote of "some merry fit of Maide Marian or els of Robin Hood").

In the forest Robin Hood with his outlaws, his Merry Men, lived almost without interference from the King's foresters or from the Nottingham sheriff. The royal deer assured them a plentiful supply of food, but they also supported themselves by levying toll on wealthy travellers, especially bishops and other ecclesiastics. To the poor and oppressed Robin was always a good friend, and they, in exchange, warned him of the approach of foes. Robin's instructions to his followers forbade them to do any manner of hurt to women of any degree, to molest husbandmen or to pillage the property of any knight and squire who was good to his subordinates. Robin Hood is said to have remained in the forest until his eighty-seventh year, when the infirmities of age forced him to enter the convent of Kirklees in Yorkshire for medical assistance. Here the traditional account of his life takes a curious turn. The prioress of the convent, who is described as a relative of the outlaw, brought about his death, purposefully, by opening a vein or artery under pretence of affording him relief by bleeding him. When Robin realized her treachery he summoned all his remaining strength to blow a blast on his horn. The familiar call reached the ears of Little John who hastened from the forest and forced his way into the chamber where the dying man lay. Then, according to the ballad, Robin Hood said:

> Give me my bent bow in my hand
> And an arrow I will let free,
> And where that arrow is taken up,
> There let my grave digged be.

A spot on the extreme edge of Kirklees Park, not far from Huddersfield, is the reputed place where the arrow fell and where the hero was buried. It is marked with a fragment of stone carved with a florid cross and a much more recent headstone.

For the best poetical expression of the consolidated legend I will call again on the work of Michael Drayton. He was not the earliest of important English writers to refer to Robin Hood (Shakespeare, Ben Jonson and Sir Philip Sidney had all mentioned him), but Drayton pulls together the story as it had settled down by Elizabethan times. Drayton, who was so much admired by his contemporaries—" golden-mouthed " was an epithet that clung to him, and Francis Meres praised him for " the purity and preciousness of his style and phrase "—belonged to the north midlands and had the feel of our county under his fingers. He was born, in the same county as Shakespeare in the year before him, at Hartshill, near Athelstone in Warwickshire, in 1563, and he died in 1631. There are strong Nottinghamshire connections in his verse. For instance, in his historical poem, the *Mortimeriados*, first published in 1596 and later entirely re-written under the name of *The Barons' Wars* (it is all about the wars between Edward II and the barons down to the capture of Mortimer at Nottingham Castle) Drayton writes descriptively of the Trent:

> Here, all along the flow'r enamell'd vales
> The silver Trent on pearly sands doth slide;

of Sherwood Forest:

> fair Sherwood, wildly bent to rove
> Twines her loose arms about the flatt'ring towers
> By the mild shadows of her scattered grove,
> Lends Winter shelter and gives Summer bowers
> As with the flood in courtesy it strove;

and especially of the Queen's Bower at Nottingham, on the decoration of which Drayton's fancy ran free in Renaissance ornament. But of course it is in Drayton's *Poly-Olbion*, in the twenty-sixth song of that work which I have already drawn on for a detailed picture of the Trent, that we find the account of Robin Hood. You may recall that the various geographical features of the country are personified in a manner that was already old fashioned when Drayton was writing. They speak; the rivers of England, the forests, address one another in Drayton's rather monotonous rhyming couplets of twelve-syllabled lines, and they argue with each other. Here, the River Trent has been speaking and has offended Sherwood Forest by singing the praises of Leicestershire's Charnwood:

Which Sherwood took to heart, and very much disdain'd,
(As one that had both long, and worthily maintain'd
The title of the great'st, and bravest of her kind)
To fall so far below one wretchedly confin'd
Within a furlong's space, . . . determineth to sing
That lusty Robin Hood, who long time like a king
Within her compass liv'd, and when he list to range
For some rich booty set, or else his air to change
To Sherwood still retir'd, his only standing court,
Whose praise the forest thus doth pleasantly report:
" The merry pranks he play'd, would ask an age to tell,
And the adventures strange that Robin Hood befell,
When Mansfield many a time for Robin hath been laid,
How he hath cousen'd them, that him would have betray'd;
How often he hath come to Nottingham disguis'd,
And cunningly escap'd, being set to be surpriz'd.
In this our spacious isle, I think there is not one,
But he hath heard some talk of him and little John;
And to the end of time, the tales shall ne'er be done,
Of Scarlock, George-à-Green, and Much the miller's son,
Of Tuck the merry friar, which many a sermon made,
In praise of Robin Hood, his out-laws, and their trade.
An hundred valiant men had this brave Robin Hood,
Still ready at his call, that bow-men were right good,
All clad in Lincoln green, with caps of red and blue,
His fellow's winded horn, not one of them but knew,
When setting to their lips their little bugles shrill,
The warbling echos wak'd from every dale and hill:
Their bauldricks set with studs, athwart their shoulders cast,
To which under their arms their sheaths were buckled fast,
A short sword at their belt, a buckler scarce a span,
Who struck below the knee, not counted then a man:
All made of Spanish yew, their bows were wondrous strong;
They not an arrow drew, but was a cloth-yard long.
Of archery they had the very perfect craft,
With broad-arrow, or but, or prick, or roving shaft,
At marks full forty score, they us'd to prick and rove,
Yet higher than the breast, for compass never strove;
And of these archers brave, there was not any one,
But he could kill a deer his swiftest speed upon,
Which they did boil and roast, in many a mighty wood,
Sharp hunger the fine sauce to their more kingly food.
Then taking them to rest, his merry men and he
Slept many a summer's night under the greenwood tree.

From wealthy abbots' chests, and churls' abundant store,
What oftentimes he took, he shar'd amongst the poor:
No lordly bishop came in lusty Robin's way,
To him before he went, but for his pass must pay:
The widow in distress he graciously reliev'd,
And remedied the wrongs of many a virgin griev'd:
He from the husband's bed no married woman wan,
But to his mistress dear, his loved Marian,
Was ever constant known, which wheresoe'er she came,
Was sovereign of the woods, chief lady of the game:
Her clothes tuck'd to the knee, and dainty braided hair,
With bow and quiver arm'd, she wander'd here and there
Amongst the forests wild; Diana never knew
Such pleasures, nor such harts as Mariana slew."

The tomboyish character of Maid Marian is as unexpected an element in the story as is the apparent sexual constancy of Robin Hood—an unusual attribute in a popular medieval hero. Perhaps, if only to acknowledge the existence of the most sophisticated treatment afforded in literature to the Hood legend, we might dismiss the hero and heroine by quoting the final sentence of Peacock's novel, *Maid Marian*, which twists history up in such a whirl of intimate relations between Robin Hood and his monarchs as to leave us in rather worse state than when we began. Peacock pretends to accept the Huntingdon title and writes: "The earl and countess of Huntingdon led a discreet and courtly life, and kept up old hospitality in all its munificence, till the death of King Richard and the usurpation of John, by placing their enemy in power, compelled them to return to their greenwood sovereignty; which, it is probable, they would have before done from choice, if their love of sylvan liberty had not been counteracted by their desire to retain the friendship of Coeur-de-Lion. Their old and tried adherents, the friar among the foremost, flocked again around their forest-banner; and in merry Sherwood they long lived together, the lady still retaining her former name of Maid Marian, though the appellation was then as much a misnomer as that of Little John."

Merry Sherwood! To the forest to-day; and first, perhaps to the part called Birklands, which owes its name to its wealth of silver birches, but has also oaks, many of them of great size, and grotesquely gnarled, and handsome beeches as well; or to the adjoining Bilhagh. These are both at the southern extremity of the surviving forest, the first being on the Welbeck and the second on the Thoresby estate. In each case tradition asserts that there are oaks still standing which were already growing in Robin Hood's time. Paying one's respects to individual trees (which is, I suggest, a disappointing and unrewarding form of pilgrimage) one finds within the area called Bilhagh the Major Oak or Queen Oak which stands in an open space half a mile or so north of Edwinstowe. Its monstrously weatherbeaten trunk (which does exert a certain spell by its evidence of sheer age) measures thirty feet in circumference at the height of five feet from the ground. Its branches cover a straight line of two hundred and forty feet, which gives them a circumference of nearly two hundred and seventy yards. Although patched and bound in a few places the Major Oak is still very much alive. Its leaves look healthy enough. But, if you let yourself in through a decent-sized aperture you discover that the trunk is completely hollow to the height of fifteen feet. A dozen people can stand inside the tree, and it is recorded that seven people have been foolish enough to have breakfast inside it and that as many as sixteen can be squashed—presumably without breakfast—into the space. There is not a great deal left of the Parliament Oak which lies just outside the bottom end of Birklands, close to the road between Edwinstowe and Mansfield. This again is of extreme antiquity and it has several traditional associations with royal history. It is said that Edward I held a parliament under its branches in 1290 (though why he should have gathered out of doors what cannot have been a very large assemblage, when the palace of Clipstone was available for the purpose, is not clear). King John is also said to have summoned a council of barons under the tree. The tale goes that while hunting in Sherwood Forest he heard of a Welsh revolt against him and that, having induced, under this tree, the barons to sanction the immediate execution of twenty-eight Welsh hostages, mostly children, who were in his custody in Nottingham Castle, he rode over to see that his instructions were obeyed before returning to Clipstone. A long avenue through the Birklands known as The Duke's Drive brings us first to a picturesque log cottage known as The Russian Hut because it was constructed in the Russian manner without the use of nails, and then to another famous oak known as The Shambles, or as Robin Hood's Larder. Here, of course, on the branches of this tree, the outlaw used to hang his illicitly killed venison, or, alternatively, the fact that a sheep stealer used to hang stolen carcasses inside it may have something to do with its name (a third alternative for which is the Slaughter Tree); and just for good measure a piece of timber not unlike a carcass in shape hung for a long time from one of its branches. The tree has suffered from fire: its trunk is charred and hollow.

The most renowned, however, of all the individual Sherwood trees is probably the Green Dale Oak, situated about half a mile south of Welbeck Abbey. The tree, which gives its name to a well-known inn at the forest village of Cuckney, is only a wreck of its former self, propped up and supported by chains. It is apparently at least eight hundred years old and may be as much as fifteen hundred, and was fully forty feet in circumference at the base. In 1724, by what seems an unnecessary piece of planning, a coach road was driven through the trunk of the oak tree, the aperture being 10 ft. 3 in. high and 6 ft. 3 in. wide. It is suggested that the opening was made because the first Duke of Portland had made a bet that there was a tree in his park through which he could drive a coach and four. From part of the wood thus produced from the mutilated tree a piece of furniture was made, called the Green Dale cabinet, which was to be seen at Welbeck Abbey.

For the sake of completeness one ought not to leave out a couple more trees in the immediate vicinity of Welbeck Abbey which have had names attached to them. Near the centre of the drive from the principal entrance at Welbeck there was once a gateway above which a pair of trees called the Porter Oaks towered like sentinels, one 90 feet high and 36 feet round, the other 100 feet in height with a girth of 40; south-east of this was the Seven Sisters, an oak which once had seven trunks varying from 80 to 112 feet in height. The loftiest was known as the Duke's Walking Stick. It is no longer there.

I said that we would make our way through the palaces of the Dukeries from south to north. Consequently the mansion which first claims our attention is that of Thoresby, the seat of Earl Manvers, and the only one of the great houses which is fully inhabited by its owner and which is used, on a reduced scale perhaps, for the purposes for which is was built. The date of its building is of a period in which the great landed proprietors of England achieved the climax of their wealth and power. It was the peak of the Victorian age.

Between 1850 and 1880, or at any rate until the agricultural depression caused by the shocking harvests of the late seventies, the landed interest had never been so prosperous. Landed rents increased by nearly thirty per cent in the course of the period, while a survey, in 1874, that became known as " The New Doomsday ", showed that half the soil of England was owned by less than eight thousand persons. In 1874 the building of Thoresby was approaching completion. It had been begun in 1864 and was the third house on the site. Thoresby Park and its house have not the long history of Rufford or of Welbeck. It was enclosed out of Sherwood Forest by the Duke of Kingston in 1683. The house that was built for him, the first Thoresby, was designed by a young man, born in Norfolk and possibly of distant Dutch descent, called William Talman. He was destined to be, between 1687 and 1700, the builder of Chatsworth and to become a bitter enemy of Sir Christopher Wren. He had been born in 1650 and his early training is unknown. Nor is there any explanation of why he should have been chosen by the Duke of Kingston to build him, in what must have been his first essay in the country house, a vast rectangular block, thirteen windows wide by nine deep, planned round a central courtyard. In any case, Talman's house (in which the daughter of Evelyn Pierrepont, first Earl of Kingston, later to become celebrated as Lady Mary Wortley Montagu, was born in 1689 and brought up) was not destined to survive very long; it was completely destroyed by fire on April 4th, 1745, and nothing was saved but documents, plate and a few pieces of the best furniture. The second Thoresby, which was the residence of the celebrated Duchess of Kingston who was tried for bigamy in 1776, was a modest affair, more like a town house, apparently, whose grounds gave Horace Walpole, in 1772, "no temptation to stop".

Modest the third Thoresby cannot be called. It must be one of the most ambitious Victorian mansions in the country. We have already encountered the architect whom Earl Manvers commissioned to produce for him a residence worthy of his position, and of its position in the Dukeries. The years of its construction were 1864-75. It was a moment of feverish constructive activity in the area. These were the very years of the fifth Duke of Portland's subterranean building across the park at Welbeck, and Clumber, having been extensively enlarged and "improved" in the years following 1857, was to undergo the same process all over again after a fire in the seventies. But even the Duke of Portland's extravagance has not left so astonishing a Victorian memorial as Thoresby is. Built near the end of Anthony Salvin's career, it is not so remarkable a landmark in the history of Victorian architecture as is his early work, Harlaxton Manor in Lincolnshire. Terrific, but hardly original.

If it looks, to the vulgar eye, a little like some vast seaside hotel or hydro, that is because the neo-Elizabethan manner of the Victorians became unduly popular with the builders of such conveniences. Built of Steetly stone, with a square, central, gabled tower that has obviously heard of Wollaton, Thoresby is too large and too grand to be anything but impressive. It consists of a block 180 feet square and has a great hall, 61 feet long, 31 feet broad and 48 feet high, which runs up through three storeys and ends in an open hammer-beam roof; it is floored with oak grown on the estate. This highly theatrical creation, into which the staircase leads under arches, contains a huge bay window and an elaborate fireplace of Steetly stone and granite carved with the history of the family from which Earl Manvers is descended. It is surrounded by magnificent pictures, including a portrait of Lady Mary Wortley Montagu, together with a fine collection of arms and armour of various states and countries. The library, too, has an elaborately carved mantelpiece, nearly 15 feet high, made, in this case, of Birklands oak. Carved on it in bold relief is a scene from Sherwood Forest, including a representation of the Major Oak and statues of Robin Hood and Little John. The principal floor of the house contains twenty-nine rooms and there are seventy-eight bedrooms. Thoresby, as I have said, is still lived in by Lord Manvers in the way in which it was meant to be lived in. During the war it housed no fewer than six hundred evacuees. On one occasion, during their residence, Lord Manvers, explaining that he got on well with the evacuees, observed with notable understatement, "we should feel lonely without them". The present Lord Manvers succeeded to the title in 1941 as the sixth earl and in order to meet death duties had to sell his estate at Holme Pierrepont (whose house and church have already entered into this account) which had been in his family since the thirteenth century.

One comes upon Thoresby rather suddenly in the course of driving through its magnificent park (twelve miles in circuit, whose superb chestnut avenues make it probably the finest in the Dukeries); it is not screened in any way by hedges or walls or groups of trees, and the towering silhouette that it presents against the forest background with its careful irregularity of outline—tower, roofs, gables and cupolas—is not easily forgotten.

The damming of the River Meden near the hall has formed an extensive and very lovely stretch of lake, covering sixty-five acres. If you drive to the western extremity of the lake you will discover a little group of two-storeyed cottages with porches and mildly Gothic windows which was built as a model village by the first Earl Manvers in 1807. It is called Budby, and thence, on a grassy eminence on the eastern side of the village, you will discover Budby Castle or Castle William, a charming piece of castellated nonsense in grey stone—a bogus fortress which must be a pleasant, if rather dark little residence.

Less than a mile eastward of Thoresby is the church which the third Lord Manvers got Salvin to build for the benefit of his tenants' souls after the completion of his own residence. The church of St. John at Perlethorpe is a large Victorian parish church in the Decorated manner with a western spire that rises to a height of nearly 130 feet.

Northwards from the hall the forest road crosses the transverse drive which divides the park of Thoresby from that of Clumber. Here, we have warned, there is now no house to see: only a long and beautiful lake, and a church that stands, surprising and inexplicable, without knowledge of the vanished house, beside it.

The enclosing of Clumber took place even later than that of Thoresby. The estate formed part of Sherwood Forest until 1707 when licence was granted by Queen Anne to John Holles, Duke of Newcastle (who lived at Welbeck) to enclose it as a park for the use of the Queen herself. Nothing very much was done about it, however, for half a century: the site of the future house was, until well after 1750, a rabbit warren, "a black heath, full of rabbits, having a narrow river running through it, with a small boggy close or two". In 1770 a house was built for the then Duke of Newcastle (who belonged—the history of the title is a bit bewildering—to the Pelham-Clinton family) by Stephen Wright, the architect of the old University Library, adjoining the Senate House at Cambridge. It appears to have been a large, rather formal building with two projecting gabled wings, each with central arched doorways. A visitor, about twenty years after it was built, writes rather confusingly: "The Duke of Newcastle's dwelling is truly magnificent, although the building is neither lofty nor very extensive."

It might also be interesting to hear of the experiences of the ordinary tourist in the Dukeries at the end of the eighteenth century. This same writer goes on: "I cannot help remarking here that, in this park, the stranger is accommodated at every cross-road with an excellent direction-post; in Thoresby park such posts appear, but for some reason they have lately had boards nailed over the inscriptions, they therefore are as intelligent as a dumb man; in Welbeck park you may get into a road, which a man might expect would lead him out of the park, but at the end of which one of these unfriendly gentlemen prevents you with his broad face and angrily says, *No road this way*: in that park I have been thrice, and twice I have been obliged to go round about the nighest way home. I mean this as no sort of censure upon the conduct of the owners of the two last mentioned domains; but as a stranger, feeling disappointment from a cause he is in no wise competent to judge of, he must observe; Such things are."

Wright's building was, in essence, the Clumber which remained standing until just before the last war. It was, however, considerably enlarged and altered in appearance—the side facing the terrace beside the lake was given an Italianate loggia—by Sir Charles Barry (the architect of the Houses of Parliament) in 1857 and, after a fire in 1879, was again refurbished by Barry's son, the second Charles Barry, who built Burlington House in London. After its Victorian embellishments Clumber was exceedingly grand. A Great Hall on the site of the portion of the building destroyed in the fire displayed a lot of marble and tessellated work; there was a huge dining-room capable of seating 150 people; the library fitted up with Spanish mahogany shelves and an elaborately panelled ceiling was worthy of its contents, for the Clumber library was bursting with illuminated manuscripts, Caxtons, Wynkyn de Wordes and other valuable books. Clumber housed, likewise, a priceless collection of paintings, of porcelain and of furniture. Nor were the gardens on any less princely a scale. The most remarkable feature was the Lincoln terrace, a quarter of a mile long, constructed, at enormous cost, of stone specially brought from Italy. A broad flight of steps led down to the eighty-seven-acre lake on whose waters rode two vessels, the *Lincoln* and the *Salamanca*. The house and its contents have been swept away. The pictures and the books were sold. The house was completely pulled down in 1937. The Duke of Newcastle also sold the park and the rest of his Nottinghamshire properties soon after he succeeded to the title in 1941. Parts of Clumber Park are, fortunately, to be preserved under the auspices of the National Trust; and a Society of Friends of Clumber has come into existence, with Earl Manvers as President, to develop the site as a centre for the arts. What remains beside the lake are the slightly dilapidated Lincoln terrace, some stable buildings and the church.

Clumber church has already been referred to in connection with other work in the county by G. F. Bodley. One can surely not be blamed, though, for stressing how the church (in which no services are now held) has gained by the disappearance of its surrounding buildings; how, standing alone on its lawn beside its lake it serves to underline the whole history and decline of the Dukeries. In itself, though its size and costliness were never remotely suitable to its situation, it certainly deserves its description as one of the most remarkable neo-Gothic creations in

England. It is very large. It would do amply as the parish church of a considerable town. It comprises an unaisled nave, two transepts, a very long chancel, lady chapel and sacristy, is 107 feet long inside and has a central tower with a spire rising to a height of 175 feet. The red facings of Runcorn stone which decorate the greyish Steetly stone of the exterior are echoed and amplified inside, where the warm red Runcorn predominates, with a slight addition of fine stone from Mansfield. The carved pulpit is a mixture of these two stones and both the choir screen and the stalls are richly decorated. On the stalls, which are made of cedar, are placed limewood figures of evangelists, doctors of the Church and great English saints. The chancel is paved with black-and-white marble and the alabaster altar has fittings of silver. Font, pulpit, the altars, and the stone sculptures were all designed by Bodley himself; the wood carving was carried out mainly by Belgian craftsmen and the stained glass, which adds greatly to the grandeur of this amazing church, is by Kempe.

CHAPTER XI

WELBECK TO THE
TOP OF THE COUNTY

THE serpentine lake—relic of the large-scale landscape gardening which went with the building of the original house in the 1770's—beside which the church stands, is situated roughly in the middle of Clumber Park. All round it, sullied though it has been by the ugly concrete roads and the curt notices that give warning of the presence of ammunition under the trees, the forest spreads. Heather, gorse and bracken; beeches, firs and larches; long stretches of open turf; man-made features, like the great Duke's Drive, four lines of lime trees three miles long; oaks. So across it, westwards—or, following the course of the stream which provides the two great neighbouring parks with their lakes and by way of the village of Carburton, with its tiny Norman chapel—to Welbeck. We must go steadily here, carefully, or we shall soon be lost. It is tempting to start at thé end, for the climax of the history of Welbeck is much the most extraordinary and interesting part of it. But it is not a feasible approach, because if we started with the fifth Duke of Portland we should get lost, literally underground, and would never find our way back to Cuckney.

It has got to begin there, even if only to find the name with which the story starts. For it was a certain Thomas de Cuckney who, in the year 1153, founded a house of Praemonstratensian Canons (the only other monastic house of this order in the county was at Broadholme, of which no traces remain). The abbey was dedicated to God and St. James and through being liberally endowed by its founder and being subsequently enriched by bequests became one of the wealthiest in the whole country. Welbeck was the seat, in this country, of the head of the Order which had been founded by St. Norbert at Prémontré, near Laon, in 1119. All that survives of the monastic buildings is a small section of the west range of cloisters, including a doorway with a pointed arch, which formed part of the basement of the great house.

At the Dissolution Welbeck Abbey was granted by Henry VIII

to Richard Whalley, whose monument in the church of the village of Screveton, from which his family came, has already been described. From Richard Whalley's heirs it eventually came—with, it always seems, almost everything else in the Midlands at the time—to the remarkable Bess of Hardwick. She, who also built (probably) Rufford within the county and, outside it, the first Chatsworth, part of Bolsover and Hardwick Hall, was born in 1518, the daughter of a country squire. When she made her first marriage he was only able to take up some forty marks for her marriage portion. She was fourteen then, and her first husband was a certain Robert Barlow or Barley, a young neighbouring landowner in Derbyshire, who died the year after his marriage and left her his estate. Elizabeth Hardwick did not marry again until she was thirty-one. It is a surprisingly long gap, sixteen years, of childless widowhood for a woman who was to develop into one of the most scheming and ambitious in English history, " proud, selfish and intriguing, a money-lender, a dealer in coals, lead and timber, who died immensely rich and yet without a friend ". Her second marriage, in 1549, was to the statesman, Sir William Cavendish. She was his third wife, and before he died she had six children by him. She persuaded him to dispose of his Suffolk estates (Cavendish is a small village lying roughly between Sudbury and Bury St. Edmunds) and began her incomparable career of architectural grandeur by building a mansion on the site of the present Chatsworth House. The tale runs that the reason for her unremitting activity in building houses was a prophecy by a gipsy that she would escape death so long as she continued building. Sir William Cavendish died fairly soon; and Bess of Hardwick went on to marry, thirdly, Sir William St. Loe, a west countryman, from whom, having stipulated that all his estates should pass to her when he died, she acquired another fortune, his children by his first wife being left penniless; and fourthly, at the age of fifty, the Earl of Shrewsbury, becoming thereby one of the richest and most powerful women in England. She was the founder of three great ducal families. But for us, in this Nottinghamshire context, it is enough to seize upon the third son of Bess and Sir William Cavendish. He was Charles Cavendish. To him Bess bequeathed the estate of Welbeck Abbey which she had bought from the Whalleys. This Charles Cavendish was knighted and his son, Bessie's grandson, was another Sir William Cavendish (1592-1676) who became, because of his services to Charles I, the first Duke of Newcastle. His father, who added to the house at Welbeck begun by Bess of Hardwick, had rendered service to King Charles by fighting and dying for him,

Clumber: lake, stables and church

chiefly within the boundaries of our county. He distinguished himself at Edgehill and was subsequently given a commission by the King to raise a regiment of horse in the north. He established himself at Newark and there so distinguished himself by his enterprise and enthusiasm against the forces of Parliament that he was appointed commander-in-chief of the King's forces in Nottinghamshire and Lincolnshire with the rank of Colonel-General. It fell to Charles Cavendish to receive Queen Henrietta Maria at Newark and personally to escort her part of the way to Oxford. But in an attempt to raise the siege of Gainsborough he was defeated by Cromwell and was killed. He was buried at Newark but later his body was taken away to Derby.

The parts of Welbeck which the great house owes to Sir Charles Cavendish are, after all the eighteenth and nineteenth-century additions, scarcely separable from the rest. But there is no mistaking the riding house and stables erected in 1623-5 by his son, the first Duke of Newcastle, who, as well as being a friend of the philosopher, Hobbes, tutor to Charles I, and an ardent admirer of the painter Vandyke, was one of the most remarkable horsemen in the history of the equestrian art. He has left to posterity an extraordinary book on the subject of horsemanship, *La Methode et Invention Nouvelle de Dresser les Chevaux,* whose illustrations, showing patterns of rearing horses trained to perform fantastic evolutions, are among the delights of seventeenth-century engraving. These illustrations also provide some of the very few surviving views of Welbeck in the seventeenth century. They show a long rectangular building with triple gables at the extremities, and numerous dormers along the front. The hall, which was at one end, was approached by an outside flight of steps, and through an ornate porch. The house looks as though it may have been moated; there was certainly some sort of a drawbridge. Most of the centre block had been built by Sir Charles Cavendish, the south wing being added by his son. The architects of the house at this stage are unknown, but Newcastle's riding house and stables, two parallel blocks with battlements, were the work of one of the members of the architectural family of Smythson whose various elements, Robert at Wollaton and John at Wiverton Hall (destroyed in the Civil War except the gatehouse of 1614, which is incorporated in the back of the present house), and also at Worksop Manor, had already contributed to the embellishment of the county. The Welbeck riding school was the work of John's son, who died in 1648, and whose epitaph in Bolsover church, over the county boundary, records that his

The fourteenth-century gatehouse at Worksop

> skill in architecture did deserve
> A fairer tombe his mem'ry to preserve
> But since his nobler gifts of piety
> To God to men justice and charity
> Are gone to heaven a building to prepare
> Not made with hands his friends contented are
> He here shall rest in hope till the world shall burne
> And intermingle ashes with his urne.

This is no place to embark on an account of the career of the first Duke of Newcastle who, even if he had not had the wife he did, we should still know as a most charming and likeable person. It was a less likeable character, King James I, whom the young William Cavendish, fresh from St. John's College, Cambridge, captivated first. Pleased with his learning and his charm of manner James created him Viscount Mansfield. Royal favour was continued during the next reign when Charles I appointed him governor of his son Charles in 1638. At Welbeck Cavendish had entertained the King, and Ben Jonson, whom he patronized, had produced a masque for the occasion. On the outbreak of the Civil War he proved his loyalty by contributing £10,000 to the King's treasury and, collecting troops at his own expense, he won Yorkshire for the Royalist cause by the victory at Adwalton Moor in 1643. The same year he captured Hull, but, after the rout of Marston Moor, he went abroad and lived in straitened circumstances. However, he had the good fortune, while abroad, to get married for the second time.

Margaret Cavendish, Duchess of Newcastle, was a lady of unusual temperament and genius and she and her husband were inordinately fond and proud of each other. She was the celebrated Duchess of Newcastle, the poetess (1624?-74) whom Horace Walpole described as a "fertile pedant", with an "unbounded passion for scribbling", and Charles Lamb as the "thrice noble, chaste and virtuous, but somewhat fantastical and original brained Margaret Newcastle", and who is charmingly enshrined in an essay on her by Virginia Woolf which tells of the Londoners, who included Samuel Pepys, crowding round her silver coach when she came from Nottinghamshire on a visit to the capital, crowding to catch a glimpse of "that romantic lady, who stands, in the picture at Welbeck, with large melancholy eyes, and something fastidious and fantastic in her bearing, touching a table with the tips of her long pointed fingers in the calm assurance of immortal fame".

She has a certain fame but it is not, alas, because people nowa-

days read, even can read, the interminable plays which she poured
out with so much confidence and disorder, her maids being
expected always to be prepared to "register her Grace's concep-
tions". She was the daughter of Sir Thomas Lucas and was
born at St. John's, near Colchester, in Essex. She met her husband in Paris, in April 1645, when she was in attendance on the
exiled Henrietta Maria. They were married the same year in
Paris and during their subsequent residence there, in Rotterdam,
and in Antwerp, were in constant pecuniary straits. She was
always trying to raise money, with little success, and lived largely
on loans from her brother-in-law, Sir Charles Cavendish. After
the Restoration she followed her husband to England where, in
spite of his Royalist devotion, Charles II only restored to him
part of his confiscated estates. The Duchess died in London and
was buried in Westminster Abbey, where a monument, in the
north transept, was erected by her adoring husband, who survived
her by three years.

I doubt whether anybody, even now, has ever properly sorted
out the Duchess of Newcastle's written works. Certainly no complete bibliography seems to exist. To compile it would probably
be a tedious labour, because her productions are extremely long
and exhausting and very numerous. Within the last couple of
hundred years the only works of hers to have been reprinted are,
in 1814, her autobiography, *True Relation of the Birth, Breeding
and Life of Margaret Cavendish, Duchess of Newcastle, written
by herself,* which was originally published as part of a book with
the charming title of *Nature's Pictures, drawn by Fancie's Pencil
to the Life* (London, 1655 or 1656); in 1872 her life of her husband;
and a selection of her poems in 1813. Even the most tireless
literary authorities admit that her plays, of which she produced
some thirty or more, are pretty well unreadable. Their characters
are not people but vague abstractions; there is practically no
action but a great deal of boring philosophizing combined with
the most astonishing coarseness of language. One of her plays,
called *The Humorous Lovers,* reached the London stage in 1667
and Pepys, who attended a performance, describes how the
Duchess made her respects to the players from her box and writes
of "her footmen in velvet coats and herself in an antique dress"
(she was obviously before her time in her "arty" costume); and
Pepys adds: "The whole story of this lady is a romance and all
she does is romantic." Husband and wife worked in the closest
possible communion of mutual adoration and admiration. Apparently three huge folio volumes of poems remain in manuscript
and the Duke's works are so mixed up with hers that it is not

easy to separate one from another. The copies of many volumes of the Duchess' works, now in the British Museum, have manuscript notes in her own handwriting.

The south wing of Welbeck, built by the Duke of Newcastle about 1630, was rebuilt in 1751, after the estate had, by several marriages (the family names involved in the history of Welbeck include, as well as Cavendish, those of Talbot, Osborne, Booth, Pierrepont, Holles, Vere, Harley, Bentinck, Wriothesley and Scott), passed into the possession of the second Duke of Portland who had married the daughter and heiress of the second Earl of Oxford. It was she who built the eighteenth-century Oxford wing which contained about twenty-five rooms, many of them in the early, rococo, Strawberry Hill kind of revived Gothic, and including a very handsome Gothic hall. Unfortunately the whole Oxford wing was destroyed by fire in 1900 and, although it was restored, the Gothic hall has completely lost its character.

The damage caused by the fire of 1900 amounted to £100,000 in the currency of the time—that would mean perhaps four times as much half a century later. It is an indication of the continuing prosperity of the owners of Welbeck Abbey that, despite the fairly recent and, one would have thought, adequate extensions by the fifth Duke (to be touched on in a moment) we are informed that after this fire "the restoration occupied nearly four years, and advantage was taken of its necessity, to re-model and *enlarge* the wing". This post-1900 work was in the hands of Sir Ernest George who also seized the opportunity of carrying out considerable alterations to the building as a whole. Since the fifth Duke's extensions are practically invisible from outside, the building, as it stands to-day, is largely a combination of late eighteenth century and early twentieth, the final appearance being principally the work of George. At practically no stage of its career has it satisfied exacting aesthetic criticisms. In 1789 it was described as "mean, ugly and ill-built". You certainly could not call it mean now, nor ill-built, but the general effect is hardly beautiful. It is muddled and haphazard.

The eighteenth-century complaint that it was built on no regular plan still holds good; and its disunity gives it little compensating romanticism of outline. There are several elaborately porticoed doorways with rival theoretical claims to being the principal entrance, but none have confidence or authority sufficient, it seems, to convince either themselves or the spectator of their pre-eminence. But, on the other hand, the building as a whole does exert a remarkable sense both of power and dignity. The ornamental waters and balustrades which lie around it; the green copper of the roofing; the distant glimpse over the mass of masonry of a cupola at a remote entrance; the smooth lawns and the well-kept roadways: all this defies the detailed confusion of the structure and lends it grace.

Such it is to-day, and such it was on a September afternoon a few years ago when a sad evisceration was taking place. A marquee had been erected on the grass overlooking the lake. A firm of Retford auctioneers had installed themselves and there were eight hundred people, it was estimated, to watch and take part in the proceedings. The disembowelling was thorough. From the Link wing came the famous Donegal carpeting, more than a hundred yards long. (It fetched £1,166.) There were purple Wilton carpets, Indian rugs, a Chippendale four-poster bedstead, green silk damask curtains, a set of Genoese gold velvet curtains—all these and a vast quantity of Welbeck seventeenth and eighteenth-century furniture and fittings.

It was not carpeting nor furniture which left Welbeck even more abruptly, something over a year later. About £500 worth of silver plate (much of which subsequently turned up in a pawn shop in Chester) was stolen by a man formerly employed at the abbey. The plate, part of which was described as belonging to the Dowager Duchess of Portland (who retains part of the abbey as her residence, while the present Duke lives in a modern house in the grounds known as Welbeck Woodhouse, built about twenty years ago), was probably not a section of the fabulous hereditary Welbeck collection. This includes a quantity of early Dutch silver, so rare as to be unmatched in Holland itself, which was brought to England from the Netherlands. The English plate in the collection begins with the flagons, chalice and paten dating from 1667-8, which was used in the private chapel and belonged to Henry Cavendish, second Duke of Newcastle. But there is one earlier piece—a gold chalice of unknown London workmanship of about 1629-30. It was in origin a domestic wine cup but became the chalice from which Charles I took his last sacrament. Of literary interest, amid all the wealth and lordly splendour, are some private modest belongings in the way of plate, an ink-stand and some spoons which belonged to Matthew Prior and somehow got left at Welbeck as a reminder of this good poet's residence at Welbeck and of his association with the Tory chief, Harley, Earl of Oxford. The Harley plate itself forms a collection on its own.

In the times of its greatness the contents of Welbeck must have been almost unbelievable. The state rooms—their very names spell grandeur, the Swan Drawing-Room, the Blue Library, the

Horsemanship Bedchamber—were filled with priceless pictures and furniture. The acres of canvas that were contained—and to some extent are still contained—in the great building had come, as if from a number of tributary streams, all pouring their various wealths into this single predestined reservoir. There were, in the most recent catalogue, just over a thousand important pictures listed. (It is interesting that that useful eighteenth-century engraver and art historian, George Vertue—whose major work, left haphazard and unsorted, has descended to us by way of the neat mind and hand of Horace Walpole—catalogued the miniatures at Welbeck and may have been responsible, as well, for the first catalogue of the oil-paintings which dates from the year 1747, when Vertue was at the height of his reputation.

This, obviously, is no place to try and describe the Welbeck paintings. The Rembrandts, the Van Dycks, the Lelys, the Knellers, belong in a context less localized than this. Instead let us rather note a matter of purely local interest which to the general student of art often seems the dullest part of the collection of paintings accumulated in a palace or great house. This is the collection of local views, of portraits not of the lords of the place in their different costumes and centuries, but of the place itself in its changing dress and surroundings, none the less varied and distinctive. It always exists, this neglected aspect of any great domestic collection, and since it could only have been accumulated on the spot, it has a peculiar and unique value. It is a great misfortune that such a cross-section, giving the appearance of a single spot as it changes through the centuries, of inestimable use to the architect, social historian, the student of landscape and of landscape gardening, and the botanist, too, should often have been dispersed. This particular sideline of the Welbeck collection is represented by some forty pictures which can reasonably be called important; not by any means because they are by celebrated painters, but because of what they contribute to our knowledge of the appearance of the house and its surroundings. We have noted the scarcity of seventeenth-century delineations of Welbeck. The painted views begin with one by Diepenbecke (1596-1675) and continue to the end of the nineteenth century; they include several by Stubbs who, over and above the portraits of horses themselves, is represented at Welbeck by a picture of the riding school. And, in a sense, the most notable local painter represented in the collection is James Baldock, a Worksop man who died at Nottingham in 1898. There is a forest painting by him, a picture of the Seven Sisters Oak; but the strangest products of his brush are the sunsets painted on the roof of the riding school, later converted into a chapel and library; this was the building put up by the first Duke of Newcastle.

The building which, surviving until the first world war, formed the climax of Welbeck's contributions to hippic or equestrian architecture was the astonishing building known as the Tan Gallop. It must have been in the same rank of importance, in the realm of the revolutionary mid-Victorian architecture of glass and cast iron, as the Duke of Devonshire's not so very distant conservatories at Chatsworth, and their offspring, the Crystal Palace itself. The Tan Gallop, though it had not the exciting, almost Byzantine rotundity of form that had those other major essays in the style, like the Palm House at Kew, must have been a very striking structure. It was nearly a quarter of a mile in length and had upwards of sixty thousand square feet of glass in its roof. The ground was strewn with tan (the spent bark from tan pits which has been used for flooring riding courses since the early eighteenth century). Apart from buildings put up for exhibitions it is hard to think of a single permanent roof in existence to-day that is as long as a quarter of a mile, and it is not surprising that this place, where the ducal horses were exercised in inclement weather, with the Duke as a spectator, was, until it was demolished, one of the wonders of the neighbourhood.

Of those buildings made for the fifth Duke which may be described as normal, that is above ground, the most striking survival is also equestrian. This is the New Riding School, which is itself no miniature structure, being 385 feet long, 112 broad and 51 feet high, its walls are of stone and windowless, and it has a steep vaulted roof of glass and iron—very little iron to glass, so that the place is exceedingly well lighted—supported on plain Doric columns of cast iron, which are ranged about eight or nine feet away from each wall. The building is regarded by historians of cast-iron architecture as one of their more important monuments. Its ornamentation includes a carved stone cornice and a metal frieze with representations of animals, birds and foliage. This place, said to be the second largest riding school in the world, for a long time existed side by side with the much larger Tan Gallop. The fifth Duke also built ranges of hot houses 800 feet in length and fruit forcing walls with glass roofs, almost as long. Of the scale of his building programme, above as well as under ground, some idea can be got by the fact that in 1875, four years before the Duke's death, there were thirty-five lodges, in neo-Tudor style, completed and six more under construction, at various points on the fringes of the estate. Their outhouses were underground.

One wonders what the solitary and mysterious fifth Duke would have to say about the bustle and clatter made by the students of No. 2 Army College as they directed their rather heavy footsteps to the college library along the stone tunnels and between the lines of the miniature railway designed to carry the produce of a vast estate to banquets in his subterranean supper rooms; or what the fifth Duke's feelings would be at the various uses made of his underground picture gallery (which is 160 feet long, 64 wide and 22 feet high). Would he be pleased to know that here, under the great gas chandeliers, there were, in those years after the second world war, troops' and staff dances (admission sixpence), cinema shows (ninepence) and mock parliaments, brains trusts and debates. The college provided, under a staff of experts, a choice of forty six-monthly courses on subjects which range from salesmanship to sculpture, distributed among some five hundred students a month. Perhaps the "building Duke" would have been glad to know that plumbing and civil engineering were taught within his own fantastic structures. Each year many thousands of students passed through the college, to carry memories of this extraordinary house into all sorts of unlikely jobs in their future lives.

The fifth Duke of Portland is so obviously a study for the psychologist that one hesitates even to raise his name in that context. No doubt the scientific explanation of his peculiarities is perfectly straightforward. It would be more to the point, perhaps, to enquire what form his crankiness, his urge to burrow, to build hugely and yet remain out of sight of his fellows, and to hide himself, would have taken if he had not been able, by virtue of his enormous wealth, to do it in so spectacular a style and to become the "invisible prince". One wonders whether a poor man with the mental complications of the fifth Duke of Portland would not somehow have put himself permanently beneath the earth before very long.

What was particularly strange in the fifth Duke's oddness was that his building mania—an almost conventional symptom of eccentricity among great territorial magnates—was combined with a reluctance to put Welbeck, and the vast extensions that he made to it, to any useful purpose except as a sort of permanent builders' yard. For eighteen years he turned Welbeck into a huge workshop and when he died a large number of buildings were still incomplete; at no time during this period did Welbeck ever seem complete or free from disfigurement. All these years the immediate surroundings of the house were covered with unsightly sheds under which carpenters, stone-masons and iron-founders were ceaselessly at work. Fifteen thousand men were employed, and the annual bill of costs amounted to £100,000, which would be getting on for half a million nowadays. Much of the building that he did was, as we shall see, of a kind that is generally associated with ostentatious hospitality, with a liking for large-scale entertainment. But the fifth Duke was a recluse. At Welbeck, huge, even before he made it huger, he lived in a suite of only four or five rooms, in which he remained shut off from the world. His means of communication with the outside was by double letter boxes on the doors, one for messages in, and for ordinary mail, and the other for his outgoing instructions. He did not like to have to come face to face with anybody or talk to them; so his notes might be about a shooting party that would arrive, enjoy itself and leave Welbeck without ever setting eyes on its host. Or he might demand some food by this same postal means and chickens were always kept roasting in the ovens in case the Duke should suddenly call for one. We are told that the Duke's abhorrence of ordinary social intercourse was accepted and understood in the neighbourhood and that if such people as the local parson accidentally encountered the Duke he would be expected to show no signs of recognition. On the other hand it is said that he conversed easily and affably with his workmen and that he presented to each of them when they started at Welbeck a donkey on which to ride, and also, for some reason, an umbrella. Another of his fads related to the indoor staff at Welbeck. The Duke was a strong advocate of vigorous outdoor exercise for all the housemaids, particularly, in winter, skating on the lake.

His oddness was most startlingly manifested in the way in which he made his journeys to London. Such journeys, obviously, had, at times, to be made but the Duke went to extraordinary lengths to avoid being seen while *en route*. If he undertook such an expedition he would get, unseen, into his carriage in the vast coach houses of Welbeck. Then, in order that he might not be observed while driving through the estate, the carriage would plunge into the underground tunnel which he had constructed beneath the lawns around the house, the parkland and fields beyond. This tunnel was a mile and a quarter long and wide enough for two carriages to pass in it; its course lay underneath the lake where it dipped sharply downhill. It was lighted by gas flares and, when it was not below the lake, by circular glass skylights which can still be seen unexpectedly and inexplicably poking through the grass of the garden and in the fields on either side of the road as one approaches the house. This was only one of several tunnels which radiate outwards from the abbey in many directions. They are rather pleasant to walk or ride in, quite dry and free from draughts and amply lighted. But to pursue the Duke on his journey. When his carriage emerged from the tunnel on its way to Worksop station the green silk blinds would be drawn and, as it proceeded along the park roads and through the streets of Worksop, the Duke would remain secure and invisible. The blinds would still be drawn when, in the station yard, the coach was lifted bodily, the Duke included, on to a special railway truck which must presumably have been some sort of "flat". In this, darkened, alone and invisible, the Duke of Portland would rattle and click, like any other piece of goods traffic, along the iron highway to the capital, where a similar ceremony of unloading him and a masked drive through the streets would ensue.

It was, of course, the building of these tunnels which marks out this wealthy recluse from any otherwise comparable building cranks. You and I, should we wish to remain unseen, and had we but a few thousands a year, could engage for our journeys a special railway carriage, lock it and lower its blinds; we could drive through London in a closed taxicab, could, indeed, live behind closed doors with a letter box or even a double letter box. But since we cannot afford to spend, say, £400,000 a year on "improving" our estate we cannot build an underground tunnel through it.

But the Duke's subterranean construction was by no means concerned only with allowing him to leave Welbeck by an underground route. His greatest energies and those of his workmen were directed towards the underground rooms of Welbeck Abbey itself, which are connected with the rest of the house by more underground passages. The first rooms that he built beneath the surface consisted of a suite of three library rooms, nearly 250 feet long. In 1875, only four years before the Duke died, work was begun, to the west of the library, on a room originally designed as a chapel but which was soon converted into a ballroom and picture gallery. It measures 174 feet by 64 and is 22 feet high and has been described as the largest private apartment in England. The ballroom completed, it was followed by what is called the Rose Corridor, a long underground conservatory with a glass roof. There are also subterranean kitchens, pantries and other offices. One of the curiosities of subterranean Welbeck is a miniature railway for conveying food and crockery along the passages; a hydraulic shaft connected with the kitchens and the underground dining-room could be supplied by means of wagons which were lowered on the shaft and ran on rails along the passage. The rails terminate in a kind of iron cupboard which was heated by steam (hot air provided warmth for the underground rooms) and in this food was kept hot until it was wanted in the adjoining room.

These corridors are, or were till recently, filled with pictures, a very large proportion of them of horses, as are the walls of the incomparable ballroom cum picture gallery itself. This fact will suggest to you that, although underground, these rooms and passages are by no means dark. Indeed, brilliant lightness, in the daytime, is one of the most striking features of the picture gallery which, although it has no windows, is flooded with daylight by means of domed skylights in the roof which gives it all that diffused, non-reflective lighting most sought after where pictures are hung. At night the underground rooms were illuminated by literally thousands of gas jets: there were 1,100 in the three library rooms alone. In these atomic days we have all of us a certain sympathy with the Duke's inclinations unimaginable to him. But, alas, these rooms and passages give no feeling of security. They are only just underground and the clear daylight that suffuses them deprives them of all comfort in a frightened epoch.

Leaving the psychologists out of it, two alternative suggestions are commonly made about the reasons for the Duke's building and for his going underground. Some people say that he merely wanted to enlarge the house without spoiling what was then its original eighteenth-century external appearance. But one would surely have a very sentimental attachment to it to be driven by such a motive for it was a muddle even then and far from lovely. The other suggestion is that at a time of widespread unemployment he wanted to give labour to as many men as possible and seized on tunnelling as a notoriously expensive and slow undertaking. But there can be little doubt that his abnormal shyness played a very large part in deciding on this course. But whatever the reason the fifth Duke of Portland made himself into a most satisfactory legend and left behind him one of the marvels of the Midlands.

Welbeck, Thoresby, Clumber—and Worksop Manor. One more building to complete the Dukeries, one which has now, perhaps, even less to offer than the site of vanished Clumber, but once greater in size than any of the others. Away from Welbeck, then, by the Manor Hills and the Lion Gate and almost into the town of Worksop; the manor lies to the south-west. Of the mansion of the Duke of Norfolk, once the senior element in the name of the Dukeries, only a tiny fragment remains. Until 1761 there stood on this site an imposing Elizabethan mansion belonging to the Earls of Shrewsbury. Old views show that it presented to its main approach a three-storey front consisting almost entirely of very tall rectangular windows, and that set back were two higher storeys with cupolas on tall drums at the sides and a smaller central tower over the front; the house had begun to be built by George, Earl of Shrewsbury and Bess of Hardwick, his wife. In October 1761 the building was tragically destroyed by a fire which is believed to have been burning for two whole days before it was discovered, and to have been caused by a fire left burning in one of the rooms to air it. A high wind was blowing and very little of the furniture or pictures was saved. The house was a total loss. One gathers that it was largely due to the taste and enthusiasm of the Duchess of Norfolk at the time that a superb Palladian creation by James Paine (1725-89) was conceived and in part carried out (a fine example of Paine's work is that early piece of civic architecture, the Mansion House at Doncaster, and Paine, who did much important work in London, also made the first plan for the great house at Kedleston which was very substantially followed by Robert Adam who succeeded him there). Paine's Worksop was intended to be the biggest palace in England and the only part of it completed—one wing, 300 feet in length, with four storeys, and a square office and stable yard—is said to have contained 500 rooms. Then the death of their heir chilled the Duke and Duchess' interest in the new house. It appears that the ninth Duke of Norfolk, who rebuilt the house, "lived becoming to his rank and fortune in retirement, chiefly at Worksop Manor, dispensing blessings to the needy, and keeping up the ancient spirit of hospitality in its primitive greatness"—at least that is what an eighteenth-century writer says, in the time of the eleventh Duke. This writer goes on, rather more critically, about circumstances by then. He says: "The present building, although only about a third of the original plan, is a magnificent structure. The plan is light and airy. The north front, which is built of a white freestone, got about three miles from the house, is rich in decoration; but everything near looks rather cold and comfortless, it has no member-like field embellishments in high cultivation. The present Duke seldom sees his princely edifice, consequently there are only two or three rooms occupied. The elegant tapestry is in a state of decay; and several of the best pictures are removed to Arundel Castle, a favourite seat of the present noble owner."

It was about fifty years after that comment was written that Worksop Manor was sold to the Duke of Newcastle. This, however, was not auspicious for the future of the house because the Duke had already come into Clumber; and perhaps two gigantic houses in the Dukeries are too much even for a duke. So the house—the whole wing of twenty-three bays—was pulled down and all that remains is the front wall, of rusticated stone work, of the ground floor, with nothing behind it except one room where the house met the stable yard at right angles. Out of the stable and other buildings in the yard a very good-sized house was constructed, which is still privately occupied. As well as retaining the sculpture on the pediment of the wall that was left, the surviving residue is given character and dignity by a fine screen in the yard of Tuscan columns.

It is curious that Worksop Manor, in any of its successive states, was never wholly satisfactory. In the original old house, in which Mary Queen of Scots spent a period of imprisonment, and in which James I was entertained on his way to London for his coronation, Horace Walpole stayed in 1756, five years before it was burnt down. He remarked sourly: " The great apartment is vast and trist, the whole leanly furnished. There is no prospect, and the barren face of the country is richly furred with evergreen plantations."

A mile up the road into the town of Worksop (pronounced locally " Wursup "). Notable breweries, the neighbouring collieries and some good medieval architecture make up Worksop, which is an unpretentious and, *qua* town, a rather unexciting place. It stands in a wide valley formed by gently rising hills and has been inhabited at least from Saxon times. It appears in Domesday Book as Werchescope. In Henry I's time the lord of the manor " built a castle on a rock of red sandstone on the northwest side of the town ". There is no sign of the fortress now, but the spot is still known as Castle Hill. It did not survive very long, for when that admirable observer and topographer John Leland was there in the mid-sixteenth century he wrote: " Werkensop a pretty market town of two streets, and metely well builded. There is a fair park hard by it, and the beginnings of a fair manor place of squarid stone in the same. The old castle on a hill by the town is clene down and scant known where it was. This town, castle, and large park, longid first to the Lovetotes, then as some say to one of the Neviles. Then were the Furnivaulx of certainty owners thereof, and after the Talbotes. The priory of the black canons there was a thing of great building and a place of sepulture to the aforesaid noblemen. Wyrkesop is called in some old writings Radeford."

Well, Radford Priory, now known as Worksop Priory, which was founded by the builder of the castle, Henry de Lovetot, has lasted better, though the church which he founded to the glory of Saints Cuthbert and Mary, on March 3rd, 1103, was fairly soon replaced by a second building whose nave we now see. When complete the church must have presented a somewhat similar appearance to the cathedral at Southwell. All that remains now is the late twelfth-century nave and the lady chapel, a long chamber attached to the south transept of the church, dating from the mid-thirteenth century. The twin Norman towers of the western façade, which had Perpendicular battlemented and pinnacled tops added to them in the fifteenth century, were probably originally surmounted with wooden spires as at Southwell. There is practically no decoration on this façade; but within, above the alternating circular and octagonal columns, the nine bays of the nave are enriched with stylized foliage on the capitals and complex moulding in the arches.

The lady chapel, a severe but exquisite example of Early English architecture, dating from about 1250, lay, roofless, until the inter-war period, just detached from the south-east corner of the church. But in 1929 the south transept of the church was reconstructed and the lady chapel once again connected with the nave. Great enterprise was shown by Worksop during these and later years in the preservation and restoration of the church and in the forming of a civic centre around the priory, a feature that was noticeably needed in a rather straggling and shapeless town. In a memorial avenue a hospital, museum and library have been built. To the south of the priory church stands the gatehouse of what was a large group of monastic buildings. This handsome structure, 60 feet broad, dates from the fourteenth century and includes a porch which is one of the most elaborate of its date in the country. It houses a staircase which led to the chambers in the upper part of the gateway. The gatehouse, which is often described in old views and accounts of Worksop as St. Mary's chapel, was restored by the Duke of Newcastle in 1893.

A fact about Worksop which one often hears referred to is that it was formerly a great centre for the cultivation of liquorice, but the growing of it seems to have died out during the eighteenth century when, we are told, " the last plantation was in the neighbourhood of Forest Lane, the pleasure ground before Mr. Roe's house ". In earlier times liquorice was regarded as one of the principal and most memorable products of the county. Of liquorice, says Fuller, under Nottinghamshire: " England affordeth hereof the best in the world for some uses; this county the first and best in England." So the county may perhaps claim liquorice in early times as it does celery, after Marshall Tallard's visitation. It is a county in many ways memorable for its food, in which, necessarily, the deer from Sherwood Forest play a traditional part, providing venison pasty to be eaten with red-currant sauce. On grand occasions roast swan is a speciality. Colwick cheese had a special place in the county's affections; and, of course, those products of Mansfield—Mansfield gooseberry pie, and Mansfield pudding. Since this is a delicacy worth knowing of, here is a recipe for it. You need: 2 oz. breadcrumbs; half-pint milk; two eggs; ½ oz. castor sugar; 3 oz. shredded suet; 3 oz. flour; 3 oz. currants; 1 tablespoon sherry or brandy; some grated nutmeg. Put the suet into the flour and mix in all the dry ingredients. Beat up the eggs, mix in the brandy and milk, and beat all well together for about three minutes. Pour into a buttered piedish and bake for about one hour. Turn out on to a dish, sprinkle with castor sugar and you have a Mansfield pudding.

On this delicious note Mansfield brings itself to our attention, the town that was once in the heart of Sherwood Forest and remained a place of only a few thousand inhabitants until the Industrial Revolution swamped its graceful centre. The market-place, although startlingly cut off from the parish church by the railway viaduct which runs through the middle of the town, still retains something of its pre-industrial appearance. At the corner of the market-place and Westgate is the Moot Hall, a stone house with a pediment, which was given to the town in 1752 by the then lady of the manor, the Countess of Oxford (of Welbeck). Subsequently, however, a neo-classical town hall of 1836 provided a new centre-piece for the square; and later still a gigantic Gothic memorial, erected to the memory of Lord George Frederick Cavendish Bentinck, son of the fourth Duke of Portland, who died in 1848, became yet another dominant feature. The town has a number of churches and chapels of different dates and denominations, of which the parish church of St. Peter, rebuilt after a fire in 1304, is the only medieval one. Mansfield has produced, besides that miller, who, according to legend, entertained Henry II with a venison pasty of the king's own deer, a number of eminent men, of whom the most enterprising was perhaps Robert Dodsley. He, greatest of the eighteenth-century publishers in London, was the son of the master of the local grammar school (founded by Queen Elizabeth), was apprenticed to a stocking weaver but ran away to London where, after working for a time as a footman, became one of the main props of our Augustan literature. Also from Mansfield came Archbishop Sterne (1598-1683) who attended Archbishop Laud on his scaffold and was the grandfather of the author of *Tristram Shandy*; and John Rogers, the inventor of great improvements in the double point net machine.

Situated at the opposite corner of the forest to Mansfield are the twin towns—that are now one, separated only by a bridge—of East and West Retford. It is simplest, and common, to call the whole place just Retford. The western element provides two handsome eighteenth-century mansions, West Retford House and West Retford Hall. Opposite the hall is the long low building, neo-Tudor of 1833, of Trinity Hospital; and south of the hall the attractive church of St. Michael whose spire Pugin described as "a poem in stone". East Retford presents a largely Victorian appearance with the town hall of 1867 in the market-place, and the old parish church heavily, too thoroughly, restored in the 1850's. There is, however, a pleasant row of Georgian houses opposite the church.

At East Retford we are, once again, on the Great North Road. And were we to follow its rather uneventful course for a few miles, through Torworth and Scrooby (an unexciting place but which Americans will presumably continue to visit because of its imperceptible associations with William Brewster, one of the two leaders of the Pilgrim Fathers) we shall be through Bawtry and so out at the top end of the county, leaving on our right those empty stretches of car-land which spread to Misterton and the Lincolnshire border.

But if, taking a turn to the left soon after the famous hostelry on the Great North Road at Barnby Moor, we head out towards Yorkshire, we find, close together, two villages which contain important early Norman monuments, Blyth and Carlton-in-Lindrick. The church of St. John at Carlton-in-Lindrick has an almost complete early Norman tower and, inside, a mixture of early Norman and transitional arches, piers and capitals.

It seems a pity to end, or nearly to end, on a mournful note, but in spite of its great beauty, Blyth is a sad place. I have no doubt that the appeals for restoring the church will have their effect and that this most ancient of Nottinghamshire's ecclesiastical buildings will be saved; but unless something has happened recently to Blyth Hall this attractive village will continue to exude an atmosphere of decay. Church and hall are connected by more than history. It has been said recently of the Norman part of Blyth church that "while Blyth is amongst the oldest of the Norman work in England in point of date, in point of style it is old fashioned and thirty or forty years behind the times, so that it exhibits features such as were constructed in Normandy when

Edward the Confessor was sitting on the English throne ". Blyth was founded in 1088 by Roger de Busli and the work of this earliest period can still be seen in the nave. But the Norman church which formed the nucleus of the Benedictine priory has suffered distressing mutilation. Not that one can call the Early English and Perpendicular additions, in themselves, disastrous, but it has left the north side of the Norman aisle, with its small windows, and primitive vaulting, as a submerged fragment. At the Reformation the conventual buildings were sold and since they included one half of the church (the parishioners had worshipped in one half and the monks in the other) this portion was pulled down and the material used elsewhere. The eastern bays of the nave and the north aisle thus found themselves isolated in the garden of Blyth Hall, whose owners used them and the great west arch as an aviary. In 1931, however, these portions were recovered by the church and it is hoped to incorporate them in containing walls. But the home of the Mellishs is going through its time of sorrow now. In the church you can see the tomb of Edward Mellish, a short, stout, cross-legged figure, who reclines sideways leaning on one arm, between fluted Corinthian pilasters, and learn of him that " he built a mansion house, a fair and stately edifice, situate on the north side of this church, where stood the seat of his father ". He did, and the house that was completed shortly before his death in 1703, and was enlarged in the nineteenth century, is now almost derelict. The army was here during the war and it has left a ruin, where a bust of, surprisingly, James Watt, looks down past the miniature iron cannons, on to the pretty, narrow lake in an overgrown garden. The Mellishs were Blyth people before Edward Mellish became rich in the Portuguese trade and built a " mansion house ". Theirs became a distinguished military family and retained its connection with the locality, moving, close by, to the misleadingly named Hodsock Priory (which never was a priory), to a house on the site of an old home of the Clifton family.

The garden at Blyth Hall, unless it has been cleared recently, is one of the strangest spots in the county and I would rather leave the explorer here, tussling with the undergrowth as he clears a way for himself from the hall to the great, grim, priory church, than any other more obviously suitable spot in this final corner of the county. Not, for instance, admiring the clean eighteenth-century formality of Serlby Hall, the home of Lord Galway, most northerly of Nottinghamshire's mansions. Nor at Styrrup, in spite of its enchanting name, because even though there may be a Roman villa with some mosaics found here, and the site of a medieval tournament ground, one of the five licensed tilting places in England, there is not much to see when you get there. Nor even would I have him stand at Gringley-on-the-Hill looking over the cars that stretch as far as the eye can see to the north. I said at the beginning, that one could find symbols of all England in the thin leaf shape of this county. And here, at the top, almost where it joins the stalk, with the forest and the Trent, the coal and the city below us, I find one where, among bamboo plants and overgrown shrubs, the remains of a Benedictine priory stand in the ruins of a garden that was once the pride of an English merchant who made his money in distant lands.

BIBLIOGRAPHY

T H I S short list of books relating to the county includes only
(*a*) a few standard works of various dates, and (*b*) some of the
most recent writings on the subject. It makes no attempt at
completeness, or to fill in the gaps between these two classes of
books. The place of publication is London unless otherwise stated.

BLACKNER, J. *A History of Nottingham, embracing Antiquities,
Trade and Manufactures.* Nottingham, 1815.
BROWN, C. *History of Nottinghamshire.* 1891.
CHAMBERS, J. D. *Nottinghamshire in the Eighteenth Century. A
Study of life and labour under the squirearchy.* 1932.
CHAMBERS, J. D. Article (" Nottingham ") in *History To-day.*
October 1951.
DEERING, C. *Nottinghamia Vetus et Nova Or An Historical
Account . . . of the Town of Nottingham, etc.* Nottingham,
1751.
FIRTH, J. B. *Highways and Byways in Nottinghamshire.* 1916.
GUILFORD, E. L. *Nottinghamshire (The Little Guides).* 1927.
INGRAM, J. H. *North Midland Country.* 1948.
MEE, A. *Nottinghamshire (The King's England).* 1945.
MOORE, H. T. *The Life and Works of D. H. Lawrence.* 1951.
NEWSTEAD. *Newstead Abbey and the Relics of Byron, etc.* Mans-
field. n.d.
NOTTINGHAM CITY. *Nottingham.* Official Handbook. Twelfth
Edition. n.d.
PEVSNER, N. *Nottinghamshire (The Buildings of England).* 1951.
PEVSNER, N. *The Leaves of Southwell.* 1945.
PRATT, W. W. *Byron at Southwell: The Making of a Poet.*
Austin: University of Texas, 1948.
ROWSE, A. L. *The English Past.* (Contains essays on " Notting-
ham " and " D. H. Lawrence at Eastwood ".) 1951.
THOROTON, R. *Antiquities of Nottinghamshire.* 1677.
THROSBY, J. *Thoroton's History of Nottinghamshire, Repub-
lished with Large Additions . . . and embellished with
Picturesque and Select Views of the Seats of the Nobility and
Gentry, Towns, Village Churches and Ruins.* Nottingham,
1790.

313

TURBERVILLE, A. S.   *Welbeck Abbey and its Owners*.   1939.
VICTORIA HISTORY.   *Victoria History of the County of Nottingham*.   1906, etc.
WARD, LOCK AND CO.   *A Pictorial and Descriptive Guide to Nottingham and Sherwood Forest, etc.*   1920.
WEST, F. H. (Archdeacon of Newark).   *Rude Forefathers. The Story of an English Village, 1660-1666.*   1949.
WOOD, A. C.   *A History of Nottinghamshire.*   Nottingham, 1948.
WOOD, A. C.   *Nottinghamshire in the Civil War.*   1937.

INDEX

315

INDEX

323

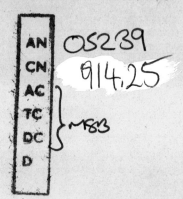